A Radical Tory

Garfield Barwick's

Reflections and Recollections

THE FEDERATION PRESS
1995

Published in Sydney by

The Federation Press
PO Box 45, Annandale, NSW, 2038.
3/56-72 John St, Leichhardt, NSW, 2040.
Ph (02) 552 2200. Fax (02) 552 1681.

Published 1995
Reprinted - paperback edition 1996

National Library of Australia
Cataloguing-in-Publication entry

Barwick, Garfield, Sir, 1903-
A radical tory: Garfield Barwick's reflections and recollections

Includes index.
ISBN 978 1 86287 236 3 (Pbk)
1. Barwick, Garfield, Sir, 1903- . 2. Judges – Australia – Biography. 3. Attorneys general – Australia – Biography. 4. Cabinet officers – Australia – Biography. 5. Australia – Politics and government – 1945- .

347.9403534092

Typeset by The Federation Press, Leichhardt, NSW.

Foreword

When, in 1948, the Commonwealth Parliament enacted legislation to nationalise the banking system, it was evident that the decisive battle for survival by the banks would be fought in the courts; the High Court of Australia and, perhaps, the Privy Council. The resolution of this issue, which was of high economic and social importance, was to turn upon constitutional questions concerning the law-making power of the Parliament. The contending parties assembled teams of the foremost lawyers of the day, Australian and English. The Australian barristers retained for the banks were chosen from a number of States. Their leader was a member of the New South Wales Bar, Barwick KC, then aged 45. To a lawyer interested in assessing Sir Garfield Barwick's professional standing, little more need be said. Between 1948 and 1958, when he entered Parliament, he dominated the Australian Bar in a manner that was to that time, and has since remained, unique. When, in 1964, the Menzies Government appointed him Chief Justice of Australia, upon the retirement of Sir Owen Dixon, he was regarded as a person of unrivalled professional eminence and experience. This was well understood by Prime Minister Menzies, who had himself been a leading Victorian barrister and who, it appears from this book, would have liked to be Chief Justice of Victoria.

From 1958 until 1963, Sir Garfield Barwick served as Attorney-General of the Commonwealth and, from 1961 until 1964, as Minister for External Affairs. Following his appointment as Chief Justice of Australia, he spent 17 years in that office, until his retirement in 1981. It seems that he considered his retirement at the age of 78 to be somewhat premature. It was forced upon him by his diabetic condition and severely failing eyesight. This is a life of extraordinary achievement and service.

The three principal phases of Sir Garfield's working life, 30 years as a barrister, six years as a Member of Parliament and a Minister, and 17 years as Chief Justice, are examined in this book in comprehensive and absorbing detail. He lived at the height of his times. He was closely involved in great events in the nation's history, and has made a distinctive contribution to that history.

For some readers, however, it will not be the account of that history that constitutes the work's principal source of interest. It is the background to the picture that is most fascinating. The effects of the Great Depression upon a young couple whose partnership capital included exceptional talent and energy but little money; the organisation and accommodation of the Bar in the years immediately before and after the Second World War; the early years of the Australian conservation movement; the style of Sir Robert Menzies as Prime Minister; the political difficulties associated with pioneering legislation on the subjects of family law and restrictive trade practices; the sensitivities involved in Australian-Asian relations; the changing character of the High Court; the ways in which the International Court of Justice transacts its business: matters such as this form the context in which the author has acted out his role in history.

It is impossible to overestimate the contribution made by Barwick KC to the corporate life of his profession. Having prospered at the Bar, he returned many times over the benefits it had conferred on him. With a small number of others he was responsible for centralising Sydney's barristers and providing new chambers for most of them in a location near the Supreme Court. This remains a subject of interest and concern to him. On the occasion of a celebration of his 90th birthday he was still proposing radical plans for re-locating Sydney's courts and barristers' chambers. Many others have benefited greatly from a career in the legal profession, but none has put more back into it.

Sir Garfield Barwick's opinions on controversial legal issues, such as the meaning of s 92 of the Commonwealth Constitution, the correct approach to the interpretation of laws imposing taxation, the nature of Federation, and the proper role of the High Court in the development of the law are, not surprisingly, expressed with clarity and vigour. Upon all these subjects there are lawyers, including judges, with different opinions. However, in considering the weight to be attached to Sir Garfield's views, it is to be remembered that relatively few people are in a position to meet him on equal terms. It sometimes appears to be assumed that one lawyer's opinion is as good, or as entitled to attention, as that of another. That view is not shared by people who have to pay for legal advice, or make important personal, commercial or governmental decisions in reliance upon it. The opinions of Sir Garfield Barwick are backed by a personal authority which comes in large part from the circumstances in which they were developed and refined. They are the result of intensive experience at the highest levels of professional and judicial activity. Barwick KC's opinions were amongst the most sought-after in Australia. In a succession of leading cases in the High Court and the Privy Council he debated issues of the kind mentioned above in close contest with the finest legal minds of his generation. As Chief Justice, he presided over the most formidable court in the land. No lawyer's views command uncritical assent, but there have been few in a position to speak with such authority.

There was a time when it was common for eminent barristers to enter political life. Names such as Menzies, Evatt, Barwick, Spender and Bowen provide examples from the 1940s and 1950s in federal politics. Times have changed. Leading practitioners appear to find politics an unappealing substitute for the rewards of professional life. It is even difficult to coax some of them onto the bench. Judicial service was once regarded as the natural culmination of a successful career in the law. Now, unfortunately, many barristers see it as a rather eccentric form of self-denial. Some of those who do not reject it absolutely say they think of it as they think of heaven: somewhere they would like to be one day, but not yet. There may not be many more careers like that described in this book.

This story of professional success and public service compels admiration. The success did not come without struggle, and the service was not rendered without occasional bitterness and conflict. By any standards, however, the achievements are remarkable.

Murray Gleeson
Supreme Court, Sydney

Contents

Part III Minister for External Affairs

Part IV Chief Justice

Prologue

It is now 1994. I was born on 22 June 1903 in Stanmore, one of the suburbs of Sydney where my parents then resided. I have recently identified and visited the house in Cannon Street, Stanmore in which I was born. I have already lived a goodly span. I have lived in Sydney for most of my ninety-one years.

In that time the city and the manner of life of its citizens have been dramatically transformed. The town in which I spent my boyhood, with its horse-drawn traffic and leisurely pace, has become a bustling metropolis with dense, almost unmanageable motorised transport — cars, buses, trucks of ever-increasing size, couriers in vans or on motorbikes or even bicycles, zipping in and out on their urgent business.

The gas-lit town was quiet, the dominant noise the clip-clop of horses' hooves, the occasional cries of the drivers and the rattle of the wood blocks with which the main streets were paved as wheels passed over them. The air was clean and unpolluted, except for the odour of freshly spread horse manure. But the streets were regularly swept, kept free of any accumulation of rubbish by cleaners with brush and pan — vulgarly called "sparrow starvers" — collecting the manure and other debris, placing it in receptacles at the kerbside.

The buildings were intimate and varied, rarely exceeding three or four storeys, well suited to the human scale of the citizenry. Now multi-storeyed buildings vie with each other for drab monotony of façade, rising well beyond the pedestrian's comprehension; they block out the sun, making tunnels for the wind and destroying the human scale of the city. It is surely not a fit place for humans to live and work, and yet much of what goes on in our society goes on here.

The city has become overpowering. It has attraction for me only when viewed from the heights of the north side, and even then I retain a nostalgic preference for what has gone. Yet fortunately many of Sydney's terrace houses survive to remind us that our forefathers lived in rented residences in close proximity to their workplaces. The harbour, now almost bereft of commercial shipping and of much of its romantic ferry traffic, remains like a jewel in contrast to the disfiguring development on parts of its shores. By permitting such high-rise development in a city which occupies a relatively narrow ridge between Wooloomooloo and Darling Harbour, we have caused too high a proportion of the population to work in the city while living in suburbs increasingly distant from it. The result is an overloaded road and rail system and a workforce condemned to spend two or more hours, often in uncomfortable conditions, commuting to and from work. Such short-sightedness says little for our intellectual capacity. Yet the Bridge and the Opera House bespeak the vision and vigour of the youthful people we are.

On the other hand the means of communication, transport and entertainment have all vastly improved, though not so as to overcome all the disadvantages. We have access to travel and entertainment our forefathers would not have dreamed of. We have taken it all in our stride, accepting each new advance as if it were an expected event. But the advantages and disadvantages of all this technology cannot yet be gauged.

In this vastly changing world, spanning nearly the entire twentieth century, I have lived out my time. It has been a full and eventful life. If I have made some contribution to this country I see it as very much that of an ordinary man doing daily what came to hand as well as his capacities and the fortunes of the time allowed. I lay no claim to special importance in Australian life, and have been reluctant to write about myself for publication, in particular anything in the nature of an autobiography.

But my grandsons have pressed me to leave them some account of it. So I began writing for family consumption only. Out of this effort this book has emerged, though I have not included matters of family life and concern.

Since retiring my sight has considerably diminished because of my longstanding diabetic condition. This alone has put me out of public circulation, though I have managed to remain an active president of the Royal NSW Institute for Deaf and Blind Children concerned with the education of children so handicapped. With the aid of a strong magnifying glass I have been able to continue my reading. But it has not been possible to handle records which might both verify and stimulate recollection. Consequently what follows in this book must depend almost entirely on recollection.

To some extent, my account of some of the incidents of a varied and busy life has been pre-empted by David Marr's *Barwick*. That book, readable enough, has been largely built on gossip and rumour, and in some places invention, certainly not on personal records, of which I have a great many, or discussion with his subject, something I must say I was unwilling to provide. Not surprisingly the book contains many errors and false assertions. In its later chapters where it touches on my days in active political life, its party-political bias leads to unwarranted assumptions and conclusions. Men in public life must accept, as

I do, the slings and arrows of outrageous journalism but ought not to be subjected to factual error, certainly not to any such error carelessly made.

It is not my intent to attempt any rectification of David Marr's text, but I must refute two statements he made about my parents. Firstly, it is said that when my parents met their families were neighbours and related by intermarriage. The falsity of this assertion would have been found if it had been checked. They were not neighbours: none of one family had met any member of the other. The Barwicks lived in the Monaro in the south of New South Wales, principally around Cooma. My father, Jabez Edward Barwick was born on 23 May 1874 at Monga, New South Wales, the son of Edward and Sarah Jane Barwick, nee Warne. The Ellicotts lived around Inverell and Moree in the north-east of New South Wales.

My mother, Lily Grace Ellicott, was born in Calala in the north west of New South Wales, on 2 January 1883, the daughter of John and Caroline Ellicott, nee Pryor. Apparently my father, in the course of his occupation as a journalist, happened to come to Moree, where thereafter he lived and worked as a printer. There he met my mother and her family. The pair married in Moree on 27 February 1902 and came to Sydney. John Ellicott junior, my mother's brother, later married my father's second cousin, Ruby Dooney, the pair meeting in my parents' home in Paddington, Sydney.

Secondly, perhaps thinking to find an explanation for my interest when Attorney-General in matrimonial causes, Marr writes that my parents' marriage had not been happy (the suggestion apparently is that this would have given me some stimulus to deal with the regulation of divorce (p 141)). On p 13 he says that my father's bankruptcy "seems to have begun an estrangement between Jabez Barwick and his wife. Within a few years, and in Jabez Barwick's lifetime, she began to describe herself as a widow".

I do not know where David Marr dug up these "facts". Like his reference to the interrelationship of the families of my parents, they are simply untrue. My parents were devoted to each other; I never knew them to have angry words. And apart from my father's journeys into the country for work, and my mother's illness, they never spent a day apart. Theirs was a successful marriage; my parents and my two brothers and I were a close-knit and happy family. My parents were dead before Marr's book appeared, but false assertions of this kind are offensive and unnecessary. The two instances are indicative of the attitude to accuracy which the would-be biographer displays throughout his book.

Since writing the above, I have read the Introduction which David Marr wrote to the paperback edition of his book, an edition published in 1992. He there discloses that the writing of the book was undertaken at the suggestion of its publishers as a "quickie" which I understand to be a superficially written book for publication against some publicised event which might enhance its sale. In this case, the event seems to have been the opening of the High Court Building in Canberra in 1981. David Marr further discloses in this Introduction his personal purpose in writing the book. I quote from his Introduction: "I began to write Sir Garfield's life with a single purpose: to pin on the man his responsibility for the crimes of 11 November 1975"; that is to say, that the book was not written as a record of fact but as a polemic to fulfil a slanderous intention. The bias of which I earlier spoke was evidently deliberate. However, as things stand at the moment, I can leave David Marr to the historians, who I fancy will be unlikely to support his views.

Acknowledgments

Whilst my vision is in general very blurred and without focus unless a person or object is very close to me, I am able to see my handwriting as I produce it, but I am quite unable to handle records either to stimulate or to verify recollection. Nonetheless I decided to handwrite the first draft of the text of this book. My calligraphy, never very good when thinking and writing, has become almost indecipherable, even by myself soon after it has been written. Consequently I have had need of great assistance in developing a final typewritten text which could be placed on a disk ready for the publishers.

My secretary (part time) Mrs Donna Camilleri has been able to decipher my handwriting and has been alert to observe repetition or ambiguity. With her word processor she has been able to furnish me with successive typewritten drafts for my correction. She has also been skilful in interpreting and incorporating my handwritten corrections. The production of this book would have been nigh impossible without her intelligent, diligent and tireless effort. I am indeed most obliged to her.

I would also like to acknowledge the great help I received from Miss Venetia Nelson who read and edited the text for me. She has respected my style of writing, such as it is, whilst at the same time making many suggestions which have improved the text.

I have appreciated the initiative of Federation Press in undertaking the publication of the book and am grateful for the co-operation I have received from Mr Christopher Holt.

The task of finding a publisher for the book and making suitable arrangements for its publication, including the selection of a suitable number of photographs from a very great number of prints for inclusion in it, was undertaken by Mr Kingsley Siebel. He is a friend I have known since my days in practice when I was putting together a law library and he was associated with a company publishing law reports and distributing textbooks. In performing these tasks he has exercised his great experience and his skill in negotiation. He has also prepared an index to the book, which I am sure will considerably increase the reader's access to its pages. This is not the first time that Mr Siebel has assisted me. He organised the publication of the booklet *Sir John Did His Duty* and I am very pleased to acknowledge my indebtedness to him for his assistance and to express my gratitude for it.

Last, I would make a more than conventional expression of gratitude to Norma. We retain the companionship begun in our youth and now in our retirement overtaken by disability (Norma with reduced mobility and in my case by reduced sight) we rely on each other's company. Consequently my immersion in the preparation of the text over a period of years and my retreat into my study for that purpose for long hours at a time have made considerable inroads on our manner of life. Norma has been most understanding and has accepted this interruption with equanimity. This I have much appreciated.

List of Illustrations

Part I

At the Bar

1 Education of a Barrister

From my very early boyhood I wanted to become a lawyer. The desire to practise the law has been the leitmotif of my life, a childhood dream that remained with me and gave me the stimulus to apply myself to study. It would be true to say that the law, its practice and administration have dominated my life; throughout my practising days as a barrister, I never contemplated following any other occupation.

Looking back now I realise that such a wholehearted concern may have narrowed my interests and confined my horizons. On several occasions I have been invited to join the board of directors of a company prominent in the business world. I declined partly because I did not consider myself to have any expertise in running such an enterprise and partly because I did not wish to dilute the attention I could give to the law. It was not until 1958, when I was fifty-five, that I yielded to a suggestion that I enter politics. Yet even when I accepted ministerial office, it was the law and its place in government that most attracted my attention. After six years in government, I chose to return to the administration of the law.

Whence came this resolve to be a lawyer? I cannot say with any certainty. Perhaps it is best assigned to one of those innate urgings to do some particular thing which develop in some humans, as it were, autogenously. Certainly it did not come from the promptings of my parents. Neither of them, nor any member of their families, had had any contact with the law. Nor had any of them any friends with such experience. However, while my parents did not prompt or urge me, they certainly did not discourage me.

For six years, as an only child, I had the undivided attention of my parents. I was early admitted to adult conversation and mingled with the many friends and relatives who crowded through our house in Paddington. To these I talked —

indeed I think in those days I must have been a vigorous conversationalist, for I remember that once I was offered a boy-proof watch (an item any boy would covet) if I would remain silent for an hour while the offeror carried on a conversation with a lady he was courting. I got the watch — seemingly such an interval of silence was unusual.

On the northern side of our terrace house a Mr Armstrong lived. He was an entertainer, playing the piano and singing songs. His aged mother lived with him and also a Miss Kelly, who was a dresser at the theatre. On the southern side a Mr Symonds and his family resided. He was a bookkeeper employed in the city, and pencilled on Saturday for a bookmaker at the races. He had a son who became one of my playmates. Further up the hill, Mr Leighton and his family occupied one of the terrace houses. Leighton was employed in business in the city. I played also with his son Frank, who later in life became an actor performing in Australian theatre. Paddington as a residential area had not then declined, as it later did. Today it has resurged as a sought-after area, much as it was in my youth by tradesmen and some professionals.

Other random memories come to me. When the Great White Fleet, an American visit of goodwill, was moored in Farm Cove, my mother's brother, Jack Ellicott, took me into the Botanic Gardens to see them. From my perch on his tall shoulders I had a splendid view of the ships. I can see them still, white and gleaming in the sunlight.

There are two memories of my mother's friend Dr Collier, who lived in West Wallsend, near Newcastle. My mother, christened Lily Grace but always affectionately known amongst family and friends as Lally, was always keen on expanding my experience by travel, meeting people and developing self-confidence. Dr Collier had as part of his surgery a dispensary where prescribed medicines were made up by the chemist as they were needed. (Today, of course, they come pre-packaged.) I must have attracted the attention of the pharmacist, because he gave me a spelling test. Both doctor and pharmacist were surprised by my accurate spelling of a number of difficult words, including "pharmacopoeia", some of which I had not heard before.

The other incident was travelling with Dr Collier in his horse-drawn buggy from West Wallsend to Newcastle where he took delivery of his first motor car. It was a black Ford, a three-pedalled affair. I rode back to West Wallsend in it, thrilled by the experience. To this day I cannot smell the distinctive odour of a new motor vehicle without recalling the smell of that new Ford and my boyhood delight in the ride. Afterwards, during my stay with him, I went on the doctor's rounds in the Ford.

I learnt to read and to spell very early and became a voracious and omnivorous reader. I still am, though diminished sight now slows my reading. While my parents did not have many books in the house, some of their friends did. On our frequent visits to them I would always read or just look at their books. This once led to my life being endangered. From handling a book in a household in which an infectious disease had recently manifested itself, I contracted diphtheria and scarlet fever at the same time. I was hastily quarantined in Little Bay Hospital and spent some weeks in an isolation ward. I still recall the shock of being given an injection of antitoxin immediately on arrival. I can see my mother standing many yards away at a railing while I stood on the ward verandah, conversing with her over the intervening space. Many people in those days died from these diseases. Fortunately for me, the treatment worked.

A pleasure in owning books, in their contribution to the totality of one's knowledge, in the very feel of them, has stayed with me ever since. The prizes I won at school or Sunday school were usually books, and I gradually formed a small library of my own.

My father, a printer, brought me reading material from the printery as well as paper offcuts on which to write and draw. I was given to drawing boats, stimulated I suppose by the yachts riding at anchor off Rushcutters Bay Park where I used to play. My father had once been employed as a journalist, a reporter for country newspapers. I think it was following this occupation that brought him to Moree where he met my mother and her family. Probably it was in Moree that he changed his occupation and became a printer, most likely in a newspaper printery.

From time to time he acted as a proofreader. He often wrote a clear and interesting account of events he had witnessed or in which he had taken part. He once rode a horse from Bega to Cooma over the Watbilliga Range. He used to give a lively account of this journey, and also wrote a brief description of it.

He was not only a literate man but he had wide interests. He had been a sprinter and a footballer — I still have a cap he won as a footballer. He was intensely interested in all sports. He kept himself fully informed about the breeding and performance of racehorses, and was a modest but level-headed punter. At billiards he was outstanding.

From my early boyhood I had taken his dinner to him when he worked back at night. I walked from our house in Glenview Street through Paddington and Woolloomooloo to Hyde Park, through it past the sewer vent (Cleopatra's Needle) opposite the eastern end of Bathurst Street. Then I would cross Elizabeth and Castlereagh Streets to the premises of SW Townsend & Co, where my father worked. The "Needle" still stands there. Whenever I pass it I reflect that it is more than eighty years since I first walked past it. It was then quite safe for a child of tender years to walk the streets alone, even in the dusk of evening. I would stay with my father talking to the other printers till he was ready to come home, then we would walk together back along the route I had come. He talked with me about many things, explaining matters of government and answering my questions about them.

My mother, a Wesleyan Methodist, attended the Bourke Street Methodist Mission, and I regularly attended its Sunday school in Flinders Street,

Darlinghurst. The Methodist Church conducted Statewide annual examinations in biblical knowledge in which I regularly competed. I won many prizes, nearly always books — biography, travel or adventure. Among these prizes were two volumes of which I became very fond. My reading of them may have stimulated or at least fortified my interest in government and my desire to become a lawyer. They were biographies of Abraham Lincoln and James Garfield, both by Thayer. Each of these men was a lawyer and each became President of the United States. Both, as it happens, were assassinated. Both came from humble circumstances and succeeded by their own efforts. Of the two men, I think Lincoln attracted me most. I still regard him as a very great man and his recorded sayings as wise.

These books told me that self-help and whole-hearted application to the daily task could lead to prominence and success in life. They taught me that lack of money did not prevent the full use of what talents one possessed. Indeed, the strictures the lack of wealth imposed on me I have come to see as a blessing in disguise. Consequently I have never bemoaned my origins or my parents' lack of capital or felt jealous of others whose parents have been better placed. Success has come from my own efforts, and there is an intrinsic satisfaction in that.

Both my parents were interested in government and in party politics. I think they differed in their perceptions. My father was of a conservative turn of mind, perhaps staid, but very rational and particularly fair-minded. My mother was ready for change and had those radical leanings so often associated with Wesleyanism. In a strange way, her readiness for change manifested itself in her domestic arrangements, in the frequency with which in their early married life she organised a change of address and in which she constantly reorganised the placement of furniture in the house. We lived in an atmosphere of novelty because of these rearrangements. She was young and vigorous, physically and mentally, strong-minded and a good administrator.

But neither of my parents was dogmatic. Both were intelligent, logical and courteous, though forceful in discussion. Federation was then new and doubtless gave rise to much talk between them and with their relatives and friends, for example on the debate between the free-traders and the protectionists, which was then topical. So I lived in an atmosphere of lively discussion, much of which I heard and at least some of which, probably in a cloudy way, understood.

City Council affairs were also then prominent in public discussion and were vigorously discussed at home. Probably through the printery, my father had a close association with a man named Walker, one of the city aldermen. Candidates for public office in those days advertised themselves by means of calico placards fixed by cotton tapes to the railings of public buildings, mainly the local hotels which were numerous on street corners. My mother had a sewing machine and was deft in its use. At City Council election time she used to sew tapes on to calico placards printed by my father. Some of these carried Mr Walker's name and particulars. In fact she showed me how to attach the tapes to the edges of the placards using her machine. I did sew on many tapes to help her out when she had many to do. So my introduction to public life was of a practical kind.

My father would take me to political meetings. These were almost always held outside a pub, where the candidate would address a street audience from the hotel verandah. There were always questions from the crowd and some banter, at times vociferous, even turbulent. I hold many recollections of such meetings from my very early boyhood. I remember these days as a time when ordinary people had a healthy and spirited involvement in public affairs, and in consequence street meetings were frequent and lively. It was, I think, a much more human involvement than occurs today when people are shut away in their homes with the TV set. All this was an early training in public life which I value immensely.

A little later, at Crown Street school, I was taught a subject called "Civics" in which I learnt a great deal about the structure of government, and that the law was at its heart. I feel sure that by the time I was nine I had a fair grasp of our system of parliamentary government and could understand much of the discussions in our house. Today children grow into adulthood without any proper education in government and are left to the paucity and imbalance of newspaper information. Many become electors while still at school, still ignorant of the structure of the government they vote to elect.

Also on Friday evenings with Father and Mother, I would travel on a horse-drawn bus from about the point where Glenmore Road enters Oxford Street opposite the Victoria Barracks to Mark Foys shop, then situated on the corner of what is now Wentworth Avenue (formerly Wexford Street), where Mother would shop. Father and I would sit in Hyde Park talking until she was ready to return home. Again we would take a horse-drawn bus to a convenient point in Oxford Street from which we could walk to our house in Glenview Street.

These many conversations with my family broadened my knowledge and my general outlook and did much for my self-confidence. I was fortunate to have a father who was a friend and mentor and with whom I could feel relaxed. If these home influences did not provide the source of my interest in law they certainly gave me a milieu in which it was fostered and developed. I think, given my talkativeness, that it was the element of advocacy in the practice of the law which particularly attracted me.

*****

My schooling, apart from the preparatory school at St John's Darlinghurst, was wholly in state schools: first a primary school in Crown Street; then, after passing the qualifying certificate and gaining an Exhibition, at Cleveland Street High School; then at Fort Street, to which I obtained a bursary.

I walked to and from all three schools, whether it was wet or fine. My path to the first two state schools followed common ground and involved walking across the front of St Vincent's Hospital, through the little green park with its pretty band rotunda which still stands there; then along Darlinghurst Road by the convict-built wall of the Darlinghurst gaol into Taylors Square.

My interest in Australian history, which has been a constant in my life, probably began by observing the marks on the stones of the gaol wall, turning over in my mind the spectacle of prisoners under guard doing such good work as is represented in that wall. Apparently each man was required to put his mark on each stone he completed and set in place. As often as time permitted, I would tarry examining the stones, counting those which had identical marks. Such an examination excited my imagination and formed the springboard for later enquiry. I would see the warders with their rifles walking along the top of the wall from the guardhouse. There were railings along this pathway on the wall which would have given them a clear view of the prisoners at work below inside the gaol. I had of course been told of the purpose of the gaol. When the gaol closed and its inhabitants were transferred to the newly built Long Bay Gaol in 1914, I was able to look over the old building, which was then open to public inspection, before the technical schools were placed there. In a ghoulish mood, I remember inspecting the gallows.

Crossing Taylors Square into Campbell Street led me past the Darlinghurst Court House. I had been told of its function and its relation to the gaol, but though I passed it daily, I have no recollection of seeing any barrister in robes walking on its front lawn. As I carried my school bag past this imposing courthouse, I little dreamt that one day I should appear as counsel in its courtrooms and that later still I should preside there over the sittings of the High Court in this very courthouse.

In my year at Cleveland Street, having crossed Taylors Square into Campbell Street, I continued down to Elizabeth Street, often speaking to friendly Chinese merchants standing or sitting in front of their business premises. I passed along Elizabeth Street to Chalmers Street, up Chalmers Street by Prince Alfred Park to the school at the corner of Cleveland and Chalmers Streets (a total distance of approximately two miles). The old building is still used as a school. Prince Alfred Park then had a pavilion where later I sometimes went roller-skating; in the southern portion of the park the school played games.

My walk to Fort Street took a different path. I walked from Glenview Street up the quite steep rise by the side of the Westbush Primary School to Victoria Street, across William Street thence through Kings Cross to the Butler Stairs which lead to the level of the wharves at Woolloomooloo; then along the road to the outer Domain, which then extended over the area now occupied by the Cahill Expressway. Having crossed this part of the Domain, I would enter the Botanic Gardens by the gate that fronts Mrs Macquarie's Road. Then through the Gardens, pausing now and then to look at a plant that attracted my attention. This passing interest in plants did not emerge into active gardening until after I married, but my later deep interest in plants and garden layout probably had its source in those daily walks through the Gardens.

I would leave the Gardens by the Centennial Gates which front Macquarie Street, then pass down Macquarie Street, past the Water Police Court to Circular Quay, across the front of the Customs House and the hotel beside it to the rear of Nock & Kirby's hardware store which was then located in George Street North. I would walk through the store, emerge from it into George Street, walk back along George Street to Essex Street (the street with steps), up that street to the gates of the school, which stood approximately where the toll barriers now stand on the bridge approaches (a total distance of approximately two and a half miles). The boys' school was housed in wooden buildings beside the old military hospital which then housed the girls' school.

Later, when the school was transferred to the new building on Taverners Hill, Petersham, I walked along the route I have earlier described down Campbell Street, along Elizabeth Street to Central Railway Station where I took a steam train to Petersham and then walked up the hill to the school.

Although these journeys were of considerable length I don't remember feeling tired or bothered about having to walk such a distance or being unduly discomforted on wet days. Perhaps at times a fellow school boy walked with me, but mostly my recollection is that I travelled alone. I could not have realised then how useful was the experience of walking to school observing life by the way in building up a breadth of interest that might later be of some consequence; and from the point of view of health it developed muscular capacity that remains with me still.

Nothing happened in my schooling at either Crown or Cleveland Street to divert me from my purpose. English, history, Latin, mathematics and science were all taught, and in all these I became tolerably proficient. At Fort Street there was no question of any discouragement of my desire to follow the law. AJ Kilgour, the Headmaster, himself a qualified barrister, very much favoured a choice of law or medicine as the career for his students. So at the end of my schooldays I remained committed to following the law.

My days at all three schools were pleasant and I made friends. But I had two disadvantages: the first was that I was small in stature and slightly built. I showed no marked aptitude for games although I played football and tennis, and for part of one year soccer, but without conspicuous success. The other was that in general I was about eighteen months younger than my peers in class. This, added to my lightness of build, meant that I was mostly the odd man out, the small or little boy good at his lessons but not readily admitted to the counsels of his larger and older fellows.

I finished my third year at Fort Street when I was fourteen and as a result had I gone straight into the final year (for which I had qualified) I would have been presented for the Leaving Certificate and university admission when I was fifteen. This the headmaster would not accept. He ruled that I should go into a remove year so as to be ready for the leaving certificate at sixteen. This was a minor disaster. The remove year was made up mostly of students who had not made the grade. I found myself going astern. I lacked the competition of boys of my own standing. I remember that a maths master, Mr Gale, who had taught me in third year, returned to the school and taught me in the final year. When he had had a good look at my work he called me out and asked what had happened to me, because apparently he realised that I had been coasting through the remove year and had not been under enough pressure to use what talents I had. He then prescribed a special extracurricular activity for me and began to knock me into shape.

I mention this because I think educators should allow an advanced student, even if younger than the general run of the class, to get ahead. Age should not be a reason to check the progress of such a student. Indeed I feel that we start substantial education too late — we should start in the pre-school years. Further, we do not place enough pressure on the student and we have too short a period of daily schooling. I do not pause to consider the cause of current practice but I do think that our attitudes need changing.

* * * * *

During my last year at school and through a large part of my first year in university, my family had suffered a very serious upset. In the preceding year or so, my father had become affected by lead from handling the moveable lead type by which printing was done at that time. He had to abandon his trade. My parents, largely through the initiative and energy of my mother, became shopkeepers in the suburb of Burwood. They had another reason to move from Paddington. They were medically advised that because of my bronchitis, with its occasional overtones of asthma, I should be moved into a drier climate. They opened a novelty shop — what these days would be called a gift shop — in Burwood Road, between Railway Parade and Belmore Street. The family lived over the shop in an area commodious enough for my parents to be able to let part of it to a member of the Fire Brigade, which then had its station at the corner of Burwood Road and Belmore Street.

The venture began to prosper. I helped in the shop before and after school. My mother did the buying and the organising, my father supporting her with any heavy work. In the meantime, he became involved in community affairs, particularly in the support of the Western Suburbs District Hospital.

When we settled in to our above-shop residence in Burwood the family joined the congregation of Burwood Methodist Church, and my brothers and I attended its very active Sunday school. The Reverend Vause Cocks was its minister. He had a flair for exciting the interest of young people and actively promoted many activities for them — plays and play readings, debates, outings and other local gatherings. A tennis club was formed and had the use of a grass court, the property of the Highways, a prominent family in the area.

During my teens I participated in these various activities. I joined the tennis club, as did Hubert Keir, George Rouse, Cedric Lewis and quite a number of others. So did Norma, who was a fellow pupil at the school. She was some three years younger than I. Her full name was Norma Mountier Symons. She was the elder of two sisters, children of William Symons (deceased) and Charlotte, nee Grant. We saw much of each other, indeed played frequently in competition tennis in a minor grade. Norma was attractively handsome, intelligent, equable and had a good sense of humour. She dressed quietly but very well. Her father had died while she was very young. Her widowed mother and her grandmother lived above the millinery shop which her mother conducted in Burwood Road on the opposite side of the railway line to the novelty shop.

As I reached my late teens we were attracted to each other and began to walk out together — indeed there cannot be any of the then pleasant streets of Strathfield or Burwood that we have not traversed together, talking about books and plays as well as local events and, later on, our own futures. Norma had been taken from school after passing the Intermediate Certificate to work in her mother's millinery business. Later she managed for her mother a second shop located in a neighbouring suburb. She studied the piano under Frank Hutchens at the Conservatorium. She was always eager to learn and had been anxious to continue her education; she has never ceased to regret that she did not. She was well capable of handling complicated concepts and to profit by tertiary education. She is an avid reader and constantly widens her horizons.

Our attachment to each other grew, I suppose you might say, imperceptibly. We found real companionship in each other's company. As my salary as an articled clerk grew, we began to go to theatres and ballet together. We saw Pavlova perform (I remember that the tickets cost me three guineas each). As time went on we both became prepared to spend a lifetime together, though we did not discuss early marriage as I had yet to qualify and accept the vagaries of a practice at the Bar.

But when in 1929 I had been in practice for two years and could, as it were, see daylight, I proposed that we marry, and we did in that year. Our mutual affection and companionship has remained firm and lively to this day, now sixty-five years on. It supports us in our declining years as we reflect on the events of the past and find satisfaction in the achievements of our children and grandchildren.

* * * * *

Before this stage was reached the family passed through the period of the pneumonic influenza epidemic which ravaged the population. I was myself laid low by it. My mother nursed friends who were more seriously affected than any of our family. The strain on her having at the same time the burden of shopkeeping was considerable, even though she was yet young and vigorous.

A year or so after efforts during the epidemic she was struck down by an attack of tuberculosis which rendered her practically speechless. Without her, it seemed impossible to carry on the business. The shop had to be sold, my mother was admitted to the RT Hall Sanitarium at Hazelbrook in the Blue Mountains, and the family was dispersed. I took my two brothers to relatives in the Monaro. Douglas, the elder, went to the Welches, my father's cousins running the local dairy and milk supply in Cooma. Russell went to my father's brother Tom and his wife Carrie at Shoe Makers Creek near Bibbenluke below Nimitabel on the road to Bombala. My father went for a time to Nyngan on the Western Plains to find employment, and later boarded out in Sydney until the family was reunited. My mother was desolated by this enforced interruption of her direct care for the family.

Stephen and Ada Keir, later of Akubra hat fame, generously took me into their home, "Tolosa", in Selbourne Street, Burwood, and treated me as one of their sons, a kindness for which I have ever been grateful. It was nonetheless a troublesome time for me, pulling my weight in their family. I visited my mother often in her mountain retreat, where the treatment consisted mainly of fresh air and exercise; streptomycin was then in the dim dístant future.

Due in no small part to her great spirit and will to survive, my mother recovered and through the remainder of her life — she lived to be ninety-three — had no recurrence of her illness. But it was more than a year before she returned to the family. Meantime, through the last months of my schooling and part of my first year in university, I remained part of the Keir family.

A near disaster occurred in the month before the Leaving Certificate examination. My lower legs quite suddenly developed painful lumps. The local doctor diagnosed what he called knotty gout. I think its technical name was *erithemen nodosum*. I was to be bandaged in hot boracic-soaked packs and confined to bed for at least fourteen days. Mrs Keir attended to me, provided these wrappings and kept me in bed. But the examination was only two weeks away. For days I lay in bed becoming increasingly anxious, not conscious of any improvement. At length I made a foolish and desperate resolution. I decided that I would get out of bed and perform some vigorous exercise of the legs. In my unscientific way, I thought that I would force the blood to flow and so clear my legs of the trouble.

So, much to Mrs Keir's strong objection, I borrowed her eldest son's bicycle and rode it along Parramatta Road (then mostly a clay surface) and through Homebush to Lidcombe and Granville. The experience was very painful indeed: I have never forgotten it. I came back tired and in bad shape. But, marvellous to relate, after a few days and a little more of the prescribed treatment, my legs cleared and I sat for the examination. But it was a narrow squeak. The incident stands out in my memory as a turning point of no small importance.

Now Fortune smiled on me. My Leaving Certificate results gained me a bursary tenable at Sydney University which paid my fees (as long as I passed the annual examinations), provided £5 annually for textbooks and entitled me to free travel on the suburban railway system between Burwood and Central during term. No doubt my parents were delighted; I certainly was. Where life would have taken me had I not received this award I often wonder. Perhaps I would still have made something of a career, but I feel certain I would not have filled the high offices it has been my lot to fill.

On the day I enrolled in the university, I wore long trousers for the first time, forsaking the bloomers and long socks I had worn as a schoolboy. The garb was symbolic. I had made a great step towards maturity, a process which was to accelerate during my three years in the Faculty of Arts and to come to fruition as I moved through Law. At sixteen, in truth, I was too young to absorb all the benefit of university life. But nonetheless in those three years my horizons were vastly expanded, my interests considerably diversified and my capacity for forming firm judgments strengthened, while the problems of life presented ever more angles and possibilities. I greatly enjoyed this process of learning and maturing. I had always been eager for knowledge and enjoyed the endeavour of acquiring it. Now there was so much more to know.

For my BA I read Latin, English Language and Literature, English History, Economics and Philosophy, of which Psychology and Physiology formed segments. The regulations allowed the student to count the first two courses in the Faculty of Law, Roman and Constitutional Law, in the required ten for a BA. I studied Latin under Professor Todd, English under Professor Mungo MacCallum, History under Professor Arnold Wood, Psychiatry and Physiology under Professor Lovell, Philosophy under Professor Francis Anderson and later Professor Bernard Muscio, and Economics under Professor Mills. They were very full years, chock-full with the excitement of learning.

I became active in the Student Christian Movement and joined in critical studies of the basics of the Christian religion. This brought me into touch with keen and enquiring minds, some from other faculties of the university. Among these was Dr Sam Angus of the Presbyterian Church. Dr Angus was a Greek scholar of note and a clergyman with radical ideas whom many in his church regarded as a heretic. Indeed, he had been charged as such before the Church Tribunal, but been acquitted. From him I learnt much of the history of the development of the gospels, and over time I became less convinced of the theology of the Christian church, as did others of my companions in the student movement. But of the validity of the Christian ethic I remained and still remain unreservedly convinced.

I graduated Bachelor of Arts in 1922, at the age of nineteen. By then our family, after Mother's return from Hazelbrook, had moved to The Broadway, Enfield, at the top of The Boulevarde, which ran almost to Strathfield Station. Again, I daily walked its length to catch a train to Central, thence to walk to the university, and in my last year there to the Law School in Phillip Street as well.

Now I had to turn my attention to securing articles of clerkship. While I was still minded to become a barrister, I thought to delay any final decision on whether to become a solicitor or a barrister till after I had graduated in Law. So to increase my options I decided to qualify as a solicitor.

Here I was fortunate. In some cases solicitors still asked substantial premiums to agree to articles of clerkship, which carried the obligation to instruct the clerk. I had no personal or family contacts which might help me in securing articles, and I would have been quite unable to pay any premium. The Dean, however, whom I consulted, gave me introductions to JW Maund of Maund & Kelymack and HW Waddell. I first called on Mr Maund. He was a bluff and, on first meeting, a grumpy man. I left him quite uncommitted. I then saw Mr Waddell. He seemed much more affable. Though he evidently had a smaller practice than Maund & Kelymack, I decided to take articles with him. Neither Mr Maund nor Mr Waddell asked for any premium.

In later years Maund became a great supporter of my practice at the Bar, and I came to know him well. He had been a distinguished footballer and was a painter of considerable talent. He had a good knowledge of Australian painting and was responsible for the introduction of Tom Roberts's painting *Bailed Up* into the Art Gallery of New South Wales. His language was always direct, forceful and at times colourful. He had a sly sense of humour. He was also a good lawyer.

Waddell practised in Challis House, Martin Place, a building with a central bow window on the upper floors. Waddell's practice occupied three rooms on the third floor. I was given the room with the bow window. I looked out on the statue of Queen Victoria on the central Post Office building on the opposite side of Martin Place. As a measure of the times, the telephone number was City 309, operated through a manual exchange. The building was served by a hydraulically operated lift, as were other buildings in Sydney at the time. For my own part I usually used the staircase.

Waddell's practice was largely conveyancing, but there was always some litigious work on hand. His father had been Colonial Treasurer for New South Wales, a circumstance which may well have helped his practice. He had a great number of grazier clients, most with money to invest. The time of my articles included the days of great activity in house-building in suburban Sydney. North Bondi, western suburbs such as Ashfield and Canterbury, and on the north side, Willoughby and Lane Cove, were being filled with brick bungalows. Financing of the builders and the purchasers from them was provided on first mortgage by insurance companies, trustee companies and trust funds in the control of solicitors and on second mortgage by individual lenders out of their own funds. Waddell had established a favourable relationship with some of these sources of first-mortgage money, including the infant Australian Prudential Association, then located in a building in King Street close to George Street on the west side. But even more importantly, his clientele of graziers was a source of considerable funds for investment on second mortgage. As a result, by the time I was articled, Waddell had developed a considerable conveyancing practice with some attendant litigation.

It became one of my duties from time to time to find the first-mortgage lender through contacts with the larger firms of solicitors who had trust moneys to invest or through insurance or trustee companies. In this way I met some of the principal solicitors and some of their managing clerks. These latter formed a group of very experienced but unqualified men, whose like does not seem now to exist.

Besides myself, there were two other clerks, one already articled and the other under promise of articles. As a solicitor could not have more than two clerks under articles at the same time, on accepting Waddell's offer I unwittingly displaced the clerk under promise of articles. The articled clerk was Theo Conybeare, with whom I had been friendly at the university. The clerk under promise was Simon (Sam) Isaacs (later a judge of the Supreme Court). With both men I established a lifelong friendship. Conybeare became chairman of the NSW Workers Compensation Commission and Isaacs a judge of the NSW Supreme Court.

Later, after Conybeare and Isaacs had transferred to other solicitors, Alf Gain joined the staff of the office as an articled clerk. Gain became a distinguished member of the NSW Bar. Tragically, he died in the aeroplane crash on Mt Dandenong in 1938.

Waddell had grazing interests near Merriwa, New South Wales. Early during my clerkship he seemed to gain confidence in me and progressively entrusted me with important decisions in the affairs of the practice. He was a bachelor, gregarious but not, as has been written, bibulous. He had a ruddy complexion but I did not at any time see him under the influence of alcohol. He went to his country property from time to time, sometimes for up to a week. On these occasions he left me in charge of his practice but always kept me apprised of his movements.

During my clerkship there was only one institution in Sydney, the MLC, which would pay interest on money deposited at call. The banks would not. Waddell always arranged with clients who provided money for investment or for settlement of transactions that the funds could be deposited at call with the MLC, crediting them in due course with the interest. As a result, his trust account carried only so much money as might be needed for the early settlement of transactions.

The confidence reposed in me and the responsibility I was given for handling these funds fostered a capacity for decision and the exercise of judgment and certainly did nothing to lessen my self-confidence. It was indeed a splendid supplement to my continuing law course with its practical emphasis.

I remember an occasion when such qualities were called into urgent use.

One morning, when Waddell had been away for a day or so, Mr Garvin, manager of the Elizabeth Street branch of the Commercial Bank, with which all our accounts were kept, rang me to ask me did I realise that the trust account was overdrawn! It was chilling news. Waddell was away. I had to act. I expressed surprise to Garvin. He asked me what was I going to do about it. I asked him what was he going to do as Conybeare was on his way to the bank with a cheque for a five-figure sum required for the settlement of a transaction that day. He would be seeking a bank cheque for that amount. Garvin asked me what did I think. I said there must be some mistake as I was sure of the honesty of the solicitor. Garvin then said he would provide Conybeare with the required bank cheque but asked me to seek no further withdrawals till we had cleared the matter up. That I was able to do as no other settlements were immediately pending.

In the practice we had no resident accountant. Mr Wilfred Allsop visited regularly and I often helped him in unravelling any matters of account. This gave me an insight into some aspects of accountancy which otherwise I would not have had. This day, I immediately rang Allsop and asked him when he had last checked the bank passbook with the deposit and cheque books. He said, somewhat apologetically, that he was somewhat behind with this. I told him briefly what I had learned and suggested that he repair the matter urgently.

I asked each clerk to work out and tell me what sums in matters controlled by him ought to be in the trust account. I did the same with transactions in my own hands. This produced the extraordinary information that there ought to have been more than £200 000 in the account which Garvin had said was overdrawn, though he had not mentioned by how much. The accountant had meantime found an almost incredible fact — that a very large number of cheques for large amounts drawn on another account, which bore a name unlikely to be confused with Waddell's, had been mistakenly debited to the trust account over a period of weeks. When I went to see him later that day Garvin was full of apologies and grateful to me for having, through my confidence that there had been a mistake, persuaded him to honour the cheque presented by Conybeare.

When Waddell returned a day or so later, I told him what had happened and said that in future, before he left on a country journey, I hoped he would see that the banking records had been brought up to date by the accountant. The incident both taught me lessons about checking facts and increased my self-reliance and capacity for decision.

Waddell had already increased my commencement pay of ten shillings a week without waiting for any prompting by me. My weekly salary progressed quite steadily so that in my third year I was receiving £9 9s per week, no small sum for an articled clerk at the time. He seemed to recognise that I accepted responsibility and attended carefully to my work. So carefully did I attend that during the law school examinations and my preparation for them I had no break from the office. When I had an examination paper in the early part of the day, I returned immediately to the office on its completion; when I had to sit for examinations in the afternoon, I worked in the office during the morning.

I was fortunate to be taught the law and its practice by men who were themselves in daily practice. No academic lawyer would have done as well for me. The Law School of my time had two professors, "Jacko" Peden, Professor of Law and Dean of the Faculty, and Archie Charteris, Professor of International Law. The school was then, as now, in the City of Sydney. It was housed in University Chambers in Phillip Street. Lectures were mostly given in the early morning and in the late afternoon, before and after the business of the courts took place. Active members of the Bar were thus able to lecture on various aspects of the law.

At the end of my period of articles, Waddell offered me a partnership with no capital contribution. The offer was generous but by then I had decided that I did not wish to practise as a solicitor. I had my mind set on joining the Bar. I declined Waddell's kind offer but asked him to introduce me to his cousin Dr George Waddell, a partner in Minter Simpson, in order that I might seek a place in Minters as a clerk for a year or so. He did so. By that time I had completed my law degree, in fact with honours and a share of the University Medal.

I saw Dr Waddell and, no doubt backed by his cousin's reference to my clerkship, made a favourable impression. Minters and Allen Allen & Hemsley had at that time followed the practice of employing graduates as clerks for a period before they sought admission to the Bar. This had advantages for the firms but chiefly it gave the clerk a chance to commend himself to solicitors who might later support him at the Bar.

But I did not get into Minters. Bernard Sugerman had been with the firm immediately before I applied. Clifford Minter, the chief voice in Minters, decided that no longer were Minters "to be made use of" by intending members of the Bar. So he vetoed my request.

A few months after my application to Minters, Waddell received an acceptance from Mr Doug Sharpe to join him in partnership. The firm became Waddell & Sharpe and later Waddell, Davies & Sharpe. By then I had left Waddell's employ, with much goodwill on both our parts. But it left me at a loose end, for I had overlooked the need to register as a student at law, which had to be effected at least two years before applying for admission to the Bar. Of course, I had served three years' articles and passed all the necessary exams. I was fully qualified to be admitted as a solicitor. And I had by this time both an Arts and a Law degree. But this was not enough. I was dissuaded by the Dean from asking the court to waive the requirement of two years' studentship and decided to wait the passage of time.

I knew that Roy Booth, a fellow Fortian, was starting up in practice in Sydney, so I applied to him for a job. He gave me a place as his "managing clerk", though I was really his only clerk and became his general factotum. So, for more than eighteen months, while I waited for the two years of studentship to elapse, I worked for Roy Booth, doing all the chores like registration and stamping of documents as well as handling transactions. When the two years had passed I left, grateful for the opportunities Roy had given me. With my studentship at law now passed, I was fully qualified for admission.

I was admitted to the Bar on 1 June 1927. The long haul from primary school to this day represented a steady if unspectacular progress. But there was now a new beginning, a new and possibly a much more searching examination to pass.

2 Early Days in Practice

As the time for applying for admission drew closer, I began to search for chambers in Phillip Street. It was not long before I found that there were no vacant rooms to be had. Many counsel, particularly young counsel, were sharing chambers. I realised that I would have to do likewise.

After many enquiries, Sybil Greenwood, sometimes known as Sybil Morrison, agreed to let me share her chambers as a temporary arrangement, for which I was most grateful. She was the only woman practising at the Bar at the time, and worked mainly in divorce. Her chambers were in Campbell House, a two-storey double-fronted building next door to St Stephens Church.

On the first floor, which was reached by a few steps from street level, WA Holman KC occupied two rooms on the right-hand side of a wide central hallway. Percy Higgins occupied the room on the left, and Sybil occupied the room on the left at the rear. After Bill Holman got to know me through my coming and going from Sybil's room, he gave me the use of his secretary's room, which was part of his suite. I occupied that room along with his secretary for some time.

This room had the advantage of Holman's quite extensive law library, to which he gave me ready access. He not only had a door into his secretary's room, but he had a door out of his main room into the hallway. He counselled me always to have two entrances to my chambers. He said he had learnt that need in politics; that I would find occasions when, if I had only one door to my room, it would not be possible to avoid two solicitors who might dislike one another meeting at my door, with the result that I might have the problem of either hastening one out of the room or delaying the other while I conversed with the first. With a second door I might avoid the two men confronting each other.

So I began in Sybil Greenwood's chambers. I was, as all young barristers are according to Gilbert, an impecunious party, a man without capital and certainly one unable to pay high rent.

The great adventure that was beginning had its obvious perils. I was to rely solely on my own abilities, attempting to master the art of advocacy, and then attract the attention of solicitors and their litigating clients. No advertising was possible, a feature of practice I have never regretted. Indeed I think the advertising which is now permissible does nothing to enhance the standing of the profession in the community. What was to happen to me must come from a confluence of my own efforts and good fortune, something without which few barristers succeed.

During my articled clerk days, the advocates at common law, or at least some prominent among them, were of a theatrical kind given to rhetoric, seeking thereby to influence the jury. I fear that at times they treated the jury much as some politicians treat the electors — as if they were only swayed by emotive considerations and unable by the exercise of common sense to form reasonable judgments. I realised early that I had little use for rhetoric, chiefly because it was somewhat beyond my talents.

I came to think that as an advocate I should adopt a quiet presentation, leaving room for raising the voice and for gesture when emphasis was needed, but concentrating on reducing to simple terms the issues to be decided and the principles of law to be applied. I thought I should act on the footing that the jury were intelligent, honest and capable of being instructed in even the most complicated matters of fact and that they could apply principles of law if these were simply expressed; that in general they would listen closely to what counsel and the judge had to say. I thought that my task would be to persuade them by logic and good sense. I realised that there is room in appropriate cases to press the jury to give effect to human values where the law seemed not to do so.

I was twenty-four when I began practice. Although I had had experience of legal practice in solicitors' offices for about five years, I had had no personal experience in the presentation in court of a client's case. I had taken every opportunity which offered during my days of clerkship to listen in court to the conduct of a case. But I had had little formal preparation for court craft.

One thing I resolved early was that in working on a case I would always work from the ground up. I would examine closely the relevant accepted wisdom of the day but not take it for gospel; I would verify it from original sources. In this way, in later days, I often found a principle which was misunderstood in its current application, or one that had been forgotten or overlooked. Following this course, I sometimes achieved results that in themselves appeared novel but which were simply built on the fundamentals of the law.

After a few days in chambers I received a brief. Monty Fowler, a friend of student days and now a solicitor, had saved a case so that he could give me my first brief. My baptism came in the form of a brief in an undefended suit for divorce brought by a male petitioner.

Mr Justice Langer Owen was the judge in divorce at this time. He was the father of Sir William Owen. In private life Langer Owen was what might be called a withdrawn man, but in court he had a somewhat caustic tongue. The rumoured story at the Bar is that he once refused to 'see' counsel (a Mr Thompson) who appeared in court in a pair of brown trousers. Counsel had had to withdraw to rearrange his dress for appearance on another day! While this looks excessive to our eyes, there remains a need for decorum in court, in dress as well as in behaviour, both for the reputation of the profession and for maintaining that dignity of proceedings essential to the administration of the law.

At the pre-trial conference with my client, Monty informed me that the man was somewhat hard of hearing. In chambers I seemed able to get through to him without having to raise my voice, but in the atmosphere of the courtroom he proved to be almost stone deaf. Whether or not the nervous tension caused by that experience accentuated his inability to hear me, the fact was that speaking across the well of the court, my small pipe, naturally thin, and perhaps more so because of my own nervousness, failed to reach the petitioner. But certainly I was not struck dumb, as I had read the Great Erskine was on his first appearance. It is said of him that only the thought that he had a young family to support got him going. At any rate, I could not get through to this client.

The judge soon realised my predicament. He kindly suggested that I approach the petitioner as he stood in the witness box. In our courts, quite unlike the practice of some American courts, counsel may not leave his place at the Bar table and approach the witness without the judge's leave. This is given when some need to approach a witness arises. Again I feel sure this is a good rule. It has its place not merely in the standing of the profession and decorum in the courts, but in the protection of the witness from the intimidation which the proximity of counsel might engender.

So, at the judge's invitation, I went close to the witness box. The petitioner was still some distance from me as the floor of the box was several steps above floor level, the situation exacerbated by my own lack of height. By raising my voice, however, I managed to get the petitioner to respond to my questions. Thus I fulfilled the requirements to justify a decree nisi, which was duly pronounced. Escorted by the petitioner and Monty Fowler I left the courtroom with a profound sense of relief. The ice had been broken!

* * * * *

Remembering my first appearance in court excites a memory of my last appearance as counsel in April 1960, thirty-one years later.

In 1960 the High Court decided by majority that the liquor licence fee charged by the State of Victoria was not an excise within the meaning of s 90 of the Australian Constitution. Fullagar, Kitto, Taylor and Menzies JJ joined to make the majority in a court of seven. Dixon CJ dissented and thought that the licence fee was an excise. He was joined by McTiernan and Windeyer JJ. Personally, I thought, and am still inclined to think, that Dixon and those with him were correct. Only the Commonwealth can impose such a tax.[1]

Dennis Hotels decided to apply to the Privy Council seeking special leave to appeal. The State of Victoria took the view that the Privy Council would have no jurisdiction to hear the appeal because of s 74 of the Constitution, that is to say, the court's decision involved a question *inter se* of the legislative powers of the Commonwealth and State.

If the licence fee did constitute an excise, then it had been unlawfully imposed and collected. The State of Victoria accordingly may have been liable to refund millions of pounds. The Premier, Sir Henry Bolte, asked Prime Minister Menzies to intervene in the case on behalf of the Commonwealth and, as I understand it, also asked if I could be persuaded as Attorney-General to represent the Commonwealth before the Privy Council.

Menzies asked me what I thought of the High Court decision. I said that I thought that Dixon's view was right. It depended on the place the fees occupied in the movement of goods towards consumption. I further thought that the English judges were likely to think the fee was an excise, moved to some extent by Dixon's views. If the Privy Council did take the matter in hand, the chances were that Dennis Hotels would succeed. He then asked me whether I would lead for the Commonwealth if it intervened; I agreed to do so. The question of the Council's jurisdiction to entertain the appeal was set down as a preliminary question on 24 April.

I immediately got in touch with the Attorneys of the States and suggested that if at all possible the law officers of each State should represent the State before the Council, all taking the same view on jurisdiction. They would thus present a united front in favour of the proposition that the Council had no jurisdiction to hear the appeal. In this I was partly successful because in the long run law officers did represent two of the States, Victoria and New South Wales. At the same time an application for special leave to appeal from a similar decision of the High Court (the *Whitehouse* appeal[2]) was set down for hearing. In the result the arguments in both cases were heard at the one hearing.

I had no opportunity for consultation with the counsel representing the States, including the law officers, before they left for London. I worked on the argument myself in Canberra. Dixon CJ had decided in *ANA No 2*,[3] at least inferentially, that s 74 only applied to the delimitation of concurrent powers, a view I had always thought insupportable. Indeed, there may be much to be said for the view that a question *inter se* could not arise in the case of concurrent powers, powers which by definition were concurrent and thus had no margins to delimit. Any inconsistency of legislation under such powers would be resolved by s 109 of the Constitution, which in that event gave the Commonwealth law paramountcy.

When there was an unsuccessful application for a certificate under s 74 in *Nelungaloo v Commonwealth*, Chief Justice Dixon delivered a reasoned judgment to the effect in substance that s 74 had no necessary application to the delimitation of an exclusive power.[4] The question in the *Dennis Hotels* case did concern an exclusive power, the power to levy duties of customs or excise (s 90). In addition, there were expressions in the Privy Council decision on the *Bank* case[5] and in Nelungaloo which might be thought adverse to the intended argument of the Commonwealth and the States. The respondent and the interveners had therefore to make good the proposition that the delimitation of an exclusive power necessarily involved a question *inter se* in the face of discouraging prior expressions.

The cases were listed for a Monday. I was to arrive in London on the preceding Friday night. I sent word to all the counsel involved in opposing jurisdiction, asking them to meet me in conference on the Saturday morning. They very kindly did so. The Commonwealth, as I thought, had a predominant interest in maintaining a wide application of s 74; and I felt myself, as Australian Attorney-General, in a position to set the argument, though I could not be the first speaker on this point.

The counsel for the respondent and intervening States had worked out an approach to the case which they explained to me. I thought it rather insufficient for success. It would be necessary in my view to attack the case somewhat differently: I laid out the argument I had already worked out for myself. Seemingly, I convinced them because they were quite willing to support my point of view. In a sense I was attempting to lead the regiment from behind. That, of course, had a degree of risk when presenting an argument which was not supported by existing authority and which to a significant extent ran in the face of discouraging expressions.

The board consisted of Lord Simonds in the chair and Lords Reid, Radcliffe, Tucker and Hodson. The applicant was represented by Mr Gowans QC, Godfrey Le Quesne (of the English Bar) and Mr O'Shea. The State of Victoria was represented by Sir Henry Winneke QC, then Solicitor-General and later successively Chief Justice and Governor of Victoria; Mr Young (later Chief Justice of Victoria) and Mr Gatehouse of the English Bar (later Mr Justice Gatehouse of the English High Court); and by Professor Zelman Cowen QC, later Sir Zelman Cowen and Governor-General of Australia.

Queensland, as respondent to the *Whitehouse* appeal, was represented by Mr Gibbs (later Sir Harry Gibbs and Chief Justice of Australia) and Mr Heald. New South Wales was represented by Mr Downing QC, Attorney-General, and Mr Holland QC (later Mr Justice Holland of the NSW Supreme Court). Western Australia, South Australia and Tasmania were represented by Mr Chambers QC, Professor Cowen and Mr Gatehouse. Mr Bennett QC and Godfrey Le Quesne represented the appellant Whitehouse. I was assisted by Mr Helsham (later Mr Justice Helsham of the NSW Supreme Court).

When the question of jurisdiction to hear an appeal in the case of *Dennis Hotels* had been set down as a preliminary matter for 24 April, the administrative officers of the Privy Council had been told that the case would last a month. Consequently, that amount of time was set aside by the Privy Council and by my department to allow me to appear and conclude the argument. But we finished the argument in a week. Judgment was delivered immediately, the Council holding that jurisdiction to hear the appeal was lacking and dismissing the petition for special leave. Supporting reasons written by Lord Radcliffe were published on 14 June.

What a contrast the two appearances afford. In the first I must have cut a lonely figure, battling with a deaf client to elicit simple personal details. In the last I was part of a galaxy of counsel arguing before the most prestigious tribunal of the United Kingdom, presenting subtle arguments on the meaning of the Australian Constitution.

I remember that on the latter occasion I had with me in London my personal secretary, Miss Wilkinson. When I returned to the hotel with my red bag containing my robes, I said to her, 'Well, Wilkie, you can put the robes away for good. I doubt if I will ever wear them again'. Little did I know that in 1964 I should wear the same gown again, though with a different wig, as Chief Justice of Australia.

* * * * *

To return to beginnings, a few weeks after my first appearance, Percy Higgins, who had retired as a country solicitor to practise at the Bar — casually as it seemed to me — asked me at quite short notice to take over from him the defendant's brief in a jury action in the Supreme Court. Unabashed by the brevity of the time for detailed preparation, I agreed to do so. Perhaps longer experience might have dictated more caution. But as it happened, in a matter of a day or so, I found myself in No 1 court before Mr Justice David Ferguson and a jury of four.

Cross-examination is an art I do not think I ever fully mastered, certainly not to the degree attained by others. Some were successful in attacking a witness in an endeavour to destroy his credibility and thus eliminate his evidence from the case. I developed no such talent. My method was to try to elicit from the witness answers which would qualify the evidence already given, minimise its effect and if possible find contradictions within it. I also sought answers which would provide material for my final address to the tribunal, whether judge or jury, according to a logical plan I had already formed. I did not seek to publicise that plan when cross-examining. Often, I think, the delay in expressing it weakened its impact. Perhaps a contrary impression had thus been allowed to be formed by the tribunal.

But I early learnt the folly of questioning too far. This affords the witness an opportunity of giving you some information you do not want, and you lose the advantage you have already gained. It was a lesson I never forgot, though the decision on when to stop remains difficult.

I was cross-examining an elderly gentleman. He had given evidence of a street accident which caused the litigation in which we were engaged. I observed that he wore heavy spectacles, indicating poor sight. Observing him closely, I thought he favoured his left eye as if it were the weaker of the two. So in a succession of questions, I placed him in relation to the position of the cars, so that they were on his left side and I had him looking mostly straight ahead. Then I made my move. I said that evidently he had weak sight. His response was to say, 'Young man, I'll not have you making fun of me'. I had to assure him that I had no such intent but needed an answer to my question. He agreed that he had weak sight. Now I had noticed that when the judge (who sat to the left of the witness box) spoke to him, he seemed to turn his head so as to bring his right eye over the bridge of his nose. My next question was, 'And your left eye is much weaker than your right?'. He said that that was not so. I then asked the question too far for I ought to have realised that I could not do much better than I had already done. But I plunged in:

'But I notice that when you wish to see the learned judge, you turn your head in order to bring your right eye to bear on him.'

'Nothing of the kind, young man. I am quite deaf in the left ear and need to do so to hear the judge.'

My first experience of cross-examination came in *Agnes v Clatsworthy*, a case that concerned the sale of a hotel. In cross-examining the plaintiff, Mrs 'A', I thought that her sex and age required me to be at least considerate if not pointedly gentle. As my questioning proceeded, courteously but persistently, I realised that the lady had a degree of cunning and was affecting not to understand my questions, thus evading them. I persisted for a time, probing the circumstances of the transaction vigorously enough but with quiet restraint. As I concluded that the lady was fencing with me and that I had demonstrated her reluctance to be frank, I thought I should call attention dramatically to that situation.

I resolved to say, firmly, "Surely, Mrs 'A', you are not as stupid as you are trying to make out". That would have been folly enough. But in my attempt at the dramatic I said, "Surely, Mrs 'A', you are not as stupid as you look". Whereupon everybody, jury, counsel and, in a mild way, the judge, reacted disapprovingly. I apologised, I hope handsomely, but I was extremely embarrassed and found it difficult to remedy the situation.

The trial proceeded smoothly enough nevertheless. I addressed the jury, putting the client's case forcibly and I think logically. But the plaintiff won.

After the verdict and the dismissal of the jury, when the judge had started to retire, the associate came forward and told me that the judge wished to see me straightaway. My heart began to beat heavily. I felt that I was in for a reproof, perhaps even a roasting. But the judge received me with a quiet smile. David Ferguson was one of the kindest of men. He complimented me on my conduct of the case, generously putting me at ease. He asked questions about me, where I had been educated, how long I had been in practice and what training in the law I had had. I was relieved and delighted by the judge's kindness.

I had mastered the intricacies of common-law pleading and over the next months began to take pleading points which were settled before a judge in chambers. These hearings lasted half an hour. Argument had therefore to be brief and to the point. Judge Ferguson was particularly expert in common-law pleading and frequently sat in chambers in pleading matters. I appeared before him on many occasions, mostly in chambers but also in jury trials.

* * * * *

When Judge Ferguson retired, I went to wish him well and to thank him, as he had always been kind and considerate to me. When I arrived at his chambers, someone was already with him and I had to wait in the associate's rooms, with his tipstaff. He was an elderly man, white-haired and rotund, reputedly well off and eking out his days looking after the judge, bringing his law books when necessary, attending to his robes and the like. I was on good terms with the old gentleman.

Alone with him this day, I said, "I suppose you'll be staying with the new judge".

His reply was swift and decisive. "No, there'll be no new judge for me".

Thinking he was moved by consideration of his age, I said, "Oh, but there's still life in the old dog".

"It's not that", he said, "I couldn't put up with a young fellow. He'd have me running here and there to get him books or this and that, and a 'Bully and Leak'.[6] But you know, it isn't like that with my judge. When he goes on circuit he only takes his notebook — and he's always right".

I do not think I ever heard a better tribute to a great judge, who knew his law, expressed it simply and used it well.

I decided early that I would spread my practice as widely as I could rather than concentrate on long cases as some of my contemporaries seemed to do. So in the beginning I appeared mostly in the Small Debts Court, the Court of Petty Sessions, Quarter Sessions and the District Court. As the practice developed, this entailed a good deal of management, because it was difficult to fit in as many appearances as I had planned, since these courts were some distance from each other. But it did give me a better cash flow. The smaller fees were usually paid more promptly than would have been the case had I been engaged in a long litigation, though perhaps that would have provided greater total remuneration.

Steadily I began to get work, not from larger firms but from solicitors whose clients were often struggling to avoid liabilities or seeking to enforce claims such as overdue rent or overdue debts. During this time I had two appearances in the High Court, one as junior to Mr Andrew Watt KC and the other on my own, successfully seeking special leave to appeal in a tenancy matter, which did not proceed further. These appearances were before a court presided over by Chief Justice Knox and included among its members Mr Justice Isaac Isaacs.

*****

After two years at the Bar when it seemed that I would receive steady work, Norma and I decided to marry. This we did in March 1929. We bought a cottage at Cheltenham, financing ourselves with first and second mortgages and exhausting what little capital we had in the process. Wedding gifts provided the main items of furniture. But near disaster was at hand. Times were turning down and recession was upon us.

The feared recession deepened into a depression and financial crisis overtook me. The elder of my two brothers had wanted to go into business running a petrol station with a partner, a friend of long standing. Both were minors. At their request I agreed to accept financial responsibility for their business, signing the necessary lease of the premises and agreements with the oil companies for the supply of fuel and oil. None of us had had any experience of handling large sums of money on our own account or of keeping personal accounts by double-entry bookkeeping. This, the vagaries of the business itself, and the economic situation, led to serious difficulties. A sum, considerable by the standards of the time, became due to the oil companies. When no funds were available to meet it I sought time from the oil companies, offering to pay the debts over a period of time. But they were unwilling to accommodate me and insisted on going to court, obtaining judgment and ultimately starting insolvency proceedings. These I resisted and in the first instance succeeded in defeating. But the matter was reopened and a sequestration order made.

Through the good offices of Ernest Street, who appeared for me in the sequestration proceedings, the Bar Council was assured that I had not myself been trading; no question of my continuing in practice arose. But of course Norma and I had to begin again. I had to buy our cottage again by arrangement with the second mortgagee, who had foreclosed.

To make matters worse, the Depression deepened. I doubt if anyone who did not pass through it can appreciate the distress it caused. Norma and I suffered along with so many others. To supplement what small income I had I did some coaching of law students and Norma went to work in her trade as a milliner. Our joint efforts and mutual determination to succeed pulled us through, though the depth of the penury we experienced was almost devastating.

The bankruptcy proceedings were not an encouragement to solicitors to brief me, and having to attend to financial affairs had distracted me to no small degree. So the growth of my practice was much retarded.

About this time I found a small room on the first floor of Chancery Chambers, which I could rent for ten shillings a week. It was at the end of a long corridor on each side of which were rooms of various sizes occupied by barristers. Outside the back window of my room, which was close to the ceiling, there was a public toilet. The sounds of flushing and the cistern filling could be heard quite plainly, and often stopped conversation when I was conducting a conference.

But my occupation of this room brought me into touch with Edgar Marks, the barrister's clerk on the first floor of Chancery Chambers. This proved good fortune indeed. He remained my clerk while I was in private practice, and became indispensable to its management. He was completely loyal, was wise in his advice, knew how to keep the secrets of all the barristers he served, indulged in no rumour-mongering and was exceptionally competent in avoiding clashes between cases in which his men were briefed. He played a notable part in my practice, for which I remain most grateful. He was a great human being, a very efficient clerk and over time a great friend to me. I owe very much to him for his support and advice during my dark days and throughout the following years of increasing workload.

The Depression was not all gloom for me. The Moratorium and Rent Restriction Acts provided a great deal of work for the Bar, particularly in the courts of Petty Sessions, the magistrate's courts. Many of the magistrates were unqualified and had learnt the law as they had graduated to become clerks in the courts. I learned to respect most of them as fair and for the most part even-handed administrators of the law.

Work under the Moratorium and Rent Acts provided many opportunities for the exercise of precise legal knowledge, particularly of the law of evidence. Quick responses to these opportunities and decisiveness in taking and arguing points of law attracted professional attention. I found myself by this means steadily increasing my practice.

One small incident occurring at this time bears repetition. I had been briefed to conduct a common-law case before a jury. On the morning on which the case was listed for hearing, I had a savage attack of dysentery. I came to the city in discomfort and told Edgar that I just could not carry on, that he had better make arrangements for a substitute. He said that they had never had a "jib" in chambers and he did not propose to have one now; I had better come with him to the hotel. Now I had been brought up as a strict Wesleyan and had never touched alcohol. But he was so confident that he could help me that I went with him.

We went to the Supreme Court House Hotel which then stood on the corner of Phillip and King Streets where the Law School now stands. He ordered a port wine and brandy in equal parts and I drank it. Although my medical friends tell me it could not have any such effect, in fact it worked on this morning; I went on and conducted the jury trial and, as far as I remember, with some success.

That episode set me off and I became a moderate drinker, slowly favouring spirits as the years added up. This experience of the efficacy of port wine and brandy to stay such an attack enabled me at a much later time to assist Zara Holt. On the occasion of a parliamentary dinner to say farewell to the retiring Governor-General, Lord De Lisle, I sat beside Zara. Just as the dinner got under way she asked me did I think she could leave the table. I did not think she should, and asked her why. She said that she and Harry had been abroad at a treasurers' gathering, had spent a little time in Honolulu on the way home and had contracted some complaint which had brought on dysentery. She did not feel she could see out the dinner. She suggested that she was small enough to bend down so that no one would notice her leaving the room. I said I thought I could help her and ordered her a brandy and port in equal parts. It came and she drank it. She remained and enjoyed her dinner. Remarkable how odd pieces of information come in handy.

My practice expanded steadily, though larger firms did not brief me for quite some time. I depended mainly on those who were often themselves battling against the odds. But one day I was briefed by Percy Williamson & Company. There were two Williamson firms, John and Percy. Both had a great deal of litigious work, but from this day on I had much work from Percy's firm and their clerk, David Seddon, became quite a constant visitor to my chambers.

When Mr Boxall, Percy's partner, met me in conference for the first time I asked him how he had come to retain me. He said that his client had been very insistent that I be instructed. He had been a juror in a common-law case which I had conducted, had been impressed by my performance and had resolved that if he were involved in litigation he would secure my services. Boxall, I think, had had some doubt as to whether his firm ought to brief me and I later learned that he had consulted Victor Maxwell (Snr), at that time a leading KC on the common-law side (subsequently a Supreme Court judge).

I gather Maxwell gave me a very good report. As it happened, he had not only heard of my work at the Bar, but he remembered that I had instructed him in a case in which Harold Waddell had briefed him. Thus I had a piece of good luck and I never forgot that kindness. The spin-off was that other large firms slowly came to brief me.

As success in the lower courts brought me to the notice of solicitors, I became involved in Supreme Court work. Consequently a considerable practice before juries developed. At the same time I worked in Equity. In my time, the Bar was divided between the common law and equity. Some specialised in land, valuation and local government; others concentrated on criminal work. Work on limited liability companies was done as part of practice in the equity jurisdiction. The Bar had not then been attracted to the intricacies of the taxation system. Indeed, when I first began to do work in connection with income tax, some of my contemporaries seemed to think that this was accountants' work and not work for barristers.

As a general rule, men working in the common law did not cross the line into equity and vice versa. So when I began to appear in both jurisdictions I picked up the rumour in the street that I was neither fish nor fowl; indeed I think some of the men on the Equity side became disturbed by my frequent appearances in that jurisdiction, particularly when my clerk would adjust hearing dates in Equity to allow me to maintain my common law lists. But my practice in this respect was part of my overall desire to be an all-rounder, to prepare myself as a senior counsel to handle the law in any of its aspects, and to do so with equal efficiency. In this fashion, I began to be at home in the courtroom, no matter which courtroom it was and no matter which aspect of the law was being administered.

But for a time I maintained one exception as far as I could, though ultimately it proved impossible. I had no desire to practise in the High Court. I feared that, partly because that court sat at Darlinghurst, I would be unable to manage my practice so as to maintain my Supreme Court work as well as many frequent appearances in the High Court.

Throughout my days at the Bar, I made a practice of taking briefs from what I would call "small" solicitors, either solicitors practising on their own or firms that were not very prominent. There were two reasons for this. First, I always remembered those who had supported me in my difficult days, and second, my refusal of these briefs might possibly damage a solicitor's business. If I were needlessly to turn down such a brief the client might easily think that had the brief been offered by a large firm I might have taken it. But following this course complicated life for me as my practice became more extensive. There was always the risk of becoming overburdened.

As the Depression lifted and as I began to build up the practice again, our affairs slowly improved, so much so that by 1937 Norma and I felt financially able to alter our house considerably and think of starting a family, something we had been in no position to do so in the earlier years. Our first child, Ross, was born in 1938.

After a year or so in the small back room in Chancery Chambers, I moved into a large room on the southern side of the corridor. Shortly afterward, another room next door fell vacant and I took it to house a secretary whom I had engaged.

Practice in those days was carried on in unkempt surroundings in paraded untidiness with handwritten opinions, written very often on the back of the case for opinion, which were still frequently delivered on brief paper twice the size of the present A4. This was a device which ensured that the solicitor or client could not use the original opinion apart from the facts and instructions on which it had been given. But the business of secretaries, typewriters and dictating machines was soon to alter all that.

My reasons for getting a secretary quite early were, first, that my handwriting, which has never been good — it gets worse when I write quickly — often had the solicitors' typists telephoning me to ask what my writing meant. This took up time, particularly as from the nature of things I did not have a copy of what I had written. I had largely to depend upon recollection suddenly called upon. Second, I have never been very methodical in the entry of fees. I had solicitors pointing out that they had had conferences with me for which I had made no charge. As I had made none, they could make none.

The third reason was that by this time I was beginning to get a few books together and wanted to have them noted up in a systematic way. So I engaged Cherry Johnson, who was introduced to me by Kevin Ellis, later Speaker of the Legislative Assembly and Deputy Chancellor of the University of New South Wales. Cherry's father was a police magistrate, and she was the first woman employed in chambers. I paid her three guineas a week. She more than earned that for me. She only had to pick up an overlooked conference or opinion (two or three guineas each) in the week to cover or nearly cover her salary.

Recently she wrote an article in the *Sydney Morning Herald* about her experience as my secretary — a very nice account indeed. I had not heard of her since she left me to marry; so after reading the article, I dropped her a note to find out what she had done with her life in the meantime. I found that she had done remarkably well. She was a writer, she had been a tutor at a university, she had raised and educated a family and was still married to the bank officer whom she married immediately after leaving my employ.

From here on my practice steadily broadened and I was regularly briefed in all the jurisdictions of the court. Cases which produced an unexpected result, particularly by the application of the law, tended to increase my practice. I began to build a reputation as a lawyer as well as an advocate. An ability to deploy the principles of the law in a practical way was appreciated. I became a leading junior. Often I was given a junior to assist me in the more complicated cases.

In time, the leading junior work became shared between Alan Taylor and Jack Shand, my seniors at the Bar by two years, and myself. In 1940 certain solicitors suggested that I should consider taking silk. At that time I declined, but later, when Frank Dwyer (much junior to me) gave his notices to take silk, I felt that it was time I took the plunge. I went to see Taylor and Shand and suggested that we three should all give our notices immediately. But they refused. At that time the silks were not getting the work. As leading juniors we were doing it; when one of us was available, the silks were not briefed. We were being paid fees very comparable to anything a silk might charge. Because of this Taylor and Shand refused to take silk with me, saying that it was too risky. When I said that nonetheless I intended to go ahead, they said that in that event I would most likely lose out. I retorted that I would not if they would come with me as there were no juniors likely to pick up our work. But they were both obdurate.

I gave my notice and was granted silk in 1942. During the next two years, so far from my work falling away, it increased. Two years later, when I had succeeded as a senior, Taylor and Shand gave their notices.

*****

During World War II, detailed control of civilian life was effected by regulations made by the Executive rather than by laws made by the Parliament. Those regulations were authorised by statute founded on the defence power of the Commonwealth. This power to make regulations was often very widely used, so much so as to excite opposition by citizens. Litigation was the result. The defence power, which supported the regulations, greatly expanded its scope in wartime. Nonetheless there were limits. It was very important in the interests of personal freedom to confine the executive government within those limits. To recognise and express such limits called for much legal expertise and, on the part of the judiciary, judgment and courage. I had many briefs for citizens to test the validity of the regulations. In some instances clients were successful, in others not. Fortunately, the then Chief Justice of New South Wales, Sir Frederick Jordan, was both a good lawyer and a man of courage, sensitive to the need to keep the executive government within its proper bounds. Doubtless such an attitude is resisted by lesser politicians but welcomed by those who understand the threat to freedom of the individual from an unrestrained executive, however well motivated.

Dr Herbert Evatt was Attorney-General in the Chifley administration during wartime. I had had an experience with him in the very early days of my practice. Seemingly in mid-life I was considered to be politically conservative. I had no reason to expect to be briefed by the Labor Government. Unfortunately, governments in Australia tend to confine their favours to those who are thought to support them politically or ideologically. So I was somewhat surprised one day when I was telephoned by Dr Evatt, asking me would I look after the Censor, who was under attack from time to time by the newspaper proprietors. This I agreed to do provided I could advise the Censor on a legal and non-political basis. I was told that this would be quite in order.

Very soon after this conversation, I was briefed by the Commonwealth Crown Solicitor on a matter in which the *Daily Telegraph* was being dealt with by the Censor, Horace Manson, for publishing the number of tons of coal lost in an industrial stoppage in the mines. I was to defend the Censor's action. I formed the view that it was indefensible. I told the Crown Solicitor that the inhibition that had been placed on the newspaper by the Censor was legally insupportable. I indicated that I would negotiate with Claude Weston KC, representing the *Daily Telegraph*, to settle the matter. Weston and I agreed that the proceedings started by the newspaper be adjourned over Christmas. I indicated terms with which I would be content, though they involved the withdrawal of the Censor's limitation on the newspaper's activity. Weston, for his part, indicated his willingness to advise their acceptance.

As soon as the Head Censor, Bonney, got word of my advice, he came from Canberra to see me. He told me in no uncertain terms that I was unwise in suggesting a settlement and that he wanted the matter litigated and the Censor's position upheld. I told him that the Censor's conduct was insupportable and that there was no solid ground in law for placing the inhibition on the newspaper. Mr Bonney must have gone to the Attorney-General to complain of my refusal to press the Censor's position. Dr Evatt rang me and asked me what sort of terms I suggested for settlement. I told him. He said they were not acceptable to him and that he wanted the matter to proceed. But I had already arranged with Mr Weston for the matter to be adjourned and that arrangement had to stand. Meantime I suggested that if the Attorney-General wanted to offer other terms he might use the services of the Crown Solicitor to negotiate with the opposition's solicitor. When I returned from vacation, the case had been settled on the terms I had proposed.

I thought that this incident would be the end of my association with the Commonwealth Censor. Later, however, when a much greater rumpus arose between the Censor and the press generally, I was briefed, but ultimately returned my brief because my advice was not acceptable to the Commonwealth. I pointed out to the Attorney-General that the relevant regulations were in my view too widely expressed and in need of restraining amendment. They had not been made by the Chifley Government but were in fact the product of the earlier administration. Once again I thought the Censor's stance insupportable. But the Censor refused my advice, saying that he proposed to fight the case in the High Court. Such a course was, I thought, doomed to failure and I strongly opposed it. As my advice was rejected, I felt entitled to withdraw from the case, putting on paper my reasons for doing so.

I understand that when Mr Alderman, who had been briefed in my place, rose to address the court on the resumption of the hearing he opened with the words, "I do not wish to be unduly rude to the Court". He got no further. Sir John Latham CJ smartly said, "Mr Alderman you won't be rude at all". With that the bails were off and the challenge to the court faded away.

After I began to appear with frequency in the Supreme and District Courts I had occasional cases before the High Court, mostly in appeals in cases I had earlier conducted in the Supreme Court. After I had made a few appearances there, one of the seniors at the Bar very kindly sought me out and told me that he understood that the High Court judges were impressed by my work but thought I was too brief in my presentations. This surprised me a little. I had a habit of condensing my submissions and no doubt expected them to be picked up quickly. Apparently I had to learn to elaborate my propositions and perhaps sometimes to repeat them, maybe in different form and tailored to catch the eye of a particular judge. But despite this encouraging message, for which I was grateful, I did not seek to build a practice in that court.

EM Mitchell, one of the leading counsel practising in the High Court, suggested that I should make some attempt to practise there. But I still made none. Quite suddenly, Mitchell died, and very soon I was being briefed in work which would have gone to him had he survived. So my practice in the High Court grew considerably, into almost unmanageable proportions. I remember an occasion when I appeared in every case in the list for the sittings except one, a situation which placed a considerable strain on my capacity to prepare myself adequately for each case.

After my appearance before the Privy Council in the *Bank* case, the availability of the appeal to the Council from Australian courts, in all cases which did not involve a question *inter se*, attracted the attention of litigants and their solicitors. So in the following years I appeared each year in several appeals to that tribunal. These were years of great personal satisfaction. I appeared at times against leading English counsel and had many opportunities for exercising my persuasive skills as an advocate and demonstrating my knowledge of the law over a wide field. From 1948 on I appeared regularly before the Privy Council and became a familiar figure in the Inns of Court, where I made many friends.

When in 1950 I called on the judges of the US Supreme Court, Mr Justice Frankfurter, a very distinguished member of the Court to whom I had been given an introduction by Sir Owen Dixon, greeted me by saying that he was delighted to meet me, and had wanted to do so for years. Not unnaturally I was greatly flattered but before I had time to savour the compliment, he added, "no man ever deserved to have as much work as you have had". I realised he meant that I was not as distinguished as the amount of work would suggest, and was appropriately deflated.

3 The Advocate's Skill

The work of the advocate demands a precise knowledge of the law and a thorough grasp of its principles. He must be able to recognise quickly which of its principles is relevant to his case and make use of it to his client's profit. Several of my cases illustrate both these points and emphasise the place of the advocate in the protection of the citizen.

Three of these cases bear upon one of the great advantages of the jury system. Trial by jury is, to my mind, still the best method of resolving disputes of fact and the determination of guilt. Jurymen (the expression includes jurywomen, of whom there were none in my practising days) bring to the task many prejudices, but because of their number and the diversity of their backgrounds, their common humanity under the guidance of a judge will tend to provide the grounds for agreement, one prejudice displacing or at least diminishing another.

All of us have our prejudices; the judge has his no less than the advocate or any member of the public. Some, by education and training, have learned to control them. But that common humanity of the jury and the great discretion they have in forming their verdict means that the letter of the law may be tempered to accommodate human values when the circumstances warrant it. One of the great responsibilities and indeed privileges of the advocate is to bring into play those human values where the letter of the law might easily diverge from the ordinary citizen's sense of what is fair and just. The existence of this capacity may lead the legal purist to criticise jury verdicts which do not seem to measure up to their legal expectation. But this capacity of the jury is in reality a useful safeguard of the citizen.

* * * * *

Very early in my practising days I had a notable example of the importance of solid knowledge of the law and attention to detail. Late one afternoon, the clerk of a solicitor who had not briefed me before brought me a brief which a leading barrister had just returned. The case was listed in the District Court at Queen's Square for 10 am the following morning. The clerk said he had been advised that the case was unwinnable; he thought so too. I was not to be disturbed by losing it. The client was the defendant.

The facts were fairly simple. The lessor of a suburban dairy had put the bailiff in to sell all the effects on the property, whether owned by the tenant or not, in order to recover overdue rent. Distraint for rent, as this was, was then still available. A limitation on the sale by the bailiff, however, was that the lessor himself could not buy any of the chattels; if he did, the sale would be void and of no effect.

Among the effects to be sold was a new milk cart. At the auction sale the lessor bought the cart and thought to cover himself by purchasing in a false name. This became known to the tenant. An action was brought by the tenant's mother claiming to be the owner of the cart. Her case was that the sale to the defendant was void and that the lessor's continued use of it amounted to a trespass. In this action, the amount of the overdue rent would not be taken into account. Of course, had the tenant sued, the amount of the unpaid rent would have been brought to account. Had the cart been sold to a stranger, the stranger would have obtained a good title. But the sale to the lessor was undoubtedly void and the property in the cart remained with its true owner.

Now trespass is a remedy given for an interference with or invasion of the possession of property. The mother, assuming her to be the owner, was not at the relevant time in actual possession; her son was. The mother gave evidence to establish her ownership. I did not challenge that. I cross-examined her to establish (1) that she had leased the cart to her son; (2) that at the time of the action he was entitled to its possession; and (3) that no physical damage had been done to the cart since the sale. I persuaded the plaintiff to say that she was charging her son £1 a week rent for the cart, and that he was up to date with his rent; she agreed that no physical harm had come to the cart.

I was opposed in the case by George Amsberg, who had shared the University Medal with me at graduation. He was later a judge of the District Court. He evidently thought that he had a "sitter", a case that he could not lose.

Judge Curlewis Snr tried the case. He was a quick-witted and well-furnished common lawyer. I called no evidence and took the point that trespass was not available to an owner out of possession as the plaintiff was. Such an owner had a different cause of action: he could sue for injury to the reversion to his interest as an owner out of possession. Judge Curlewis conceded that this was a sound point. But he said he would allow an amendment so that the plaintiff could sue as a reversioner. I said I would not oppose the amendment.

The judge said that in that event the plaintiff should succeed. But I submitted that injury to the reversion could only be to the title or to the physical condition of the chattel. In this instance, as the sale to the lessor was void, there was thus no injury to the reversioner's title.

The plaintiff had agreed that the vehicle had not been physically harmed. Therefore no damage to the reversioner had occurred. The plaintiff might have an action in detinue but only if there had been due demand before action was brought. There was none. Amsberg complained bitterly that the point had been sprung on him. He called for and was given an adjournment to consider his position. He could not answer the point and Judge Curlewis dismissed the plaintiff's action.

Just what ultimately happened I do not know. No doubt the legal costs of the unsuccessful action proved a factor in any bargaining about the cart. To the solicitor this result looked a bit like a miracle. After that I received quite a number of briefs from him.

* * * * *

The second case was a jury trial, and illustrates my point about a jury being able to temper the rigour of the law. A well-known solicitor who had consulted me, mostly on conveyancing and company matters, one day asked me to defend a client of his who was charged with fraudulent dealings with a bank and with misapplication of money of a partnership of which he was a member. I was told that the client had made damaging statements to police and it was probable that he would be found guilty. It was fairly clear that his client did not have a very good case and that I might not be able to do much for him. But the solicitor said he must be fully defended. So I agreed to do my best for him.

Just as he was leaving my room the solicitor said, "Of course his partners will give him a good character". When I queried this he said, "Yes, they certainly will". I doubt whether the solicitor realised the great importance of that information. Good character is evidence on the issue of guilt or innocence. It was because of a slip in relation to this principle on the part of the judge who presided over the first trial of Mr Justice Murphy that there was a new trial.

The prosecution's complaint was that the accused had misused thousands of pounds of the partnership money, including some belonging to a bank. He was a member of the Royal Sydney Golf Club and thus known to some of the judges. Judge Hilary Studdert, who did not know the accused, was chosen to try the case. He was a fine criminal lawyer and a good judge. He and I had long been friends, with chambers on the same floor of Chancery Chambers. He was known, however, as a very severe judge when sentencing.

I saw the accused, heard his story and realised I could not call him to give evidence. He would have to make an unsworn statement from the dock. This relic of a time when an accused could not give evidence on his own behalf enables an accused to make an unsworn statement about which he cannot be cross-examined. The jury has to receive what he says as evidence and give it such weight as they think proper in the circumstances.

As I could not call the accused, he would make such a statement. I could not determine what he would do, though with the judge's leave I might assist him. But there was one piece of favourable evidence that could be put forward — sworn evidence of his good character. Now both the accused's partners were called as witnesses for the prosecution. They would thus be available for cross-examination and their evidence of good character could be obtained from them by that means. I accepted the solicitor's statement of what the partners would do and proposed to act upon it. I did not see or speak with them.

I decided not to ask either of them anything about the accused's character when I was cross-examining. I decided that although the partners had given evidence for the prosecution I would call them as witnesses for the accused and thus obtain their evidence as to good character. This was an unusual course, but to my mind one obviously of advantage to the accused. It carried some risk as I had not had an interview with either of the partners. But, given the position in which the accused found himself, the risk was reasonable. The dramatic effect of calling the partners would lend emphasis to their evidence. I carefully observed each man as he gave evidence for the Crown. I felt a little uncertain about the attitude of one of them.

The accused had been in the cells overnight, for him a particularly uncomfortable experience, and he had been upset by it. He made his unsworn statement, which must be made before any evidence is called for the defence. He said that he was a returned soldier and told the jury about the quality of his service and spoke favourably of his life. He had not concluded his statement at the lunch break. When the judge had left the bench, my client gave me a piece of paper and asked me to read it. The piece of paper had written on it: "Shall I emphasise the returned soldier angle a little more? I don't like the look of this jury. Is there any chance of a non-suit?".

Now in a civil case, when the plaintiff has called all the evidence in support of his case, it is possible to non-suit him by successfully arguing that even if all that evidence were accepted, it would not make out the plaintiff's case. But the idea of a non-suit was quite misplaced in a criminal trial. Its equivalent is for the judge to rule that the accused has no case to answer. There was no ground to do that in this case. The request, however, did indicate that the accused felt himself to be in a desperate situation.

After lunch I told him it would not hurt for him to speak further of his war service but that there was no question of a non-suit. So he went on and concluded his statement. Then I asked the court attendant to call the first of the partners. The Crown Prosecutor, Mr Crawford KC, objected. Was I asking that this witness be recalled for further cross-examination, in which case I would need the judge's permission? But I was doing no such thing. I was calling the witness as a witness for the accused. Whereupon the Crown Prosecutor complained that without his consent I must have been interviewing Crown witnesses. This was not so. The judge, at my request, told the prosecutor that I had every right to call a witness and did not have to get the Crown Prosecutor's consent. The partner gave his evidence, saying that he had known the accused for a long time, that he bore a very good character and had a good reputation in the city.

Then I called the other partner, of whom I had been slightly apprehensive. Very cautiously I asked him how long had he known the accused.

"I was at school with him, I was at the war with him, I've known him all my life."

"Putting aside the present circumstances, how have you found him?" I remember very well the precise words I used and those he used.

"He is one of the best fellows I have ever met", he said, and added words commending his character and reputation. I was astonished by that answer. It was extremely generous but quite evidently sincerely meant.

This concluded the evidence. Now I had to address the jury. I had quickly to change tack, capitalising on the answer I had just received. I reminded the jury that we had a criminal trial on our hands. They were asked to find that the defendant was a criminal. That would be something that he could not shake off for the rest of life. There needed to be something evil to justify such a description. It was not enough to have the appearance of evil; it must exist. Yet they had heard that he had a fine character and reputation; that he was one of the best fellows his partner had met. I remember saying to them, "You are all men well on in life; as you sit there you might like to cast your minds down the years. There must have been a day when appearances were against you, where someone could think that you had done something very wrong. Quite likely there was somebody who thought you were a good man when appearances belied the reality".

The accused was acquitted. The foreman of the jury, after they had been discharged by the judge, came over to me and thanked me for that speech. Needless to say, I was very pleased. It is one of the delights of the advocate to turn seeming defeat into victory.

The accused bustled out of court without so much as offering to shake my hand. I received no thanks from him. Queen Elizabeth I, in a letter to James VI of Scotland, wrote: "Who longest draws the thread of life and views the strange accidents that time makes, does not find out a rarer gift than thankfulness is, that is most precious and seldomest found".

I would respectfully agree.

* * * * *

I received more from the client in the following case. While I was still a junior counsel, a Newcastle firm of solicitors who had supported me for some years briefed me in a damages claim against the Broken Hill Proprietary. The client was a workman who had been working in the Newcastle steel mill where very heavy coils of steel rod were being made. The steel came out of the furnace white-hot and was immediately coiled. This day the coil had sprung and knocked the client over. His left hand was severed at the wrist and on the other hand all the fingers were severed at the palm, leaving him with only his thumb on that hand with a pad of flesh. This was a most severe injury. The client was in his forties, and could no longer follow his former, or perhaps any, occupation. He was a widower and had two sons to support.

Where an accident occurs at work the worker may make a worker's compensation claim and he can sue the employer at common law for damages. But in that case he must establish negligence on the part of the employer. The amount payable under the Workers' Compensation Act is limited by that Act; the damages at common law, assessed by a jury, are unlimited unless the jury's assessment is found by the court to be unreasonable. If the workman accepts worker's compensation, he is not able to sue at common law for general damages unless he starts his action within twelve months of receiving compensation. A judge may give leave to proceed with a common-law claim although more than twelve months have elapsed, but such leave is not always given, and a special case for it has to be made out.

Very much more than twelve months had elapsed from his acceptance of compensation before his action commenced. So an application had first to be made for leave to proceed. The application came before Mr Justice Bavin. It was opposed by Jack Shand on behalf of the employer. Bavin had been Premier of the State and had probably had much more political than legal experience. In my appearances before him I had found him a fair-minded man.

Ignorance of the need to sue within twelve months was not necessarily sufficient ground to grant the application, and there was nothing else of an exculpatory nature. I drew rather strongly upon the extent of the appellant's injuries and their effect on his employability, contrasting the relatively small amount payable under the Workers' Compensation Act with what might be thought adequate damages. If the appellant were able to establish negligence, I submitted that it would be proper to assume such negligence and contrast what damages were then likely with the amount of worker's compensation. I remember then appealing to His Honour's sense of fairness. To this he responded and granted the necessary leave. This was a hurdle well cleared.

The next step was that the defendant applied to move the trial from Newcastle to Maitland, probably to avoid any prejudice there might be in Newcastle against BHP. It may also have been thought that dairy farmers, who were most likely to be called as jurors in Maitland, would be less likely to think in large amounts of damage than might be the case among city men. Although this move was opposed it succeeded and the case was set down to be tried in Maitland.

I had a young man reading with me then, Chris Langsworth, who subsequently became the chairman of the Workers' Compensation Commission. He was given a complementary brief as my junior. I remember saying to Langsworth as we were driving up to Maitland that I would open the case to the jury so strongly that they would not be able for one moment to fail to think of this man with no hand on one arm and only a stump and a thumb on the other. I felt I had to encourage the minds of the jurors to contemplate large figures when they came to assess damages.

Mr Justice Heron, later Sir Leslie and Chief Justice of the State, presided over the trial. Opening the case, I put before the jury the picture of a fingerless man, unable to do up a button or to grip anything in his hand. I remember that the judge told a member of the Bar, who told me, that he never wanted to sit through an opening like mine again. It disturbed him too when I drew a gaunt picture of this man's injuries without prospect of employment. There were difficulties in proving negligence on the part of the employer and the plaintiff might easily have failed on that score, but we were able to satisfy the jury that there had been insufficient precautions taken to prevent the injury.

In the end, the plaintiff received £7500, the largest verdict awarded up to that time in New South Wales for personal injury. These days, partly because of inflation, much larger sums are handed out, both by judges and by juries. In this case the amount represented the wages the plaintiff would have earned during the balance of his working life and about £3000 general damages in addition.

The sequel was a notable contrast to the earlier case. This man came to see me personally in my chambers in Sydney to thank me for what I had done for him. He was a very straightforward man of great courage. I learnt later that he became able to extract a cigarette from a packet and light it. He had been a keen fisherman and after his injuries learnt to land a bream using his thumb and the pad of flesh. He also learnt to type with his thumb. He married the daughter of a publican and bought a hotel in the Hunter District. He succeeded in business and put his boys through university. He was a great example of the human capacity to overcome disability.

Whenever I went to Newcastle Court, which was fairly often, I travelled to Newcastle by train. If my former client knew that I was coming, he would invariably meet me at the railway station and proudly tell me of his progress. If by chance he missed me at the station, he would be outside the court when I came out at four o'clock. I came greatly to appreciate my contacts with him. The gratitude that this quite simple man expressed was truly moving.

* * * * *

In the 1940s Mr Justice Maxwell was appointed a Royal Commissioner to inquire into the liquor trade in New South Wales. Mr William Dovey KC was briefed to assist him. Wartime conditions caused shortages in the supply of beer and spirituous liquors; government intervention by regulation of the liquor trade exacerbated the situation. The almost inevitable result was a considerable black market in alcohol.

The inquiry promised to be wide-ranging and therefore likely to involve the breweries, at that time the proprietors of most of the retail outlets. The breweries joined together to prepare themselves for an onslaught. One of the larger firms of solicitors was directed to offer me a brief to look after the interests of the breweries before the Royal Commission. Because of the financial interests involved, the fee I was offered was very large indeed. I once described it as a prince's ransom. I was at first reluctant to take it, as a case of such magnitude did not readily fit into my schedule of work. But more importantly, I had a brother who was the licensee of a city hotel and who I felt sure would have been involved in dealings in liquor which might be in breach of the regulations. He was a first-class publican but very adventurous. I rated the possibility of his being involved in the inquiry very high and I did not wish to suffer the possible embarrassment of appearing in the proceedings.

So I refused the breweries' brief. This upset the solicitors but they understood my reasons. They briefed another leader of the Bar and asked me to accept a brief at a very considerable fee to advise that leader on strategy. This was a very attractive offer as it would not interfere with my other work and would not place me in the limelight. But I realised that it would be quite impossible to keep from the profession, and indeed from the public, knowledge of the fact that I was behind the breweries' case. So I turned down this offer also.

The Royal Commission, as it appeared to many, steadily deteriorated into a witch-hunt of individuals in the liquor trade. Certainly among the profession and probably among the public, the Royal Commission earned something of the reputation of the Star Chamber. I find it remarkable that the public accept the conduct of Royal Commissions as a means of obtaining evidence, bearing in mind that our forebears revolted against the Star Chamber, which was a standing Royal Commission of its day. Press and politicians alike seem quite anxious to call for Royal Commissions into all manner of activities, not pausing to consider that the powers of a Royal Commissioner are easily abused. Indeed the public spectacle of witnesses squirming under questioning by the Commissioner or by his assisting counsel provides dramatic copy for the daily press, to the delectation of many of its readers.

During the course of the Commission a firm of solicitors asked me to accept a brief to protect a witness who was to be called before the Commission. He was a publican suspected of trafficking in liquor. I was tempted to accept as I always felt an obligation to protect the citizen and on this occasion I felt that witnesses particularly needed protection. But I had refused the breweries and felt that I should stand quite clear of the Commission's proceedings.

As part of the Commissioner's recommendation at the end of the inquiry several witnesses, including the publican for whom I had been offered a brief, were to be charged with perjury. I was offered a brief to defend him. It obviously presented difficulties, but I had refused to look after him when he was in need and felt a distinct obligation to accept the brief. When I examined it, no ray of hope appeared. The client had virtually admitted to false swearing.

Jack Shand and Sam Isaacs were also briefed for other of these witnesses. Before I had done much work on my case, Shand approached me and said that all our clients were in dire straits. Did I think it possible that we could find a point of law which might help? So we arranged a joint conference in my chambers.

The charge of false swearing on oath was said to have occurred not in a court of law but in this Royal Commission. The first thing therefore was to check the validity of the Royal Commission itself as it was the source of the Commissioner's authority to administer an oath. A facsimile of the Commission was produced; it seemed to conform to the statutory requirements. One of these was that it be issued under the *great* seal of the State and tested accordingly. In these respects it was in order. The Commission had been extended. Sometimes governments make a slip in extending a Royal Commission, doing so by Executive Council minute instead of letters patent, which would not conform to the statutory requirements. When a facsimile of the letters extending the Commission was produced, the letters patent had been executed under the *public* seal, not under the *great* seal. That difference caught my eye.

While my colleagues were still in my chambers, I rang the secretary to the Attorney-General (his name was Hamilton), and asked him would he ask the Chief Secretary's Department whether the State had one seal or two. Shortly afterwards Hamilton rang and said, "You've thrown the Chief Secretary's department into a flap". My colleagues agreed that there might be something in this divergence. We did not have the time to make the necessary inspection of the government gazettes which such an inquiry would entail, so a young barrister (now a professor of law) was briefed to do this.

Before Queen Anne's reign, when the sovereign died his great seal was broken up. There was then no executive authority in the land until the new sovereign made his own great seal and authorised its use. The procedure to devise and authorise the great seal was long entrenched and quite elaborate, and derived from days when the main form of attestation was by seal. Today, with commercial corporations as well as with public authorities, formal attestation is still in many instances by seal. In Queen Anne's time, however, the inconvenience of having an interregnum while the new seal was being prepared caused the passage of a statute allowing the new monarch to continue to use the former monarch's seal until such time as a new seal was approved for use. Thus continuity of authority was maintained. But when Edward VIII came to the throne, he did not have a new seal made before he abdicated. Consequently George V's seal continued to be used until George VI prepared his own.

On the death of the sovereign, because of Queen Anne's statute, the Governor in an Australian State could continue to use the great seal of the deceased monarch. When the new seal of the reigning monarch had been made and its use authorised in England, the State Governor would request the colonial office to obtain a new seal. The procedure then adopted was that the Privy Council would resolve that a seal for the State be designed and submitted for approval. On approval of the new seal an authority to the Governor to use it would be issued. A request was then made for the return of the old seal so it could be destroyed.

What the search of the records revealed was that after the abdication the Agent-General for New South Wales, apparently on his own initiative, approached the Deputy Master of the Mint who, without much ado, designed a new seal. This was fabricated and sent out to the NSW Premier without any approval or authority by the Privy Council for its use. It was this seal that was on the Royal Commission.

Now this was quite a point, but unfortunately it was too large a point. That is always a dangerous thing for a lawyer. This seal was on some of the judges' commissions. The discovery of this point had to be followed up by putting together the necessary legal evidence to establish it. This was done. The discovery of the apparent defect and the changes in the nomenclature of the State's seal provided a possible source of defence, and at the least, of embarrassment to the prosecution.

My client was tried in No 2 High Court before Judge Holt. Mr William Dovey KC, who had assisted the Commission, was appointed to prosecute. A conviction seemed fairly certain. Soon after the case began, I asked leave of the judge to prove on the *voir dire* the facts that would establish that in point of law the Royal Commission was invalid. The idea of a voir dire is that it allows of proof before the judge in the absence of the jury, the judge to decide the legal points.

The point being sprung on the prosecution sent it into some disarray. Mr Dovey was tall, had a very fine resonant voice and a good presence. However, on this occasion he was speaking in dulcet tones, quietly as befitted a prosecutor who was certain of getting a result. He objected to a voir dire during the Crown case but said that of course the defence could prove these facts in its own case. Now that meant that the jury would decide the validity of the Royal Commission. Thus the legal question was transferred from the judge, where it ought to have remained, something that neither the judge nor Dovey seemed to realise.

Immediately I asked the judge to rule that this was so, which he did, something that surprised me because he was quite a good lawyer and was by then an experienced judge. Though the point might not be of much weight with a jury, it did at least give me a talking point. But as my main attack on the prosecution I set out to bring before the jury the oppressive nature of the conduct of the Royal Commission.

The transcript of evidence before the Royal Commissioner, in so far as it affected my client, was tendered by the prosecution and thus available to me when addressing the jury. I could also point out the difference between the descriptions of the seals on the two letters patent, reminding the jury that it had to be satisfied beyond a reasonable doubt of the validity of the Royal Commission and its extension. But the main thrust of my address was to emphasise how the witness had been treated.

The result was that my client was acquitted, much to the astonishment of the Crown and its advisers. In all probability the jury acquitted because of the oppressive nature of the questioning which had produced the damaging admissions. The verdict was an example of the jury's ability in what they considered a proper case to resort to human values and temper the application of strict legality.

* * * * *

During World War II the government controlled the community by regulations made under the Defence Act, relying on the expansion of the defence power in wartime. Right from the time when the High Court decided that the price of bread could be fixed by the Commonwealth in wartime as an exercise of the defence power, those making regulations under that power have tended to stretch the power to its limits. But even in wartime it has limits and an important function of the courts is to be watchful that those limits are not exceeded. Fortunately Sir Frederick Jordan, Chief Justice of New South Wales during the war, was alive to this need. He was quite courageously prepared to declare invalid any regulations which stepped beyond the proper limits. I had many experiences with the regulations in which I appeared before Sir Frederick, but I shall mention just two — one more amusing than significant, the other of more consequence.

In the first case, a publican was charged with having refused to supply on demand beer at the regulation price. He had a large quantity of beer which he was probably selling in the black market. One day a government inspector entered his bar and demanded of the bartender a bottle of beer for which he tendered the regulation price. Told that there was no beer, he spoke to the publican but was told the same thing. Thereupon the inspector disclosed his identity and asked to inspect the cellar, where a considerable quantity of beer was evident. The inspector was told that the beer was all earmarked for a party later on. He did not swallow this and said he would now take a bottle. He gave the publican the money for it, with a parting indication that the publican would be reported.

I had Jack Smyth as my junior. The charge was failing to supply the beer. Smyth had suggested that a good point was that the officer did not fail to get his beer. I did not really think much of this point. We had other more complicated legal points to put before the full court which included Jordan CJ, Rogers J and, I think, Kenneth Street J. We did not do well with our other points and Smyth whispered, "Why don't you try the other point?". So I submitted that on the facts, the accused had not failed to provide the beer. By majority the case was won on that point, which shows that sometimes in litigation it is not wise to abandon any point.

The other case was a challenge by a client to the validity of the manpower regulations, which were very extreme. The Commonwealth made no attempt by evidence to establish the need for them to be as extensive as they were. In argument emphasis was placed on the extremity of the regulations and the absence of any justifying material. The full court's decision disallowing the regulations was expressed by Jordan CJ.

One of the dangers in writing judgments is that occasionally judges are tempted to use florid expressions. I remember being told by Victor Maxwell Snr that when he was appointed to the bench, John Harvey (then Chief Judge in Equity and a great judge) had said, "Well Victor, if ever you're tempted to put a purple patch in a judgment, put it in and put the judgment away for the night. Next morning whatever you might think take it out because it will lead to trouble". I know how wise that advice has proved.

On this occasion, Jordan wrote a very strong judgment and he described the regulation as imposing "serfdom" on the population. The strength of his language did not help when the Crown took the case to the High Court. There the respondent failed completely; the regulations were upheld. I felt that that court was overborne by the state of the war (El Alamein had not then been won) and felt less need to confine the Executive within bounds. Indeed I remember that Dixon CJ subsequently in an indirect way criticised Jordan for his decision in this case. I thought Jordan was right and that he had the right judicial attitude towards the exercise of executive power. The courts exist to protect the citizen against its excesses.

I tell of the details of the following case because of the extraordinary attitude which the prisoner adopted at the end of his unsuccessful attempt to overturn the verdict of the jury and because of the humorous aspect of his ultimate state of mind. To respect his privacy, I have called him "John Doe".

One day I received a letter from an inmate of Long Bay Gaol. He told me that he had been convicted of attempted murder and was serving a life sentence, but that he was innocent and had been given a further appeal (the course provided for under s 475 of the State Crimes Act). He wanted me to appear for him and said I need not worry about my fees, his friends would see me paid.

I was intrigued by this letter. Over the years I maintained a friendship with Reginald Downing, who was for years Minister for Justice and Attorney-General in Labor administrations. I have been delighted that the court complex in Liverpool Street bears his name in recognition of the great service he rendered in the law and in political life.

I told Reg Downing of the letter I had received and asked him about the writer. He said that some members of the police and some inmates of Long Bay Gaol had grave doubts about John Doe's guilt. The police knew him as a petty criminal but not in connection with violent conduct. The use of a gun, which had been involved in his conviction, seemed out of character. Downing thought it would be a good thing if I appeared for Doe.

The evidence against John Doe was that on the day in question two men presented themselves at a pawnbroker's shop in Surry Hills. One undoubtedly had a pistol. A demand of some kind was made on the pawnbroker, a relatively young man. Whatever was said between them, the callers were not satisfied. The pistol was discharged at the pawnbroker at point-blank range. He was wily enough to duck, and the bullet missed him. He ran below the level of the counter, jumped through his shop window to the footpath and disappeared. The two men also fled. But a hat was left on the counter. That undoubtedly was John Doe's hat. In a line-up, he was identified by the pawnbroker.

The two men were tried together for attempted murder. Neither gave evidence. Doe vigorously denied his presence at the scene. He challenged the pawnbroker's identification and claimed to have been elsewhere at the time of the shooting. But he gave no explanation of the hat. His co-accused stated from the dock that Doe was not present at the time. But the solicitor defending Doe did not call the co-accused to the witness box to make that statement on oath. The jury convicted both men. When sentenced, Doe reacted very vociferously indeed.

It was the unexplained presence of John Doe's hat which was the central evidence against him. An appeal by Doe to the Court of Criminal Appeal was unsuccessful.

Some years later, and before the inquiry before Judge Studdert began, a prisoner then serving a long sentence in Long Bay wrote to Mr Downing and was later interviewed by him. This prisoner said that he was the second man at the pawnbroker's shop and that he was wearing Doe's hat, which he had borrowed from him. Mr Downing told the prisoner that he would not consider making any concession to him because of what he was prepared to say. However, the prisoner insisted on his story. When subsequently he was asked to put the hat on his head in court, he did so. Quite obviously, it did not fit. His response was that this was not unusual. He never bought a hat. He usually stole one and would not be fussy about its size or fit.

But Doe and his friends maintained an agitation which ultimately resulted in a special inquiry by Judge Studdert. Both Doe and the other prisoner gave evidence saying that the hat had been borrowed, a fact which Doe confirmed in his evidence. Judge Studdert found against the prisoner, not feeling convinced by the new evidence. Nonetheless, disquiet continued because of persisting agitation on Doe's behalf. The proceedings in which I was briefed were the result.

In due course I received from a solicitor a brief which included the transcripts of the trial, the appeal to the Court of Criminal Appeal, the inquiry before Judge Studdert and Doe's account of his hat. The new proceedings were heard by a full court presided over by Jordan CJ. In conformity with State practice in the hearing of criminal appeals, John Doe, as an appellant, was present in court throughout. I did my best for him but to no avail: the verdict of the jury proved too strong an obstacle. After the result was known, Doe wrote thanking me for my efforts on his behalf and offering the opinion that had I appeared for him at his trial he would not have been convicted.

John Doe appealed to the High Court. Again I appeared for him, and again I failed to convince the court. The appeal was dismissed. Some days after the result had been conveyed to him, John Doe wrote to me again. He expressed his gratitude for my effort for him and then, somewhat remarkably, said that all avenues having been explored he was now resigned to his fate: he had come to accept that it was better that the finality of the jury's verdict should be maintained than that an exception be made in his case. I must say I was impressed by this attitude in a man now to serve the remainder of a life sentence, and one who most fervently maintained his innocence. I have kept that letter in my personal archives. Incidentally, my fees were duly paid. I later learnt that a public concert had been held to raise them.

Some months later I met Reg Downing on the corner of Elizabeth and King Streets. He remarked on the result of the John Doe proceedings. I said that I had failed to overcome the force of the jury's verdict but that I had serious doubts about Doe's guilt, so much so that I thought that Downing might well consider releasing him. Downing, who was a first-class minister and a compassionate man, made no response to my suggestion at the time and, in the hurly-burly of practice, the matter passed from my mind.

A couple of years later, I had occasion to see the Premier, Mr Cahill, and Reg Downing together in the Premier's office in Macquarie Street. Over a cup of coffee, I said to Downing, "What did you do about John Doe?"

"I did as you suggested. I let him go. It's strange that you should mention him because a few weeks ago, on a winter's day, I was coming out of the Attorney-General's office in Macquarie Street when a well-dressed man, overcoat and all, greeted me in the street with, 'How are you, Mr Downing?'. I didn't recognise the speaker and said so. 'You've forgotten me, I'm John Doe'."

Reg Downing then recalled him and asked him how he was getting along.

"Well, Mr Downing, I've learnt my lesson. I had got into bad company. Now I keep on the right side of the law and am doing all right".

"What are you doing?" asked Downing.

"Oh", said the former prisoner, "I'm an SP bookie".

This is an amusing sidelight on the illegal practice of unlicensed bookmaking, but his view is probably shared by many Sydneysiders: SP betting is regarded as being on the right side of the law.

* * * * *

These and the later *Bank Nationalisation* case were successes, but I had many failures; perhaps if the full tally were known, there would be many more losses than successes. In trial work I frequently appeared for defendants, at times with the principal function of keeping the damages within reasonable bounds. Some failures were due to poor advocacy, others to poor material with which to work. Some were publicly noticeable, others — the majority — merely of concern to the individuals or corporations concerned. Some were most difficult to win, for example the Communist Party Suppression Act. In that case I was not consulted before being briefed to appear in the High Court. The Act under challenge recited much material of a factual kind. But the court could not be bound by these recited facts as if they had been judicially established. It may be that if those facts had been so established the Commonwealth power to pass the Act might have been upheld, or at least by more than one judge.

My argument about the validity of the Act was unconvincing. Only the Chief Justice was prepared to uphold its validity on the grounds set out in his reasons rather than on my argument. Latham CJ, while still in office, once told me that my argument in the Communist Party case was the worst he had heard from me. I have no reason to question his judgment.

In the 1950s I failed adequately to explain to the Privy Council the method of local government rating on the basis of the unimproved capital value of the land, a system used in Fiji and widely used in Australia, but not in England. I was appearing for CSR in an appeal against the decision of the Supreme Court of Fiji upholding a rate assessment made substantially on the improved value of the property rather than the unimproved value of the land.

Rating on unimproved value is based on the Henry George idea of taxing the unearned increase reflected in the unimproved value of the land, due not to the efforts of the owner but to increased community facilities or general economic conditions. In my view I ought to have won the case, but I failed to convince the Privy Council and lost. I had as my junior Leslie Scarman (later Lord Scarman, Lord of Appeal) and Brian McKenna, later Mr Justice McKenna of the English High Court.

Then there was the Dobell case where Mary Edwards and Joe Walinsky challenged the decision of the Archibald Trustees in awarding the prize to William Dobell for his painting of fellow artist Joshua Smith. I was briefed for the plaintiffs by Dr Frank Lovat. He was much more familiar with art, particularly with painting, than I was, and he helped me greatly in the conduct of the case. I was also assisted by Mr McDonald, curator of the National Gallery of Victoria.

I saw Dobell's portrait in the Sydney Art Gallery among the other contestant paintings. It impressed me by the brilliance of its colouring. I did not then know Joshua Smith and could not tell whether the almost emaciated figure really resembled him. But however that might be, the painting leapt off the canvas. Smith was himself an accomplished portrait painter.

After I had been briefed, Lovat and I had conferences with the plaintiffs and with McDonald. I went to the gallery with Lovat to view the painting. My immediate reaction was to say, "This thing has faded, its brilliance has diminished". McDonald asked me why I thought so. I told him of my earlier view. He agreed that it had faded somewhat and said it would continue to do so because it had been "varnished". Mastic had been applied while the pigments were still green, a circumstance which might suggest that the canvas was not painted for entry to the competition but that the decision to enter was an afterthought.

The Archibald Prize, according to its initiator, was to be for a portrait of a person of some prominence, which suggests that the entry be objectively held. The basis of the challenge by the plaintiffs was that the painting was not a portrait but a caricature — two distant concepts, but narrowly separated.

Frank Kitto and Conybeare appeared for the Archibald Trustees and Frank Dwyer for Dobell. Mr Justice Roper heard the case sitting in Equity in the old district courtroom adjacent to the female block in Queen's Square, Macquarie Street.

The case had already been made into a *cause célèbre* by the journalists. A daily audience filled the courtroom to overflowing. The two rows of seats in front of the public area were filled by ladies prominent in the social and artistic world of Sydney. Among them was Lady Hannah Lloyd Jones, whose husband and children had been painted by Dobell. She also owned Dobell's *Blue Lady*, which I have seen, a very beautiful painting indeed. She daily sat immediately behind me.

The challenged canvas was exhibited in the courtroom on an easel. At times Joshua Smith was asked to stand beside it. At least on a superficial view, it differed significantly from the actual appearance of the sitter. Joshua was quite unlikely to have worn a jacket in any way resembling that depicted. He was known to take his religion seriously, and to live by it. The emaciated face, the Kings Cross lighting in the background, that jacket and the placement of skinny arms cruciform in front of him provided much material for the argument that the painting was no more than a caricature, not a portrait recording the actual appearance of the sitter.

One day as I entered the courtroom, I noticed Dr Benjafield near the entrance. The doctor was a frequenter of the courts, often giving evidence of medical facts or opinion in personal injury cases. I asked him if he would venture an opinion in the witness box about the relationship of the canvas to the sitter. He said he had a firm opinion about that and was willing to give it. Accordingly I called him as a witness for the plaintiffs. He said that the canvas represented what the sitter's corpse would be like when he had been dead some days.

Among the defence witnesses was a man named Haefliger, a *Sydney Morning Herald* art critic. When facing the canvas in the courtroom he was rapturous in its praise. It told him things about Joshua Smith he had not known, among other things that Joshua had a square personality.

I asked him to expound his concept of a square personality. Each time he offered a synonym I was able to trip him and indicate its inadequacy. After several unsuccessful attempts he said that I was being unfair to him in a matter of art. I responded that on the contrary I was dealing with a matter of language. Was he having difficulty with the English language? He bridled somewhat at this and tried again. After several more attempts to explain, I said that perhaps I could help him. Would he accept that a square personality was the antithesis of a circular personality. "You've got it exactly" came from the witness and I laughed, to his considerable discomfiture.

At the time I was friendly with a cartoonist named Frith then producing three-dimensional cartoons for press publication. His method was to model his subject in plasticine. A photograph of the model gave the resulting cartoon in print a sense of a third dimension and brought out the elements of its caricature. Frith lent me a plasticine head of the then Leader of the Opposition, whose features included a prominent nose. The identity of the model could readily be seen from the nose, but the extent of its prominence clearly indicated that a cartoonist had been at work. I had this model in a shoebox on the Bar table.

At one point in my cross-examination of Haefliger I exhibited this model and asked him into what category of art he would place it. He said he could not take it seriously, it was a joke. At this point Frith, who was in the audience, stood up and said loudly, "Young man, answer the question. That is a serious work of art", and he was straightaway bundled out of court. Haefliger maintained his attitude and did not answer my question.

Such incidents lent colour to the proceedings but helped the plaintiffs very little. The fineness of the distinction between a caricature and a portrait, and the material derived from Smith's evident unlikeness to the figure on the canvas provided scope for an advocate. I think I did my best. I lost because of the narrowness of that margin, but I cannot think that the trustees had been unanimous in deciding to award the prize.

The judge found that the Archibald bequest did not require the competing canvasses to be in truth portraits. It meant only that they must be, in the opinion of the trustees — or I suppose a majority of them — a portrait. Thus all the evidence given in the cases had to be regarded as irrelevant. Having so decided, the judge had completed his function, finding for the defendant trustees and Dobell. Privately, he volunteered the opinion that the canvas was a portrait.

Naturally the plaintiffs were dissatisfied. Such a result was quite unexpected. As to the true nature of the canvas, it was only an opinion of a judge, an *obiter dictum* at a time when he really was, in the lawyer's phrase, *functus officio*.

From my point of view, I had failed. I could not blame the material I had, so it must go down as poor advocacy.

4 Landmark Cases

By 1945, commercial air transport had been developed in Australia by private enterprise. The Holyman family, which had maritime interests in and around Australia, inaugurated an airline with interstate flights. Reg Ansett, when the Transport Act of Victoria had prevented him continuing his car passenger service from Hamilton to Melbourne, had started an airline in Victoria, and Butler had, with Holyman's assistance, begun an airline serving parts of New South Wales. Qantas, as a private venture, ran air services within Queensland and the Northern Territory.

Mr Chifley, the incumbent Prime Minister, decided to nationalise the interstate airlines. He sought to do so by the *Australian National Airlines Act* 1945. If that Act became effective, the interests Holyman had built up in the airline company Australian National Airlines would be taken over and the Commonwealth Government would have a monopoly of interstate air transport.

By this time the High Court in a series of decisions had supported the validity of the various State Transport Acts which had controlled, *inter alia*, interstate road transport. Notwithstanding the provisions of s 92 of the Constitution, these Acts required licences to operate transport vehicles including those engaged in interstate transport, the grant of such licences being at the discretion of a State official. The decisions of the court which dealt with these Acts were collectively referred to by lawyers as the *Transport* cases.

The Holyman interests naturally contested the Commonwealth's power to nationalise interstate air transport, relying on the express provisions of s 92.

I had in the early years of practice considered the scope of this section and had in fact worked on a case which involved consideration of its effect on interstate road transport (Greenstar Trading Co). Although I had not appeared in the case, I had worked for Percy Spender on its preparation. The validity of a Transport Act of New South Wales was upheld in that case.

Jerry Walsh, a partner in Malleson Stewart, Solicitors of Melbourne, called on me one day in 1945. He asked me if I would write an opinion for his firm on the validity of the Australian National Airlines Act. I was then very busy and told him that I had no time really in which to write an opinion. But I said to him, "Why do you need an opinion?". He asked what did I mean.

"Well", I said, "the Act purports absolutely to forbid you to fly and carry passengers and goods from one State to another. That operation clearly is an exercise in interstate trade and commerce and it seems to me quite clear that the Commonwealth may not forbid you to engage in it".

He questioned the certainty with which I spoke and reminded me of the *Transport* cases. I said I didn't think they really had much to do with the question. They were no more than an attempt to regulate vehicular transport and, as the court seemed to think, were laws about vehicles, and any impact they had on interstate transport was, so it seemed, thought to be no more than consequential. In any case, any prohibition contained in the transport legislation seemed to have been regarded by the court as merely part of a regulatory scheme. Whether or not those Acts were valid did not now, in my view, need to be considered. At the lowest, the Airlines Act was a case of absolute prohibition, not one of regulation. He said that there were other views about that.

I said I supposed there were. "Do you mean to say that the Commonwealth can prevent me from swimming across the Murray from New South Wales to Victoria?"

"I don't suppose so", he said.

"Well, how then can they tell me I mustn't fly over the Murray?"

"But this flying of passengers and goods is not a matter of trade."

"Oh", said I, "good gracious, I suppose one of the earliest forms of commerce is carriage of goods and people for reward. Well, you've got the benefit of my opinion. I've no time to write it and perhaps you may think it's not so worthwhile because it is, as it were, off the cuff. For what it's worth, I am of the opinion that the Act is invalid".

He went off. He had probably had other opinions from quite notable members of the Victorian Bar who I suspect had expressed the view that the *Transport* cases would in some way justify the new Airlines Act.

In due course I was briefed to appear in the challenging litigation begun by Australian National Airlines. During the preparation of the case, a singularly fortunate event occurred. During wartime, the Commonwealth had by regulation forbidden people to travel from one part of Australia to another without a permit. People had no automatic right to this permit; its grant was at the discretion of an official. A young woman named Dulcie Johnson, wishing to visit her personal friend in another State, had travelled between Cook in South Australia and Kalgoorlie in Western Australia without a permit, for which she was prosecuted by the Commonwealth before a magistrate in Perth. Mr Seaman, the magistrate, decided that the constitutional guarantee of freedom of interstate movement —

"intercourse" in the constitutional language of s 92[1] — rendered the regulation invalid in relationship to the facts of the case. Somewhat courageously, he dismissed the prosecution.

Seaman's decision was given some publicity. When I read of it in the Sydney newspapers, I immediately rang Jerry Walsh and said I thought there was a possibility that the Commonwealth might appeal this decision and that it would be wise for those he represented to support the young woman. The Commonwealth did appeal.

At that time Dr Evatt was Attorney-General. Mr Spicer KC (later Attorney-General and Chief Judge of the Industrial Court), along with Mr Sugerman KC (later president of the Court of Appeal of New South Wales), appeared for the Commonwealth. David Maughan KC was briefed to lead me for the young woman. The case came before the High Court in Sydney, which decided unanimously that paragraph 3(a) of the regulations, as it prevented a person travelling interstate, was invalid because of s 92.[2] This was of course a very large step towards success in the *Airlines* case itself.

I think Dr Evatt, always suspicious of the motives of those he dealt with, thought that I had put the young woman up to making her journey. But I had not. That she did so was, from the Holyman litigation point of view, purely accidental.

There were three separate cases brought in the High Court challenging the validity of the Australian National Airlines Act, the plaintiff in each case being an airline. Three separate groups of barristers were briefed for the plaintiffs. I was given the brief in the first case to be listed. With me were Dr Coppel KC and Reginald Sholl (later Sir Reginald Sholl and a judge of the Supreme Court of Victoria). The Commonwealth was represented in the first case by Jim Tait KC (later Sir James Tait), PD Phillips and TW Smith (later Mr Justice Smith of the Supreme Court of Victoria). In the second case, Ham KC, Dean KC (afterwards Mr Justice Dean of the Supreme Court of Victoria), and Ward of South Australia (later Ward KC) were for the plaintiffs. In the third case, the plaintiffs were represented by David Maughan KC, Claude Weston KC and John Holmes (later Mr Justice Holmes of the NSW Supreme Court). Sugerman KC and Dignan (later a judge of the NSW Worker's Compensation Commission) appeared for the Commonwealth in all other cases.

I had decided upon a direct attack, much along the lines I had outlined to Walsh in our initial conversation. In particular I would not acknowledge the relevance of the *Transport* cases. My argument almost took the stand that the invalidity of an attempt to prevent commercial transport interstate of goods and passengers was obviously a breach of the constitutional guarantee of freedom of interstate trade, commerce and intercourse. But of course during argument I had to deal with some of the decided cases. The Commonwealth for its part used the *Transport* cases and the ideas on which they were based as some support for its case.

The cases took some time to argue. As the time for reply approached, I did something I had never done before or since. I wrote out my reply in full. I well remember writing it in a school notebook, which it practically filled. Kevin Ward had appeared in the *James* cases (all important challenges under s 92). I respected his judgment as an advocate and his knowledge and experience of the operation of s 92. I asked him if he would read my proposed reply. I remember that we walked together in the Fitzroy Gardens discussing it. He agreed with the thrust of the argument. I then showed it to Claude Weston, who took the view that it would fail and that I should think again. David Maughan thought it would be difficult to make the argument stick but said that I might well succeed in making it do so. Indeed, he encouraged me to persist with it. I destroyed the notebook and put an argument founded on its contents.

In the event the plaintiffs won. The attempt at a national monopoly of interstate transport failed. But the court decided that the Act was valid in so far as it incorporated the new ANA (which later became Trans-Australia Airlines, then Australian Airlines and ultimately Qantas) and authorised it to conduct an interstate airline.

I had then, and still have, some doubt as to the correctness of this part of the court's decision. The Commonwealth had and still has no power to provide for the incorporation of companies as itself the substance of its legislation. While it may possibly be correct to say that a power to make laws on interstate trade and commerce would enable the Commonwealth to pass a law authorising the Executive to trade interstate, the effect of the Airlines Act was to create a trading corporation with power to trade interstate. Also, I doubted whether the Chifley Government intended to start a competitive airline: it wanted, I rather thought, a national monopoly or nothing. There was much to be said for the proposition that upon its proper construction the Act did just that and nothing else. Its substance was to authorise a monopoly.

But I did not feel so strongly about this aspect of the court's judgment as to advise an appeal. However, Holyman and his other advisers were keen to prevent the Commonwealth starting up an airline which might provide competition with its own interstate operation. Accordingly, I was instructed to draft a petition to the Privy Council for special leave to appeal against as much of the court's decision as upheld any part of the Airlines Act.

I thought Holyman's best course, rather than pursue the appeal, was to buy up the intrastate "feeder" lines as soon as he could. I did not think that an airline devoted exclusively to interstate operation could succeed if it was unable to control at least some of the intrastate airlines. I overlooked the position of Qantas, which controlled Queensland intrastate lines. Qantas is a private company, so any constitutional limitations on the Federal Parliament in relation to interstate trade were not thought to apply to its operations.

Ultimately these intrastate operations supported the new ANA. Also, East West Airlines, controlled by Mr Shand, supported TAA. However, Holyman did in fact buy up some intrastate lines, but not the Ansett operation which ultimately took over Butler's operations. So TAA did survive.

Holyman's solicitors offered me the opportunity to go to London in support of the petition. But I had no wish to go. Though my own practice was then considerable, I thought an extended absence might well endanger it. Malleson Stewart briefed Sir Walter Moncton KC, to whom I wrote expressing arguments which could be put in support of the petition. But the Privy Council refused special leave to appeal.

The decision on the ANA Act was of the first importance — to use the jargon of the day, it was a landmark case, and I had enjoyed my part in its production.

* * * * *

The *Banking Act* 1947 was introduced by the Chifley Government and passed by Federal Parliament in that year. Section 48 of the Act read:

> Except with the consent of the Treasurer, a bank shall not conduct any banking business for a State or for any Authority of a State, including a local government authority.

This section virtually (though not in terms) required the State governments, their authorities and their municipal councils to bank with the Commonwealth Bank, a bank wholly owned by the Commonwealth.

The Melbourne City Council opposed such a course, preferring to maintain its own freedom to bank with whichever bank it would. It challenged in the High Court the validity of this section of the Banking Act. Like all legislative powers given to the Commonwealth, the banking power was subject to the Constitution.[3]

I was briefed by Malleson Stewart to lead Dr Coppel KC and Douglas Menzies of the Victorian Bar (Menzies was later a judge of the High Court) for the plaintiff corporation. Harold Mason, Jim Tait, Victor Windeyer (later Sir Victor Windeyer, a judge of the High Court) and John Holmes (see p 53) appeared for the Commonwealth.

With Dr Coppel and Menzies, I held conferences in Melbourne in the autumn of that year. We laid out the argument for the plaintiff, basing it on two propositions: first, that the Commonwealth could not deny a State the ability to bank with a bank of its choice or require the State to bank with the Commonwealth Bank. The legislative power with regard to banking, so ran the argument, did not extend so far as to enable such a fundamental activity of the State to be controlled by the Commonwealth. Our argument could be expressed by saying that the federal nature of the Constitution required such a limiting implication to be made upon all the powers given to the Commonwealth by ss 51 and 52, both of which are prefaced with the words "subject to this Constitution". That Constitution was essentially federal, with both Commonwealth and State as enduring elements.

The second proposition was that s 48 was textually inseverable so that if the limitation on banking services for a State was constitutionally insupportable, the limitation on the local government authorities must also be invalid, even if there might possibly be power to control the banking activities of local government, treated in isolation — a point it was unnecessary to argue or decide for then present purposes.

In the ordinary course, this case would have been listed and heard in the second half of the year. There were no elements of urgency. But the Chief Justice, for a supposed reason of urgency, fixed its hearing for a date during the July vacation of the court.

I had become accustomed for some years to ski in Kosciusko State Park for a week or longer during the court vacation in July; from 1944 I had been one of the park's trustees. When I was told of the date fixed for the case, I told Tom Trumble, senior partner in Mallesons, that I would be skiing and would not be available to argue the case. He protested, but I said that the argument had already been laid out and that Coppel and Menzies were quite capable of presenting it.

That year I stayed with a group of friends in Betts Camp which lay between the Kosciusko Hotel and the Chalet at Charlotte's Pass, a few miles from either resort. We spent the days skiing on the range, returning to the camp in the late afternoon. Several times during that week Tom Trumble rang me, asking me to change my mind. I remained obdurate. The weather had been good. I was in good company and I was enjoying the skiing. Also, I had had a busy year and needed some respite.

On the Friday a group of us set off in the early morning to ski to the hut on Spencers Creek which flows into the Snowy. This meant crossing an area known as the Guthries, a part of the eastern side of the Snowy River Valley. I had lent my skis to a friend and was using a pair borrowed from Johnny Abbotsmith, who worked in the snowfields during the winter season. His "boards" were a little shorter than my own and seemed to call for a somewhat different control, though they did have some advantages. The days had been sunny and warm, the nights freezing. Consequently, parts of the snowfields exposed to sunlight, particularly on western-facing slopes, tended to thaw during the day and to freeze during the night, forming an icy surface where the snow cover was relatively thin or completely blown away. Skiing on such a surface is both difficult and dangerous.

When we began to descend the Guthries on the western-facing slope this day, I ran out of an area well covered in snow on to an area of ice. I immediately saw the danger but, in a show of vanity, thought I could master the situation. So instead of attempting to halt, even to sit down, I ran on. Inevitably I lost control of the skis. My skis were completely everted, my knees twisted outward to the point where I felt as if a cartilage had snapped in one of them. I knew that when I cooled off, not only would the knee be painful — as it eventually became — but that I would be unable to use it in skiing. But I was warm enough to go along with the party for the rest of the day, exercising particular care. But as the afternoon wore on, I decided I must get treatment at the Hotel. So I left the others and set off on my own down through the Perisher area to the main road. I reached the hotel at dusk. My knee was bound up by a doctor and I had dinner.

Not long afterwards Tom Trumble rang again, asking me to return to Melbourne for the hearing, which was to begin on Monday, emphasising that this was my last chance. Since my skiing was ruined, I agreed, to Tom's great satisfaction.

I went to bed, arranging for the hotel staff to wake me at midnight and to provide me with sandwiches. I left the hotel about 1 am and drove myself through the night to Cheltenham. Later that day, Saturday, I went into chambers to refresh myself on the points of the case. I flew to Melbourne on the Sunday evening. I well remember that flight. The night was very stormy and for a time there was doubt whether the plane could take off at all. We had a very bumpy ride. Planes did not then fly at such altitudes as they do today and consequently felt the weather more. In fact some passengers had been offloaded because of the prospect of heavy weather.

I appeared in court on the Monday morning, hobbling because my knee had stiffened and become painful. Some medical friends had proposed surgery, but I would not agree. Though sometimes on a cold day I can still feel pain from it, it causes me no inconvenience.

We won the *Melbourne Corporation* case. The court's judgment was published on a Friday, 13 August.[4] It broke new ground. I suspect, though I have no means of knowing, that Evatt advised Chifley that the court's decision represented a serious challenge to his Banking Act, an act which was near to the Prime Minister's heart. I doubt if the decision's influence was so great. The case so far as the Banking Act was concerned dealt only with the inability of the Commonwealth to force the States to bank with a specified bank, though it did establish a fundamental principle of our constitutional law not limited to banking. It emphasised the essential federal quality of our Constitution.

But whatever advice he received, Chifley acted swiftly. On the Saturday, 14 August, he announced the nationalisation of the banks. This move was not only legally disputed with success in the *Banks* case,[5] but electorally at least contributed to the change of government in 1949, an election which returned Menzies to government.

Douglas Menzies, who was RG Menzies' cousin, appeared with me on this case and in the *Bank Nationalisation* case both in Australia and in London, for the State of Victoria (intervening and supporting the banks' case). Out of our working together on these cases, and in opposing each other in others, our friendship and that of our wives and families grew. It flourished and continued till Douglas Menzies' death on 1974. His wife Helen had predeceased him. That friendship became a large part of my life, a part I shall ever cherish.

My mishap that day on the Guthries and its consequence at least contributed to my later selection to lead the group of counsel who appeared for the banks, both in Australia and later in London, in their challenge to bank nationalisation.

* * * * *

One afternoon as I was returning from court, I was stopped in Phillip Street by a junior who had a considerable practice and who later became a judge of the NSW Supreme Court. He seemed quite agitated. He had appeared for a respondent in the High Court and had just heard the result. The appeal had been allowed and the court had made an order whose terms disturbed him no end. He obviously wanted to unburden himself and I stopped and listened.

As he recounted them, the facts were that a married man with a family and in good employment had many years before formed an association with a young single woman, who held a very important secretarial position in the city. They may have become lovers, but that was not charged or proved and ought not to have affected the matter in litigation. But the man fell victim of tuberculosis and ultimately lost his job and became bedridden. The young woman, now no doubt no longer young but still unmarried and gainfully employed, did not desert him but saw him frequently and began to lend him substantial sums of money to enable him to pay interest on the mortgage of his house and to contribute to the upkeep of his family. In this way, a considerable sum became due to the lady.

As his health declined, the man insisted that the lady have some acknowledgment of the debt and signed promissory notes in her favour. Under his will he left all his personal effects to his widow and the equity in the house to the lady, whom he appointed his executrix.

After his death, his widow made an application under the Testators Family Maintenance Act for provision to be made for her out of the deceased's estate. However, when the amount due to the executrix was taken into account, there was nothing left out of which any provision could be made for the widow.

In the course of the matter before the trial judge, the existence of the loans and the authenticity of the promissory notes were challenged. The executrix, who gave evidence of the loans and the making of the promissory notes, was very closely cross-examined in an endeavour to establish that there was no debt due to her. However, the trial judge believed her and affirmatively found that there was money due to her in sufficient amount to make the estate insolvent. Accordingly, he dismissed the application.

The widow appealed to the Supreme Court but her appeal was dismissed. She then obtained special leave to appeal from the High Court. The court allowed the appeal, gave the whole estate to the widow and ordered the executrix to pay all the costs. These would inevitably amount to a very large sum, seeing that they would cover the costs of all the earlier proceedings. My friend was incensed by what he regarded as rank injustice because the court had virtually made the executrix provide the estate for the widow. If the normal course had been followed, the executrix, entitled to defend the will, would be awarded the costs and there would have been no estate remaining.

As I listened I too became incensed by what the court had done, so much so that I told my friend that if his instructing solicitor was able to provide an instructing solicitor in London and a junior counsel, I would appear on a petition for special leave to appeal without any fee and likewise on an appeal if leave were granted. In the event, one of London's leading solicitors briefed me with a junior. The brief carried no fee. I understand the junior received no fee. He was John Sparrow, then a leading Equity counsel and later Warden of All Souls, Oxford.

In the course of the High Court's judgment, there was the following passage which I quote verbatim:

> The respondent also produced some promissory notes, but they may be bound up with the illicit cohabitation between her and the deceased and their validity may be doubtful. Her debt is not one the existence and validity of which had been admitted, nor had it been proved in a court of law. It could not therefore be assumed. No tenderness need be shown to a creditor whose debt grew out of a liaison between her and a married man. The widow's application should not be refused because the result might be to disturb the arrangements which the deceased had made with a view to simplifying the discharge of his obligations to the respondent. She should be left to prove her debt if she can.

To my mind, these were inaccurate and unsustainable words. There had been no specific issue of adultery at the original hearing. In particular, the validity of the promissory notes had not been attacked because of it. In any case, there had been no proof of adultery, certainly not in relation to the promissory notes, but more importantly, the trial judge had believed the executrix when she said on oath that she had lent the money and her account of the making of the promissory notes.

I got leave to appeal from a board of three Lords of Appeal (Lords Normand, Oaksey and Radcliffe). The following year I appeared for the executrix on the appeal. As John Sparrow by this time was installed at All Souls, for junior I had Peter Foster, subsequently Mr Justice Foster of the High Court of England. I received no fee and I understand that neither John Sparrow nor Peter Foster received any fee and the London solicitors no recompense.

In presenting argument on the appeal I made the passage quoted above from the High Court's judgment fairly prominent, as I had done in seeking special leave to appeal. It excited immediate comment from their lordships. On one occasion in the appeal, one of them asked me had adultery been an issue. I said it had not. I was asked was there any evidence of it. I said that the cynical could say so because the lady went to the man's house almost every weekend over a period of years. This brought from that lord the retort that in his book, such a matter had to be charged as well as proved. Then he added, "By the way, is it the law that if I lend my mistress £100 I can never recover it?" I said that I had no doubt that it was not the law but the contrary would appear from what I read in the High Court's judgment.

Then another lord asked me if the trial judge had believed the executrix on the creation of the debt and the promissory notes. I said that he had.

"Then", said that lord, "how can you say that her debt has not been proved?".

"Truly my Lord", I replied, "I cannot, but it has been said".

I was opposed in the appeal by Sir Frank Soskice, later Lord Stowhill. He had been Attorney-General in a Labor administration, and was a great friend of Hugh Gaitskell and became one of mine. When Frank Soskice felt that the tide in the case had turned against him he became a little rhetorical and began to talk about the widow's mite with a degree of emotion. Lord Porter, who was presiding, said to Sir Frank, "May I intervene to make a remark?". Of course, said Frank. Lord Porter said, "You know, Sir Frank, when I have anything to decide I put aside all sentiment and all emotion. I think that that is a good general rule". This to an English counsel in the circumstances was quite a rebuke. Frank politely said, "If that is a rebuke my Lord, let me accept it". Lord Porter smilingly said, "It is not a rebuke, Sir Frank, only a reminder". And there was no more emotional rhetoric.

In the end, the appeal was allowed and the High Court's orders were set aside.

* * * * *

The other case was of a different kind. It was an application for special leave to appeal and it was indeed the last case that I conducted as a private practitioner.

It concerns the will left by Surgeon Harris, who arrived with the Second Fleet in 1790. In a well-known story, when Harris was charged with the commission of an offence the clerk who drew up the charge sheet expressed it as "For that on the . . . day of . . . *ultimo*" something was done. But in truth it ought to have read "the . . . day of . . . *instant"*. In a day of high technicality this discrepancy brought an acquittal. Surgeon Harris was very pleased with his good fortune. He said that if ever he had an estate he would call it "Ultimo"; and he did. His house, "Ultimo House", still stands and is now part of a technical college. The suburb Ultimo largely embraces the estate Surgeon Harris acquired; Harris Street is its main thoroughfare. The Harris family provided a Lord Mayor of Sydney and became very well known in the colony.

In his will Harris left a number of life estates and the remainder to those Presbyterians who had left certain ports in Northern Ireland between certain dates. The NSW Supreme Court, both at first instance and on appeal, decided that this gift in remainder was a valid charitable trust. About forty-two years after the full court decision, the last of the life tenants died and the remainder fell to be distributed.

By this time the Harris family had grown to a considerable number of people. Their representative, through a solicitor, sought my opinion on two points. One, whether the gift was a valid charitable gift (because if not charitable, it was otherwise void) and second, whether after this long lapse of time anything could be done about reversing the decision of the Supreme Court. I advised that in my opinion the gift in remainder was plainly not a charitable gift and was invalid. If that were correct the whole estate was distributable among the next of kin. I thought that in any case the High Court would be unlikely to grant special leave to appeal but that the Privy Council might well do so.

I appeared in London in 1955 with Kenneth Jacobs as my junior to support a petition for special leave to appeal. Jacobs later became president of the NSW Court of Appeal and later still, a judge of the High Court. The Board of the Privy Council before whom we appeared was chaired by Lord Gavin Simonds. He had had extensive experience in the law of trusts. We were opposed by Gordon Wallace QC for the Presbyterian Church, which was claiming the estate.

Our first task was to convince the Board that the gift of the remainder did not constitute a charitable trust. Of course the members of the Board soon reminded me about the lapse of time. But I pointed out that nobody had been hurt or disadvantaged by the lapse of time as the last of the life tenants had only just passed away. I also said that this practice of the Supreme Court in giving rulings on the validity of a gift in remainder when the actual parties concerned to challenge it were not present or even identified was not very satisfactory and that I would later on say more about the lapse of time.

I sensed at a given point that I had probably satisfied the Board that this was not a valid charitable trust; I passed on to the question of the lapse of time, dealing with it as I have already indicated. I told them Surgeon Harris's story because the will referred to "Ultimo" in describing the estate of the deceased. I think their lordships were intrigued by this sidelight of Australian history. When my colleague Wallace came to address them I felt the die was cast, and indeed it was. Special leave to appeal forty-two years after the Supreme Court's decision was granted.

Before the appeal came before the Privy Council I had become Attorney-General, so I did not argue it. Kenneth Jacobs did, and succeeded. The considerable estate was distributed among the Harris next of kin.

In a way both of these cases indicate the benefit there is in an external final court of appeal. Such a tribunal seems better able to take large and dispassionate views. Of course nationalist feelings naturally and quite properly have put an end to the appeal to the Privy Council. But one cannot help feeling that the Australian community has lost the good offices of a very experienced and distinguished tribunal.

5 The Banks Nationalisation Case

When the Chifley Government announced its intention, on 13 August 1947, to nationalise the banking system, the individual banks sought legal assistance in preparing to defend their interests. Each customarily employed a firm of solicitors and some had given general retainers to members of the Bar. General consultation began immediately, and in due course the legislation was presented to Parliament. Then a group of barristers was assembled and detailed consultation began; at the same time the English banks had assembled a team of English counsel and solicitors. Early on I was briefed by Allen Allen & Hemsley and told by Norman Cowper of that firm that by arrangement I was to be the leader of the Australian barristers.

The form of the Nationalisation Act raised an immediate problem for the banks: it became operative as soon as the Royal Assent was received, thus automatically putting an end to private banking. An application was immediately made to the High Court to restrain the government from carrying out the terms of the Act until its constitutional validity had been authoritatively determined. Negotiations were at the same time commenced between counsel to get an undertaking by the government not to implement the Act pending that determination. Though at first refused, such an undertaking was given on the morning when the banks' application to the court was to be heard. The application thus became unnecessary.

As the High Court decided that it was invalid, and the Privy Council held that it lacked jurisdiction to hear an appeal from that decision, the Act never came into force and consequently the affairs of the private banks were never affected by its terms.

A number of possible grounds of total or partial invalidity were canvassed by counsel, but s 92 of the Constitution was early thought to be the likeliest source of total invalidity:

> On the imposition of uniform duties of customs, trade, commerce and intercourse among the States, whether by means of internal carriage or ocean navigation, shall be absolutely free . . .

Section 92 had been frequently discussed by the High Court right from the early days of the Commonwealth. The cases mostly concerned compulsory marketing schemes or restrictions on commercial motor transport, and in the cases described in the previous chapter, on personal travel throughout the Commonwealth and commercial air transport between the States. In the course of these decisions judges had expressed themselves in various ways. Mr Justice Dixon was the consistent supporter of the application of s 92, though as a rule he was in the minority. I had myself conducted or been engaged in some of these cases and of necessity was familiar with all of them and consequently with the attitudes of the individual judges towards the operation of s 92.

Although throughout 1947 I was heavily engaged in general practice, I did preparatory work for the presentation of argument on behalf of the banks. I considered that the court had never adopted the correct attitude to the application of s 92 and had formed my own view of how the section ought to be applied. The problem in point of advocacy was whether an attempt should be made to have that view accepted by the High Court. The judges had variously decided cases involving the application of the section, sometimes on the basis of the subject-matter of the legislation, sometimes on the parliamentary motivation in its passage, and sometimes on the nature of the legislation, that is, whether it was regulatory or prohibitive. There was a general tendency to seek to define what the section required trade etc to be free from rather than to consider what a prescription of absolute freedom required.

To my mind the proper approach to determining the validity of an act *vis-à-vis* s 92 is first to work out the legislation's full operation on interstate trade etc and having done so to determine whether that operation left the individual free to engage in it. This involved the difficult question of what restraints or burdens upon the individual's conduct of such trade etc were permissible, while leaving the individual absolutely free in relation to that trade. This meant considering what is involved in the concept of "freedom" in a civilised society. It does not constitute unbridled licence to act according to the individual's own decisions. The delineation of that margin between what is not an invasion of freedom and what is merely accepted regulation of it is a singularly difficult question about which minds are likely to differ.

But I did not think the argument in the High Court was one in which I should attempt to secure from the judges acceptance of so radical a change from what had already been decided. I felt it would be wise to accept the propriety of what had been decided by them and be content to rely on the absolute nature of the prohibition imposed by the banking legislation.

I felt little difficulty in being able to convince the court that banking is part of trade etc and that interstate banking, although dealing with the transmission of intangibles, is part of that interstate trade etc which had the protection of s 92.

I made my own assessment of the likely attitudes of the various judges to nationalising the banks. I considered that Rich, Starke, Dixon, Williams and Fullagar JJ would be disposed to find invalidity on one or more grounds and that my task would be to aid them towards such a conclusion. Latham CJ I thought would be disposed to support the legislation, and if he did so, McTiernan J would follow him. It was therefore important that we convince Latham.

I asked the banks' solicitors to engage Richard (Dick) Eggleston so that he and I could work together developing the argument on s 92. I wanted to prepare a proposition on it which, being consistent with what he had already decided, Latham could not reject.

The Banking Act prohibited all private banking except in the unlikely event that the Commonwealth Treasurer permitted it. Latham had subscribed in *Gratwick v Johnson*[1] and in the *Airlines* case[2] to a distinction between an absolute prohibition and a regulation. He had accepted the invalidating operation of s 92 in each of these cases. So we worked out a specific formula which coincided with Latham's expressed views and which we thought he could scarcely dispute:

> On the decided cases as they stand, at least the proposition is correct that s 92 is infringed whenever an individual or a corporation is engaged in inter-State trade, commerce or intercourse and, either by direct prohibition, or by regulation with the object, purpose or motive of effecting such a prohibition, the carrying on of such business by him or it is forbidden. It is the individual's freedom to move from place to place and to conduct his business across State lines that is protected or guaranteed by s 92 . . .

We took the ambiguous word "regulation" as sufficient to denote those laws which, though affecting interstate trade etc, left it absolutely free.

The banks were to be supported by two States, Victoria and South Australia, both of which had transport and marketing legislation and were wedded to maintaining the transport and marketing decisions.

The cases brought in the High Court were listed to commence in Melbourne at the beginning of term in February 1948. I well remember the fortnight in February 1948 when the conferences of counsel and solicitors took place in Melbourne. It was fiercely hot with blistering northerly winds and it continued like this throughout February and March. The counsel and solicitors all met daily during this fortnight in a room in the Union Bank in Collins Street on the corner of Queen Street.

There was ample room for discussion during these conferences about the transport and marketing decisions and their impact on the argument of the banks' case. For my part, I had thought these decisions irrelevant to the result of the present case and had reasons for not attacking them.

The banks with English headquarters sent out to Australia to these conferences Kenneth Diplock, then a leading junior at the English Bar and about to become a KC, and Emrys Lloyd, a partner in Farrers, one of London's great firms of solicitors. These lawyers brought to the conferences the views of English counsel on how the case might be conducted.

Out of this association great friendships were formed which lasted until Kenneth died in 1985 and Emrys in 1987. Kenneth became in due course Lord Diplock and ultimately senior law lord. He was a fine lawyer of a practical rather than an academic kind. He was also a good horseman. I rode with him in the Puckridge hunt during the hearing of the *Banking Nationalisation* case (referred to from here on as the *Banks* case) in London. He arranged a horse for me from a livery stable at Wimbledon; for exercise during the hearing I rode each week on Wimbledon Common or in Richmond Park.

My argument before the High Court reflected my knowledge of its members and my estimate of their likely reaction to the legislation. Thus some things could be taken for granted. But it was critically important that the full operation of the legislation should be appreciated; consequently I spent a deal of time expounding this. The legislation raised many questions about legislative power and acquisition of property, as well as the operation of s 92. The argument on these topics was distributed among the counsel for the banks.

By its absolute prohibition of private banking, the Act created a government monopoly. The legislation on the *Transport* and *Marketing* cases provided for a regulatory system of licensing of private transport operations supported by a prohibition of unlicensed operation. Thus it could be said that the statutes in those cases attempted a regime of regulation as distinct from outright prohibition. Therefore Latham's support of those cases might be accommodated to the acceptance of the proposition that an outright prohibition of interstate banking, as distinct from its regulation, was invalid.

So my argument in attacking the validity of the Banking Act need not disturb the existing decisions while not expressly conceding their propriety.

As matters stood in 1948, it had been decided that the Commonwealth as well as the States was bound by s 92. All legislative power given to the Commonwealth by ss 51 and 52 is said to be "subject to this Constitution". Thus there was an area of legislative power denied to all the legislatures federal and State, a circumstance which did not favour a wide application of the section.

Understandably, the press treated the *Banks* case in the High Court as a *cause célèbre* and no doubt were looking for quotable dramatic rhetorical expressions from the Bar table. They thought of the case as a political spectacular. On the day the case opened in Melbourne, the court was crowded. Not only was there an abundance of journalists, but Melbourne society was represented by rows of well-dressed and splendidly hatted ladies. They fully occupied the benches at the side of the courtroom.

I was, however, determined to keep the argument to legal principle and to ignore the political overtones. It was to be no more than a dry legal debate. So I am afraid I disappointed my audience. I opened the case in a matter-of-fact way: no rhetoric of any kind, no generalities or throwaway lines. The dull approach was, I am sure, disappointing, and it was not long before I lost my audience. One reporter wrote that I made the case sound like a minor contest between citizens. He little thought how congratulatory I took his description to be.

Although there was only one hearing, there were in fact three separate cases, each with its own group of counsel.

With Evatt, Attorney-General for the Commonwealth, were Professor KH Bailey, Solicitor-General of the Commonwealth. With them in the first action, were Weston KC, Holmes and Benjafield; in the second action, Harold Mason KC and BP Macfarlan; in the third action, Tait KC and Gowans; in the fourth and fifth actions, PD Phillips KC and Menhennitt.

For the banks in the three actions besides myself there were Dr Coppel; Frank Kitto (later a judge of the High Court); Adam (later Mr Justice Adam of the Supreme Court of Victoria); Alan Taylor (later judge of the High Court); Ashburner (later a member of the Industrial Arbitration Commission); Eggleston (later Sir Richard, a judge of the Federal Court); and Bernard Riley.

Coppel, Kitto, Taylor and Hudson in turn addressed the court, supporting my argument but adding argument on the several points which had been allotted to them. Both the leaders for the intervening States also presented argument.

The Attorney-General's argument occupied a great number of days in a highly repetitive fashion. He was anything but a born advocate and his delivery was dull and tiresome. The case dragged on for forty days, from 9 February to 15 April, a time of singularly hot weather. During this time Sir Isaac Isaacs, former Chief Justice and Governor-General, died at the age of ninety-two, an odd coincidence bearing in mind a central feature of the litigation.

On 15 August 1948 the High Court delivered judgment by majority, finding the legislation invalid. Latham CJ and McTiernan J dissented and held the legislation valid. In the course of his judgment Latham completely misquoted the proposition that had been put to the court and then demolished the misrepresentation.

The Commonwealth Government immediately sought special leave of the Privy Council to appeal. It was an unlikely step for a Labor Government to seek the assistance of an external court, but the Chifley Government did. Norman Cowper offered me a brief to appear in London to oppose the petition for special leave. At first I declined to accept it. I took the view that the Privy Council would be certain to grant the Government of Australia special leave to test the decision of the High Court on the validity of its legislation and that the banks were unlikely to successfully oppose the petition. I advised Cowper that the banks should send a good draftsman to London to make certain that the documents lodged there were in shape in accordance with the known views of Australian counsel. My suggestion was accepted and Frank Kitto and Dr Coppel from Melbourne were dispatched to London.

However, the National Bank, an old supporter of mine, was not prepared to accept the advice I had given. I was pressed to accept the brief and to go to London, but because of the pressure of my own work I could not do so immediately. Accordingly, Norma and I joined the *Strathnaver* in Fremantle. On board were Douglas Menzies, briefed by the State of Victoria, "Tacky" Hannan, Solicitor-General of South Australia, Norman and Mrs Cowper, Ralph and Mrs Burt of Blake & Riggall, Solicitors, of Melbourne, and Tom and Mrs Trumble of Malleson Stewart, Solicitors, of Melbourne. The journey took a little over three weeks and was most pleasant. We had a team of friends, conditions were very good, the ship was lively with parties, games and swimming, plenty of relaxing amusement. We called at Colombo, Bombay, Aden, passed through the Suez Canal to Port Said, then through the Mediterranean to Tilbury. My father, aged 74, died while we were still at sea. This was the first trip abroad for Norma and me, though before marriage Norma had visited New Zealand.

I had calculated that while the clients were paying my wife's fare to London, I would be responsible for the cost of her residence there. We calculated at the time that we would be back in Sydney within three months. We had young children, our son Ross aged ten and our daughter Diane aged four. Fortunately, Norma had relatives — an uncle by marriage, a widower, and his daughter, Mrs Mavis Blau, who had always been very close to Norma. Though unrelated by blood, they were like cousins. Mrs Blau (always known by the family as "Cousie") and her father occupied our house in Cheltenham looking after the children. In the event, however, it was more than ten months before we returned home. At times we both worried about the children and I fretted about what might be happening to my practice. But as it happened, the children had such care and attention that they scarce missed us at all and my absence did little if any harm to my practice.

Each time we went ashore at a port during the journey to London, I noticed the hovering presence of Norman Cowper. He organised our sightseeing in Colombo and Bombay. His evident solicitude was most notable at Aden where I insisted on taking a taxi to see the ancient wells by night.

When we berthed at Port Said, Cowper asked me not to go deep into the town. There had been riots in Cairo and Port Said and British vessels had not been calling there until shortly before our arrival. It was thought that matters had not so far settled down as to make it safe for Westerners to be abroad in Port Said at night. But Douglas Menzies and I, accompanied by Norma, hired a barouche and toured the town. We were the last passengers left ashore and were escorted back to the ship by the local gendarmerie. When we were approaching the articulated pontoon over which we had to pass to reach the ship's gangway,

Norma became a little apprehensive and nervously took my arm, so that I am sure we looked like a pair of newlyweds. A young Egyptian selling roses proposed that I buy a bunch for two shillings, but I refused. He persisted, walking along with us. As we neared the pontoon, exasperated by my refusal to buy, he said quite sharply, "You love the bloody girl, you buy the bloody flowers", at the same time offering to sell me his remaining four bunches for two shillings. When we reached the gangway, Cowper and Trumble were hanging over the taffrail anxiously awaiting our return. By then it was in the advancing hours of the morning.

I relate these small incidents because of what subsequently occurred in London at the end of my argument to the Privy Council. I did not then realise that Cowper, who was accounted worldly-wise, had been delegated to secure my personal safety, and to ensure that I remained available to appear in the Privy Council. I guess that on the voyage he thought me a fractious colt.

I had asked to be accommodated at Claridge's for the month or so I expected to be in London. Our ship arrived a day late. We found in our rooms in the hotel an invitation to a reception to be given in the hotel in honour of the visiting lawyers and their wives that very evening, 7.00 for 7.30. We presented ourselves at the door on the reception room at 7.15. We were asked our names by a tall, liveried man who, when told them, turned to the assembly within the room and, in a stentorian voice, said: "Mr and Mrs Barwick".

There were, as we later ascertained, well over a hundred people in the room. On this announcement we became conscious that all eyes were focused on us. I think they were expecting somebody closer to a greybeard as the principal lawyer from Australia. They saw of course a man of modest stature, clean-shaven and almost boyish-looking — at least I would like to think so. Beside him they saw a handsome young woman, well but not elaborately dressed and of a height only slightly less than that of her husband. This shock over, we were greeted in a warm and friendly manner, being passed round from one to another in what to us was a kaleidoscopic fashion. We had a splendid evening, greeting not only new faces but refreshing ourselves with those of our lawyer friends who had either preceded or accompanied us. Before the evening was out, we had received invitations to visit, both in the country and in the town. But, though very pleasurable, the evening was nervously exhausting and at its conclusion we gladly sought the rest of our first night in London.

I had brought with me, besides the brief for the banks, briefs in two applications for special leave to appeal. In one, the client was Grace Bros — a case concerning the acquisition by the Commonwealth of the Grace Building in King and York Streets, Sydney. The other concerned the price to be paid for the wheat compulsorily acquired under the wartime Wheat Pool, *Nelungaloo v Commonwealth.*[3] In the first of these, I was to be led by Cyril Radcliffe, and in the second to be opposed by Harold Mason, both of whom were in the company that evening.

In the succeeding days I was busy meeting the English counsel and solicitors and in conferring about the banks' opposition to the grant of special leave. Sir Cyril Radcliffe KC (later Lord Radcliffe), Sir Walter Monckton KC, Sir Valentine Holmes KC and Kenneth Diplock, now KC, were the senior English counsel and Brian McKenna, later Sir Brian McKenna, judge of the English High Court, the one junior. Douglas Menzies was to be led by Sir David Fyfe KC for the State of Victoria and Tacky Hannan was to have as his junior Mr Barrington, later a county court judge. I also met the English instructing solicitors.

Cyril Radcliffe thought that there was a possibility of persuading the Privy Council to reject the Commonwealth's application in point of discretion. I took the view that, the High Court not having been unanimous, the Council would not refuse the Australian Government an opportunity to appeal against its decision, particularly in so far-reaching a matter as its constitutional power with respect to banking. But of course the endeavour to persuade the Privy Council to refuse leave had to be made.

Apparently the two groups of solicitors, English and Australian, differed on who should lead the banks' opposition, the English preferring Cyril Radcliffe and the Australians myself. Ultimately I was asked to attend a conference of all solicitors and to express my view on the matter. I had no doubt that Cyril Radcliffe should lead. Not only was he the outstanding English advocate of the day, but he thought the petition might possibly be defeated, while I did not. I said I had myself one particular objective which was to reduce, if not destroy, Sir John Latham's influence with the Council. To weaken his dissent from the majority view would be of considerable advantage, or so I thought. It was settled that Cyril Radcliffe should lead and I would follow.

The Board to hear the petition was presided over by Lord Wright and otherwise consisted of Lords Porter, Simonds, Du Parc, Uthwatt, Morton and Cohen. The Australian Attorney-General opened and I thought was well received, particularly by Lord Wright. Then Cyril Radcliffe put the argument for the banks' opposition. He was an outstanding advocate and a brilliant lawyer. This day he gave a polished performance; his language was clear and concise and his delivery easy.

He completed his address about three-thirty and I got up to follow him. Doubtless I provided an anti-climax. The Board had heard England's best and now it heard my flat Australian voice! I rather suspected the members of the Council to be thinking, "We've just heard Radcliffe in good form, why must we hear more — and from a Counsel we little know". But if such thoughts were passing through their minds they were far too polite to show it.

I had never argued from a lectern to a Bench sitting on the same level as that on which I was standing. I later learnt to use this situation to my advantage. But this afternoon I made the mistake of folding my arms and resting them on the lectern. Thereafter I felt unable to withdraw either of them to make a gesture or emphasise a point. It almost made me tongue-tied. The period until four, the time for adjournment, was agonising, one of the worst I had experienced. I had never felt so ineffective, and the polite silence of my hearers only made matters worse.

I had a very troubled night. Next morning I opened up again, working as always without script or notes. I did not repeat the mistake of folding my arms. After about twenty minutes Lord Andrew Uthwatt (who had for a time attended school in Australia, a circumstance of which I understand him to have been proud) made some remark to me and I made a joke in reply. It changed the atmosphere. Sir Valentine Holmes, himself a great advocate with nonconforming habits, later told me that it was a magical moment, one of the rarities in his recollection. He said I had broken through a barrier and gathered strength with the Privy Council thereafter.

Incidentally, Valentine Holmes and I became good friends in the ensuing months. His habit of life was to go at the end of the working day to a wine bar in Fleet Street, Pomenoys, and have a drink with his clerk. I suspect that he was the prototype of some part of Rumpole of the Bailey. Many times I invited Val to parties that Norma and I gave while in London. He would always accept but never turn up. Once I asked Walter Monckton what was the trouble. He told me not to be concerned, that Val never came to any of their parties. This I had to accept but continued issuing an invitation to him.

On the evening before our departure for Australia in 1949, we gave a final party. Early in the evening Walter Monckton came across the room to me and pointing to Val Holmes chatting to a fellow guest, said, "That's the nicest compliment Val could pay you". I did very much appreciate his gesture in attending the party.

During the fortnight preceding this party, Val and I had met in the Temple. He said, "I hear you are going to the Derby". I said we were; that we were going into the middle to see the people on the flat. He said, "You'll enjoy that and they will enjoy you. You will not condescend to them". I deeply appreciated that perceptive remark.

I took occasion to examine Latham's judgment and indicated how he had transformed the proposition we had put and demolished something we had not. When I set out the proposition we had actually put and contrasted it with the one Latham had recorded and rejected, consternation overcame the government team. As I continued to elaborate what Latham had done Evatt sent urgently for the transcript of the argument in the High Court, only to find that I was precisely right. I made my point, and my thrust, I am sure, went home. Any weight Latham might have carried was at least reduced if not displaced altogether. After that there was little I could do beyond supporting Radcliffe's argument. I ended up that day much more content than I had the previous afternoon.

Special leave to appeal was immediately granted. Norma and I then expected to return home but thought to do a little sightseeing before doing so.

During 1948 I had seen a Sydney ophthalmic specialist about my sight, which I thought to be intermittently weakening. He made a close inspection of the retina of each eye. When examining one of them, he quite evidently showed some concern. Noticing this I said "There's a mark on that retina". "There is", he said, "how did you know that?". I said that a general practitioner once told me of it, but had been unable to offer me a diagnosis. The specialist said, "You have had a crisis in your arteries at some stage". This I doubted, but knowing I was to go to London, he gave me a referral to a Harley Street specialist.

This incident troubled me but I decided not to consult a physician on the matter till I had completed my argument in London. But on the day following the conclusion of the hearing, I consulted a Harley Street man, a well-known specialist. He also could offer no conclusive diagnosis of the mark. His best assessment was that I had been born with it; otherwise he gave me a fair bill of health. I left his surgery much relieved.

The following day Norma and I took the Flying Scotsman to Edinburgh where the hired car we had arranged awaited us. We toured Scotland as far as Aberdeen, returning along the west side of Loch Lomond — a thoroughly enjoyable experience, the deciduous trees not having yet lost their leaves even though it was then November.

Norma had had no enthusiasm to visit Scotland. In her mother's house there had been a monochrome print of shaggy cattle on a windy Scottish moor. That for her represented Scotland. However, the Pass of Killiecrankie in autumn changed all that. At Aberfeldy we visited a tweed mill; I bought some lengths of tweed. During the course of doing so, Norma asked might she buy our daughter a kilt. I asked what right had our daughter to a kilt. Norma, by now roused to admiration of the country, replied, "You forget my grandfather was James Duff Shaw Grant. That surely entitles my daughter to a tartan". So we bought a length of Grant Hunting tartan.

On our return from this journey, the banks' solicitors, both English and Australian, indicated that they desired Australian counsel to remain in London to prepare for the hearing of the appeal, likely to occur in the spring of the following year. In some alarm, Norma telephoned our home — in those days a time-consuming business talking on an indifferent line. But her relatives assured her that all was well with the children who, we were told, were not missing us at all! They agreed to stay on in our house till we returned.

After a few weeks we left Claridge's and went to a very large apartment in St James' Court in Buckingham Gate. This apartment we shared, until almost the end of the argument on the appeal, with Frank and Eleanor Kitto. This had been arranged with the consent of all of us to enable Frank and me to work together on the preparation of the case-book on s 92. The book was to set out the argument in summary. It would later be included with other summaries in a book to be filed and exchanged for the Commonwealth's case-book.

Before concentrated work on the case began, its various aspects were apportioned to different groups of counsel. It was agreed that I should deal with the argument based on s 92. In Australia I had asked for Eggleston to assist me. But the bank had not briefed Eggleston to work in London. Now I asked that Frank Kitto be nominated. I knew that we would need his skills as a draftsman and an exponent of the English language. He was also an outstanding lawyer.

While s 92 was thought only to bind the States, it might have been possible to decide constitutional validity by reference to the subject-matter of the legislation in question. The Transport statutes might be regarded as having motor vehicles and their use as their subject-matter. Any impact of such legislation on interstate trade might be regarded as merely consequential and be ignored. But when it was authoritatively decided by the Privy Council that the Commonwealth also was bound by s 92,[4] a different approach had to be found. This time the area withdrawn from legislative control was said by the majority of the court to comprise only those laws which were "aimed at" interstate trade and commerce. They might be expressed as only laws discriminating against such trade etc.[5] The decision whether the law was so "aimed" had to be made upon examination of the terms of the legislation itself.

This was a very unsatisfactory criterion on which to determine legislative validity. Apart from all else, it was based on the view, or at any rate produced the result, that the constitutional provision meant that interstate trade and commerce had to be relatively free. The force of the word "absolutely" in the section scarce left such a view possible. It was akin to the view that s 92 only protects interstate trade etc from discriminatory laws.

As I earlier indicated, I thought that the proper approach to the problem was to establish the operation of the statute upon interstate trade and commerce and, having done so, to ask whether such operation left that trade etc free. In other words, was the impact of that operation on interstate trade compatible with the concept of freedom of the individual in a civilised and complex society? That there are restraints which may be imposed in such a society which do not deny the individual's freedom must be conceded. The problem is to develop a criterion by which such acceptable restraints may be identified.

It had already been authoritatively decided, as I thought correctly, that the concept of freedom of interstate trade and commerce included or entailed the freedom of the individual to engage in it. Indeed, I cannot think that any other view is possible.

Now, dealing with the matter in the ultimate tribunal, I considered it advisable, if not necessary, to offer a general discussion of the meaning and operation of s 92. Perhaps the proposition we had worked out to present to the High Court was sufficient, the Act completely prohibiting the individual to engage in interstate banking. The contest between prohibition and regulation might be enough. There was really no need to define precisely the margins of permissible lesser legislative interferences with trade. The word "regulation" in that proposition was ambiguous, though for purposes of argument fairly serviceable. But I felt it was necessary to have some explanation of what restraints or burdens the section in principle allowed.

This involved the consideration of what restrictions the law may impose on the individual while at the same time leaving him free. This in turn called for an examination of the concept of freedom of the individual in a developed and civilised society.

A citizen is not unfree because he may not defame his neighbour or because he cannot drive on the wrong side of the road or must obey the red light at a traffic intersection, or because, being infected with an infectious disease, he is required to remain apart from his fellows. Freedom is quite consistent with many community-imposed restraints which are in turn designed to maintain the freedom of the members of society. The problem is in expressing in words a proposition which will identify those restraints which though restricting action are nonetheless consistent with freedom in the sense in which it should be understood in a civilised society. Though the question of the consistency or inconsistency of any restraint of the individual is essentially a practical one, the formulation of a yardstick by which to gauge the inconsistency is extremely difficult. Perhaps it may be thought better not to attempt the formulation of a universally applicable criterion, allowing each case as it arises to make its contribution to an increasing understanding of what may and what may not be permissible.

To anticipate the result of the case in this respect, the Privy Council was content to use the concept of regulation, without any definition, as adequate to cover these permissible restraints, those which did not render trade and commerce unfree.

So at the outset of the work on a case-book we had a clear idea of the direction the argument should take. Our argument, if carried to its logical conclusion, would deny the validity of the statutes dealt with in the *Transport* and *Marketing* cases. But there was no need to carry the argument that far in preparing the book.

Frank and I discussed the contents and form of the case-book as its draft emerged, almost daily. This made us very conscious of the risks that would arise if different counsel expressed views on the s 92 question. But I had no power to keep the argument in our own hands. The counsel employed by the English solicitors and counsel for each of the supporting States had a right to address the Privy Council on the point. But I was to have two unexpected pieces of good fortune.

While Frank and I worked on the case-book relating to s 92, others were working on case-books dealing with the other points of the case. From time to time we were involved in discussions about these other aspects, but none but Frank and myself discussed the s 92 question until after the case-book was ready to be filed.

In outlining our argument, Frank showed outstanding skill in the choice of expressions. The need not to go against the interests of the supporting States had its influence both on the expression of the argument in the case-book and in due course in its presentation.

Ultimately, the various parts of the case-book were brought together. The book had to be authenticated by the signature of a senior and a junior counsel. All counsel gathered one evening in Stone building in Lincoln's Inn to settle the book. David Fyfe presided; we dealt with each draft book in turn. About most of them there was some discussion. The s 92 part was the last to be considered. No one wished to offer any comment on our draft. When this became apparent, Val Holmes said that if no one else wanted to say anything about this book, he did. He said it was the best case-book he had ever read: it not merely put the argument, it educated those who were to read it.

Now although it was only necessary for the book to be signed by two counsel, all seemed anxious to sign it; and all did, including counsel for the supporting States. The book thus authenticated and printed, was exchanged with the Commonwealth's book. Both were then filed with the Registrar of the Privy Council.

After the case-books had been exchanged, I was asked by several of the counsel, particularly by some English counsel, if they might see the typescript of the argument I was to put before the Council. When I told them that there would be no typescript, there was some disquiet. I have never worked from a typescript and often had few, if any, notes. Knowledge of this probably added to their disquiet. As I sensed their anxiety, I said that if we all gathered one evening I would give them a conspectus of the argument as I intended to put it. This was welcomed and arranged. We all assembled, again in Stone building, and I gave a fairly full run down of what I proposed to put to the Council. There were some comments, particularly from Kenneth Diplock, who of all the English counsel present was the most familiar with the cases on s 92. At the end of the evening I think that the disquiet had been somewhat allayed but not completely removed.

Next morning Douglas Menzies came to see me. He was quite agitated. He said he could not be a party to my argument because it would destroy the Transport and Marketing cases. I conceded that it could. He said he intended cabling Melbourne for instructions. Douglas had not spotted the logical outcome of the argument the case-book presented, but my conspectus of it had alerted him to the possibilities. I reminded him that he had signed the book. He immediately saw the difficulty he was in. However, I said that I had thought out a course of arguing the case successfully without involving an attack on the Transport and Marketing cases. I then proposed that if he, and his leader Fyfe and Tacky Hannan, would agree to adopt my argument on the basis that the Nationalisation Act contained an absolute prohibition and themselves present no argument, I would undertake not to bring down the *Transport* and *Marketing* cases unless I was in dire extremity, a situation I did not expect. The formula I proposed would safeguard the States' positions, leaving room to treat the *Transport* and *Marketing* cases as no more than permissibly regulatory. I thought the terms of the formula I proposed were unlikely to attract the attention of the Council, while at the same time safeguarding the intervening counsel.

Douglas realised this. Also, he and his leader would not be called on till I had fully developed the argument so that he would by then be satisfied that I had carried out my undertaking.

He took a little time to turn this over but finally agreed; later Hannan did likewise. So I not only retained the support of the two States, but I had ensured that there would be no separate argument on s 92 presented on their behalf. This was indeed a piece of good fortune.

I fully realised the extent of the restraint that my undertaking imposed upon me but was satisfied that nonetheless I could successfully put the banks' case without drawing attention to the relationship of the argument to the situation of the *Transport* and *Marketing* cases.

There remained the English counsel. It would have been presumptuous on my part to suggest to them that they should leave the entire field of s 92 to me. After the conspectus I had given at the meeting in Lincolns Inn, none of the counsel suggested any conference with me or indicated to me any particular attitudes they intended to take. I had to proceed on the footing that some one or more of the English counsel might present an argument of their own on s 92. This possibility was never absent from my mind as I presented my argument to the Privy Council.

However, after I had been speaking for some days, Walter Monckton came to me asking me if I contemplated anyone following me. I think he thought I might be considering asking Frank to do so. I said that I was not. He then said that my presentation of the case so far had been a "tour de force" and that he would not follow, nor would anyone else. While I own up to great pleasure on receiving such a compliment, particularly from one who was himself a great advocate, I was better pleased to know that there was no risk of a discordant voice in connection with s 92. This was again a great piece of good fortune.

Thus the only argument presented on s 92 was the one we put. Both David Fyfe and Tacky Hannan adopted my argument on the footing that the Nationalisation Act imposed an absolute prohibition.

* * * * *

Dr Evatt opened the case for the Commonwealth on 14 March 1948 before a Board of seven law lords presided over by Lord Porter. They were, in addition to the Chairman, Lords Simonds, Du Parc, Normand, Morton of Henryton, Uthwatt and MacDermott. The Board adjourned over Easter. Evatt, by then, had been addressing it for eighteen days. During the recess, Lords Du Parc and Uthwatt unexpectedly died. On resumption after the recess, the argument continued before the remaining five law lords.

Evatt did one very effective thing during his argument. He had successively read to the Board Dixon's dissenting judgments on the *Transport* and *Marketing* cases. In my opinion formed at the time, he thus destroyed Dixon as a reliable authority. Indeed, I thought him so successful in this respect that I resolved not to rely during my own argument on anything Dixon had written; and as well as I recall, I did not do so.

Evatt earlier decided to have some of his own judgments as a judge of the High Court read to the Board. Rather than do this himself, Kenneth Bailey read them, for this purpose standing at the lectern, Evatt sitting on the side bench. On one occasion, one of the lords asked Bailey a question about some aspect of the judgment he was reading. Before Bailey could respond, Evatt rose from his seat, quite abruptly displaced Bailey at the lectern and proceeded to answer the question. It was quite natural that Evatt should wish to give his own explanation. But it was the manner in which he treated Bailey which excited attention. I thought the lords were not only surprised by his action but looked on it with distaste. At the lowest, it was an extremely insensitive thing to have done, particularly to Bailey who was a most gentle and courteous man.

At the conclusion of Evatt's argument, DN Pritt KC addressed the Board.

The Commonwealth had as I thought the initial advantage of appealing to English lawyers who were used to the omnipotence of Parliament as it exists at Westminster and were naturally disinclined to support restraints upon its legislative powers, particularly a restraint as wide-ranging as the banks were claiming s 92 to be. On the other hand, the banks had the advantage of the High Court's judgments.

Cyril Radcliffe opened for the banks, dealing with questions of power, compensation and jurisdiction, relying in this respect on s 74 of the Constitution. In the course of his presentation of an argument dealing with the compulsory acquisition of the property of the banks (required by the Constitution to be on just terms), he pointed out that one section said that the Commonwealth could acquire the business of a bank and another that the Treasurer, by notice, could prevent a bank from doing any business. He said, "My Lords, remarkably like money or your life; of course a well-recognised form of acquisition of property but hitherto not thought to be on just terms". Cyril Radcliffe's remark was a powerful thrust and typical of his capacity as an advocate.

I followed, feeling much more comfortable than I had in the argument on the petition. I built the argument largely on the decisions of the Privy Council, but particularly on *James v Cowan*.[6] But apart from maintaining that in operating their banking business, the banks were engaged in interstate trade and commerce, I followed the line I have already set out in the preparation of the case-book. The operation of the statute rather than its subject-matter, its purpose, or motivation was the critical fact. What did it do to the individual's capacity to engage in interstate trade etc? Having answered that question, was the trade etc and the individual's capacity to engage in it absolutely free? The absolute prohibition of private banking clearly provided a negative answer.

I had of course to tread a difficult path, not only in presenting my argument but in answering the various questions put to me by the members of the Council if I was to honour my undertaking to Douglas Menzies. To do so prevented me from attempting any assault on the *Transport* and *Marketing* cases though of necessity they were mentioned in the course of the argument.

Soon after I began, members of the Board began to probe my argument, asking questions which sought concrete and practical answers. I well remember the first such question, by Lord Fergus Morton. I immediately set out to answer it. But he protested that he did not mean to embarrass me and that I could give him my answer at some later stage. But I said I wished to deal with it straight away. I think Lord Moreton thought I was impetuous and foolish, the matter in hand being complex.

It seems that the practice of the English Bar and of Canadians appearing before the Privy Council was to defer providing an answer and hopefully providing one later — and the Council was prepared to go along with this practice. However, I managed to answer the question straight away and felt I had gone at least some distance in satisfying His Lordship's concern. Indeed, I think the feature that distinguished the Australian advocates from both the English and the Canadians was our ability and willingness to respond forthwith to questioning.

Several years later, when I was in the robing room of the Privy Council during a recess in the argument of a case, I overheard two English solicitors discussing me, one saying to the other, "I wish we had him: he can answer questions". Although this was not intended for my ears, I derived personal satisfaction from hearing it.

Later still, when appearing for an appellant before a Board presided over by Gavin Simonds, as soon as I opened the case, the Board interrogated me for a full hour. At the end of that time, Lord Simonds expressed his apologies for having thus detained me, but adding that the time had been well spent. I am sure that this ability of the Australian advocates to enter into dialogue with the Bench was both noticed and appreciated and impressed both the Temple and the solicitors.

In what became after 1948 my frequent appearances in the Privy Council, after having opened an appeal, as it were, generally, I put forward specific propositions. When I began to do so, the presiding lord would generally say, "At dictation speed" and the lords began to write down my propositions. Because of this, it was said in the Temple that I was the counsel from whom their Lordships took dictation, somewhat misleading but intended as a compliment.

Those of us who had appeared before the High Court presided over successively by Latham and Dixon had become used to carrying on a dialogue with the Bench and indeed profited by it. But not all Australian advocates enjoyed such interrogation. I remember when later presiding over the High Court, counsel protesting when asked a question, and saying that he preferred to present his argument without interruption. To my mind, dialogue rather than speeches heard in silence is to be preferred. For one thing, such exchanges are more likely to promote sound judgment. At any rate, during the *Banks* case I answered many questions and I think by answering them, made my argument clearer to my listeners.

I have already told of Walter Monckton's reaction to my address. I concluded it on a Thursday afternoon. I felt I had succeeded. So apparently did Norman Cowper, who heard it all. He had had anxious times when we called at the ports on the way over; when I had hunted in England; when I had skied in Switzerland. After disrobing on this Thursday, I set out for our flat in Buckingham Gate, walking along Downing Street to the Horse Guards Parade and intending to go through St James Park. When I was just short of No 10, Norman caught up with me. He had missed me in the robing room. He grasped my hand somewhat fervently. He was flushed with excitement and said, "Now you little bastard, you can break your bloody neck as far as I'm concerned". I knew this did not spring from ingratitude or malice, but from genuine relief. I had survived to present the argument which he too thought had been successful. Norman and I were good friends and remained so till his death. He was an intense man, and a good lawyer. This day, I think he felt he could relax. I must say I too felt very relieved: my immediate task was at an end and I felt I had not fallen down in the doing.

About this time, Cyril Radcliffe was appointed a Law Lord — a singular distinction, for in all the years only one other man had gone from practice at the Bar to the House of Lords: that was Lord Macnaghten. Radcliffe's elevation in the middle of the case was, I felt, somewhat inconsiderate of the parties' interests. He was due to respond to the Commonwealth's argument on s 74. But of course on appointment he had immediately to withdraw from the case. It was first suggested that I do that reply, but I declined. However, Walter Monckton, with the able assistance of Brian McKenna, stepped into the breach and did very well. The argument on s 74 proved successful and the Board in the long run found itself to be without jurisdiction to hear the appeal. However, in giving judgment, it expressed its views on the operation of s 92 favourably to our contention, although this did not constitute a binding precedent.

I remember being invited by Allen Allen & Hemsley to attend on the evening of 26 October at the Bank of New South Wales's head office in George Street, Sydney, to hear the result of the case, expected to be received from London that evening. A considerable number of people were present. Fairly early in the evening the result came. The banks had won, or rather, the Commonwealth had lost. At the time we did not know the Privy Council's reasons for disallowing the appeal. But the news was received with much enthusiasm. I remember I did not stay for the party which followed as I was in the middle of a case on which I had to work that evening.

I am inclined to think that at this time the Board's reasons for rejecting the appeal were based on its view of the operation of s 92 and that it was later that the argument on the privative effect of s 74 was made the basis of the judgment. I think this because of the subsequent publication of the views on s 92 which in the event were no more than *obiter dicta*. They were later turned into a binding precedent when we successfully argued *Hughes v Vale*[7] which finally disposed of the *Transport* cases.

*****

I have already mentioned the friendship between Kenneth Diplock and me which began during the period he was in Melbourne and endured until his death in 1985. He was devoted to hunting and to point-to-point racing. For the rest, he was consumed by the law, its practice and its administration. He was a fine and a decisive judge. Over the years we dined together when I was in London, at times in his apartment in the Temple. In the 1970s I sat as a member of a Board of the Privy Council over which he presided.

With Walter and Biddy Monckton I developed a friendship which lasted with Biddy beyond Walter's death. He was among the most charming of men, devoted to the law, an outstanding advocate, fond of and skilful at cricket. My last meeting with him was when he was Chairman of the Midland Bank in 1960. I was by then Attorney-General of the Commonwealth. I lunched with him at the bank at the conclusion of an argument in *Dennis Hotels v State of Victoria*.[8]

I have already mentioned the friendship of Val Holmes, who has long since passed away.

Emrys Lloyd, a partner in Farrers, was slightly built and of Welsh extraction. He was educated at Winchester and New College, Cambridge. He had been an outstanding athlete, having competed successfully in two sports at the same Olympic Games. He was a champion with the foils and coxed a successful eight. In fact, I think he had several Olympics to his credit. But he was a most modest man and few with whom he came into even close contact, so much as suspected, let alone heard from him, his Olympic prowess. In the years I knew him he was in great demand in England and Europe as a referee in fencing contests.

He was diffident in offering his views in the preparation of the *Banks* case, though he developed a clear understanding of the constitutional problems and held his views on them quite firmly. But those who heeded him soon realised his wisdom and sound legal knowledge. With him and his wife Elizabeth, Norma and I formed a very close friendship. Elizabeth was a graduate of Oxford University. She was the only daughter of PG Doyne, an ophthalmic surgeon of international reputation. I think many ophthalmic practitioners in Australia had been instructed by Mr Doyne. He also was an outstanding fencer. Norma and I came to know him and his wife and visited them at their home outside Henley. We remain in frequent contact with Elizabeth.

Through Emrys I came to know Sir Leslie Farrer (since deceased) and his son Matthew, now Sir Matthew, and his cousin Bill Farrer. Matthew is now head of Farrers.

One other friendship grew out of these associations. After Sir Leslie Farrer retired as senior partner of Farrers, Joe Burrell became the senior. He and I formed a very close friendship over the years. He (also a Wykehamist and graduate of New College) was a very congenial companion, a very good lawyer with a strong sense of humour, and a capacity for enjoying life in the company of friends.

Among those other friendships were Robert (now Sir Robert) Gatehouse, a judge of the High Court in England and his then wife, Henrietta, who now lives in Italy.

With Brian McKenna a very deep friendship developed. He was a splendid lawyer. He was just and exhibited great independence of mind. Sorrowfully, I think his willingness to be outspoken cost him his chance of promotion through the ranks of the judicial hierarchy. He retired early from the Bench and I fear appeared a lonely figure in the Temple. But we maintained a lively correspondence till his death in 1990.

When all is said and done, these and other friendships we formed were the real rewards of my participation in the argument of the *Banks* case.

6 Knighthood

In 1953, Douglas Menzies and I decided we would take our families together on a caravan expedition during the May school holidays. We both arranged our practices so as to be free to do so. I hired a caravan in Sydney and Douglas one in Melbourne. We planned to meet and travel together in Victoria. In due course we arrived at a house in Euroa — Ned Kelly country — owned by Douglas's brother-in-law Malcolm Cameron, a grazier, one of whose sons with the same Christian name is now a Member of the House of Representatives. Malcolm was away at the time but his wife Helen, Menzies' sister, was there. We camped in the grounds of the house, which contained a swimming pool. For some meals we dined in the house, for the rest we camped. The weather was good. We were all having a most enjoyable time, the two families getting on very well together.

Then a telegram addressed to me interrupted our halcyon days. I had left my itinerary with my clerk and thought the telegram must be from him. But it was from the Commonwealth Honours Secretariat in Canberra and informed me that the Queen would be pleased to make me a Knight Bachelor and desired an answer whether or not I would accept the honour. If I declined, I was to state my reasons for doing so.

I was astonished. I had not the least inkling that anything of the kind was afoot. I was then almost fifty years of age, in high practice in Australia and in the Privy Council in London. I had been an adviser to governments on constitutional questions and was fairly prominent in the affairs of the legal profession throughout Australia. I felt proud that my work and the practice of the law should have been so acknowledged but surprised that I should have been singled out for such an honour.

I did not feel I wanted a title. I had often joined in jesting about the "characters" who were knighted. Like many, I suspected that some honours were bought, if not by financial contribution to party funds or to some approved charity, then by the performance of some favour to the party in government. But in any case, and apart from my personal disinclination to accept, I immediately realised the difficulties a title would create for me and my family. None of the judges in New South Wales, not even the Chief Justice, nor any of the members of the High Court other than its Chief Justice, had been knighted. There was no barrister then in practice in Australia who had been so honoured. Though I had no egalitarian sentiments, I felt I could well do without a knighthood.

I discussed the matter with Douglas over a few days. Although Douglas was the Prime Minister's cousin and the initiative for the grant of the honour must have come from the Prime Minister, I am sure that Douglas had no foreknowledge. Indeed, he assured me he had not. But he insisted that I should accept. I remember him saying that the offer of the knighthood was a compliment to the Australian Bar and, in particular, to my own New South Wales Bar, and that if I did not accept, such an honour was unlikely ever to be offered to a practising man. He went so far as to say that I owed a duty to the profession, of which he said I was an acknowledged leader, to accept and to put up with such disabilities as the possession of a knighthood might entail. He emphasised what he considered was the unique position I had attained in the Australian profession. I could scarce dispute what he said.

I had no ideological aversion to knighthood. I did not share the egalitarianism of many of my legal colleagues, and I certainly had no Anglophobia. I recognised the great benefits we had obtained from our British origins: our democratic parliamentary constitution, the rule of law and such good sense and tolerance as we possessed. I believe that all should be equal before the law, and should have what is called equal opportunity in life, though in truth that is scarcely attainable. But I accept that we are all different from each other; so are the talents with which we are endowed, individual and distinct both in quality and extent.

I spent some anxious hours quietly turning the matter over in my mind. While the children disported themselves in the swimming pool, Norma and I mulled over the possibilities of one course and the other. Norma, as ever, would support me whatever I decided. She had no desire for a title but if I accepted, she would live with it as best she could.

In the end, though with continuing misgivings, I came to accept Douglas's reasons but jestingly said to him, "Well, I will not myself send an accepting telegram. As you feel so strongly, you can do so on my behalf". And he did.

I had a disturbed mind about the matter during the interval which elapsed between that day at Euroa and the day in July 1953 when the public announcement was made. Complete secrecy about the knighthood had been maintained. On that day I went into chambers full of apprehension. My colleagues on my floor of chambers included some Anglophobes and some egalitarians, to each of whom the knighthood would, I felt, be offensive in principle. However much I disagreed with their views, I respected them and was anxious to maintain their acceptance of me and their friendship and goodwill. So you may imagine my great relief and pleasure at what ensued.

As I emerged from the lift that morning, I was met by a welcoming committee of my colleagues. I was warmly greeted and enthusiastically addressed as "Corona" — Sir Garfield, Sir Gar, Cigar, Corona, so the progression ran — and enquiry was made for the health of my children, who were "cigarettes". I not only received their congratulations, but I felt their friendly encouragement. A little later, along with a few close friends, they gave me a formal dinner and presented me with a silver tray on which all their signatures had been etched. It remains one of my proud possessions, always on display on the sideboard of our dining room.

But I had yet to face the Bench, a bench quite unused in those days to addressing any counsel as Sir this or Sir that. My first appearance after the announcement was in a district court in Sydney before Judge John Nield, a friend whose ability, courage and integrity I greatly respected and admired. He had decided a case against the client whom I now represented; I had not appeared at that hearing. The legislation governing the district courts provided for an application to the trial judge for a new trial to correct any error that may have been made earlier. I was of the opinion that an error had been made, but before Judge Nield I took the course of pointing out the legal mistake without specifically saying that His Honour had made it.

As I developed the point, Nield, a quick-witted lawyer, realised that he had in truth made this mistake and quickly, and perhaps to anticipate my saying so, said: "Yes, exactly, Sir Garwick", much to his embarrassment and my unobservable amusement.

The confusion of my two names is quite frequent and indeed easy to make. My mother had been addressed as Mrs Barfield long before this. A mayor in a country town, who had not had a knight on his hands for some time, managed to introduce me as Sir Arthur Tremayne — why I do not know. But I sympathise with people who have tripped up on my names.

The judges of the High Court and the Supreme Court were all generous towards me and I think realised the awkwardness I felt. I was surprised at the ease with which my new rank was accepted and at the speed with which I became acclimatised, as it were, to the new form of address.

I received a great number of congratulatory messages, I think as many as five hundred from all parts of the country. The daunting task of replying to each one personally, as I did, in the middle of a busy practice, took some time. I wrote the last letter one evening on the island of Mauritius as I was on my way to London to argue a case in the Privy Council.

When I stood for Parliament in 1958, the local branch of the Liberal Party was very concerned about the electoral effect my knighthood might have. Knighthoods were by no means common in Canberra, or for that matter in political affairs in Australia at the time. Parramatta was a mixed electorate, and an undemocratic or elitist air would not have helped my prospects. But I said to the local Liberals, with whose anxiety I sympathised, "Well, if I am no good as a Member, it will not matter; I'll not last. But if I prove to be any good as a parliamentary representative, I think that the knighthood will give rise to what might be called a mark of affection. People will be able to address me by my Christian name and not appear presumptuous or unduly familiar". And so it proved. At that time the now current fashion for Christian names had not developed. For my part I dislike the fashion and resort to it only with my intimate friends, acquaintances and relations.

I never found the title to operate at any time as a barrier or impediment to the establishment of good personal relations with all manner of men and women in the electorate, or for that matter elsewhere. I have never required anyone to address me by the title, or ever announced myself by it; nor have I discouraged its use. My impression is that it is used by all manner of people quite naturally and without diffidence.

I recall the scene when the Queen dubbed me knight in the ballroom of Government House, Sydney, in 1954. Someone took a photograph of the event through a door opening on to the front terrace of the House. The photographer caught me kneeling under the touch of the sword. I was extremely nervous. The Queen was new and young and if she was nervous, as well she might be, for this may have been her first investiture, she did not show it.

In some ways I regret the Hawke Government's removal of the knighthood from the ranks of the Order of Australia. I had nothing to do with its introduction by the Fraser Government. But I think there is room in a democracy such as ours for special ranks to mark special achievement and service to the community and to distinguish between the levels of merit and achievement attained. Such a knighthood, that is, knighthood in the Order of Australia, could not have been bought nor be solely the result of government patronage. Also, the chivalrous obligation of duty to the community which a knighthood should carry is likely to be performed by such a knight who had received the honour for genuine public service of a high order and having been judged worthy of it by an independent Council of the Order. Perhaps in saying so I may be taking too rosy a view of human nature. But I prefer to set my estimate of my fellow citizens higher than the cynics might.

Somehow, I think as Australians we unnecessarily consider ourselves demeaned by looking up to somebody. We do it readily enough in sporting activities but not in public service, sometimes I think even in family life. We too readily dub due deference as a mere cringe or describe it as pulling the forelock. The possibility of the improvement of standards of behaviour by example is reduced by this attitude. As the national immaturity which has created such attitudes passes and a more nationally adult society develops — a society which does not have any semblance of a sense of inferiority — the regime of a rough and, to a degree, coarse egalitarianism may disappear.

Now, forty years on, I can see in retrospect that my apprehensions of 1953 did not eventuate, neither then nor at any subsequent time. Nor have I ever been conscious of my possession of a title causing embarrassment to my wife or my children. My wife has accepted the courtesy title of Lady quite naturally, and its possession and use have not in any way changed the naturalness and warmth with which she behaves. I think those with whom she has associated, which in my parliamentary days included a great number of the constituents, have accepted her for her own worth and have not been repulsed or felt repulsed by her use of the title. So I found nothing offensive in my accepting a distinction which the quality of my own work had brought to me. Neither of us has any regret that I made the decision I did at Euroa in 1953.

7 Housing the Bar

When I was called to the Bar in 1927, most of its members were housed in chambers in the southern part of Phillip Street, though possibly a few were still in Elizabeth Street. Doubtless in early times these streets were chosen as the home of the Bar because of their proximity to the Supreme Court House in King and Elizabeth Streets.

In 1927, as I remember Phillip Street, on the eastern side there was Oxford Chambers at the corner of King and Phillip (housing a small number of barristers in a two-storey building which I think had formerly been the Oxford Hotel), then Denman Chambers, a four-storey building containing a number of chambers. Then there was an area of land on which was a single-storey cottage standing back somewhat from the building alignment. It was occupied by a Dr Fiaschi and displayed a blue light indicating that he treated venereal disease. Phillip Street was then a haunt of the women of the town. I had been accosted four or five times between University Chambers and the corner of Phillip and King Streets as I made my way about 6pm toward Central Station. So I suppose Dr Fiaschi had a clientele close at hand. It is on this land that Wentworth Chambers now stands.

Next to Fiaschi's cottage there was Selborne Chambers, a multi-storey building, the lower floors housing barristers. Next there was Chancery Chambers, with seven storeys of chambers above Hughes' car-hire service. Then there was a vacant block on which later a building for the Teachers Federation was built; next door was Campbell House, a two-storey building with a basement, in which the caretaker and his wife lived. The first floor contained four rooms, occupied by barristers. On the top floor a professional coach taught classics.

Next stood St Stephen's Church and further down Phillip Street houses or small buildings, in one of which I remember that Holdship & Holdship, Solicitors, practised. The Stamp Office occupied a stone-fronted building about halfway from the present Martin Place alignment to that of Hunter Street. In 1927 Martin Place did not cross Phillip Street; indeed, it had not then crossed Elizabeth Street.

On the western side of Phillip Street there was the Supreme Court House Hotel on the corner of King and Phillip, then Paris House which contained refreshment rooms, then a building in which I think the Pioneers Club had premises, then University Chambers which, on its Phillip Street frontage, had a number of floors of barristers' chambers, but on its upper floors housed the University Law School including its library, and above that the State Department of Labour and Industry. Next door there was Northfield Chambers, a small two-storey building, then Lyndon Chambers and a row of terrace houses, in one of which a man called Blunt ran an agency for the disposal of medical practices. I remember that David Maughan had chambers in one of these houses.

My present recollection is that the old Wentworth Chambers, a dilapidated timber structure which housed barristers' chambers and which provided a thoroughfare in earlier days from Elizabeth to Phillip Street, was still standing in 1927. I had often walked through the building, as an articled clerk, on my way to the Registrar-General's premises opposite St Mary's Cathedral. Wentworth Chambers may have stood on part of the area now occupied by Martin Place.

Years later when I was in Chalfont Chambers (between Martin Place and Hunter Streets), I often went on my way home into the Tudor Hotel on the western side of Phillip Street for a drink with fellow barristers. Sometimes a group of us would tarry in an upstairs bar beyond the statutory six o'clock closing time, yarning more than drinking.

One evening in 1947 while we were there after hours — and I can pinpoint the occasion as being during the time argument in *Gratwick v Johnson*[1] was being prepared — David Maughan, who was leading me in that case, put his head into the Bar room to ask me something. I remember Gerald Donovan, afterwards a judge of the District Court, and a well-furnished student of the law, as well as a first-class golfer, extending Maughan an invitation to join us. But he had all the caution of an Equity practitioner and declined. He then took himself off.

No more than a few moments later a police officer arrived. All of us were in breach of the law. The officer began to take names. But there was one occupant of the room who was not a barrister. He was a sizeable man with a cloth cap. When the officer confronted him with a polite request for his name, the reply was "Jack Lang". The officer bridled, though accustomed to being the butt of jokes on such an occasion. He said sharply that he would not be trifled with and that unless the man gave him his proper name he would "lumber" him. The man asserted firmly that his name was Jack Lang. The officer moved as if to make an arrest, when the man, who proved to be a seaman, produced his papers — and his name was Jack Lang! We all quietly enjoyed the officer's discomfiture. When he had left, we speculated on what David Maughan would have done had he accepted Donovan's invitation.

When the country had settled down after the Second World War, the city's commercial interests began to move eastward. It became apparent that soon land in Phillip Street would attract commercial attention and development and that rentals would become increasingly high. In those days, barristers had become accustomed to fairly low rents in the various, somewhat makeshift chambers. The *Sun* newspaper had already put up the building later occupied by the GIO. The number of barristers had increased, and available chambers in Phillip Street became quite inadequate to house the Bar. Some barristers had taken chambers in a building on the south side of King Street between Castlereagh and Pitt. It became clear that soon the Bar would be dispersed through commercial parts of the city, though within acceptable walking distance of the Supreme Court.

When there was the possibility of a site for a new courthouse for the Supreme Court in College Street, I had the idea of finding a site in Darlinghurst north of Liverpool Street on which to construct low-level buildings, perhaps round a hollow square, to provide chambers that would house the whole Bar. But it all fell through, largely through lack of interest.

But in the 1950s, Ken Manning and I began to concern ourselves with the housing of the whole Bar in Phillip Street once more. We had the singular advantage in this connection of a friendship with Frederick Deer, then Assistant Manager of the MLC Company. He was also a non-practising member of the Bar and had its interests at heart. Manning and I conceived the idea of forming a company which would put up a building in Phillip Street and in which only barristers would take shares. The main obstacle was the difficulty, financial and physical, of getting the necessary land.

About this time I became the president of the Bar Association of New South Wales. I proposed some changes: that the presidency be limited to a term of two years, that the custom of writing letters to the press about legal matters should cease, unless there was real cause, and that we should resume an earlier practice under which the executive officers called on the dignitaries of the State and city.

The proposal was that, accompanied by the Honorary Secretary and Honorary Treasurer, I should call on the Governor, the Chief Justice, the Premier and the Lord Mayor. I had no difficulty about the first two, but some counsellors opposed calling on the Premier and, though less strongly, on the Lord Mayor. They seemed to think that such an official call smacked of acceptance by the Bar of the incumbent's political views. I disputed this, and I won the argument. We duly made a call on each of these dignitaries.

The call is, of course, a formal occasion; matters of substance are not raised. The call on Governor, Chief Justice and Lord Mayor went off amiably, as did the call on Premier Joseph Cahill. But I sensed that the Premier particularly appreciated our call and was pleased we had done so. I thought he felt honoured by it.

When the following year we repeated the call on the Premier he asked if there was anything he could do for us. Surprised, and having confirmed that this meant I could make substantial requests, I asked that the Mint, which it had been suggested be demolished to make way for a courthouse, be spared, and that we could acquire on a long lease land the government owned in Phillip Street (the land where Dr Fiaschi's house had stood) in order to put up a building to house the Bar. The Premier said he would take both matters on board.

Subsequently there was no question of demolishing the Mint. It has since been refurbished and houses a museum of Australiana. In due course a Bill was put through Parliament to give the Bar, in the embodiment of Wentworth Chambers Pty Ltd (which was inaugurated on 24 October 1952), the title to a 99-year building lease of this piece of land. We could not have asked for more.

The articles of Wentworth Chambers Pty Ltd provided that each shareholder should contribute £1000 to the capital of the company, which was originally £500,000. The shares were to be called for their full amount during construction of a proposed building. But the venture met with resistance. To start with, there was not enough enthusiasm among the barristers to ensure successful flotation of the company without substantial financial inducement. A potent objection came from seniors who were heads of a floor of chambers. They did not wish their particular community of barristers to be broken up; the proposal for the building did not necessarily ensure a disposition of chambers like that they already enjoyed.

As an inducement to encourage subscription to the capital, the articles stipulated a fixed rent of sixteen shillings per square foot per annum for each room. The rooms were to be all of equal size. The subscriber for each share would be granted a lease for ninety-nine years of a room of 200 square feet at this fixed rent.

After plans had been completed and tenders obtained we were ready to sign up a well-known firm of builders for a fixed price. But we still did not have the required number of subscribers for the shares. Manning and I were quite desolated by this lack of response after all our efforts. We faced the unpleasant fact that, in accordance with the terms of our prospectus, we could not accept the tender for construction and would have to abandon the project, return the funds we had already collected and remit any outstanding obligations of subscribers. I thought, however, that once the building was under way, some of the indifference and most of the objections would dissipate.

I got Manning's agreement to treating a subscription by a group of us for the whole of the shortfall as a substantial compliance with the undertaking in the prospectus. We realised that to do this was to bypass the real intention of that undertaking, but we thought that in the circumstances we were justified. I called a meeting of three other seniors besides Manning and myself and asked them to join us in taking up the twenty-two or three outstanding shares. In various proportions they agreed to do so. Manning and I decided that we should regard the undertaking of the prospectus as satisfied and let the building contract to the successful tenderer, John Grant & Sons, an old, and as we then understood, a financially well-established firm. Building began in August 1954.

I very well remember that this meeting of seniors was held on the eve of my departure to London to argue cases in the Privy Council. Two or three months after my departure, I received a cable from Manning to tell me that the outstanding shares had been taken up and that the liability of the group in respect of them was at an end.

In the design of the building we had followed the philosophy that a barrister does not need a very large room in which to work and to be consulted. Also, we felt that the then existing practice of each barrister duplicating the library of every other barrister was uneconomic and profited the booksellers more than the individual barrister. We therefore encouraged the formation of a common library on each floor of chambers. This made it more likely that the small working rooms would be adequate.

The MLC through the good offices of Fred Deer provided us with a mortgage which, with the addition of the initial payments on the shares, provided enough working capital to begin construction. The calls on the shares provided the rest of the building costs. Unfortunately, during the period of construction, John Grant & Sons, which was then building a number of city projects, went into liquidation. Apparently they had overstretched themselves. The board of Wentworth had the trauma of finding new builders in mid-stream and losing part of the benefit of the original tender. But, though difficult, all was rearranged and the building progressed to finality. It was opened on 20 August 1957 in the presence of Lord Morton of Henryton, a Lord of Appeal in Ordinary.

Shortly before the building was completed, Manning and I heard that Selborne Chambers, next door on the northern side, was to come on to the market. The company that owned it was in liquidation. The obvious thing now was to buy the property and replace the building with a new set of chambers. We managed with some difficulty to secure a loan from the Commercial Bank, and signed contracts in March 1956. This time we had no difficulty in selling the number of shares needed to finance the building and to repay the loan by the bank. The multi-storey building which now stands interconnects with Wentworth Chambers. Unlike the latter it has two basements. With our then available resources it had been too costly to excavate a second basement under Wentworth: both sites are solid sandstone. Unlike the land on which Wentworth Chambers is built, Selborne is built on freehold. It was opened to tenants in July 1963.

When Wentworth was nearing completion, Manning and I proposed that its basement be made available for a Bar common-room at no cost to the Bar Council. The rental value of this basement at the time was £1600 a year. The resolution was that it be made available rent-free, the Bar would equip and furnish it, and it would be available only to members of the Bar. We resisted a request that solicitors be invited into the common-room.

To make ends meet, we had to let the ground floor in Wentworth and two floors in Selborne when it was completed. Wentworth's ground floor was taken by Custom Credit and the State Crown rented the rooms in Selborne, partly as a gesture of support of the Bar.

Some years later, Sydney University proposed placing limitations on its intake of students into the Law School. A reason given for this was shortage of space and the lack of any possibility of increasing it. Without first mentioning the matter to the directors of Wentworth, Reg Downing, who as Attorney-General was a member of the University Senate, offered the University Law School occupation of the two floors in Selborne, on the footing, I assumed, that the proposal to limit the intake of students would be abandoned. Quite obviously the government felt politically affected by any such limitation and made this offer at least in part for political reasons. When Reg Downing informed me of what the government proposed, and indeed had agreed to do, I very strongly objected; the company could not agree to the presence of law students in the Selborne building, with their considerable demands on the lifting capacity at the very time when barristers needed it most. Without the company's agreement, the government's arrangements with the Law School could not be implemented.

I must say Downing was quite angry at my opposition. He reminded me — and quite justly — that the government had co-operated with the company, indeed had been generous in doing so. But I remained firm and the proposed use by the university of part of Selborne fell through. In the end, the university did not cut back its intake. Just how the matter was arranged I do not know.

While Wentworth Chambers was being built I was appearing before the Privy Council and meeting many members of the English Bar. The Temple had not then been fully rebuilt after the wartime bombing. Various parts of it, both Inner and Middle, including the Temple Church, were damaged, as were parts of Lincoln's and Gray's.

I conceived the idea that it might be a good thing if some of the original masonry of the buildings of the Inns were incorporated in Wentworth Chambers to mark the continued life of the institutions of the Bar and the Common Law in New South Wales, and also the fundamental attachment of the Australian people to the rule of law — to which the Inns of Court throughout history had contributed so much. Accordingly, I canvassed this possibility with members of the four Inns. As a result I was given four pieces of masonry for incorporation in the new building: a finial from the roof of the Hall at Lincoln's Inn; a piece of a Purbeck marble column of the Round Temple Church; a piece of masonry from the organ loft of the rectangular section of the Temple Church; and a piece of carved Portland stone from the fabric of Gray's Inn.

Then I thought that it would further emphasise the spirit of continuity if the heraldic emblems of the Inns were exhibited in or on the new building. I applied to the Masters of each bench, Middle, Inner, Lincoln's and Gray's, for permission to do so. This being granted, I realised the company could not afford to have the emblems cut in stone. So I asked the Inns if I might have plaster reproductions made of their armorial bearings.

About this time I was dining one evening with the benchers of Gray's Inn. One of them said to me, "What is this I hear, Barwick, about plaster casts?" I explained my idea. The speaker then said, "Barwick, I have never thought of you as chicken-hearted. Why don't you ask us to provide you with stone replicas, suitably coloured?" I said I had not wished to trespass on their generosity, but I was prepared, after his invitation, to make the request. Thereafter each Inn provided me with a coloured stone replica of its heraldic emblem, for which I expressed profound gratitude.

The four heraldic emblems of the Inns of Court are on the southern wall of the entrance to Wentworth Chambers and are protected by an armour-plated glass shield. Nearby is a plaque containing a statement which I drafted and which emphasises that sense of continuity of which I have spoken.

> These stones bearing the arms of the honourable societies of Lincoln's Inn, the Inner Temple, the Middle Temple and of Grays Inn are the gift of the four Inns of Court. They are here displayed to mark the continuity in this land of the common law of England and of the traditions of the Bar, its independence and its sense of duty to serve the citizens and to assist in the maintenance of the rule of law.

A slice of Purbeck marble of the Round Church now provides the threshold to the common-room. The finial from the hall of Lincoln's Inn stands in the common-room foyer. The Portland stone from Gray's is displayed on the southern wall of the anteroom to the common-room and the stone from the rectangular part of the Temple Church (actually part of the organ loft) is on the same wall.

* * * * *

One of our hopes in promoting the Bar common-room, which on the completion of Selborne was extended to include one of the basements of that building, was that members of the Bench would be prepared from time to time to lunch, or perhaps even to dine, there as the judges do in the Inns in London, particularly those who are benchers. Historically, much progress in the common law took place through discussions on legal problems in the Inns. I think that these proved more effective and displayed more wisdom than do the law reform commissions of today. Of course, we realised that the refusal of Australian journalists to accord integrity to public men would open the door to criticism if the judiciary lunched or dined with the Bar. But we thought that nonetheless the judiciary could properly drop in to the common-room from time to time where juniors of the Bar could meet them socially and where legal principle, and even recent decisions of the courts, could be discussed.

But it did not work out as we had hoped. I think the failure was partly due to the inability of some members of the Bar to respect the dignity and place of the judge when engaging in friendly discussion. The exercise of close personal contact and informal discussion without invasion of judicial dignity often proves too much for the populist egalitarianism which is current in public life. And of course on the other hand it is not given to all judicial officers to unbend and join in friendly discussion without endangering the position of their office. Just the same, some members of the judiciary do on occasions join in social functions held in the common-room, but little real discussion of the law can be expected then to take place.

We had also hoped to promote a communal sense among the members of the Bar. Their chambers would be in close proximity, which we felt was essential to maintaining the Bar's ethical standards and promoting that friendship and mutual trust between barristers which so much profits the administration of the law. But the two buildings have become quite inadequate to house the Bar. Chambers are now to be found not merely out of Phillip Street, but in commercial or even retail areas of the city. I'd like to be young again and free to apply myself to providing a new solution for the housing of the Bar in a manner which will maintain and emphasise its corporate life and the contribution it makes by its independence and integrity to the administration of the law.

Unfortunately, the law reformers, or at least some of them, treat the members of the Bar as indistinguishable from the solicitors. So do many journalists. In New South Wales, solicitors have a right of audience in all the courts. If they wish to perform as advocates they may do so — and in fact some do, mainly in the Local and District Courts. But the Bar is not to be distinguished from the solicitors by the fact that barristers mostly work in the courts as advocates. It is to be distinguished because, not having direct contact, and particularly commercial contact with the citizen client, it is able to exercise an independence of judgment and action, and at the same time perform both its obligations to the court and its duty to the solicitor's client. From the exercise of this independence, both the administration of the law and the interests of the citizen can profit immensely.

Also, the Bar tends to become a community of lawyers who know each other and in many cases are close friends. This allows the area of dispute in litigation to be reduced by agreement. The sense of community and mutual respect and trust can contribute greatly to the speed at which litigation is brought to an end. The members of the Bar, or at least many of the senior of them, are conscious of their obligation to speed rather than delay the process of the law. It would be a sad day if the Bar as an institution were to disappear or be overwhelmed. But failure of the Bar to perform the obligations I have described must not only endanger its standing but may ultimately bring about its disappearance.

I remember a case where, because I had discussions with the opposing counsel, we finished in two days a case estimated to take a month. I do not pretend that the Bar always performs in this fashion. But that such an event does occur is due almost entirely to the independence of the Bar and its willingness to keep litigation to its essentials, with the aim of its disposal in the shortest time possible. The community would lose much by the disappearance or dilution of the Bar.

As I view the scene in the law today, I fear for the future of the Bar as an institution. For one thing, the tendency of large firms of solicitors to form their own advisory services poses a distinct threat to its continuance. But perhaps at least of equal importance is the cost of chambers in close proximity to the Supreme Court. The hard fact is that rents in the city of Sydney, including the areas between Castlereagh and Macquarie Streets, are far too high for barristers' chambers. The Bar mostly draws its members from men with little or no capital or income beyond what they can produce from practice. High capital cost of establishment and high rents, particularly during those lean years which the young barrister must expect, must tend in the long run to damage the institution of the Bar. Young men and women who otherwise would take the venture into practice and bear with its early vicissitudes are likely to be dissuaded and to turn to the inducements offered by the solicitors.

This is a problem that the leaders of the Bar should take in hand and solve. For one thing, somewhat as the Inns of Court do, they could provide funds to subsidise the student and the pupil and indeed the young practitioner. This should not be impossible if the leaders share with me a belief in the importance to the community of the institution.

For another thing, it is a time for large thinking. Traditionally, chambers have clustered round the Supreme Court. That doubtless has had its significance in the life of the Bar. But, though traditional, there is no reason now, with modern communications, why this proximity should be maintained. A centre for the Bar could be considered outside the centre of the city. The Supreme Court itself could be moved to the south-west, where the centre of population is. Many government offices have done so.

Part II

Attorney-General

8 I Turn to Politics

My nomination in 1958 for preselection for a federal constituency doubtless surprised my colleagues in the law, and also many in the community who knew me only as a barrister. Though I had always been interested in government, and kept myself abreast of current affairs, I had shown no interest in active politics. My political views I had kept to myself.

Throughout my practising days I had adhered to a self-imposed rule that I would not identify myself with any particular group in the community: religious, social or political. The independence of the Bar is compromised by the overt political identification of its members. The barrister, if he is wise, puts aside his own views and makes no political or moral judgments of the client's cause; otherwise he must warp that detached judgment to which the client is entitled. I have always deeply treasured this independence, and tried to live up to the motto of the NSW Bar: "The servant of all, the servant of none".

By 1957 I was fifty-four. I had advised and acted for governments of both political persuasions. I was known in legal circles throughout Australia and in London and, through my work, also in the Australian commercial community. I was counted among the leaders of the Bar in Australia. I had no great desire to join the Bench.

After thirty years of practice it might be thought that the excitement of a new case to conduct and new problems to resolve had lessened. But it had not. I continued to enjoy practice and the personal satisfaction it brought. Yet it was possible that at some time in the future I might come to be bored by the repetition of it all. And it was also possible that I might become condescending to the younger and less experienced men who by then would be appointed to the Bench.

I had found myself once in this uncomfortable situation in a suit in Equity before a new, young and confident judge. I had cited a decision of a certain judge. The young judge, perhaps a little too conscious of the talents he had been given, snapped back at me, "Well, he was wrong". I made a quick and foolish decision to rebuff him. Without pausing to choose my words, I retorted, "Of course, it is your Honour's privilege to dismiss Sir John Harvey's decision out of hand. In my book, Sir John Harvey was a great judge of long experience whose decisions I respect". The young man flushed and I am sure felt the import of my thrust.

As I walked to chambers at lunchtime that day, I realised that I ought not to have spoken as I had. I also realised that long years of advocacy had sharpened my reactive processes, making cerebration quick and apt in an unguarded moment to become impulsive. In the following weeks I often reflected on the possibilities of the future, bringing as it would increasingly frequent appearance before men my junior in years and experience.

But no dying excitement of practice or consciousness of the risks of a surviving senior counsel practising before a youthful Bench would have led me to contemplate leaving the Bar: and certainly not for any such reason as entering politics. I had always declined proposals to join the board of commercial concerns. By 1957, the only appointments I had accepted outside the Bar were as a trustee of the Kosciusko State Park (1944) and as a member of the board of Royal Prince Alfred Hospital (1951). These scarcely distracted me from complete attention to my practice. Though I was interested in rural matters, I had resisted buying a country property; I realised the distraction even hobby farming may involve.

One day in 1955 Ian Baillieu, a longtime Australian friend of mine in England, said, very earnestly:

"Chum, you'll soon have to exercise one of your options. You'll need to make a choice about your future. You could come here to practise and you'd stand a chance of being appointed some day to the Lords. Or you could break out of the law as others have and join me in commerce. Or you can carry on a while at the Australian Bar and in time accept a seat on the High Court, which I am sure will come your way, or you could follow what I know is your great interest and go farming in Australia. But the time has arrived for making a choice, for exercising one of the options."

I made no decision then, but continued happily and busily with my practice. A little earlier I had received a suggestion from two leading London firms of solicitors that I should set up in practice in London. It was an attractive prospect. I had enjoyed my appearances before the Privy Council and I had quite a few friends at the English Bar. I suspect that my work on the *Banking Nationalisation* case had excited much attention in legal circles. I felt that I might get by in practice there, but in the end doubted my capacity to carry off such a drastic change. I also felt that London would not afford my children the opportunities they would have in Australia. When I finally decided against transferring to London, this last consideration loomed large in my thinking.

Long before, in the 1930s, Bill Holman, then at the Bar, had said to me one day in his resonant voice, "Gar, you should go to London".

"But what about Eton and Harrow? I have not been to either."

"The English would accept you for your own worth. As far as Eton and Harrow are concerned, they would simply say 'poor chap, he has not had the opportunity'. They would not hold against you the fact that you had not attended either school or for that matter an English university."

But I stayed in Sydney, not sufficiently venturesome then to try my luck abroad.

* * * * *

During 1956 I began to feel that there was something wrong with my health, but I could not really point to any cause. I began to be often thirsty, drinking a good deal of water, and I developed an almost overwhelming craving for chocolate.

That year I was briefed to appear for the Colonial Sugar Refining Company in an appeal from the Supreme Court of Fiji to the Privy Council (see p 48).

During the hearing I had frequently to interrupt my address to take a glass of water because I was becoming exceptionally dry in the mouth. By the time I made my final address my mouth had got so dry that my tongue literally clove to the roof of my mouth, making speech difficult. I must say it was a frightening experience, and my juniors were alarmed also.

When the argument concluded I went straight from Downing Street to Harley Street where I had an old friend, Harold Dodd, an eminent venous surgeon. He put me in touch with another physician and between them they diagnosed a very advanced state of diabetes. Mr Dodd organised me into the London Clinic, to which I went straight from Harley Street, collecting my overnight gear on the way.

At the clinic I was placed under the care of Dr Geoffrey Lawrence, which was one of the fortunate circumstances of my life. Himself a diabetic, Lawrence was eminent in the treatment of the disease. He had developed it during his university days. By the time he graduated in medicine he knew that his life would be short, for before the discovery of the beneficial use of insulin that was the fate of diabetics. So he bought himself a practice in Italy, intending to practise there till he died, a young man in the sun. But meantime Banting and Best developed the use of insulin — one of the great medical developments of the age. Lawrence's friends, hearing of Banting and Best's success, persuaded him to come home and use the new treatment. He did, and he became world-famous for his own development and use of insulin.

I was extremely fortunate tc have come under his care. He was not only a good physician but a good teacher. He taught me in the week I was in London Clinic how to regulate my life, how to use insulin and within what parameters of food and exercise I should keep myself. When my blood was tested on admission it was found to contain a very great number of ketones, poisons, as a result of the presence over time of sugars in the blood. These were so numerous that Dr

Lawrence told me when discharging me that had I not been treated he did not think I would have lived out the year. But the week in London Clinic taking insulin — for I was taught to give myself an injection the second day I was there — balanced my blood.

The change was miraculous. I now had to regulate my life in a very disciplined way, something not so difficult perhaps for one who lived by the rule "in all things moderation". I remember writing to Norma to break the news to her, which I am sure came as a great shock. She for her part began to read about the treatment of diabetes; she became quite expert in the management of the diet and ever since has remained watchful that my meals were regular and my diet suitable. Her care and attention in these respects are as evident today as they were from the beginning.

Dr Lawrence also told me that I need never contemplate not having a daily injection of insulin, that I was bound to it for life. Subsequently I made one or two excursions into drugs taken orally, but these did not prove successful; with those breaks excepted, I have had a daily injection from that time to the present.

I have managed to live with my diabetes, even allowing for the rigours of my practice. But no one outside my wife and immediate family knew anything of my condition. I presented myself as a normal healthy person.

* * * * *

While my future was thus open, events I had not counted on, in 1954 and 1957, conspired to direct me towards politics. Before describing these events I need to give some account of my political views.

I have been identified as a conservative in politics. Yet in the Depression years I sympathised very greatly with those who endured unemployment and social hardship, and, indeed, suffered with them. I felt that Jack Lang was right in wanting a moratorium for the payment of the government's obligations. I was impressed with Lang's capacity to persuade his hearers to his view. He concentrated on essential facts, simply explained, though he had an unpleasant voice which he used vociferously to get his message across. Of course, he appealed to the emotional antipathy of rich and poor, painting what seemed to me an exaggerated view of each.

But any tendencies natural to young people which I might have had to think along socialist lines soon evaporated as I came to see more clearly the possible consequences of wholehearted government intervention and the increased cost of government which socialist theories involved. I think the hard realities of life with their practical human considerations displaced theorising. In the succeeding years I thought much about theories of government. I was to become convinced that an economy in the modern world could not be planned and that socialist endeavours to do so were doomed to failure. I had been familiarised with parliamentary democracy in a constitutional monarchy and accepted it as the best form of government yet devised by man. I did not care for the presidential and congressional form practised in America. In any case, I came to realise that in a world where human nature remained unreformed, where humans had not been "born again", socialism must ultimately end in disaster, in a sterile halt to enterprise and individual endeavour, if not indeed in a loss of personal freedom such as we have witnessed in the communist world. Self-interest remains the mainspring of most human activity. The protection of the individual's capacity to promote his interests, as long as they are not harmful to the community, is a function of government, but the planning of his life and economy is not.

At the same time I came to realise the defects of a capitalist society. I did not countenance the extreme views of *laissez-faire*; I recognised the community's claim to protection from the harmful exercise of the individual's self-interest. Capitalism could not be wholly unregulated: some government intervention was therefore called for. Ideally the result was a balance between the conflicting claims of the individual and the community.

But the blemishes of capitalism, considerable as they might be and at times distressing in their results, were far outweighed by its advantages and by the disadvantages of socialism. Undoubtedly I felt capitalism to be a system which encourages and rewards the strong and venturesome and is like to exert a process of natural selection which may disadvantage the timid and the weak. Undoubtedly the possible products of capitalism called for compassionate community support for those who fell by the wayside. I witnessed the work of beneficent Labor governments in New South Wales which, in general, had confined their intervention to remedial legislation more practical than ideological. With much of the legislation of those years I felt in sympathy and perhaps did not realise the creeping paralysis of human endeavour which was in progress. Certainly I was not stirred into any personal revolt.

Over the years I also became aware of the power of the leaders of the trade union movement to dislocate industry and make it uncompetitive. By the combination of wage demands which an internationally competitive industry could not afford and work practices which drastically reduced productivity, consumer goods became unduly expensive, which in turn led to claims for increased wages. The unions had performed a very necessary service in ending unfair and unsafe work practices and had gained for their members wages and conditions more appropriate to the work they did. In what is properly a bargaining area, their strength enabled the bargaining to be between groups of equal strength. While some of this impressive improvement had been achieved by the use of industrial muscle, much had resulted from fair compromise or negotiation and some from legislation, passed or conceived by Labor administrations.

But I had become aware that the use of industrial muscle could both divide the community, perhaps as much as had the earlier bad working conditions, and by destroying competitiveness bring great harm to the country generally, not to mention the employees themselves. I had witnessed the ever-increasing use of work bans and restrictions, which the trade union leaders found to be more effective than strikes. I had been consulted professionally on the constitutional validity of a proposed bans clause for consideration in awards. But both the use and the threat of the use of industrial muscle had disrupted the balance between employer and employee in wage bargaining. The trade unions had become the more powerful of the negotiators. Indeed, the trade unions were becoming as oppressive as the employers were said to have been in pre-union days. The balance now needed to be restored.

* * * * *

In 1954 Sir Eric Harrison resigned his seat in the House of Representatives for the division of Wentworth. He had accepted the post of High Commissioner for Australia in London. Mr Lyle Moore, then a prominent figure in the world of real estate, was Chairman of the NSW Branch of the Liberal Party. He approached me with the suggestion that I nominate for preselection in the Liberal Party cause for the division of Wentworth. He said that he thought that with my standing at the Bar and the support of the central office of the party, I would be assured of preselection and that Wentworth was a "safe" seat. I declined. I was amused but not surprised that Lyle Moore should assume I was a Liberal. I had no party affiliation and indeed had never been a member of the Liberal Party.

Not only was I then disinclined to leave practice and enter politics, but, as it happened, Norma and I were in the course of building a new house in Maher's Road, Beecroft, and had no wish to live in the Eastern Suburbs. I held the view that the member should reside in or close to his electorate and be readily accessible to his constituents. After my conversation with Mr Moore I heard no more of the matter. I did not disclose to anyone other than my wife that I had been approached. Events, however, were to catch up with me.

Towards the end of 1957, upon his acceptance of the post of Australian Ambassador to the United States, Sir Howard Beale resigned his seat of Parramatta in the House of Representatives. Then one day, without any prior arrangement, I was visited by Senator Spooner, Government Leader in the Senate and prominent in the NSW Branch of the Liberal Party. He asked me to consider nominating for preselection for Parramatta. Again, while he could give no firm assurance, he said I would have a fairly good chance. I told him I was not inclined. He urged me to accept and asked me to think about it.

By this time we had settled into our new home in Beecroft which, though not actually within the division of Parramatta, was only a few hundred yards outside its northern limits. But there were many things to be considered. The future of my family bulked large among them. My son and daughter were still at school, Ross at Barker College and Diane at Burwood Methodist Ladies College. I had not accumulated so much capital that, bearing in mind my gifts to Mundroola Pty Ltd,[1] I could look after my family without any income from personal exertion.

Then there was my own inexperience of political life and my lack of any base in the Liberal Party. I had on hand a great deal of work which I could not simply drop. I also had diabetes. Though I had nonetheless been able to cope with my practice, would the same be true of the onslaught of political life? On top of all this, I had serious doubts whether I could fit in with those who would necessarily be my parliamentary colleagues, all of whom I must accept without having any say in their selection. Having considered all these things, I told Senator Spooner that I was not of a mind to submit myself for preselection.

Over the Christmas period of 1957 I went with my family to a small settlement on the south coast of New South Wales where I was building a small cottage. The area was then known as Red Head but is now known as Bendalong. I had not mentioned Spooner's proposal to my family.

My duties as a trustee of Kosciusko State Park required my presence there during the early days of January 1958. I would have to travel through Braidwood, Queanbeyan and Cooma to Kosciusko, where I was to meet my fellow trustee, Sam Clayton, head of the State Department of Conservation. We were to ride on an inspection of some areas about which some question had arisen.

While at Bendalong I told Norma of Senator Spooner's approach, merely as a piece of information. Then I received a message from Menzies asking me to meet him in Sydney as soon as possible. I arranged to be in Sydney on a Saturday morning early in January, intending to go on the next day to the park.

The Prime Minister met me in my chambers early after lunch. He had come, he said, to urge me to nominate for Parramatta. We discussed the pros and cons till late in the afternoon. I mentioned some of my difficulties but, perhaps wrongly, I did not disclose to him (neither then nor at any other time) my diabetes. I had hidden it carefully from my legal associates and would not want it known in political circles because of possible unfavourable repercussions. Only my immediate family knew of it. I maintained this reticence till I was about to retire as Chief Justice in 1981.

Menzies and I had had a number of earlier contacts. We had appeared against each other in the High Court in a civil case during the time he was out of office. Later I had taken over from him a case in the Supreme Court of Victoria. He had consulted me in connection with the retention or disposal of the government's interests in BP and in AWA and also, more recently, in connection with the double dissolution of 1951. While I had appeared for his government in the *Communist Party Dissolution* case, I had not met him at all during that case. But we had had conversations at the time I was briefed for the security service in the Petrov Royal Commission.

Menzies mentioned the personal advantages he thought I could bring to the government. He stressed that I had little more to achieve in practice in the law, and that he thought I would find satisfaction in a political career. He said that to choose to nominate was not to make an irreversible choice — that if I did not take to parliamentary life I could leave it and return to practice. He said that the government would profit by my legal, particularly my constitutional, knowledge. He gave me his frank estimation of many of the members of the government and said that if I succeeded in parliamentary life it might be possible for me in time to succeed to his office when he had left it. For my part, I stressed the difficulties I have described.

We discussed the whole matter frankly and at length and parted as the shadows were falling. One matter I did specially take up with him. I knew from a remark he had made to me on another occasion that he strongly disapproved of the appointment of a practising politician to judicial office. He had at the outset been vocal about the appointment of William McKell as Governor-General, chiefly because he was at the time Premier of New South Wales. I know he came to respect McKell for the way he conducted himself in that office. I wished at least to keep open the chance of being appointed to the judiciary. I thought that at this time I would have satisfied Menzies' most stringent requirements for appointment to the Bench. But once I became a politician it might be different. So I asked him to assure me that if I went into politics he would never deny my appointment to a judicial office on those grounds alone. He said quite firmly that I could have that assurance. He reminded me of it in 1964.

I had told Menzies that it would take me some months to clear my desk of current work, particularly my work in the Privy Council, so that if elected I would for some time frequently be absent from the House. He saw no difficulty in this.

When we parted at the end of the afternoon no decision had been made. I told him I was moved by what he had said but was still unsure what to do. I wanted time to consult my family and to think about the matter further. I said I would let him know when I had made up my mind.

I went home to Beecroft and had a meal by myself. I could not telephone Norma as there was then no telephone connection to the partly-finished cottage. I went early to bed, awoke at midnight and set off by car, driving myself to the Chalet at Kosciusko. I had a fast trip and during the journey naturally turned over Menzies' suggestion. I arrived at the Chalet for early breakfast with Sam Clayton. After breakfast we saddled up and set off on an inspection of part of the top area of the park. We did not return till dark. In all, I figure we rode more than 20 miles that day, some of it over fairly rough country. I remember how tired I was that night. Next day Sam and I rode again to see another part of the park but this day we rode only a little more than half the distance of the day before.

Over these two days at odd intervals I talked with Sam about the possibility of my nominating for Parramatta. He had had a long experience in the NSW public service and as a well-trusted officer had come into close personal contact with many politicians, particularly with Sir William McKell. I profited no end from his wisdom and his pungent assessments of the work of some of those with whom he had had official dealings. He saw no obstacles to my success as a politician, though he warned me of many of its pitfalls.

Back with my family, I told them of my talk with the Prime Minister. We canvassed together the financial aspects of the future if I chose to go into politics. In 1958 a member's parliamentary salary, and more significantly his retirement benefits, were much less than they are now. It was not until the acceptance of the Richardson Report in 1960 that parliamentary salaries rose almost spectacularly. In particular, I emphasised to the family, especially to our son, that if I went into Parliament there would be no more accumulation of money. We would have an income on which we could live but it would provide no surplus. I had always led Ross to believe that, as the Fort Street motto suggests, he would have to make his own way, though in fact I was providing for both children through Mundroola. Ross has made his own way and very successfully too.

I elaborated for Norma the duties that would fall upon her in working the electorate, new duties in a new and strange environment. In the long run, it was agreed that I should make the change. If any of us were more certain than any other that I should do so, it was our son. Now, in the whirligig of time, he at the age of fifty was preselected to contest the division of Parramatta, though its boundaries no longer favour the Liberal side of politics. But fortunately or unfortunately according to one's point of view, he was unsuccessful in the general election, though he cut the Labor margin by about 50 per cent.

I let the matter simmer in my own mind for a day or so. One of the things I weighed, and I am sure Norma did also, was whether, with my diabetic condition, I could stand the stress of political life. We both realised the risk of the onset of hypoglycemia without warning. Ultimately, with her concurrence, I decided to make the change: it could satisfy my sense of public concern and obligation and give opportunity for my interest in government. One morning, I set off to walk through the bush for between a quarter and a half mile to a little shack where a lady who acted as postmistress lived. I sent the Prime Minister a telegram: "Barkus is willing". So the die was cast.

My entry into politics was to a degree experimental. I had no specific political ambitions nor any specific political causes in mind, though of course I wanted to succeed, particularly if I filled a ministerial post. But I felt no regret in forgoing the daily round of legal practice or, strangely enough, the inevitable loss of regular contact with my legal friends. The break would in any case be partly obscured by the months it would take me to finish the work I had on hand.

The next step was the preselection meeting at the Liberal Party rooms in Ash Street. I was assisted by the then secretary of the NSW Branch, John Carrick, later to become a senator and a knight, still a prominent man in public life and a close friend. Of course I made a speech to explain the qualifications I thought myself to have.

I remember one incident during my speech which amused me at the time and still does. While I was answering questions posed by the members of the preselection committee, John Mant, a solicitor and a friend of mine, suddenly asked me what I thought of Mr John Kerr's suggestion of a Melanesian federation. Mant was sitting in the front row of the meeting, a little to my left, as I faced the audience. For a second I was nonplussed, for I had not given any thought to the matter. So I played for time, asking Mant to speak up as I had not fully caught his question. He was a little taken aback by the suggestion that he had been mumbling. He paused a moment before repeating his question very distinctly. By then I had thought the matter through. There is possibly no more difficult form of government to operate than a federation. To impose it upon Melanesians as they emerged into the international hurly-burly did not make sense. So I said, "I do not like it". I think the incident might have persuaded John Mant that I had the potential of a politician.

At any rate, I was selected, and received congratulations from many present, including John Carrick.

* * * * *

Now came a very great change in our lifestyle. We were a close-knit family. We were all of us fond of motoring and holidaying together. At that time Norma had a 2.4 Jaguar and I had a 3.4 Jaguar, and Ross had his own car. We had a fine house and saw many friends in it. It was splendidly furnished by Norma and we lived quite graciously. Now we virtually became public property.

Norma had not had anything to do with public life and, in particular, public speaking. We had of course worked together in the family for its benefit and we had shared many social occasions. She had travelled a great deal with me and was accustomed to meeting people. She was always well liked and well received. She had made many friends in Australia and abroad, friendships she has maintained throughout the years. But now she would have electoral duties to perform. She accepted them cheerfully. On the first occasion she had to make a speech she asked me to write her out a few lines. The next time she had a speaking engagement it was a case of giving her some points, but after that she began to speak quite well without any prompting from me. Indeed, the ladies of Parramatta would tell me quietly that she did very well at public speaking. She moved around the electorate and was, as I say, well liked. She attended many women's gatherings. Much electioneering was done by running house parties, and these she organised. We formed many acquaintanceships with residents of the electorate, several of which have lasted to this day. I have always been deeply grateful for the way she held the fort for me in the electorate.

Then followed my introduction to the electorate. Howard Beale took me to see Mr Phillip Jeffrey, the father of the Liberal Party in Parramatta. He was a very able businessman of considerable political acuity, and well known and respected in the electorate. His family had long been prominent in the social life of Parramatta. He had been associated with every election in the division since Federation, and was now to manage my campaign for the by-election.

Since Federation Parramatta had been represented by a non-Labor man except for one period of three years. After Joseph Cook, who became Prime Minister, there was Eric Bowden, who held ministerial office, Fred Stewart, who was a minister and then Howard Beale, who had the portfolio of Supply. My successor, Nigel Bowen, became a minister and was close to being chosen as Prime Minister. He was later knighted, on appointment as the first Chief Judge of the Federal Court.

Phillip Jeffrey took me round the shopkeepers of Parramatta and to the clubs. I addressed a number of meetings and spoke in Church Street on shopping mornings. I was assisted by Mr Jim Clough, then the Member in the State House for the seat of Parramatta. But the Cahill Government had by then started the government housing settlement in the Dundas Valley. This valley had been a delightful semi-rural area. Mr Thynne Reid, of Hardie's, had a large house at the head of the valley. I have heard it said that he offered the Cahill Government his house and £40,000 to preserve the Dundas Valley as "lung country" — as an open public resort. If so, his offer was not accepted. The housing settlement to which folk from inner-city suburbs such as Golden Grove, Waterloo and Erskineville were brought to live effectively ended the Liberal Party's tenure of the Parramatta seat in the State House and made a very significant change in the texture of the federal division.

I did a doorknock through this settlement, with little electoral success. But at least I made contact with a large number of its residents. I can say that, though in a sense a dull chore, I enjoyed the experience, meeting many people who perhaps would not have attended public meetings, and of course putting before them relevant government policies. I fought four elections in the division during my time in Parliament. My vote in the Dundas Valley area showed some improvement during that time.

I remember at my first public meeting of the campaign, receiving a good lesson in the political need to choose words carefully when addressing an audience. I was anxious on this occasion to dispel any suggestion that, because of my professional life, I was remote, without personal warmth and unused to popular contact. I therefore set out to emphasise the human side of a barrister's practice. So far I think I was on the right trail. But, in pursuit of this objective, I said that "I have *touched* a great number of people in my time". Some wag in the audience, who apparently had some knowledge of the level of the fees I charged, called out loudly "and how!", to the immense amusement of all around him.

I was opposed in the by-election, and indeed in subsequent elections, by a very nice man, Dan Mahoney, who was prominent in local government affairs. I think he was then Mayor of Parramatta. He and his wife became and over time remained good friends of us both.

I won the by-election by a good margin, though a much smaller one than that by which Howard Beale had won his election in 1955. He had forewarned me somewhat portentously that I would not get the same result as he had. For the moment he was right. But in 1963 I obtained the best majority of any Liberal candidate in Australia with the exception of John Cramer in Bennelong.

9 Cabinet Minister under Menzies

I was introduced into the House of Representatives by Roy Wheeler, a stockbroker, the Member for Mitchell, which adjoined Parramatta on the west, and by Mr Armitage, the Member for the division which adjoined Parramatta on the east. They accompanied me, with customary mild protest on my part, from the door into King's Hall to the Speaker's chair to be sworn. On the way, Dr Evatt, Leader of the Opposition, rising from his seat on the Opposition side of the table, shook my hand.

I was allotted a room which Fred Chaney and Bill Falkander already occupied. It was quite a small room on the Senate side of the House. It was really overcrowded by the three of us. The seat I was to occupy in the House was in the back row on the Government side near the door leading into Kings Hall. Fred Chaney sat next to me on my left.

I knew a few members on the Government side, but really only Dr Evatt and Mr Whitlam of the Opposition. Whenever I was able to get to sittings of the House I listened to the debates, trying to absorb the atmosphere and make some assessment of the personalities on both sides. The House, however, was rarely full: mostly, except at question time and perhaps on the adjournment at evening, there would scarce be a quorum present.

While I was clearing up my practice, particularly while I was in London, I was often absent from the House. Because of the position of my seat, near the door to Kings Hall, my absence was readily observed. One evening, driving to a function in the electorate, I was listening to Parliament on the car radio. I heard Arthur Calwell say that unless the Member for Parramatta was seen more regularly in his place what was said of his distinguished predecessor in the law would be repeated about him. I knew what he meant. Percy Spender, standing as an independent, had defeated Archdale Parkhill for the seat of Warringah in 1937. Now Percy Spender, who was a KC, was in quite heavy practice at that time. Then the only way of travelling to Canberra was by road or rail, both methods time-consuming. There were then no regular flights. In order to continue his practice while attending to parliamentary duties, Spender quite frequently made a dash for Canberra by train or car, in some fashion caught the Speaker's eye, and, getting the call, made a speech which often trod on corns. He would dart off immediately afterwards, making back to Sydney in all haste. Because of these flying visits and the often critical speeches, Artie Fadden christened Spender the "Butcher Bird", the propensity of that bird being to fly into a room, defecate on the floor and fly out.

Well, hearing Calwell's remark about me, and recalling the epithet attached to Spender, I decided to make some fun for myself. I decided to ask a question in some sense as a retort to Calwell's remark. The Labor Party was at the time very much in the political wilderness and its members were showing it in their performances in the House. On the following Tuesday morning I saw Harold Holt, then Leader of the House, and asked him whether my proposal was in order. He approved it and, himself fond of fun, thought it not such a bad effort.

Thus encouraged, when the House sat, I asked the Minister for Territories, Paul Hasluck: "Is there any way in which bird of paradise feathers could be obtained to feather the moulting Members of the Opposition who are feeling the cold winds of political adversity?". Choosing to ask Hasluck rather than the Prime Minister was a mistake — and I paid for it. The Prime Minister had a splendid sense of fun and would have made something of my question. But Hasluck, in a very staid fashion, offered the House a detailed explanation of the relevant regulations of the Territory, which absolutely forbade the gathering and export of bird of paradise feathers. Consequently such feathers could not be available for my proposed purpose. My joke fell flat. Fadden came up to me immediately to reprove me as a tyro member for asking a question affecting the Leader of the Opposition. But when I explained myself and referred to Calwell's remark about me he relented somewhat. But he was right. It was not seemly for a novice to take a pot shot at the Leader of the Opposition. This was the only question I ever asked. My ears still tingle at the memory.

Evatt I had known since my early days at the Bar, well before he took silk. I had appeared as his junior and had had a difficult experience with him. I had opposed him in the *Banks* case[1] both in Australia and in London. I had represented ASIO in the Petrov Commission, in which he behaved so strangely. I had also appeared for the government in the *Communist Party* case[2] in which Dr Evatt successfully appeared to establish the invalidity of the Communist Party Dissolution Act of 1950.

I realised that I had come to the parliamentary scene late in life after I had become prominent in my own profession. I was already set in my ways and used to following my own paths, perhaps too insensitive to the attitudes of others. To become a good parliamentarian accepting all members as of equal significance called for tolerance and understanding. I am sure that I did not become one. Menzies, Holt, McEwen and Calwell were good parliamentarians. They respected the institution and to a significant extent a bond existed between them and others on both sides of the House, derived from their common membership of it. But otherwise there was little common ground between the parties. They dined at opposite ends of the dining room and drank at opposite ends of the bar. But, for all that, there was then less positive hostility and less vilification of one another than occurs now.

Over the next six years I made some friends on the other side of the House. I doubt if I made any enemies, though I was conscious at times that some looked askance at me. Perhaps I did not commend myself to Eddie Ward. I became conscious that I was an object of curiosity among some members and that there was speculation about my motives in joining them. But that was to be expected, and though at times I was conscious of it, mostly it did not trouble me.

This was of course a new world for me. I had once addressed the Upper House in Sydney on behalf of some grazier clients, which gave me some experience of the atmosphere of that chamber. On that occasion a member of the Lower House made a very amusing remark. As tradition required, I was robed, including a full-bottomed wig. The president of the Legislative Council was similarly attired. I was to address the House on the effects upon my clients' business affairs of a Bill affecting the wool industry then before the House. My brief was to canvass the substance of the Bill, something the rules of the House did not allow, so I had to watch the president, whom I expected to keep me within those rules. I thought he might give some small sign before he interrupted me. This would allow me a few seconds in which to retreat. For his part the president, alert to what I might attempt, was watching with some intensity.

As we thus watched each other, a member of the Lower House standing in the doorway enquired of a councillor what was afoot. He was told that what was in hand was a Bill concerning wool. "How very right", he said, "with that pair of merino rams glaring at each other".

I made no speeches as a backbencher other than my maiden speech. My absences abroad and the acceptance of the attorney-generalship at the end of 1958 left me no time for doing so. I made one personal explanation denying Eddie Ward's assertion that I was in receipt of an annuity or some such payment from the private banks.

I decided to make my maiden speech when my professional work was over and my attendance in the House more regular. I decided against anything in the nature of a declaration of attitude or expectation. I had no special political gospel to proclaim. The law and the Constitution would be a relatively flat topic. I decided to speak on the Budget, the Supply Bills being then before the House. It was Fadden's last budget and it provided for a small deficit, of £100 million, as a stimulus to the economy. I thought some indication of my appreciation of national finance would not be amiss, though hardly a source of excitement.

I planned to speak after dinner and arranged accordingly with the Whips. I had not spoken with the Prime Minister since my admission. On this evening I went in to see him before the time for speaking arrived. We did not discuss the substance of the speech, the nature of which I indicated, but he did advise me to keep my voice up in speaking. He said my experience of speaking in the much smaller space of a courtroom would cause me to drop my voice. He said he would sit at the table during my speech and if my voice began to drop he would pass his finger upwards past his right temple. In the event, he had no need to signal me. I spoke as I had always done in court, with a minimum of notes. I commended the budget as honest and appropriate to the nation's needs. I concluded the speech with a compliment to the retiring Treasurer, who came up to me afterwards to congratulate me.

In retrospect, I think it would have been wiser for me to have discussed the substance of my maiden speech with the Prime Minister. I think it must have been a very dull speech. I was followed by Gough Whitlam, who spoke of me as a distinguished lawyer.

The general election was called for 22 November. I conducted what to my unpractised eye seemed to be a vigorous campaign, assisted by that wise and staunch campaign manager, Mr Phil Jeffrey, and by Norma.

Throughout my time in the House I meticulously followed the practice of writing a personal letter with personal salutation and signature to each newcomer to the rolls, to each constituent or family bereaved by death and to each elector who became naturalised. I made it my business to attend naturalisation ceremonies and to offer advice and encouragement to the migrants.

I remember regularly counselling them not to employ their native tongue in public, but to speak English, however much they might speak their native language in their households or private gatherings. I felt — and said — that Australians were used only to English and that conversation in public between others in a foreign language might engender suspicion and or even dislike. Nowadays we seem to encourage the migrants to use their native language in public. Here I feel we have failed to remember the great unifying force of a common language and the risk to national unity of a babel of language in the public streets. National unity is hard enough to achieve by a people who have no history of armed conflict in their own land. I doubt the wisdom of accepting migrants who cannot already speak English. Apart from all else, this policy has involved us in great expenditure in teaching migrants to speak English and oddly enough in teaching their children to speak their native tongue.

* * * * *

After the electoral results of 1958 showed the Liberals with a clear majority, the Prime Minister asked me to see him. We had had only one discussion since I had made my speech. One morning in August 1958, after question time, I had left the Chamber by the door into King's Hall when the Prime Minister caught up with me. He said he expected I had noticed that he had a vacancy on the High Court to fill. (Sir Dudley Williams had retired.) He asked me did I want it. I said no, I had no present yearning for the Bench. I said that had I felt like it, I might possibly have been Chief Justice of New South Wales. He said, "You wouldn't turn down such an appointment, would you?". "Yes", I said, "I would".

He replied quite feelingly, "I'd have been delighted to be Chief Justice of Victoria" — a remark which surprised me at the time, but one I remembered in a later discussion in 1964. He then said he had two names before him and asked me what I thought of them. I knew and liked both men. I said that I thought that one of them, while he had had the lesser experience of the two, would be better in the work of the court. The matter was left at that. I knew he felt warmly towards the other of the two men and had been critical of the work in the Petrov Commission of the man I had preferred. I wondered what he would do. In the result, no doubt for reasons of his own, he did recommend the one I favoured.

When I called on Menzies at his request he said that he wished me to be the Attorney-General in the new Ministry and a member of Cabinet. While he had given me no express assurances of a portfolio, I could not say I was surprised by the offer. But I was surprised to be told that I was to be a member of Cabinet. In my understanding of Westminster government, I had not thought of the Attorney-General as necessarily a member of Cabinet. Indeed, because of the independence of this office, it may be better that the Attorney should not be a member of Cabinet, since his presence might in some circumstances affect that independence.

Because of this impression, I remember immediately saying to Menzies, "Aren't you taking a risk?", for I was a raw recruit and had made no mark as a backbencher. I was even a new member of the party. He replied, "No, I am not, but you are". In retrospect, he was right: the risks were in my corner. I was walking into an area with which I was unfamiliar and for which I think I was ill-prepared.

What I did not immediately appreciate, for I had done no counting of heads, was that to fit me into the Cabinet a minister would have to be displaced. I found out that Alan Fairhall, a very capable minister later to be a successful Minister of Defence, was put out of Cabinet to make a place for me. Alan, whom I came to like and respect, showed absolutely no resentment. He straight away came to see me, offering congratulations and asking me to take over his Sydney driver, Bert Reid. Reid drove me faithfully and efficiently until late in my chief justiceship. In Canberra, Ray Coppin was assigned to me as a driver. Both were loyal and capable men.

I walked out of the Prime Minister's room elated and apprehensive. My training, right from the time I had been an articled clerk, had prepared me for making decisions and taking responsibility. I had learned to be decisive and to realise the perils of indecision. Self-confidence had developed, as well as firm views on matters of principle. But as I set about organising myself for the new role, I had no time for reflection. I had to get busy doing what had to be done.

But I did realise, even as I plunged into this new and fast-flowing stream of ministerial life, that I would be living dangerously from now on.

My room as Attorney-General was on the second floor on the House, right at the rear of the corridor. It was so far from the Chamber that when the bells rang for a division or a quorum, I had to run part of the way to reach the Chamber before its doors were closed. It was a small room containing little more than a small desk and a couple of chairs.

My secretarial staff consisted solely of Miss Wilkinson, an experienced secretary who for some time had been assistant secretary to the Prime Minister and more recently secretary to the former Attorney-General. I would hazard a guess that "Wilkie", as I came to call her, as indeed all who knew her affectionately did, would then have been in her mid-fifties. I was to find her competent, loyal and politically wise. I had no press officer or research assistant, except that at times Miss Wilkinson had an assistant. I found the professional officers of the Department quite adequate for my research needs. As for the press, I informed them at the outset that I would send for them when I had anything of public interest to say and I asked them meantime to keep away from my officers.

My spartan personal entourage never resulted in any inefficiency or caused anything to be left undone. Working with me, they fully coped with the demands of my office.

At the swearing-in ceremony by Sir William Slim, I received the congratulations of all my colleagues. I was genuinely surprised at the warmth of their welcome. I would not have been surprised if I had been, as it were, put on the shelf until I had proved myself. But I found no trace of resentment or suspicion and none of them seemed to want to distance himself from me.

After the ceremony the whole Ministry assembled in the Cabinet room and the Prime Minister spoke of the responsibilities of ministers. He advised us to take great heed of what our heads of department had to say, though emphasising the need for exercising our own judgment and making our own decisions: taking advice did not mean that it must be accepted or one's own judgment overborne. The form of government to be followed would be what I would call "ministerial". The work of the Cabinet would be confined to decisions of general policy and to the resolution of any ministerial or departmental differences. While there would be regular party meetings to keep members informed, there was no caucus domination as might occur elsewhere.

We tend to use the expression "ministerial responsibility" rather loosely. Its proper use is to describe the constitutional need to have ministerial advisers to the Governor-General who are members of Parliament and who take responsibility to Parliament for the advice given to the Governor-General and for the action taken upon it. For this the Ministry as a whole is responsible. The parliamentary control of the Ministry is by the grant or refusal of supply or by resolution withdrawing confidence in it. But the expression can also refer to the decisions and actions of the ministers individually in administering their portfolios. In this instance, the responsibility is to the Ministry as a whole and perhaps in a more general way to the party in government. But the House of Representatives may express its disapproval of the Ministry by passing at any time a resolution of no confidence in it.

Menzies by this time had been in office for ten years. I suppose it could be said that the directions he gave and his manner of giving them to the assembled ministry exemplified his great prowess as an advocate. He was able to explain in simple and direct terms matters of principle and practice, however apparently complex they might be. I knew Menzies to be devoted to the maintenance of the rule of law, to be a traditionalist and a federalist in matters of government. Indeed I saw nothing of him which led me to think that he attempted a presidential form of government, though I suppose as Prime Minister he attracted special public attention. His considerable political wisdom was usually treated by the press as craftiness.

I was surprised at the almost homely atmosphere Menzies created at this first assembly of his new Ministry. There was none of the arrogance or domination the press tried to attribute to him; he was friendly without being condescending. As I came to know him, he was a less complicated man that one might expect. I found a degree of shyness in him: he was very sentimental when dealing with friends or when speaking of them. In my own relationship with him I found him open to receiving new ideas, quick to understand, and when convinced, prepared to be enthusiastic. His Presbyterian upbringing was reflected in high standards of behaviour; his innate liberal conservatism appeared even in his dress. As well, he could be a genial companion with a strong sense of humour, a propensity which made discussion in the Cabinet under his chairmanship friendly, however forcibly views might be expressed. He was a proper man. I never heard him tell a blue story, though I have seen him enjoying hearing one well told. He did not swear and expressed himself in correct English.

I well remember my first Cabinet meeting, held in Melbourne. On the agenda was a request by the Dutch Government for a right of overflight of Australia for its military planes destined for West New Guinea. Richard Casey introduced the item. As a new boy, I thought it proper to remain silent during the discussion. I knew that the Americans had refused the Dutch a right of overflight and that the British were likely to and in the long run did refuse them logistical support. I assumed this to be common knowledge among my colleagues.

Suddenly Menzies said, “What do you think, Mr Attorney?”. The form of address was new and the suddenness of the enquiry disconcerting. But I had a view and felt confident enough of it to answer, “I would refuse them”. Mentioning the position of the Americans and of the British, I concluded, “I think it would be foolish to support Dutch colonialism”. A silence fell on the meeting, even though the others thought that overflight should be refused. But though there had been Australian co-operation with Dutch colonial administration, Cabinet decided to refuse overflight.

Thinking back over the events of that day, I realise that Menzies valued and doubtless appreciated my reticence but, anxious to encourage me and to assist my acceptance by my fellows, he felt he should project me into the discussion. Also thinking back, I realise that I must have sounded abrupt and too certain in the expression of my views. Perhaps I was.

But Menzies' action on this occasion was not in the least out of character. In the succeeding years I had much opportunity to observe his conduct of a Cabinet. He was a good chairman, anxious to obtain the views of its members. Rarely was his own view put forward before discussions had taken place, though doubtless on most occasions he had one.

* * * * *

Professor Bailey was at that time head of the Attorney-General's Department and Solicitor-General, two offices then held by the same person. My own experience of him made me admire his knowledge of the law, his sense of loyalty and his uprightness. He was gentle and not assertive. I enjoyed working with him and gained much knowledge of the working of the Department from him.

My unfamiliarity with the ways of the Department soon produced odd results. For example, when I received a letter from a minister asking for an opinion on some legal point, I worked on the point, formed an opinion, wrote it out and sent it direct to the Minister. When this had occurred on several occasions, one day Bailey called on me and said almost laconically, "Minister, you've been advising the Treasurer and some other Ministers".

"Yes", I said, "I have."

"But you have a department."

"What do you mean?"

"Well, it's customary for the papers to go to the Department for their views."

"Do you mean you want an opportunity to say I'm wrong?"

"Not at all, but that is the regular practice. The officers wish to offer their assistance and advice."

"I see. You want me when I receive a request for advice from a minister to ask the Department to prepare a reply."

"Precisely."

"Does that mean that I don't work at it myself?"

"No, when the advice comes back from the officer, we could discuss it — you and myself, or if you wish, the officer concerned. You could then form your own view and settle the form of the official advice."

Thereafter this procedure was followed — and from my point of view, substantially.

I soon found that other ministers began to call on me bringing me their legal problems. I welcomed this because I needed to know my colleagues and to find out exactly what their work involved. The frequency of these visits increased considerably and took up a good deal of my time. Apparently, before my appointment the practice had been for ministers to ask the Prime Minister for his view. This shift by which ministers came to me took some of the load from him. It came back to me by the usual underground channels of Canberra that the Prime Minister was saying that he now had an attorney who was willing and able to give advice to his colleagues.

As I was a member of Cabinet, and not all of the ministers who called on me were, I was often asked to help get through Cabinet some proposal they were making to it. One of the ministers with whom I had frequent contact was John McEwen, who sought my legal advice from time to time, and occasionally on matters of substance. I came to like and respect him and we were always on secure terms with each other.

One of the interesting matters that came to my attention had to do with worker's compensation and involved the Treasury. Under the Commonwealth provisions, a worker, though entitled to worker's compensation, was able to sue at common law for negligence on the part of the Commonwealth. But he must do so within twelve months of his receipt of a payment of compensation, otherwise the Commonwealth could plead the time limitation.

A young soldier had been injured during gunnery practice. He was hit by metal in the groin, causing damage to his genitals. He was hospitalised but discharged without being told that the injury might mean he could not have children. He was paid compensation according to the statutory provisions. Some time later he discovered that he was permanently sterile. He made a claim at common law though more than twelve months had elapsed since he had first received compensation.

Treasury decided that the limitation should be pleaded. It had actually instructed the Attorney-General's Department to do so and the plea had been lodged. Journalists became interested in the situation and the Melbourne *Truth* took the matter in hand, much to the discomfiture of the Treasurer. I was asked by Harold Holt to do something to relieve the situation. I pointed out that the course followed by his Department had been wrong. In the first place it was for the Attorney-General to decide what pleas would be pleaded unless there was some policy matter which had to go to Cabinet. Second, the pleas in this case should be withdrawn and the soldier given the right to proceed at common law. This was done. Later I wrote to the Treasurer saying that in future the Attorney-General would not plead the inhibiting provisions unless it was felt that the Commonwealth had been substantially disadvantaged by the lapse of time. That, as far as I know, remained the position, certainly through my own time.

I found great interest in watching Menzies handling John McEwen, the leader of our Coalition partner. I came to see the fundamental weakness of coalition government, as it must frequently cause compromise on the part of the major party and the inhibition of initiatives that the majority member would otherwise have taken. By the time I joined the Cabinet McEwen had decided to find support for the Country Party in the secondary industries. Somewhat inconsistently, given the fundamental interests of primary industry, as Minister for Trade he favoured and encouraged the maintenance of tariffs, something one would not have expected of a country man. His view of the manufacturing industry must have been that it had little hope of developing a great export trade and should be content with serving the local population with useful import substitution, aided in this by the level of tariffs.

When Dean Rusk was in Canberra for an ANZUS meeting in 1963, I organised a meeting with him for McEwen, which I also attended. Rusk I think perceived the weakness in our economy caused by our failure to process our raw materials and export secondary products, relying on exporting raw materials. I recall him saying to McEwen, "But surely you do not wish your country to be no more than a quarry" — a perceptive remark, the full weight of which I suspect McEwen did not comprehend. At any rate, I saw no consequence of it. McEwen was of course intent on increasing our external trade, but I do not think he had come to realise that a secondary industry exporting manufactures to the world at competitive prices and of competitive quality was unlikely to be built behind a tariff wall.

In Cabinet, Menzies seemed to ensure that McEwen expressed a view on the matter in hand. I thought he at times tried to persuade McEwen to his own point of view, but he avoided any confrontation. It was part of his general practice of chairmanship by consensus.

It was a Cabinet rule that papers should be presented for consideration four days before the meeting at which they were to be discussed. It was a good rule because it gave ministers time to discuss matters with their departments and to be alerted to any possible ramifications. The rule could be broken for special reasons. On one such occasion I had a proposal to commute a death sentence for murder imposed by the Supreme Court of the ACT. This was probably the first time, at least in recent days, that the question of commuting such a sentence had arisen in Federal Cabinet. At the time the criminal law operating in Canberra was identical with that in New South Wales, where murder still carried the death sentence.

This murder was of a particularly unpleasant kind. There was a strong popular feeling in Canberra favouring execution, a feeling I knew to be shared by some members of Cabinet. As I was anxious to avoid a Cabinet leak, with resultant pressure from the press, I arranged with Menzies to waive the four-day rule and asked him not to bring on the item in Cabinet before nine o'clock in the evening. As this was the first occasion in recent times that a Federal Cabinet had had to consider commuting a death sentence, I presented a paper setting out the principles on which I thought Cabinet should act. After considerable discussion, and the expression of some opposition, the Cabinet accepted my recommendation. I was grateful to my colleagues for their willingness for the reasons I gave them to discuss the matter immediately and at short notice.

The place of the Prime Minister in such a system of Cabinet policy-making and ministerial decision and action is worth considering. As I have said, Menzies did not seek to be or act as a president. He was content to be the chairman of Cabinet and leader of the party. He liked the prominence this gave him and was guilty at times of referring to the government as "my government". This has become common. I think it would be a salutary exercise and an antidote to presidential aspirations and pretensions if the government were regularly referred to as Her Majesty's or His Excellency's government. To some this may appear pedantic but to my mind it has substance; and at least would be a useful discipline. After all, we seem to have little difficulty in referring to Her Majesty's Opposition.

The press tend to attribute everything to the Prime Minister, as if he were a president. This is a pity, because it tends to turn politics into a game, a personal contest between individuals to the great neglect of ideas and policies. It tends to trivialise occasions. Even more serious is the circumstance that the press want to be players in that game. As a result, the public get more comment than information, not the colourless communication of fact, carefully ascertained and retailed. Accurate and objective information is really indispensable to the stable operation of a democracy.

10 Matters Matrimonial

Percy Joske had had extensive experience of matrimonial causes in his practice as a barrister, and had written a well-received textbook on the subject. Before my arrival in the House, he had prepared a private member's Bill to exercise the legislative power of the Federal Parliament on "Divorce and Matrimonial Causes and in relation thereto parental rights and the custody and guardianship of infants".[1] Later he had persuaded Menzies, with whom he was very friendly, to take over his bill as a government measure but without the Whip; that is to say, the members were to have a conscience vote.

Joske's Bill sought to find a common denominator of the grounds for divorce provided by the State Acts, making some minor changes in some of them. It proposed no major changes in the law; the motive was to get uniformity of the law throughout the Commonwealth. The State laws were built exclusively on the grounds of proved fault as the reason for dissolution of marriage.

Shortly after my appointment as Attorney-General Menzies asked me to take over this Bill. On my asking him, he said I would be quite free to make the Bill conform to my own wishes, subject of course to Cabinet approval. When my colleagues heard that I was taking on the carriage of the Bill, some expressed their sympathy and told me that it was likely to put an end to my political life. Federal politicians had been avoiding the Matrimonial Causes area for fifty years. It was regarded as a political hot potato, with religious as well as social and party-political overtones. But, buoyed by a novice's ignorance, I felt undaunted.

I had handled cases in divorce, alimony and custody but had not had any extensive practice in that jurisdiction. I remember that during the public discussions of my Bill Archbishop Woods of Melbourne discussed the Bill and my relationship to it with the Prime Minister. Among other things, Menzies assured the archbishop that I was happily married and a good family man. He suggested I call on Woods the next time I was in Melbourne. I did and we had a cordial and useful discussion.

As I contemplated the formation of a federal law of divorce, I had to bring into my conscious thinking what was my own subconscious philosophy of marriage and divorce. This was quite an exercise, for my personal experience had not made me form any particular philosophy about it. I enjoyed a stable, happy and satisfying relationship with my wife and children. I had been brought up, as had my wife, in the Methodist Church, from which we had derived and retained moral values, particularly those concerned with marriage and family life.

My philosophy then and now was to regard marriage, and the creation and maintenance of a family, as basic to a stable and well-ordered community. I could not think that promiscuity and irregular and perhaps temporary liaisons were consistent with that stability and orderliness. Nor could I accept that children of a single parent born outside marriage would not be severely disadvantaged. I felt that the nurture of children in a family atmosphere and with the guidance of both parents and the sense of mutual tolerance which a family can provide were all essential to the community's strength and the stability of its future. I also felt that in the development of a family there is great scope for the exercise of sound judgment, which I would place, along with wisdom, at the summit of the hierarchy of human talents.

I had of course to build on the premise of dissolubility. I could not yield to the doctrine of indissolubility and build upon that. The civil authority had for a century acted upon the basis of dissolubility by judicial decree. In other words, the question for me was a secular one. In proposing legislation by Parliament, of necessity religious dogma could not dominate, though of course in making any political judgment the religious beliefs and sensibilities of the community had to be kept in mind, and the community's moral standards respected. The starting point for me was that marriage must derive its force and sanction from parliamentary law. Parliament could legislate for its dissolution, but the statutory provisions I proposed must be acceptable to the community as a whole.

The States had provided that breach of the marriage obligation by one of the spouses in one of the respects specified in the relevant legislation was a necessary condition of dissolution. The Australian community's concept of marriage and its obligations were founded on adherence to monogamy, and designed, as the *Book of Common Prayer* so eloquently recites, for the mutual comfort of the pair and for the procreation and nurture of children.

Before making any decision about the contents of a divorce Bill, I read a good deal, including Shepherd's *Marriage Made for Man*. I considered laws in force in Britain, the United States and Canada. I realised that there was a growing interest among lawyers and sociologists in the idea of the breakdown of marriage as a basis for its dissolution. Where breakdown was apparently irreversible, these people were disposed to treat this as an acceptable reason for divorce, whether or not either party had committed any matrimonial fault. Where a marriage had broken down without hope of reconciliation, the community, I thought, as well as the estranged spouses, might have an interest in terminating the relationship and, perhaps more importantly, opening the door to the formation of a new and more stable and fruitful marriage.

As soon as it was known that I was taking on the Bill, I was approached by various groups seeking alteration of the law by making dissolution either easier or more difficult. The Salvation Army asked me not to provide that a single act of adultery was sufficient to warrant dissolution. They were prepared to demonstrate from their experience that many marriages were maintained and indeed maintained more stably after an act of adultery by one of the spouses. I had considerable sympathy with their views, but I told them that divorce upon proof of a single act of adultery was too entrenched in the community for me to accept what they proposed. I knew that in Victoria more than one such act on the part of the husband was required. While I felt that this distinction between the sexes was unacceptable, I could see no grounds for requiring more than one act of adultery generally on the part of either spouse. However, as I was by that time moving towards favouring marriage counselling, I felt that, given the intervention of marriage guidance counsellors, the existence of the legislative possibility of divorce for a single act of adultery would not preclude the rebuilding of marriages the Salvation Army spoke of. Perhaps these cases had been helped by their own counsellors.

Of course, there may be serious breaches of marital obligation which are not specifically nominated as statutory grounds of dissolution. For such cases the separation ground might well be disadvantageous to one of the spouses and leave a sense of unfair treatment. But although I was conscious of this, the advantage to the community of clearing the way for a new liaison, and perhaps a new family, had to be weighed in considering the advisability of adopting the separation ground.

I finally concluded that if it were demonstrable that a marriage had irretrievably broken down, whether or not any of the current statutory matrimonial faults, or for that matter any other faults, had occurred, a dissolution should be available. I thought it best, however, that the marriage should be able to be dissolved at the instance of an aggrieved spouse; that is, I thought that if the aggrieved spouse felt unable to overlook a fault, and felt that the marriage was consequently at an end, dissolution by judicial decree should remain available. So I was content to retain statutory prescriptions of matrimonial fault, with some changes, for example reducing the period of desertion from three years to two, and in another instance dispensing with the ground altogether, for example non-compliance with an order for restitution of conjugal rights. Of course, litigation to establish one of these statutory grounds could be fraught with bitterness and the enforced disclosure of sordid aspects of the marriage. But I proposed to leave the choice to the party who claimed to be aggrieved.

If irreversible breakdown was allowed as a ground for divorce, the question arose of how would it be established, in particular, how would it be established without acrimonious controversy. There was precedent in the existing Australian legislation for accepting unilateral separation, as by desertion, as enough to warrant dissolution — hence the traditional ground based on desertion for three years. In a sense, the marriage was taken to have broken down if such desertion was evident. But of course the remedy was only available to the deserted spouse.

Left to myself, I think I would have been satisfied to provide that the marriage had broken down — and irreversibly — upon a separation of three years, that is, if the parties were mutually and physically separated and not persuaded after marriage guidance to resume cohabitation. The further two years of legal proceedings would mean that dissolution would not be effective under five years.

But I felt that I would not be able to carry the community with me if the Bill so provided. So I opted for a five-year period of separation as sufficient evidence of breakdown. With the time taken for the divorce proceedings, this really meant that seven or eight years would most likely elapse between the actual separation and the dissolution. I felt that this was the best I could achieve in the face of deeply entrenched and understandable community views.

New South Wales had a statutory provision for an order for the restitution of conjugal rights. Divorce could follow on the sole ground of failure of the spouse to return as ordered. I knew that this was much used as an easy path to divorce; in fact I suspect it was often used collusively to achieve what in substance was a divorce by consent. I resolved not to include such a provision in the Bill. This was a fairly bold course because the New South Wales profession found it fairly attractive as a way to divorce. As compensation, I reduced the period of desertion from three years to two.

*****

The changes gave me a great deal of trouble and called for much public education on my part. In promoting the Bill I addressed numerous bodies in the community on my proposals. Some churchmen were against them, particularly Archbishop Fox, leader of the Roman Catholic Church in Victoria, who vigorously expressed his opposition. A medical man and his wife, both resident in Victoria and both Catholics, maintained strong opposition throughout the Bill's passage through Parliament. After the Bill had been passed and received the Royal assent, they petitioned the Queen to disallow the Act pursuant to the power reserved to her by s 59 of the Constitution.

I had had some contact with Cardinal Gilroy and, though I was not a member of his church, we got on well. He knew that I was well known to and well regarded by Premier Cahill. In the week that Cahill died I happened to be a patient in Prince Alfred Hospital. While there Cardinal Gilroy wrote to me, referring to Cahill's death but mainly saying that he was still "grieved" that I persisted with clause 23(m), the separation ground. I wrote back saying that he and I could not discuss the propriety of this ground. His premise was indissolubility which, for his purposes, I understood and respected. My premise as a secular lawyer was dissolubility and it had now been publicly and legislatively accepted for more than a century. I said that he would not commit the sin of criticising my conclusion on his premise; that the matter would have to be discussed if at all on my premise, which I realised he might not be able to accept. Then I set out why on my premise this ground was justifiable. In reply I received a very gentle letter from the Cardinal in which he said that I was right, we could not discuss the matter. Thereafter the Roman Catholic Church in New South Wales gave me no particular bother.

The Anglican Church strongly opposed my reduction of desertion period from three to two years. I called on the Anglican Primate, Archbishop Gough, to explain why the reduction was desirable, after which the Archbishop expressed himself content. I asked him if there were any other provisions of the Bill with which he or the church was dissatisfied. He did not indicate that there were any.

But very soon after that interview, Gough issued a public statement roundly condemning me as encouraging young people to enter into marriage with no resolution to maintain it. I must say I was unduly incensed by this attack, bearing in mind the recent interview. I decided on the instant to make a public statement in which I said, among other things, that I thought young people were less cynical than their priests. I discussed the statement with Professor Bailey, a man prominent in the councils of the Anglican Church. He agreed that I should publish it as he knew of my interview with Gough. Publish I did, and I became known in some circles as the "bishop basher". In retrospect, the statement was too vigorous and it would have been better to have ignored Archbishop Gough's attack, even though I felt betrayed.

One evening some time later I was having one of my customary discussions with Menzies. He said, very quietly, "Gar, you're having trouble with this Bill of yours".

"Yes, I am."

"With one particular clause?"

"Yes, that's right."

"Well, is it worth all this?"

"Yes", I said, "I think it is. I think it's right to persist with this clause."

"Well", said Menzies, "you know how it is with me. I am an old Presbyterian and, with me, all divorce is dirty."

"But", I said, "I cannot act on that basis." I showed him some of my correspondence with Cardinal Gilroy, in which I explained my reason for including this ground. Menzies read it and then read it again. I sent him a copy. We had no more discussion about this clause or any other part of the Bill.

When the petition of the Victorian doctor and his wife arrived in Yarralumla, the Governor-General, Lord Slim, sent it to me as Attorney-General to advise him what he should do with it. In the case of a petition to the Queen for the exercise of prerogative power the Governor-General would deal with it himself as advised by the Attorney-General. But this was not such a petition. As it was based on s 59 of the Constitution it had to go to the Palace for the Queen's personal attention. The question arose as to who should advise Her Majesty on what to do with it. For this there was no precedent. In the days when the Commonwealth formed part of the British Empire it would have been for the British Government to advise the Queen, but with Australia's independence it was for the Australian Government, through the Prime Minister, to advise her. So at my request Menzies wrote to advise the Queen to reject the petition, and it was done.

Some members of the Victorian Branch of the Liberal Party, including some members of Parliament, were very much against the Bill. One afternoon in Melbourne I addressed a large meeting of the branch. The Premier, Henry Bolte, was there, my federal colleague Peter Howson, and other Victorian members. There were a number of women present. At the end only one person rose to oppose the Bill, a woman who said she was against all divorce. I said that in that event we would find no common ground for discussion. The meeting seemed on the whole friendly, and I felt I had convinced at least some.

Two days later I received a letter from a woman I did not know, but who had attended the meeting: "I went there a hundred per cent opposed to you. I came away in your favour. If you were to sit down before the television camera and talk as you talked to us, I don't think you'd have any trouble with this Bill." I liked that. I felt it was a nice tribute to my own capacity to explain things clearly and convincingly.

It also confirmed my strong opinion that clearly expressed sound argument has more electoral effect than all the advertising and ballyhoo of professional electioneering. The problem is to find the opportunity to meet people in circumstances where you can present such argument. People are more receptive and rational than the electoral minders will credit. But unfortunately, due in no small measure to the attitudes of some journalists to offer comment rather than information, many voters lack a knowledge of the facts by reference to which they could exercise intelligent judgment.

* * * * *

I am very conscious that as a rule it is the children of a broken marriage who suffer the most. Too easy it is for the estranged parents to place their own convenience before their children's welfare. One might expect that parents would do anything for their children, even to the point of honourably bearing the frustrations of an unsuccessful marriage, and many do. But if they could or

> you can tell me whether in providing the separation ground I favour the guilty at the expense of the innocent.
>
> A man and woman married, both adult and each having his or her own business. After marriage, each continued individually in business. After a time, the woman became pregnant. She said, "I am going to do away with this child. It would be bad for business". He said, "I didn't marry you for this. I would like children. I will not agree to your doing away with the child". She insisted that she would and he said, "If you do all will be over between us. Now it is a matter for you to think about".
>
> Well, she had an abortion without his consent, and he left her. Some fifteen years later he, for the first time, formed a close friendship with another woman. His wife remained in business. When he found that the lady with whom he was now associating was pregnant, he wrote to his wife telling her of his situation and asking her to divorce him. His desertion or his adultery would provide grounds. He offered to pay any costs involved. She wrote back that she wanted nothing more from life and would see that he got nothing more from life. She refused to divorce him.
>
> Now, Mr Pressman, who was guilty and who innocent in these circumstances? And did I do wrong in making provision that enables that man to gain his freedom to marry and thereby legitimise the child?

There was utter silence. The pressman, brash as he was, said, "Oh, that's very difficult". I said, "I don't think it is. I think the answer to my last question is very clear."

* * * * *

During the progress of the Matrimonial Causes Bill through the House I conceived the idea of a Marriage Act which would provide a nationally uniform legal framework for the celebration and incidents of marriage. Such an act would exercise the legislative power given by s 51(xxi) of the Constitution, which had not been exercised before. I obtained from Cabinet the authority to prepare a Bill for this purpose and set my officers to begin the work.

I laid down the principles to be followed: marriage was to derive its validity from the national law. That law must select and authorise the person to celebrate it, and there must be both record and certification of the ceremony. There was to be no marriage outside that law. While I was most anxious that the civil nature of marriage should be upheld, where for religious or other reasons the parties wanted a further ceremony, provision was to be made for a second ceremony, but only if the validity of the civil marriage was acknowledged. Religious denominations were to be recognised by the Attorney-General, who had to be apprised of and satisfied with the form of marriage ceremony they conducted. When recognised, the clergy of that denomination were to be authorised to celebrate marriage according to the approved form.

The marriageable age was to be eighteen for the male and sixteen for the female. Marriage should not be celebrated where either party was under twenty-one without the consent of parents or guardians. Birth certificates had to be shown to the celebrant, who would also have a book of certificates which would act as a marriage register. Each certificate was to be watermarked with the Commonwealth Coat of Arms, thus indicating the authority giving validity to the marriage. By appointing the priests and ministers of the Christian churches as marriage celebrants, the desire for marriage in a church could be satisfied.

The law was to apply and be observed by all, including members of the Jewish faith. In some instances Jews were outside the scope of State marriage legislation. But the Commonwealth Act should be all-embracing; all Australians should be within its scope. I therefore set out to learn about the Jewish faith. I had many conversations with its rabbis and laity. A rabbi is a lawyer, not a priest in the ecclesiastical tradition of the Christian church; he alone is allowed to read the Law. I found that each synagogue is independent of all other congregations. Each chooses a rabbi, who is engaged under a contract with the laity and can be dismissed by them. There is no hierarchy of rabbis, so I had to contemplate dealing with each congregation.

The members of some congregations had some differences with their rabbis. Some asserted that marriage was a lay matter, whereas the rabbis insisted that it was a rabbinical matter, and thus for them to celebrate. The Australian Council of Jewry, based in Melbourne, for a time claimed the right to speak on the matter for all Jews, but its position was not universally accepted.

I could not find any accommodation of the two opposed views. I conducted an informal plebiscite throughout the congregations, offering various formulae to bridge the gap, but I found no majority for any formula large enough to settle the matter. In the end I took it on myself to decide that celebration of marriages under the Act between Jews was to be a rabbinical matter and that the rabbi would be authorised to celebrate it. Jews, both orthodox and liberal, seemed to accept this solution.

* * * * *

With the licensing of lay celebrants, marriage celebrations without any clerical participation has come into favour. It seems to me that the demand for this comes from those who have no religious commitment or who, because of earlier divorce, are unacceptable to priests or pastors. Many others for whom the significance of marriage has been weakened — something to which the Family Law Act has contributed — prefer a ceremony performed by a layman and often in unusual places. It is proper that this community demand be satisfied, but in my own view the need for and the selection of lay celebrants should be closely monitored. But in my time no such demand was apparent. To a degree it has been created by later events.

In some of the State legislation the clerks or registrars of the Courts of Petty Sessions and the registrars of births, deaths and marriages had been authorised to perform the marriage ceremony in the courthouse or registry. This useful facility was reflected in the Bill, in which a form of marriage ceremony which I personally settled was provided. A room in the local courthouse in Canberra was suitably furnished and decorated as a venue for marriage ceremonies.

But though I saw no general demand for lay celebrants, I realised that there was a distinct possibility of continuing difference in a Jewish congregation if there was no acceptable rabbi available to perform marriages. A similar difficulty might also arise in Christian congregations. To meet these possibilities, I provided in the Bill a power in the Attorney-General to appoint a marriage celebrant. Though expressed in general terms, in my mind at the time this was merely a reserve power to be exercised in emergencies; during my years of office I had no occasion to exercise it. A later Attorney-General, however, used the power to appoint a large number of celebrants in all manner of lay occupations. It soon became apparent that the performance of the marriage ceremony could be a lucrative sideline occupation. The celebration of marriage now takes place in a variety of environments, some most informal, if not bizarre.

When it became known that the Bill was to require the production to the celebrant in all cases of birth certificates, I received some complaints from the clergy. One Anglican canon was very vociferous on the point. He rang me more than once, and on one occasion said, "Why can't you leave it to the celebrant to be satisfied of the adulthood of the partners?" I reminded him that when Lord Hardwick produced his Marriage Act in 1840 he provided that marriage could be celebrated without parental consent if it appeared to the celebrant that the parties were over age. The resulting scandal of clergymen marrying minors was something I was not prepared to risk.

While the Bill was under consideration, Norma became aware of my talk with the canon. She was fond of ceramic antiques, and shortly after the canon's protest happened to attend an antique fair held in the Savings Bank in Martin Place. She saw a small piece of Staffordshire representing the chancel of a church, showing the end window. Standing before a table stood the priest in robes holding a book. On his right at the end of the table two young people, boy and girl, stood holding hands. They were obviously under age. At the other end of the table was a clerk suitably dressed. The piece carried a plaque with the following words: "The New Marriage Act. John Frill and Ann Boke aged 21. That is right says the Parson, Amen said the clerk." It is quite evident that the parson and clerk are winking at one another.

The piece was not for sale, but Norma managed to seek out its owner, who was a dealer, and persuaded him to part with it, telling him of my interest in the subject and its topicality. It remains in our cabinet as a pleasant reminder of the days spent in preparing and piloting the Marriage Act.

* * * * *

There was one novel provision in the Bill to which I should refer. Usually under English law a child born when the parents were not married is illegitimate, a status which has had some consequences in the law and in the community at large. But if the parents subsequently marry, that marriage will legitimate the child provided the parents could have been married at the time the child was born. But of course not all parents of an illegitimate child could satisfy that condition. I thought this was harsh and that it would be right to provide that a subsequent marriage of the parents would legitimise the child, irrespective of whether or not they could have married at the time of the birth.

When I directed the officers to make such provision in the Bill, I was very quickly visited by the senior draftsman. He emphatically told me that such a provision would be invalid — outside the purview of the power to legislate on marriage. I contested this but said that in any case I would leave it to the court to decide. The provision was enacted.

In due course the State of Victoria challenged its validity. I did not appear to argue the case but asked the Solicitor-General to represent the Commonwealth. The court which heard the case was composed of six judges divided evenly: three for validity and three for invalidity. In such a case the view of the Chief Justice would normally prevail. Sir Owen Dixon CJ was among those who thought the provision invalid. But there were seven judges in office at the time and the court decided not to give judgment but to order that the matter be reargued. On the rehearing there was a majority for validity. The provision still stands as part of the Act: the subsequent marriage of the parents in all cases legitimises the child.

The Bill went through the House and the Senate without major incident. One member of the House, however, did ask me in a vigorous speech to provide that the bride and groom should put their fingerprints on the marriage certificate. This was for the purpose of personal identification. He had been a police officer and claimed to have had difficulty identifying the parties when bigamy was prosecuted. Indeed, the member had a point, because the identification of a person may become critical in such proceedings and personal identity is not always easy to prove. But I did not think I could adopt the suggestion. Fingerprinting is associated in the public mind with crime and in the context of marriage would have been regarded with aversion.

As well as I know, the Marriage Act has functioned successfully and has been accepted by the community, though I do think that as a people we have loosened the bonds which in its solemnity the marriage ceremony clerically performed formerly helped to forge.

11 Petrov, ASIO and the Crimes Act

In April 1954, Vladimir Petrov, Third Secretary in the Russian Embassy in Canberra, defected and sought asylum in Australia. His defection was induced by the Australian Security Intelligence Organisation (ASIO), aided by a medical doctor, Dr Bialoguski, because he was thought to be able to provide considerable information on the operation of Russian intelligence officers in Australia. In the outcome, Petrov furnished much more information on other countries than he did on Australia.

The Prime Minister was first informed of the defection by Brigadier Spry, the Director-General of ASIO, on Sunday, 3 April. Spry advised Menzies that it would be wise to have a Royal Commission to inquire into the degree to which the Russians had been engaged in espionage in Australia. Menzies accepted this advice and informed Parliament when it met the following week of the defection and the appointment of a Royal Commission. There had been a Russian defection in Canada earlier which had been followed by a Royal Commission into Russian activities in that country.

Petrov had defected without informing his wife of his intention. Upon learning of Petrov's defection, the staff of the Russian Embassy had taken his wife to the Embassy preliminary to her return to Russia. Petrov had been taken to a safe house under the protection of ASIO officers. In due course his wife was put on a BOAC airliner at a time when she was intending to go to Russia and not to stay in Australia. She was accompanied on the plane by armed guards.

When the plane reached Darwin it had to be serviced and refuelled, for which purpose all the passengers were taken into a passengers' lounge. ASIO managed to get a telephone conversation between Petrov and his wife while she was on the ground, as the result of which she decided to stay in Australia and seek asylum.

This change of plan was accompanied by dramatic incidents including the disarming of the Russian guards.

There was a general federal election afoot at the time. An incident such as the defection of a Russian intelligence officer needed sensitive handling. The Royal Commissioners were carefully chosen: Mr Justice William (Bill) Owen of New South Wales, Mr Justice Ligertwood of South Australia, and Mr Justice Philp of Queensland, all very experienced trial judges. They sat for preliminary hearings in Canberra soon after their appointment and then began taking evidence in Melbourne and later on in Sydney.

Two of Dr Evatt's staff were implicated by a document removed from the Russian Embassy and brought by Petrov to ASIO on his defection. Evatt, formerly Commonwealth Attorney-General and Minister for External Affairs, decided to appear in the Royal Commission for his staff. The Communist Party was represented by Edward Hill, a high official of that party and a barrister and solicitor in Victoria. The government appointed Mr Victor Windeyer KC (later a Justice of the High Court) and Mr Bernard Riley of the Sydney Bar to assist the Royal Commission.

I was in heavy practice at the time and learned of these events from the press accounts. In a general way I followed the progress of the Royal Commission, but I had had no contact with any of the people involved in the defection or the Royal Commission.

At the time of Petrov's defection McCarthyism was abroad in America. This posed a problem for the Commissioners, who were anxious that they should not appear to be tinged with McCarthyist witch-hunting, and it also affected the way the assisting counsel acted towards ASIO.

After the Commission had been in operation for some time, it held public sessions in Sydney. But when Petrov was disclosing security information, particularly when it concerned other countries, it held private sessions from which all but the witnesses and assisting counsel were excluded.

Without prior warning, Menzies asked me to call on him late one afternoon at the Hotel Australia. I found him very critical of the way in which Windeyer and Riley were performing. Like the Commissioners themselves, they adopted a very non-partisan stand, and Menzies felt that they were not adequately protecting ASIO's interests. He therefore asked me to accept a brief for ASIO.

I did not feel able to do so because I was very heavily engaged in court work and the Commission looked as though it would go on for some time. But Menzies pressed me very strongly, and ultimately persuaded me to accept. I had as my junior Mr Ray Reynolds, later Mr Justice Reynolds of the New South Wales Supreme Court. It took a great deal of work to bring myself up to date with the affairs of the Commission. There was already a voluminous transcript of evidence; interviews with the principal officers of ASIO were necessary and time-consuming. Also I had to rearrange a great deal of my work on hand.

Through my conferences with Brigadier Spry, his deputy Richards, and other ASIO officers, I acquired a good working knowledge of its operations but in particular of the Petrov operation which had triggered the Royal Commission. I found Spry to be energetic, imaginative and efficient; he was also alert and maintained a proper standard of integrity. Richards was thorough and efficient. Both men I thought were fully honest and carried out their tasks conscientiously and in a level-headed fashion.

The agent who had been principally engaged in the operation with Petrov, Dr Bialoguski, was a very capable person and behaved in the operation with considerable skill, indeed with a degree of panache. Subsequently he became well known in musical circles in London. During the course of the Commission I formed the view that he was not being adequately protected by the assisting counsel and took one or two steps to ensure that an unfair impression of him and about his part in the affair was not left uncorrected in the records.

As the Commission proceeded, therefore, I came to have a more active part in it, cross-examining people like the journalist Rupert Lockwood, fairly extensively. Here, the aloof stance of the Commissioners made my task almost impossible. I could bring the witness to the point where he could not avoid the final damaging answer but when he would not answer but stand uncomfortably mute the Commissioners would not exercise any compulsion to make him answer. For a cross-examining advocate this is most frustrating, and so it proved for me.

Fairly soon after I joined the proceedings, Dr Evatt came into conflict with the Commissioners for some of his public utterances. They decided to exclude him from the proceedings for what they considered to be his contemptuous behaviour. I felt at the time that Dr Evatt was unhinged. He was not fully in control of himself in what he said or did. He was labouring under a paranoid delusion that he had lost the Prime Ministership on the defeat of the Labor Party in the 1954 election because of the Petrov defection, which he claimed to have been a politically-contrived and conspiratorially-organised event.

I spoke to the Commissioners myself and suggested that Evatt not be excluded, but they were justifiably solicitous for the dignity and standing of the Royal Commission and were adamant. After that he sat on the solicitors' bench behind Mr Hill, prompting him and suggesting to him questions he should ask, particularly during the cross-examinations of Dr Bialoguski. Some of these questions were childish in the extreme and as I was sitting near Hill I could not fail to hear what Evatt was proposing.

Petrov had said that he met Madame Ollier of the French Embassy at a particular place in Queanbeyan on a particular day. The purpose of the meeting was to persuade her to reveal French secret codes. While she was for a time ambivalent about this, in the end she did not do so. She had returned to France by the time the Royal Commission was under way. Evatt claimed that she had been in some other place in New South Wales at the specified time and that the meeting was Petrov's invention. Evatt always made this alleged false statement of Petrov central to his attack on Petrov's credibility and the acceptability of his revelations. On her return to France Madame Ollier was the subject of official inquiry. She said in evidence that she did meet Petrov in Queanbeyan at the time and place he stated.

Later as Attorney-General, I tried to get the French authorities to release the depositions taken from Madame Ollier at this inquiry, but the French have always refused to let these papers become public. It may be that some later historian will obtain access to these depositions. The Royal Commission found Petrov truthful and accurate; confirmation of his account of the meeting with Madame Ollier would help that assessment.

The Commission's public hearings went on for many days and created a great deal of public attention. In Sydney the sittings were in the main courtroom of the old court at Darlinghurst, and the available public seating was almost invariably fully occupied. Although I found my work in the Commission very interesting, I did not feel that I had achieved a great deal. No doubt I secured the protection of ASIO according to my brief. I was glad, however, to return to general practice at its conclusion.

As Attorney-General I became closely associated with ASIO, although the organisation was strictly attached to the Prime Minister. I think all the contacts between the Prime Minister and the organisation were made through me and I made almost all decisions on any operations, subject of course to the Prime Minister's knowledge, which I constantly maintained; if need be he confirmed my decisions. I can understand Chifley entrusting the authority of the Director-General to a judge of a Supreme Court, though I do not think such an appointment helps the political independence of the judiciary. But in my case I thought that from the point of view of government it was an extremely risky thing to have an official not under immediate ministerial control deciding on the activities of a security organisation. Of course in this country, where government is expected to be open and subject to public scrutiny, such a body is likely to be adversely viewed and misstatements about it and its operations are only too likely. In the five years I was Attorney-General and in direct control with Brigadier Spry, I was ever conscious of the anomaly of an organisation, albeit properly under ministerial control, whose activities were shrouded by complete silence so far as the public is concerned. Yet I realised the practical necessity that this be so because of the very nature of its work.

The proceedings of the Royal Commission and its report left no room for doubt that the Russian Embassy in Australia had been promoting espionage and intrusion into the secrets of the Australian Government. In this activity they had sought to engage Australian citizens and they found some members of the Communist Party ready enough to assist them, that party being prone to subvert a democratic government. While those proceedings did not lead to any criminal charges, it alerted the Australian Government and the Australian people to the need to be watchful of such intelligence operations on the part of foreign governments in Australia and I think aided public acceptability of an organisation such as ASIO, particularly as it operated during the time of the Menzies Governments. Some of the suggestions of the Royal Commissioners led to my recasting of the Commonwealth Crimes Act.

* * * * *

Soon after my entry into the House of Representatives I noticed unanswered questions on the notice paper seeking information on telephone-tapping by ASIO. I realised that such questions ought not to be answered, but their reiteration on the notice paper, left unanswered, seemed to me a potential embarrassment to the Government and, in any case, an undesirable parliamentary phenomenon. As a backbencher there was little I could do about it. I had no desire to promote myself by speaking about it in the House.

I had and still hold firm views about the citizen's privacy, which should not be invaded except for the clearest need of national security or other compelling community considerations. Too often we hear of that privacy being broken, at times ruthlessly, by journalists who arrogate to themselves the attitudes of a Spanish inquisitor. Indeed, my views are so strong that, quite contrary to much current opinion, I would make it actionable to publish any false statement or insinuation of any kind whose publication causes injury, whether mental or material. The only defence should be that the defendant had taken all reasonable steps to verify the truth of the statement published and that there was public benefit in the knowledge of the facts. The onus of proving falsity would be on the plaintiff, the onus of proving truth or due inquiry and public benefit upon the defendant. This would not displace liability for defamation in which personal or corporate reputation was involved.

So I had reservations about giving ASIO the right to tap telephones. On the other hand, I accepted that there were elements in the community who were not only prepared but anxious to subvert our way of life, dividing us as a people and weakening the development of national unity. I accepted that these subversive efforts were organised and that they operated clandestinely.

I was therefore prepared to accept the need for an organisation like ASIO to keep tabs on such people as well as on any international spy in our midst. The problem was to devise a way of controlling ASIO's invasive activities. My own endeavours were aimed at finding the proper balance between maintaining individual privacy and protecting the community from the subversion of its institutions.

When I became Attorney-General and thus ministerially involved with ASIO, I asked Brigadier Spry how telephone interception was done and who had originally authorised it. I learnt that Prime Minister Chifley had inaugurated it and given the director of the security service the discretionary authority to do so.

The first director was Mr Justice Reed of the South Australian Supreme Court, so perhaps understandably Chifley was content to give him that discretion. The authority, however, had continued under Menzies, so that when I became involved, the director exercised an uncontrolled discretion to intercept telephones for security purposes. He appeared to be under no obligation to inform the Prime Minister or the Attorney-General of the identity of any person or body subject to telephone surveillance nor to give any report on this activity. As far as I could find, neither the Prime Minister nor the Attorney-General were in fact informed — certainly not as a matter of routine. I must say, however, that when I looked into the details of ASIO's phone-tapping it was clear to me that the director had acted very responsibly in deciding to intercept telephonic communication.

I took the opportunity when next in London to discuss telephone surveillance with the head of MI5. He strongly supported it and emphasised that it was indispensable in the work of a security service: it was essential to know who was talking to whom as well as the particulars of their conversations. I found him convincing. My subsequent experience of ASIO's work did not weaken this impression.

The English authorities took the view that telephone interception fell within the Royal Prerogative and needed no parliamentary authority. Their justification was that historically the access of the public to the Royal Courier Service, the predecessor to the Royal Mail, was given on terms that the Sovereign could open any mail, no doubt as a counter-measure to anti-Royalist plotting. So inspection of letters carried by the Royal Mail was taken to be within the Royal Prerogative — a view still held in Great Britain. The British extended this prerogative to communication by telephone, the telephone service being also provided by the executive government. I was not prepared to accept this view for Australia. I could see no logic or authority justifying the inclusion of telephone interception within the ambit of this Royal Prerogative, even if indeed that prerogative applied to our mail services. So I questioned the validity of ASIO's practice.

About this time I read an American book called *The Eavesdroppers* by Dash, Schwartz and Knowlton.[1] It alerted me to the possibilities of unregulated telephone interception. In America where telephones are installed by private companies, all forms of spying by telephone were practised by politicians, industrialists, businessmen and activists of one sort or another. Spying was carried on also by other undercover electronic devices over which, in Australia, the Commonwealth would probably have no legislative power. Much later I met Professor Samuel Dash and had some illuminating conversations with him. Indeed I have maintained a friendship with him.

Having formed the view that ASIO's phone-tapping should be controlled by legislation, and having ascertained how the tapping was done in the Postmaster-General's telephone system, I raised the matter with the Prime Minister. He was alarmed at the idea and immediately conjured up the political consequences of such statutory control. But the Government was presently at risk. It neither knew nor wished to know the extent or identity of any particular telephone interception. Yet it must take responsibility — and prominently in the Parliament — for what was being done, particularly if it were being done amiss. Suppose, I said, that some malevolent employee in the telephone service covertly slipped in a "bridge" between a citizen's line — particularly a prominent citizen's line — and that of ASIO and then contrived public knowledge of its existence. How would the Government rebut the suggestion of its complicity in this invasion of privacy? It would have no more than its own and, doubtfully, ASIO's denial. I pointed out that there were already questions on the notice paper relating to telephone interception which were unanswered. But they were a reminder of the difficulties of the situation.

The Prime Minister became impressed by my persistence and asked me how I would go about effecting statutory control. I said I would cast the legislation in the form of a prohibition, under criminal penalty, of phone-tapping except by ASIO, in that respect placed under the close supervision of the Attorney-General. I would inaugurate a recorded system of authorisation of ASIO, but I did not go into any detail. I had not then honed into anything like final form the detail of a system such as I subsequently established for granting a warrant for a telephone tap and for a report on its outcome. Menzies suggested that I prepare a paper for Cabinet along the lines I had indicated which, in principle, he would support.

In making this suggestion, I was not carrying out any request by ASIO, whose director showed no particular enthusiasm for my suggestion but offered no opposition to it.

I had to consider whether it was proper or advisable that the Attorney-General should be informed of the identifying factors of a telephone tap. Also, ought he to know of the results of the intercept? I was not anxious to be burdened with that knowledge. And I realised that some in my Department, in assisting me, might gain such knowledge. There was always the risk of a leak.

I concluded that there was really no alternative to me and perhaps some of my officers knowing the particulars of the phone taps. I had considered the possibility of giving a judge the authority to issue a warrant, but I rejected the idea because, in my view, a judge should not be given what is in fact an executive function unassociated with the exercise of judicial power. Also, it would probably be inevitable that the judge would have to work in secret in considering an application for a warrant. Security and judicial work do not comfortably mix. There was the possibility of selecting some retired service man of distinction and entrusting him with the task. But the public are sceptical of such a course and there would be the problem of succession as such an officer retired. But I thought the public would accept the representative nature of the Attorney-General's office and had in this, as in other matters, to take the political risk of the quality of the person holding office. The Attorney-General in the last resort is accountable to Parliament. So I opted for placing the responsibility of controlling this activity in the Attorney-General.

I prepared a Cabinet paper outlining the legislation, arguing its justification and asserting its philosophy. It was successfully argued before and adopted by Cabinet. By then the essential features of the proposed Bill had been worked out. It would forbid all telephone-tapping except by ASIO on the warrant of the Attorney-General. In contrast with today's experience, there were no leaks of my proposal and thus no media dramatics. The legislation went through the Legislation Committee of Cabinet and I promoted it in Parliament.

The Bill passed through both Chambers of Parliament with surprisingly little opposition and became law as the *Telephone Interception Act* 1958. It worked satisfactorily in my time in office and, though not having any information on the matter, I assume it still does.

I devised a very tight administrative control over the grant of a warrant to tap which required due reporting of its use. Whether or not the warrant was renewed, the director was required to destroy the tapes recording the intercept, except such part of them as was essentially relevant to the security work of the organisation. Thus non-security material was not kept nor was any record made of it. This may seem unnecessarily dramatic but I was anxious that the record be complete and, in the case of subsequent enquiry, available. Also, I needed to impress on ASIO the importance and unusual significance of allowing an interception.

I specified the kind of tape which must be used to record the intercept. Samuel Dash's book pointed out that the ordinary narrow tape, where the message is recorded longitudinally, readily lent itself to faking. Such a tape in the expert's hands could be cut and rearranged very quickly to convey a vastly different message from the one which had been recorded. There was available a wide tape where the message is recorded transversely. This was incapable of being falsified. Accordingly, I required it to be used.

I treated the control under the statute as personal to the Attorney-General in his capacity as the holder of an independent office. Thus I did not regard myself as under any obligation or, indeed, free to inform any of my colleagues, including the Prime Minister, of any particulars of any interception or even of the number of interceptions which had been made, or of anything learnt from them. I never did so. I should add as indicative of the attitude of my colleagues that none, including the Prime Minister, ever sought such information, and it goes without saying that no one, including the Prime Minister, ever asked or suggested that any telephone be tapped.

It will be apparent that even if few telephone interceptions were involved, my control of them under the scheme to which I rigidly adhered involved a good deal of work. It had all to be done personally: none of it was in any respect delegated.

During the preparation of the Bill I received quite pressing requests through Government channels from police for access to telephone tapping as a means of investigating crime. I consistently refused to expand the Bill to allow this. In the first place, I was not then convinced that police should be allowed to tap telephones, and second, to bring police interception under the necessary rigid control would have involved the Attorney-General in an overwhelming volume of work. Recently the question of telephone interception by police has arisen in public discussion. I have reached my own conclusions about this and would like to offer them here.

The libertarians would deny the propriety of any such interception. Their insistence upon an absolute right of "privacy" would deny the community the ability to protect itself either against subversion, even if internationally inspired, or against breach of the criminal law which the community has established. Probably, to be logical, they would oppose the principle I had adopted in statutory authorisation of phone-tapping for national security reasons. Of course, the description "national security" is both elastic and to a degree vague. The possibility of abuse tends to lend colour to the denigration of the reasons given for its justification. But then it is rare for human regulation to be absolutely beyond abuse. It seems to me, however, that the libertarians' extreme view of the complete inviolability of individual's privacy must in the end lead to anarchy.

I feel that the preservation of the community, its unity and its safety, is of paramount concern not merely to the community as a whole but to each individual member of it. The individual member derives his or her significance from that membership. However much the individual may become a recluse, he or she is inevitably and vitally dependent on the existence of the community and its security as a social manifestation. Just as there must be bounds to the claims of the community so there must be bounds to the claims of the individual. From the balance of these claims, a just society results. In their imbalance there is either tyranny or unacceptable instability, if not actual anarchy. The reference here to the community or its social manifestation is not a reference to the "state" as conceived by some political systems or some political dogma, but rather to the body of the citizens taken as an organised group expressing itself through social and political institutions. The government apparatus is basically no more than representative and has no separate claim to the possession of power or authority beyond that representative capacity.

If it is correct that crime — the activity of those who will not conform to accepted mores as expressed in the law — by its extent or persistence calls for action to contain it, then measures considered necessary by the community, though they call for some intrusion into individual privacy, must be accepted. I would now be prepared to accept that in the investigation of some major crimes a stage may be reached where knowledge of what a suspected individual or some person in likely association with him or her is saying to others or being told by others becomes essential.

* * * * *

In 1959 I was asked by Cabinet to prepare amendments to the Crimes Act to remedy defects in the law which had been exposed in the course of the Petrov Commission. When I studied the Commonwealth Crimes Act I realised that besides these defects there were considerable gaps in the Commonwealth criminal law and that because of this deficiency the Commonwealth might be called on to rely on State authorities to deal with certain crimes. State criminal law would be set in motion by the State Attorney-General; serious stalemates could arise if a State opposed what the Commonwealth wished to do.

I proposed to Cabinet that it authorise me to make a wider overhaul of the Crimes Act, which it did. In due course I produced a Bill which did not exceed any traditional bounds but which did furnish the Commonwealth with powers it had not so far had.

I tightened up the Official Secrets Act in one or two particulars in which I thought the existing provisions were markedly defective. I have never favoured leaks of government secrets or leaks in anticipation of government action. Those who leak confidential information and those who take the leaked information and use it for their own advantage are, I think, worthy of the contempt of their fellows. But I realise that a contrived leak is at times a course adopted by ministers, possibly as a way of sounding public reaction to some contemplated change. I had not myself used this device. I thought the government should be free to formulate its policy and action within the confines of its own government apparatus, however publicly accountable for its subsequent actions it might be.

The inclusion of the amendments of the law and perhaps in some sense inclusion of treason as a federal offence gave rise to opposition by a section of the public. The magazine *Quadrant* and one of its principal supporters, Sir John Latham, were quite conspicuous in public criticism of my Bill. However, I maintained the terms of the Bill.

In these days of increasing advertisement in the media, sensationalism and the publication of "exclusive" stories no doubt boosts circulation, and thus advertising rates and revenue. Because of the use of the byline, glamorous "exposures" promote the reputation of individual journalists. Because advertising by business is tax-deductible, the community partly pays for the advertising material with which we have now become so familiar, and which is indirectly encouraged by published speculations so often founded on leaks. Disloyalty in the public service is thus encouraged by a press seeking leaks. When to this is added the manoeuvres of party politics, the conduct of government business becomes increasingly difficult and time is taken up warding off attacks, often based on misrepresentations.

I strongly favour public discussion of matters under consideration by the government, and there is undoubtedly room for active journalists to point out relevant information. Reliable information is what the public needs. It can profit too from opinions, including the opinions of journalists. But it does not need and cannot really profit by comments disguised as statements of fact. My antipathy to leaks does not involve any repression of disclosure and discussion of facts otherwise obtained and verified. Nor does it involve any discouragement of public protest, though this can too often be grounded on misinformation. Unfortunately, recent experience suggests that even juries are unwilling to take a strict view of the illegality of such leaks, too often succumbing to the imagined benefit of public knowledge not otherwise available.

I had no difficulty in obtaining the approval of Cabinet to the Bill I ultimately produced, including the changes to the law on official secrets. But although I thought the Bill itself of no great significance I had a very torrid time steering it through the House, particularly through the committee stages. The Labor Opposition bridled at the tightening of the official secrets provision and at the criminal sanctions which the Bill provided, without any coherent conceptual reason for doing so.

I had a particularly difficult experience with the crime of treason. The Bill in this respect merely made the traditional crime a Commonwealth offence. This was challenged by the Opposition as reactionary and unnecessary. In considering this opposition, I included an occasion for bringing a charge of treason which, as things presently stood, the Commonwealth could only ask a State Attorney-General to prosecute. I thought such a situation lessened the dignity of the Commonwealth.

The Member for Eden Monaro, Allan Fraser, was seated at the table opposite me. When I was emphasising the need to protect Royal personages he interjected. I thought he said something to the effect that I should not worry about the Royal Family. I immediately repeated what I thought I had heard him say. I do not think I then fully realised how deeply the members of the Labor Party react to any suggestion of disloyalty to the Crown.

The reaction to my repeating what I thought Fraser had said brought pandemonium. The claim was that Fraser had not said what I had attributed to him. Gordon Freeth and Fred Osborne were both seated on the front bench immediately behind. Each of them claimed to have heard what I thought I had heard. When the *Hansard* "green" turned up next morning, it reported that Fraser had said "Don't hide behind the Royal Family." In the upshot, I made amends by appearing in the House that morning, though I stated my belief that I had said what I heard.

The debate on this Bill and its clauses was a very tiring one because feeling ran very high in the House. Towards its conclusion I felt singularly tired. I sat down at one stage with my head in my hands. Holt, always a kind man, came to the table and suggested that I leave the Chamber and rest awhile. I went out with him (not as has been said with Jack McEwen). The media said I was in tears. I certainly was very upset and had tears in my eyes.

This experience remained in my mind for some time. It brought home to me the delicate balance of blood sugars in my system. I realised that there were distinct limits to the amount of intense pressure I could handle: it was to form a factor in my later decision to quit politics.

Holt, as Leader of the House, had suggested to me at the outset of the committee stage that I should impose a guillotine, but I thought I would rather see a day's debating and at the end of that time decide whether the guillotine was necessary.

It was during the debate in committee that Mr Whitlam, who led the Opposition attack, called me a "bumptious little bastard". This was said at the start of a division, while Fred Chaney was acting Chairman of Committees. On the day he lacked self-control when he was not getting his own way, and vented his petulant displeasure. There was nothing that Chaney could have done about the incident.

But next morning the Speaker, Jack McLeay, attended by the Clerk of the House, asked me whether I was prepared to have Whitlam's outburst removed from the *Hansard* report. I agreed that in the interests of the House it could, but I asked that the "green" containing the outburst be retained in the records. This McLeay agreed to do.

On the second day of the debate in committee I did lay down a guillotine, and by its assistance, passed the Bill through the committee stage.

So far as my recollection goes, for all the noisy opposition to the Bill as it went through the House, there never has been any suggestion from a later government that any of the sections relating to official secrets introduced by me should be revised or deleted. The importance of having statutory offences should not be overlooked. The question is not whether there is present or expected need to enforce them. There is great deterrence in the very existence of the provisions themselves. In general citizens do not like performing illegal acts. The absence of relevant statutory provision can be an encouragement to the performance of acts which the community has need to proscribe.

12 Company Law and Trade Practices

One area of my work as Attorney-General was in company law and trade practices. Before I took the portfolio, there had been moves among the States for the drafting of a uniform Companies Act, that is to say, a Bill which each State could enact and thus bring uniformity to company law within the Commonwealth. The Commonwealth was not conceived as having power to pass a Companies Act, so the only path to uniformity was through State co-operation and State enactment of laws in identical terms.

The proposal was well ahead when I took office, but I participated in the final stage of the draft Bill. I would have wanted the State Attorneys to take a course somewhat opposed to the one they had decided to take. It concerned the doctrine of *ultra vires* and the content of the Articles of Association for a company with limited liability.

The invention of limited liability made an enormous contribution to the growth of commerce in the modern world. Without it, much of the enterprise which has taken place could not have happened. The risks of failure in the development of new techniques or the opening up of new areas of business are far too large to be taken on the shoulders of individuals, who would be personally responsible for all the liabilities which a failed enterprise might accumulate. Thus a corporation whose shareholders' liability is limited to a stated amount, usually the agreed amount of the contribution to the shareholding, enabled the assumption of many risks which otherwise could not have been contemplated.

A company with limited liability of its members drew its powers, apart from some statutory powers, from the terms of the articles of association, which stated the purposes for which the company was incorporated. Early on, the courts decided that acts of the company which did not properly fall within the scope of the objects stated in the articles were *ultra vires* — beyond the corporation's power — and therefore void. This was undoubtedly inconvenient for commerce and placed on the boards of directors and those dealing with the company the need to interpret the terms of the articles and confine the company's activities within the bounds of the articles as they were likely to be interpreted by the courts. The possibility of genuine error is obvious.

To get over this difficulty and to minimise the risks of an act of the company being held to be *ultra vires*, the draftsmen of articles began to insert more and more objects as objects of the company until in the long run the objects were stated with such width and generality that the corporation could safely do almost anything it wanted to do without running the risks of *ultra vires*.

This, of course, helped the conduct of commerce quite considerably, and quite justifiably, but it also produced the increasingly familiar phenomenon of the diversification of a corporation's activities, which now quite often include activities completely different from the basic reason for which the corporation had been formed and for which capital was provided by shareholders. Also, such diversification calls for managerial skills and other expertise beyond what the corporation's principal business would require. Much of this diversification takes place as a result of corporate takeover or merger.

I have spoken elsewhere of the need to control mergers to ensure they do not take place in circumstances inimical to the public interest. But here I would emphasise the effect on the corporation's shareholders of this process of diversification without reference to them. As things stand, the person who contributes capital to a corporation for the purpose of starting and running a brewery may find that his capital is ultimately deployed, directly or indirectly, in running a hardware store or a vineyard. Of course all the shareholders of corporations at any one time are not all original subscribers; they may have bought later but before this diversification.

To meet what I think is a situation which calls for attention, I would suggest that as between the board of directors and the company, the articles of association should be required to nominate the company's principal object and that the further articles be read as incidental only to that object and not in themselves substantive objects. The proposal is that the directors of the corporation be confined to acts which fairly fall within the scope of the principal objects or a purpose incidental to it.

So that the board of the corporation should not be embroiled in the uncertainties of language and its interpretation, provision can be made that an act which might honestly and fairly be thought to fall within the principal object or be incidental to it would be valid, although in point of law according to the view of the court it did not. Further, those dealing with the company would not be concerned with this limitation on the directors' powers. The doctrine of *ultra vires* would not apply to transactions with strangers, but the director would be responsible to the company for the consequences of any act outside the limited scope of the director's powers. Thus the commercial dealings of the company would not be at risk. Its adoption of such a legislation would mean that the board, if it wished to diversify, would have to consult its shareholders before any diversification was made.

But it was far too late for any attempt to completely revise the philosophy of the proposed Bill. The Attorneys virtually abandoned the doctrine of *ultra vires*. Consequently corporations appear now to be able to do anything they decide to do, and do so without frequently consulting their shareholders.

I remain of the view that both the public interest and that of the shareholders require some such limitation on the ability of a board to employ the company's funds in ventures not contemplated when they were furnished or their shares acquired.

But although not a party to the creation of the meetings of Attorneys-General, during my term of office I set up a Standing Committee of Attorneys-General designed to increase uniformity of State legislation, and used these meetings to produce uniformity in several departments of the law. In some instances, such attempts failed because a State enamoured of its own law was unwilling to vary it to secure uniformity. An endeavour was made to persuade the States to concur in the plan I developed to control restrictive practices, but ultimately Victorian officials put paid to that endeavour. Nonetheless some useful work was done by the Standing Committee.

* * * * *

My work on trade practices I regard as potentially some of the most important work I did, but it was frustrated in the end by the course of political events.

As I have already said, I am convinced that free enterprise based on individual initiative sustained by the rewards which enterprise and effort produce is much preferable to government planning of the economy. Planning along socialist lines is not only not conducive to the creation of wealth but it concentrates on its distribution. In the long run such planning is inimical to the creation of wealth and is likely to lead to stagnation. In any case, the modern economy cannot be successfully planned, if for no other reason that no human can know and provide for all the many elements which affect and control it.

Yet there always remains a need for government to express in tangible form the compassion of the community for those who for any reason are unable to provide for themselves the necessities and comforts of a civilised society.

I am also convinced that free enterprise essentially depends on effective competition. The human tendency to minimise the effort competition consistently demands is an all too common feature of the business community. This is also evident at times in the work force. Such a tendency results in stultifying practices which restrict competition and ultimately, if unchecked, produces monopolies, whether in goods, labour or services. Consequently I felt that some legislation was necessary to curtail restrictive practices and the tendency to monopolise. Ideally it should extend to the work force as well as to commerce and industry. The politician's problem is to restrict government intervention to what is reasonably necessary to protect free enterprise. But any tendency for government to plan or participate in business activities should be resisted.

Many in the Liberal Party and many people in business will not readily accept the kind of government intervention required by any attempt to regulate restrictive practices and monopolisation. But nonetheless, for the health of the economy, I felt that national government should attempt such control. So I tried to induce my colleagues to accept a legislative scheme of trade practices regulation. I was encouraged in this by some discussion in the community at that time about the impact of restrictive practices on the price and availability of goods and services. During 1959 I raised the matter with Menzies. After long discussion he agreed that I could make a study of the subject and prepare a proposal for consideration by Cabinet and the parliamentary party.

When in 1960 I attended the General Assembly of the United Nations in New York, I used the opportunity to examine American legislation and practices and also to visit Canada and Britain. To do the footwork I took with me Mr Richardson, an officer of my Department who was later to have a distinguished career as Professor of Law at the Australian National University, as an Australian ambassador and as a member of the Administrative Review Tribunal. He was a very competent and well-furnished lawyer and keen to work with me. I found him careful in the collection of material and level-headed in his judgments.

I did not care for the American method of control which imposed penalties on businessmen for infraction of the regime imposed by Congress. This law was necessarily expressed in universal terms, and often of ambiguous import. By its very nature, law on this subject was difficult to interpret and apply. It made illegal certain business activities described in the legislation in general terms, placing on business the need to form a judgment about the meaning and scope of the law on pain of a criminal penalty if an error of judgment were made. I also felt that the American system allowed the Justice Department too much opportunity to impel businessmen into making arrangements at times perhaps legally unnecessary but which were wise from a business point of view, given the great cost of litigation. I could see possible injustice arising from the departmental ability to apply such pressure. I believed that when litigation resulted, far too much time was taken up, both by the Justice Department in its investigations and by the courts in contested cases, in establishing exactly what was being done in business.

I also felt that the American legislation gave an incentive to those in business to shroud their activities with complexity, sometimes with make-believe, to keep the investigator at bay. The real question in considering restrictive practices is the impact on the community, economically and socially, of anti-competitive practices. In other words, the real question for examination and decision was what harm pursuit of the individual practices might do to the public.

I thought the American anti-trust legislation as it was administered was useful in preventing monopolisation and in reducing inordinate diversification by major corporations. My own philosophy favoured small business, where the relationship of employer and employee was likely to be close and to produce mutual trust, indispensable in a healthy and productive economy. I was not and am not prepared to concede that there are necessarily benefits to the community, or increased efficiency, from the so-called economies of scale. No doubt in some circumstances the nature of a product or the means of producing and marketing it will demand larger corporate participation. Through such corporations capital may be provided and efficient production and distribution secured. But where possible, small or medium-sized enterprises will be more satisfactory, both humanly and economically.

I formed much the same view of the Canadian legislation as I had of the American. On the other hand, I was favourably impressed with aspects of the United Kingdom legislation. I was able to discuss all this legislation and the manner of its operation with Richardson. In the end we devised a scheme of our own which I hoped would avoid what we thought were the objectionable features of the legislation we had studied.

I had concluded that not all restrictive trade practices were harmful to the free-enterprise system, or at any rate so harmful that they called for government interference. The real problem was to identify those features which, in their actual operation, were likely to be harmful to free enterprise or, in the language of legislation, to be against the public interest. The notion of the public interest, though lacking in precision, is broad enough to allow a competent tribunal to decide whether a particular practice should be proscribed as socially or economically harmful.

Though there is scarce any advantage in categorising one's philosophy, if it had to be done mine was in the order of modern liberal conservatism that says that governments should, by and large, keep out of business and allow competition to affect the price of goods and services and thus regulate the economy. But it allows a proper place for government intervention — not participation — in business by legislation which explicitly defines the occasion for intervention by duly constituted and independent authority. It may not be enough merely to maintain an even playing field. Restraint of the exuberance of the marketplace and tendencies to distort its operation must be part of government activity.

My proposal therefore placed the main emphasis on the public interest. But it was also designed to avoid costly investigative processes and to avoid involving business people committing possible illegality before harm to the public interest of what they were doing had been established.

The plan was to list a series of practices, broadly described, which were to be in one part of the list proscribed absolutely and in all circumstances and in the other part defined as being possibly but not necessarily harmful to the public interest. This latter group of practices would not be proscribed until found by a competent tribunal to be, in their own circumstances, harmful to the public interest. The plan then provided for disclosure by businesses that they followed or employed one or more of these secondly designated practices. This was not to require an unwieldy body of information but only a simple description of the nature of the practice which would satisfy the statutory descriptions. For example, if the business were selling its goods on terms that the buyer resold at a stated price or subject to some restrictive condition, the required information would simply be that the business followed the practice of retail price maintenance, with a statement of its essential nature. There was no call for elaborate detail. The information would be recorded on a register kept in the Attorney-General's Department, which I assumed would have the responsibility of administering the legislation. The register would be absolutely confidential, protected by severe penalties for disclosure. Having been registered, the disclosed practice could be continued without restriction or penalty until it was found by the appropriate tribunal to be harmful to the public interest. Thereafter, to carry it on was prohibited and attracted a criminal penalty. I could see no need to make business conduct criminal unless it were done in defiance of an order of a duly constituted tribunal.

The question for investigation would therefore be whether the actual practice as carried on was inimical to the public interest. I did not believe it could be said categorically of any of the practices described in the second list that they would necessarily be harmful to the public interest.

In order to ensure adequate disclosure of the restrictive practices, it was necessary to impose penalties for non-disclosure. The suggestion was that if the trader did not disclose that he carried on a described restrictive practice he would lose the right to assert later that the practice was not in fact harmful to the public interest.

This part of the scheme was not completely understood and caused considerable opposition. In retrospect, I think it would have been better to have been content to place heavy penalties, both monetary and custodial, on non-disclosure while retaining the trader's right to justify the practice as not harmful to the public interest. Had the drafting stage been reached, such a modification might well have been made.

Part of the scheme — in my view an important part — was the regulation of mergers. We had formed the view that some aggregations by merger were on the one hand steps towards monopoly, or at best moves towards a restriction of competition, and on the other hand tended to an inefficiency detrimental to the public interest. The latter feature, it seemed to me, stemmed from the inclusion under one management of a diversity of businesses lacking any homogeneous elements. Also, while there may be advantage in a large organisation, I thought that, on the whole, size was not in itself desirable. For one thing, stable industrial relations would be better promoted by the proximity to each other of management and workforce, something less likely in large enterprises.

So I felt at the time, and believe even more strongly today, that it would be wise to regulate mergers. Few have no disadvantage that calls for investigation and intervention. In fact, if some of the aggregated industries were today dismembered, I suspect that not only would they be more profitable in total than they are presently in their aggregated form, but their products might be better, their services more efficient and their industrial relations smoother.

The ease with which mergers can take place encourages a diversion of energy from the creation of goods and services, and the improvement of production, to a mere playing with paper, which provides easy gains for the individual but often harm for the community. Doubtless the formation of a judgment whether particular mergers are against the public interest requires a great deal of skill, experience and sensitivity. But such expertise exists and could be harnessed into the necessary tribunal to make such a judgment, not only efficiently but quickly and decisively — one thing to be avoided is protracted litigation and indecision.

* * * * *

In 1960-61 the Government found it necessary to impose credit restrictions in a too buoyant economy. This proved singularly unpopular with the business community. The effects of the credit squeeze were clearly reflected in the general elections which took place at the end of that year. The Government majority was cut to two. After providing a Speaker, there was a working majority of one.

By late 1960 Richardson and I had completed our thinking about this legislation and I was ready to enter the drafting stage. But while the Government was able to carry on, it was obviously inappropriate to launch trade practices legislation in the atmosphere which followed that general election, legislation which it was feared would further alienate the Government's traditional business supporters. Many of these people had voted against the Government to teach it a lesson rather than to overturn it. Political wisdom, however, required a pause in the development of trade practices regulation.

I discussed the matter with Menzies after the new Ministry was sworn in. He knew that I had worked out a scheme but I had yet to discuss its detail with him. While I indicated to him my own inclination that the Commonwealth could provide a useful Bill relying on its own constitutional power, I said that it might be wise, particularly in the post-electoral atmosphere, to seek to supplement the Commonwealth power by State co-operation in the passage of complementary legislation. I suggested that I take my proposed scheme to the Standing Committee of Attorneys-General. This would give the Government the necessary breathing space as the effect of the electoral setback passed. Also, if successful in securing State co-operation, any uncertainty about constitutional power would be removed. Menzies agreed. Accordingly, through 1962, I carried on negotiations for State co-operation through the meetings of the Standing Committee. But the delay placed me at considerable disadvantage in dealing with parliamentary questions and increased the Opposition's scepticism about my sincerity in suggesting the legislation.

The endeavour to obtain the support of the States for my scheme was ultimately frustrated, partly by the pressures brought by the business interests on State Governments, particularly the Victorian Government, and by the preference by the NSW Labor Government for public disclosure of the information provided under the scheme by business and recorded in the register. That Government was unwilling to accept the confidentiality of the register. No doubt there is virtue in public awareness of matters of public concern. I did not, however, favour using the fear of publicity as a weapon in the control of restrictive practices. I do not think those who engage in monopoly or trade practices ought to be regarded as common criminals. Granted that what they are doing may be against the public interest and a source of undue private gain, I still think the fear of public disclosure should not be used against them before their activities are independently considered and passed upon.

My scheme was outlined to Parliament in a ministerial statement made with Menzies' approval on 6 December 1962. It engendered a good deal of discussion and called for many explanations, particularly to traders who were fearful of its ramifications and were generally opposed to it. I made many speeches explaining it, impressing on my audiences the need for controlling restrictive practices harmful to the public interest if the system of free enterprise with maximum competition was to be maintained.

In retrospect, it can be said that in the long run my acceptance of the portfolio of External Affairs helped to set back the cause of rational trade practices legislation by many years. In 1963, after the general election, the Prime Minister was not prepared to have me continue as Attorney-General even for the short time it would take me to produce legislation on trade practices according to my scheme. The reason given was that I had been successful in External Affairs. The Government, he said, could not continue to receive criticism that I was only half an External Affairs minister, the rest of my time being devoted to the work of the Attorney-General.

When I asked him directly, the Prime Minister had no criticism of my work in either portfolio, but insisted that I must yield the attorney-generalship. I deeply regretted this decision, and I tried to persuade him to change it. I sought at least a six months' extension as Attorney-General to pilot my trade practices legislation. I said that no matter who he appointed Attorney-General in my place, "the tycoons will eat him up and spit him out". I said they had tried to do that to me and had not succeeded: I had maintained my ground. But the Prime Minister was adamant. I had to bow to the situation.

What has followed, I think, has been unfortunate. The legislation which my successor produced was inadequate. The present legislation, built to a large extent upon the American pattern, was produced by an Attorney-General who did not favour free enterprise but espoused socialist planning. Also, it is grounded on a very wide view of the Commonwealth's corporate power under the Constitution which may yet invite challenge. But that legislation notwithstanding, we have seen a growth of takeovers and diversifications dangerously financed on excessive borrowing, which has not only been harmful to the community as a whole but has injured the reputation and acceptance of sections of the commercial community, including the banking system itself. Perhaps the justification for the proposal to control mergers and to discourage diversification is much more evident.

13 The Snowy Mountains

My earliest contact with the high country of the Snowy Mountains was in 1929 when Norma and I on our honeymoon drove to the summit of Kosciusko in our small Fiat car. We also played golf on the nine-hole course in front of the Hotel Kosciusko.

Later, during a January vacation, Richard Webb (a lecturer in veterinary science at Sydney University) and I, accompanied by Jack Kenny of the New South Wales Bar, rode from the chalet across the Kosciusko summit and down Hannalls Spur from Mt Abbott into the Geehi Valley, passing out of the valley by the Geehi walls along a stock route into the Upper Murray Valley by Khancoban and up Bradley's Gap into Pretty Plain where we fished for trout for some days. We finally worked our way back to the chalet. This trip confirmed my own fondness for this alpine region and familiarised me with the condition of some of the higher levels of the New South Wales Alps. During other vacations I had fished for Murray Cod from a small power boat in the flooded Goodradigee above the Burrinjuck Dam.

Early in my practising days, I skied on occasions during July vacations in the Snowy Mountains. I joined a party based in Alpine Hut on Dead Horse Creek. From this base, we traversed the main range visiting the various shepherds' huts as well as skiing up Jagungal, known locally as the Big Bogong, at the northern end of the Range.

Before the Snowy Mountains Scheme was first mooted I was consulted by the New South Wales Government and asked to advise whether New South Wales could lawfully dam the Snowy, which flowed into and through Victoria to the sea. I advised that New South Wales could do so, provided it allowed enough water to pass into Victoria to service the Orbost flats on which I understood maize to be grown. It seemed that Victoria neither made, nor was likely to make, any other use of the waters of the Snowy. From my instructions there seemed little difficulty in New South Wales complying with this restriction. But the cost of the scheme proved to be daunting to the New South Wales Government.

Bill McKell, the Premier, had become interested in land conservation, and particularly of the high country, largely through the efforts of Sam Clayton, who became head of the State Department of Conservation, the inauguration of which McKell had supported. In 1944 the McKell Government set aside the whole alpine area as a national park to be known as the Kosciusko National Park. It was to be controlled by a trust comprised of the departmental heads or representatives of the Treasury, Lands, Conservation and Forestry Departments — along with two members of the public. McKell, who in some way had become aware of my interest in the high country, persuaded me to become one of those trustees. A journalist named Noel Roberts, with an interest in arachnology, was appointed the other non-departmental trustee. When I went skiing I would take the opportunity to make observations and inspections of interest to the trustees. There was no financial contribution to the cost of my visits to the snowfields, nor did I ever receive any payment for the performance of any duty for the Park Trust.

The Park Trust had the then unusual duty of repairing the damage done by overgrazing in the high country, particularly by sheep. In early days when snow leases of alpine areas were granted, the graziers who were the successful bidders tended to be large landholders and used the leases only as relief country on which to graze flocks when pasture on their holdings, because of seasonal condition, was low. So, while large flocks were at times agisted on the alps, the high country was not necessarily grazed every year, and then only for fairly brief periods and usually with little harm to the land and its grasses. But the grazing came to take place every year, and the number of sheep as compared to cattle increased. The result was serious depletion of the grassed areas.

The high country in its natural state contained many sphagnum bog areas. The sphagnum moss held vast quantities of water accumulated during winter, and the spring thaw released it very slowly as summer progressed. This storage and slow release was of considerable significance in maintaining the grazed areas, and the flow of the streams originating in the high country. Many graziers did not appreciate these functions of the bogs and used fires to dry them out. The restoration of these areas of sphagnum moss became an important part of the Trust's restoration work.

The Snowy Mountains Authority, through the fervour of its chief, William Hudson, soon required the removal of all stock throughout the whole area. On its own initiative the Trust first withdrew all stock from the higher altitudes, allowing grazing to continue, subject to the oversight of its rangers, in the lower country. When it began operating, the Trust had had to put up a few buildings to enable its work to be done. As far as possible it used the local granite as its building material and was able to carry out its construction work by its own employees without having to observe the lines of demarcation between trades obtaining in the closely settled areas. Thus the Trust's ability to carry out some of the necessary work was maximised.

The arrival of the Snowy Mountains Authority, however, put an end to that. Trade union leaders arrived with their insistence on observance of industrial demarcation lines. The Trust could no longer use their handyman employees but had to employ plumbers, electricians and other tradesmen to carry out its operations. As it did not have the funds to do this, its programme of construction had to be for the most part abandoned as such strict demarcation did not create jobs: it just destroyed them. The Trust felt obliged to yield to the Authority in withdrawing all stock from the area of the park, though in the view of its staff the grazing of stock, particularly cattle, in the lower areas and the presence of stockmen were beneficial.

With the departure of the graziers, an available workforce able to deal with vermin, both animal and vegetable, was withdrawn. There was no protective controlled burning, and wildfires caused by lightning strikes were fed by an increasingly dense undergrowth. On the other hand, grazing no longer occurred and to a degree erosion was reduced. Strong views are held by the conservationists on the one hand and the grazing interests on the other, the latter emphasising the lesser damage done by cattle as opposed to that which can be done by sheep.

As part of the process of restoring the high country and preparing it for the eventual arrival of tourists, the Park Trust at one stage examined the possibility of extending and deepening the pools in the streams flowing in many parts of the area. To this end I made a tour of the park, extending over some weeks, accompanied by a fresh-fisheries expert named Tubb. We examined many locations where we thought that by adding obstacles, such as rocks or tree trunks to these streams, larger and deeper pools might eventuate, thus improving the possibilities of fly fishing and the size of the trout with which many such streams abound.

In the course of this tour Tubb and I observed a large flat near the headwaters of Spencers Creek where there was a large shallow area of water which it seemed to us could be deepened by partially blocking the entry of the water into Spencers Creek. There were ample quantities of granite boulders in the vicinity which could readily be put in place to provide the barrage we contemplated. We thought the resulting lake would make an ideal locality for trout and thus provide a good area for fly fishermen.

Before recommending such a course, at Tubb's suggestion we consulted with the water authorities of the State telling them of our proposal. It was as well that we sought this advice. We were told that there was a geological fault in the area of Spencers Creek and that it would not be possible to hold water so as to form the lake we had in mind. This put an end to our proposal. This information formed part of my own equipment in dealing as a fellow member of Cabinet with a Snowy Mountains Authority proposal to dam Spencers Creek.

My duties as a trustee of the Park was one of the most pleasant experiences of my life. It not only brought me into touch with practical conservationists including my fellow trustees, but it also took me into this lovely countryside during summer, meeting the rangers and stockmen who were most interesting and knowledgeable about the high country. Riding on inspections mostly twice a year confirmed my fondness for the alpine climate and scenery. I mostly rode with Sam Clayton, as I have already described. Riding in the high country, in the summer, sometimes camping under the stars, was an experience which lives on fondly in my memory. Sam was a great conservationist of the useful kind. He was deeply principled, and adamant about the need to resuscitate and develop our land. I learnt much from him about soil and forest conservation, and came to respect his judgment in this area. I also rode with Baida Byles, a forrester and a grand character, particularly in the Alpine Ash areas of the mountains. I was pleased to hear, some time ago, that Sam Clayton had been awarded the McKell Medal for Conservation — indeed, the first to receive it. Sam died only recently, on the edge of ninety years of age.

When in 1958 Prime Minister Menzies offered me the post of Attorney-General and a seat in Cabinet, I discussed with him the retention or abandonment of activities in which I was then engaged. I agreed to resign from the Board of the Royal Prince Alfred Hospital, of which I had been a member since 1950, but expressed a desire to remain on the Board of the Royal New South Wales Institute for Deaf and Blind Children. This offered no difficulty. But the trusteeship of the Kosciusko National Park needed special consideration. I wished to retain it. But I pointed out that Senator Spooner, who would be a Cabinet colleague, was in charge of the Snowy Mountains Authority; that the respective activities and responsibilities of the Park Trust and the Authority could raise the possibility of a conflict of interest. Also, there was perhaps an anomaly in my being at the same time a State official and a federal Cabinet minister. After discussion, Menzies thought that I should retain the trusteeship and leave the possibility of conflict to await its arrival. So I remained a trustee and continued to perform my duties as such until I was appointed Chief Justice in 1964, in all a period of twenty years.

Ultimately the possibility of a conflict of interest did emerge. To supplement the storage capacity of the Guthega dam, the Authority decided to dam Spencers Creek. At some stage the fault of which Tubb and I had become aware came to the knowledge of the Authority. It was decided to freeze the bed of the dam by the use of electric power generated by use of the dam's storage. The frozen bed could retain the water stored by the dam and thus overcome the consequences of the geological fault. But the net yield of electricity would be considerably reduced. Indeed, I understood that the entire operation would increase the total wattage available from the whole scheme by no more than at best 5 per cent.

But if the Spencers Creek dam were built, its water would submerge the Edgeworth David Moraine, a unique geological feature named after its discoverer, Professor Edgeworth David. The Authority had to have Cabinet authority to build the dam. Senator Spooner initiated the discussion supporting the proposal. I disclosed my State interest as a trustee of the park and my strong opposition, both as a member of Cabinet and as a trustee, to what was proposed. Of course the dam would be an engineering triumph, but it would damage what today is included in "the environment". The possibilities of breakdown in the elaborate form of construction and the small net yield of electrical energy did not seem commensurate with the environmental cost. In the end the dam was not built.

A further involvement in the affairs of the Snowy Mountains Authority saw me on the other side as assisting in furthering one of its projects. In 1963 Senator Spooner asked me if I would join him in a negotiation with the New South Wales Government. He explained that under the agreements for the Snowy Mountain Scheme New South Wales had undertaken to build the last in a series of dams, which had to be built on New South Wales territory. The Authority was limited to the area of the Kosciusko State Park; its boundary fell short of the site for this dam.

Although New South Wales was bound to pay for the construction of the dam it was refusing to do so, partly because of lack of funds. Senator Spooner explained that the flow of the rivers in the Snowy Mountains area was insufficient to allow the generation of hydro-electricity for more than two hours a day, one hour in the morning and one in the evening, corresponding with peak demand in New South Wales and Victoria. But even with this very restricted generation of electricity, the water would have to be reused and could not be allowed to flow beyond the dam capacity of the scheme.

The truth was that the storage of water for irrigation and hydro-electricity were two inconsistent purposes, bearing in mind the terrain and the available supply of running water. The solution was to keep the last dam in the series (that to be built at Blowering on the Tumut River) empty so that the water used in generating electricity would be caught in the empty dam and later pumped back to higher levels by electricity generated at the seaboard. The scheme had already developed to the point where it was urgent that this last dam at Blowering be built. It would also give employment to the considerable group of technicians and skilled workmen which the Authority had built up, who would otherwise be disbanded.

The negotiation which was proposed was to secure the building of the dam and use the Snowy Mountains team rather than the State Public Works Department. Spooner explained that the Prime Minister was quite unlikely to agree to relieving the State of its obligation to build this dam out of its own funds. We could, however, offer to lend it the £11 million estimated as the cost, provided they would employ the Authority's team in its construction. He said that the negotiation must be very secret and no hint of it must reach Menzies.

This posed a problem. I was being asked to engage in an intrigue which was based on the need to keep the Prime Minister uninformed. The State Premier was unlikely to favour the proposal as he would be asked to bypass his own Minister for Public Works. But Spooner pressed on me the national importance of getting this dam built, otherwise the scheme on which so much had been spent could not be fully operated. The generation of electricity would need to be forgone completely. I decided to go along with the Senator and I accepted the personal risks it involved.

Negotiations took place over several weeks with the Premier, Jack Renshaw, and the Attorney-General, Reg Downing. Though our proposal involved them in difficulty with the Minister for Public Works, both Renshaw and Downing were men of goodwill and understood the urgency of building this dam. In the end we succeeded. New South Wales agreed to borrow £11 million from the Commonwealth and spend it on construction by the Snowy Mountains team.

The agreement had then to be ratified by Cabinet. At the meeting where Spooner introduced the proposal, there was immediate opposition from Menzies. Spooner was not the most adept at presenting the problem and he was having difficulty with Menzies; he also seemed unsure of the reactions of Cabinet members. Throughout his presentation I remained silent. All of a sudden Menzies said to me, "What do you think of this, Attorney?" I replied that I had been listening amazed — I did not know what the fuss was about. We wanted the dam built, we wanted our people to build it, the State was prepared to accept a loan of its cost and pay interest on it at the same rate that we would have to pay. The Snowy Scheme otherwise might not work. Why the opposition?

Menzies said, "You're in this, are you?", and of course he had smelt a rat. But nonetheless we carried the day and Cabinet ratified the agreement. The dam was built and the scheme began to work even though the extent of electricity-generation was extremely limited.

In retrospect, I have had much interest and pleasure from my association with the Snowy Mountains. I have taken part in the rehabilitation of its land area, in the return of pastures with the natural grasses, the redevelopment of the sphagnum moss bogs and the glorious summer wildflowers. As well as a Park Trustee I have played my part in the development of the Perisher Valley, Smiggins, and in so far as the Trust authorised it, in the development of Thredbo. To the extent I have mentioned, I have had a part in the use of its waters for land irrigation and electricity generation. I remain grateful to the McKell administration for the opportunities it provided over the twenty years I served as a Trustee.

Part III

Minister for External Affairs

14 Muscle Men and Portuguese Sailors

In the second half of 1959, when I had been Attorney-General for less than a year, Richard Casey, who was Minister for External Affairs (a name I prefer to Foreign Affairs because it is more comprehensive), was about to go to the General Assembly of the United Nations in New York. Casey and I had become friendly. He asked me would I look after his portfolio while he was away. I said that I would not because it might excite jealousy: I was new in the Cabinet and had already advanced quickly; I saw no need to exacerbate the situation I felt had been created. Casey expressed his disappointment.

The next day Menzies caught me up in a corridor and said Casey had told him of the conversation. He thought I was wrong. I had been accepted by the party and the Ministry; there was no jealousy about my promotion. Looking after Casey's Department would be good experience for me and he thought I should do it. I was conscious of the uneasy relationship between Menzies and Casey and wondered if the suggestion was related to this. But Menzies was quite definite in his reassurances. I decided to accept.

Looking back, I wonder if even then Menzies had me in mind for External Affairs. I had no ambitions in that direction, being fully involved in the legal matters of the Attorney-General's Department, and I gave no thought to what the future might hold. For the next three or four months I was acting Minister for External Affairs, making such ministerial decisions as came up.

The drafting of the Antarctic Treaty was one of the first tasks. The substance of the treaty had already been decided by international agreement but the detail had yet to be settled. It was a critical piece of work. I had quickly to immerse myself in the geography of the Antarctic. The standard globe rotates on a north-south axis and was useless for surveying the Antarctic Territory. I needed one that rotated also on the equatorial axis. Such could not be found in Australia and I had one flown out from London at my own expense; it is now in my son's possession. I found it extremely useful in the settlement of the draft treaty.

It was during this time that a decision had to be made on a resolution affecting South Africa's membership of the United Nations. Until this time Australia had been supportive of the resolution, as had Great Britain; but in consultation with the officers, I formed the view that Great Britain was likely at a later Assembly to drop its support. It seemed to me that we should prepare for such a change, which might come about without prior consultation. So I decided that on this occasion Australia should abstain.

The morning after the results of the resolution became known in Canberra, the phone rang and Menzies' voice said, "Is Casey tearing up our foreign policy, changing our vote on South Africa?" I was bound to say, "Casey didn't do that, I did". Before he could explode I added, "I'll tell you why I did it. I suspected the British Government might alter their vote and wanted to be in a good position to meet the change". This seemed to satisfy him but he said, "always remember we need friends and that calls for friendly loyalty". I could not disagree — we are a small and vulnerable people. But I was able to say that the South Africans knew of our intended vote and had no difficulty with what we had done. As it happened, the next year the British Government did change its vote, and Menzies said to me that we were fortunate to have changed our vote already.

* * * * *

In 1959 Richard Casey became Lord Casey of Berwick and went to Britain to sit in the House of Lords. I remember that this raised a certain legal question. One weekend when I was at our cottage at Bendalong, I received a message from Mrs Rowbotham's little bush post office that the Prime Minister wanted me to telephone him. Mrs Rowbotham's cottage was a quarter-mile's walk away. I tramped up the bush track, rang Menzies and asked him what he wanted. He said he had forgotten to ask me before I left Canberra whether Casey could be a member of the House of Representatives and a member of the House of Lords at the same time. Well, I must say I was a little put out at having to tramp through the bush to have this message because I was booked to be back in Canberra on the Monday afternoon. I said that as far as I remembered my law he could be both at once, but that I would verify it and see him on Monday. Indeed, the Constitution apparently contemplates that a minister in a State government might be a member of the Federal House because s 44 expressly precludes the minister's receipt of a salary as being a disqualification for being a member.

When Casey did finally resign from the House of Representatives Menzies asked me to accept External Affairs. I said I would be prepared to do so but only if I could also retain the attorney-generalship. I had much work going ahead in that portfolio and had no wish to relinquish it. Menzies said I would kill myself if I tried to handle both. So I declined, and Menzies carried the portfolio himself until the result of the 1961 election was known.

In September 1960 Menzies asked me if I would attend the UN General Assembly on his behalf. Norma and I went to New York where Jim Plimsoll, one of our great diplomats, was the Australian representative at the United Nations. We lived at his house on Second Avenue. Later, as Minister, I bought a well-placed apartment in Beekman Place on East River for our representative at the United Nations.

The 1960 General Assembly was notable for the attendance by the prime ministers or heads of state of a great number of countries. That year Khrushchev and other Eastern Bloc leaders attended the Assembly. I think the Americans were very apprehensive that some physical injury might be done to these people, so they closed First Avenue each morning when the Russians and other delegates were driving from their hotels to the Assembly. It was quite a spectacle, and in a sense amusing, to see a great motorcade travelling at tremendous speed to the United Nations building. The surface of First Avenue undulates, and steam from underground piping emerges here and there, giving the scene an evil and unearthly appearance. The Russians seemed to be moving at breakneck speed through intermittent clouds of wispy vapour.

At the rostrum each head of state took the opportunity to declaim his ideological viewpoint and to express himself highly critical of those who did not share his view. Rhetoric there was aplenty. Mr K, as we called Khrushchev, made a great speech, all of which unfortunately I did not hear. This was the occasion when he took his shoe off to use as a mallet on the rostrum.

South Africa's representative was its Foreign Minister. He made a very challenging and wide-ranging speech, accusing those who criticised apartheid of hypocrisy, forcefully describing the manner in which they segregated the indigenous people in their own countries. I remember him vehemently going round one country after another. Two that came in for particular attack were India and Japan. Towards the end of his speech Krishna Menon, Foreign Minister in Nehru's Government, moved from his place in the Assembly, came over to me and said, "You know, you are the worst of them all, the way you treat your Aboriginals, and the speaker hasn't mentioned you". I dismissed this, defending the Australian position, but of course I had no chance of convincing him. But the incident reinforced my own view that we ought to move at least to integrate the less than full-blood Aborigines into our community.

At each General Assembly it is customary for each delegation to give a reception to which it invites representatives of other delegations. One evening I was invited to a reception given by one of the African states. Outside the hotel I found the South African representative hesitating about going in because he had forgotten to bring his security pass. His real objection was that Mr K would be there with all his muscle men. But I persuaded him to come in with me and franked him in with my pass.

Inside we were greeted by the African representative dressed in his colourful Kenti cloth. He greeted the South African like a long-lost brother, but it was quite evident that he had not identified the man but was being affable on principle, and I said so. In the reception room we found Khrushchev surrounded by a press of people, with photographers taking flashlight shots. The South African and I sat at a small round table at the side of the room which had a lit candle on it. All of a sudden Mr K decided to leave. Krishna Menon, who always walked with a stick, was on the edge of the crowd. When it unexpectedly surged with Mr K, he was bumped, lost his balance and fell across our table. The candle was knocked over and went out, and candle grease spilt on the South African's clothes. I knew there was no love lost between him and Menon, but there followed a pretty lively altercation, each abusing the other vehemently. But soon it was overtaken by the enormous movement of people as Mr K went towards the exit door.

For our own reception, I informed Plimsoll that I wanted the Russians told I would not have any muscle men inside the reception room, and that I would not have any pressmen or any cameras admitted other than our own departmental photographers. As it turned out, Mr K did not attend because he was still listening, as the shadows fell, to an interminable speech by Fidel Castro. The evening passed pleasantly without incident.

The matter then agitating the General Assembly was the disturbances in the Congo. Dag Hammarskjöld, the UN Secretary-General, had taken an initiative in the affairs of the Congo and there were murmurings about it. I decided to make a contribution to the debate. I made a speech commending restraint and suggesting that the Congo should be allowed a time of calm in which to sort out its affairs without outside interference.

Each participating country makes a general speech in the Assembly surveying the international scene — a *tour d'horizen*. I booked a time to make such a speech on behalf of Australia. A day or so beforehand, I received a message that Menzies was coming to the General Assembly. There was no suggestion that I defer my speech but it seemed only proper that I should leave it to the Prime Minister to make when he arrived. When Menzies arrived we discussed the position reached in the General Assembly. He met a number of heads of state, among them Pakistan's Foreign Minister, Bhutto.

I was present at a conversation in which Bhutto put forward some views about India and Nehru which I thought unnecessarily provocative. But there was no time to discuss them with Menzies as he left immediately afterwards for Washington for the weekend. There he met President Eisenhower, Harold Macmillan, and Christian Herter, the US Secretary of State. Over the weekend the idea of proposing a resolution critical of India was developed and reduced to form. I gather that apart from Herter there were no officers present.

On the Monday morning I met Menzies at the United Nations before the day's proceedings opened. He produced a text of this proposed resolution, notice of which he said he wanted lodged straight away. I said that we could not put the resolution forward without first seeing what support it would have. Also, I saw difficulties and ramifications which needed discussion. Brian Hill, a departmental officer (later Ambassador to Vietnam), agreed that we should shop around for support. Menzies, however, went ahead and lodged the resolution, a move which proved disastrous. Nehru made a bitter attack on Australia and its Prime Minister.

The next evening I was to accompany Menzies to the theatre. Cables had come with news of harsh criticism of the Prime Minister in the Australian press. Menzies was badly affected. I remember that at the theatre he was very downcast, remarking to me that he felt desolated that his own people had been so critical of him. A lighter end to the evening was meeting Mary Martin, the lead actress, who was a friend of Menzies.

* * * * *

The 1961 election brought near disaster. We had imposed a credit squeeze to prevent the economy getting out of hand and this had displeased a great number of our own supporters, particularly people in business. For a time it looked as though we would have a hung Parliament.

By the Sunday midday I had made up my mind that we would lose office and went to my Attorney-General's office in Phillip Street and tidied up departmental affairs. Menzies rang and asked me to come to Canberra that evening to discuss how we would manage an evenly divided House. When I arrived, at about nine o'clock, I was greeted by Ray Coppin, my driver, with a brand-new ministerial car. (I had been putting up with an old Humber.)

"What a pal you are", I said. "Here I am about to lose office and you produce a new car".

"You won't lose office", said Ray. "Have you heard the latest information from Moreton?" Moreton was Jim Killen's seat. I said I had heard from Jim Killen almost every hour telling me he would win, but I didn't accept it.

I got in the car and we drove on towards the city. After a while Ray, who was a Roman Catholic, said, "If you don't win Moreton I'll throw my beads away". This was loyalty beyond the normal.

The next day I began some discussion with Menzies about how we would manage. We had little hope of luring a member of the Opposition into the Speaker's chair and thus having an extra voting member. But Killen did win Moreton, ironically on Communist Party preferences — Jim was an ardent anti-communist. This gave us a majority of two, a working majority of one after providing a Speaker.

In the succeeding months we carried on government as if we had a clear majority. The back bench not only behaved itself politically but actually looked after its health to ensure that no one was lost by death or illness. Arthur Calwell said to me once, "You chaps are governing as if you had a majority of twenty-five", and I agreed.

Once again Menzies asked me if I would take External Affairs. Again I said only if I could remain Attorney-General. He repeated that two portfolios would endanger my health and reminded me that times were very different from the days when Latham and Evatt had held both: each job was now far more demanding. I said I would accept if I were given two assistant ministers, one in each portfolio, to do the routine work under my direction. Menzies agreed to appoint Gordon Freeth, Minister for the Interior, to assist me in Attorney-General, and Senator John Gorton, Minister for the Navy, in External Affairs (later to be Prime Minister). Of the two, Gorton was headstrong. I had to tell him that he could not overrule the Department if there was a difference — something I could not risk.

* * * * *

So I became Minister for External Affairs. I inherited a bizarre case, the destiny of two Portuguese sailors who in that year had deserted from a Portuguese naval vessel in Port Darwin. They jumped ship but were apprehended as unlawful immigrants. Menzies had ordered their deportation to Portugal, where doubtless they would have been treated as deserters.

By the time of my appointment the local press had taken up the case. Journalists had become clamorous for their retention in Australia, asserting that if returned to Portugal under Salazar's dictatorship they would face torture and summary execution. The matter had considerable prominence in the daily press, and I as Minister got the flack. I remember that in one issue of an afternoon paper, the front page was wholly given to a photograph of my head and shoulders with the glaring caption: "This man has their lives in his hand". But I did not seek to shelter behind the fact that the direction to deport had been given by the Prime Minister and not by me, though I suppose that, had I been so minded, I could have countermanded his direction. But this I was not inclined to do. I thought that we owed it to a friendly power — Portugal is the oldest (and continuing) ally of Great Britain — to return to its custody deserting members of its defence force. I did not know precisely what Portuguese law provided in such a case. Salazar I knew to be a dictator but I was not prepared to accept the journalists' assertions as to the characteristics of his rule. But another factor entered in.

About this time, sixteen Malays who had illegally entered Australia several years earlier and had remained, as far as appeared, quite peaceably in the Northern Territory, were discovered and apprehended as illegal immigrants. Alexander Downer, the Minister for Immigration, ordered deportation. This I thought harsh and unnecessary. But Downer refused to yield to press pressure and the expressed views of some citizens. He had, however, voiced to me his strong disapproval of the proposed deportation of the Portuguese and now expressed the hope that I might see my way clear to allow them to remain.

For my part, I felt that, at the outset of my administration of my new portfolio, I could well do without the controversy and the press's suggestion of uncaring indifference to the fate of fellow humans. Nonetheless, had it not been for the fortuitous contretemps of the Malay immigrants, I do not believe I would have yielded to the pressures. But I saw in the situation a chance of leaving the Malays here at the price of allowing the Portuguese to remain. I formed a plan which came to successful fruition.

Portugal at this time was only represented in Australia by a consul. I arranged for him to call on me and told him that I wanted Salazar to tell me that he did not want the deserters returned to Portugal, that he had no objection to my allowing them to remain in Australia, notwithstanding their desertion. The Consul saw many objections and was disinclined to forward my message. I pointed out that the affair was being blown up by the Australian press to the disadvantage of Salazar and his regime. Deportation would give the journalists continuing opportunity to blackguard the Portuguese administration and Salazar personally. Also the situation was increasingly involving my own reputation. I pressed the Consul and finally persuaded him to pass on my message to Salazar. After some delay, there was success: a message from Salazar saying that he did not want the sailors returned to Portugal and had no objection to my allowing them to remain in Australia.

Now I sought an interview with Alexander Downer. I well remember the occasion. It was an evening when I had a formal dinner engagement in Canberra. The House was sitting and I had notified the Whip of my whereabouts for the evening. Before going to my flat in Northbourne Avenue to dress, I saw Downer, said I had a matter of ministerial interest to discuss with him and asked him to remain in his room in the House when it had risen for the day until I returned from dinner.

I returned to the House between midnight and 1 am. There was no one in sight and only the Minister's car and my own in front of the building. I repeated that I thought that Downer should not deport the Malays. They had been here a long time and as far as I knew had not misbehaved. I said I knew that he felt that the Portuguese should not be returned to Salazar. I said I had so far been unwilling to alter the Prime Minister's direction, but I had found grounds on which I could properly allow the Portuguese to remain. But in that event I would want him to allow the Malays to stay. We talked this over until about 3 am., when we reached agreement that there would be no deportation either way. I did tell Downer about the message from Salazar, but did not feel it necessary to say how I had got it.

When we parted outside the House and took to our cars there was neither person nor other car in sight. Next morning on the front terrace of the House a journalist approached me and said, "What were you and Mr Downer discussing last night after the House rose?" I told him it was none of his business and sent him off. Surely, the bricks of the House have eyes and ears!

After this nothing was heard of the Portuguese, but in 1968 one of them, Da Costa, came suddenly back into view. He was charged with the murder of his companion, Andreas Koklas, near the Barkly Highway, on or about 13 January 1968. Koklas had been battered to death by a heavy stone. His partly decomposed body was found on 13 February by two Aborigines. Da Costa pleaded not guilty but was found guilty by a jury. He sought from the High Court leave to appeal on the ground that there had been an irregularity in the reception of the evidence of the Aborigine.

After lengthy denials to the police, Da Costa ultimately admitted killing Koklas after a dispute about sharing the expenses of a car journey. He had called Koklas, as a Greek, a "money-hungry bastard" and there had been a fight. He had thrown a large stone at him and when Koklas did not get up had covered him with leaves and driven off. He had sold Koklas's watch and transistor radio and later tried to draw money from his bank account. It was this that had set the police on his trail. He admitted:

> We had an argument on the Barkly. I did not know that he was dead. I just panicked and shot off. I will never forget what he said to me. I did not want to kill anybody. Andreas and I were friends and I just panicked. I am sorry to have wasted your time. I should have known better. I should have told you before. I suppose my life is finished now. There is no need to talk about it. You know all about it.

The appeal, naturally, was rejected. All this was a strange but remote outcome of the decision to allow the Portuguese sailors to remain in Australia. Perhaps one might wonder whether or not their return to Portugal might not have been so bad a course to pursue.

15 West New Guinea Indonesia and Malaysia

My first ministerial involvement with the problem of West New Guinea (Irian Jaya) was in 1958 at my first attendance in Cabinet, where in answer to an enquiry by the Prime Minister I said it would be foolish to support Dutch colonialism there.

My contemplation of what our policy should be in relation to Indonesia continued while I was acting Minister for External Affairs. I discussed the matter with departmental officers, and at the UN General Assembly I talked with officials of Indonesia and other South East Asian countries. But I had as yet no specific ministerial responsibility for our policy on West New Guinea.

In 1960 I was due to return from London after having argued the *Dennis Hotels* case[1] before the Privy Council. When the case finished sooner than expected, Menzies asked me to come home through parts of Asia and South East Asia in a leisurely fashion, taking the opportunity to find out what the leaders in those countries were thinking about Soekarno and his claim to West New Guinea.

My first call was Karachi. I had the pleasure of sailing on Karachi Harbour with Roden Cutler, the Australian High Commissioner to Pakistan and later Governor of New South Wales. The tremendous courage of this man is attested by his Victoria Cross. He had a leg amputated as a result of war injuries, but this did not stop him sailing. In Karachi he entered his boat down a very hazardous set of wet and slimy steps. I must say I admired his performance.

My discussion with Cutler about local political affairs had prepared me for my interview with Ayub Khan, the Pakistan President, his ministers and other political leaders.

Khan was a striking figure, a soldier and a military dictator, but I felt that according to his country's standards and state of development he was benign in his administration. He seemed genuinely anxious to return to a representative form of government, though he did not favour the direct election of parliamentary representatives, preferring a collegiate model. He thought by this means to avoid the election of the old politicians whom he said had corrupted earlier governments.

About West New Guinea he thought that the Indonesians ought to have the whole of the territories which had formed the Dutch colony if they were to feel that their revolution was complete and that they had secured full independence from the former colonial power. Possession of the whole of this territory might help international perception of their independence, particularly among the Asian countries. I was to find this perception the prevailing one among the heads of departments to whom I talked.

Like the other leaders, Khan had reservations about Soekarno personally and was suspicious of his relationship with the Communists and the Eastern powers, but he thought that a considerable number of Indonesians had a strong desire for the control of West New Guinea and that it was not simply a political ploy of Soekarno's. He thought Soekarno had neither the drive nor the capacity to expand Indonesian territory beyond the bounds of the former Dutch colony. Although he expressed this view with some reservations, for want of fuller information, he accepted that any change in the status of West New Guinea must come by agreement between the Dutch and the Indonesian governments, certainly not by armed incursion or military threat. He was uncertain of Dutch motives in wishing to retain West New Guinea, and he placed no emphasis on self-determination for the indigenous people.

In Delhi, as in all the Asian cities I visited, I was not only well received but given much hospitality. I met Nehru and his daughter, Mrs Gandhi, and a large number of ministers, politicians and officials. There was a good deal of frank discussion, not only about Indonesia and West New Guinea but generally about India-Australia relations. Nehru was predictably anti-colonial. He had been consumed by the struggle for Indian independence and I felt that his views were coloured and that any continuance of Dutch colonialism in West New Guinea was in his view unthinkable. He seemed to realise the ethnic difference between the people of West New Guinea and the various people of the Indonesian archipelago, but this did not seem to alter his views. He did not seem to me to give much weight to self-determination for the Papuans or to give much credence to the Dutch claim to protect the indigenous people. In fact I found a striking lack of concern about the rights of indigenous people in all these discussions with Asian leaders. It made me wonder whether this is a peculiarly Western concern.

I put to Nehru the possibility that Soekarno would not be content with the acquisition of West New Guinea but would have designs on further territories. He did not seem to accept this as a real possibility but I felt that his judgment may have been affected by his anti-colonialism and possibly by some personal relationship with Soekarno — after all, they were fellow revolutionaries. He certainly expressed no antagonism to him, nor did I notice any distrust. I did get the impression that Nehru thought there was substantial support among informed Indonesians for the territorial claim.

I had a string of discussions with Nehru's Foreign Minister and his Treasurer, as well as with other ministers and public servants. None saw any room for continuing Dutch colonialism. Differing views were expressed about Soekarno personally and about his motives and the possibility of an expansionist drive. My impression was that he was regarded more as a rabble-rouser than a statesman and that the Indian ministers were not confident about his future direction and in particular his relationship with the Communist Bloc.

My next port of call was Kuala Lumpur where Tom Critchley was in post. His residence faced a golf course where he quite often partnered the Tunku, Abdul Rahman, so he was able to introduce me informally. Tom had been Ambassador to Indonesia and was conversant with those in authority there and with conditions generally. He favoured a warmer relationship between Australia and Indonesia, and a friendly approach to resolve the future of West New Guinea, thinking there was merit in the Indonesians' claim to the territory.

Like Khan, the Tunku and his ministers had no enthusiasm for Soekarno personally and much suspicion about his motives in relation to West New Guinea, but they had some sympathy for the view that Indonesian independence needed possession of the entire Dutch territory. There were some reservations about the possibility of Indonesian expansionist intentions, but Indonesia's logistical incapacity was thought to make any further territorial claim unlikely.

In all these opinions the prevailing anti-colonial sentiment possibly accounted for much of the support given to the Indonesian claim. On the other hand, Indonesia was a near neighbour and the relationship between the two countries was by no means settled. I felt the Tunku did not account Soekarno as any better than a rabid nationalist and as quite possibly an ally of the communist powers. This view was reflected in the cautious terms he used in supporting Indonesia's claim to West New Guinea. The confrontation of 1963 had yet to develop. But in the meantime the Tunku was obviously very wary, particularly as he felt Soekarno to be quite unpredictable. But again, no one wanted military activity in the area.

In Singapore Mr Jockel, the Australian High Commissioner, arranged an interview with Lee Kuan Yew, mainly on the footing that I was Attorney-General and a fellow lawyer. Lee had at this time no soft spot for Australians; indeed I doubt if he had met Menzies or received Casey. But I got on very well with him. As our relationship warmed, he gave me his forthright views on the communist problem, the workings of the Soviet Bloc and relations between Australia and Asia. I talked very comfortably with Lee not only because we were both lawyers but because we were both Anglophiles and had come to realise that socialism is not the answer to the attainment of human happiness. I thought him wise, logical in his reasoning and moderate in his statements. He was fortunate in having a vigorous Chinese population willing to work in a regime depending upon a high degree of self-reliance. Lee took much the same view of Soekarno and the West New Guinea question as the people I had already seen.

My interview with Lee was the beginning of a friendly relationship which has lasted throughout the intervening years. I have come to respect him and his judgment much more as time has gone by. His success in creating wealth for Singapore has been outstanding, given that there is an autocratic element in his government. He has been more interested in creating wealth than in trying to redistribute it before it is made, something some of our politicians here have tried to do.

I remember asking the British agent in Singapore during this visit what was the level of unemployment in Singapore. He said there was none.

"Surely", I said, "that's nonsense".

"Not at all. If a Chinese loses his job, next morning he will sit on the kerb with a banana leaf and a couple of bananas — he is in business. He will do something for himself straight away."

I remember thinking to myself, the day Australia adopts that attitude, we will really take off.

In Jakarta, besides a long interview with President Soekarno which Dr Subandrio attended, I met and had discussions with Abdul Nasution, Ruslan Abdulgani, Dr Johannes Leimena and others. I constantly searched for the motivation of the West New Guinea claim and for any indication of territorial expansionism. I also watched for any communist association. All of those with whom there were discussions were ardent nationalists. All had had a part in the revolution; some, like Abdulgani, bore evidence of having been tortured.

The Communists strongly supported that nationalism and were likely to seek a part in the national revolution. Some leaders, like Nasution, openly disclaimed any friendship with or countenance of the Communists; others were prepared to use them in support of their nationalistic aims. One continually sought to ascertain whether Soekarno had identified himself with them and their doctrines. I found this a confusing area; the lines between an understandable nationalism and a subversive communism were quite blurred, the more so when the nationalists were not always careful themselves to draw a dividing line. Perhaps in the exigencies of the situation that ambivalence was seen as necessary among the group of ministers, which included both Moslems and Christians. Leimena and Nasution I understood to be Christians. Soekarno was a Moslem. (The cap he always wore may have been as much to hide his baldness as to declare his religion.) Though the discussions were usually frank I felt that our Anglo-Saxon ways and values tended to arouse suspicion and at times incredulity on the part of the Indonesian leaders.

Of course, all the ministers had strong views about the Dutch. The revolution was too recent for the inevitable bitterness of such a conflict to have subsided. They were clearly unable as yet to deal objectively with the Dutch; in their minds what they sought could only be obtained by revolutionary violence.

Soekarno was a powerful public speaker, able to rouse his audience to a high pitch of excitement, an intense nationalist, prepared in promoting that nationalism to co-operate with the Communists and to make compromises with them. He was prepared to threaten violence and even engage in warfare, expecting thereby to wear down his Dutch opponents. I doubt if he paid much attention to Australian attitudes, though by pressing them on him in personal conversation I felt I had made a mark. But allowing for the need for strong action to reach his goals, he had done well for Indonesia. For one thing, he had given them a national language, Bahasa Malay, an achievement for which I think he can claim historical recognition. I thought him devious and unpredictable, perhaps because he did not have a sufficiently confident grasp of economics. Administration was not his forte and he no longer had the services of Hatta. For perhaps the same reason, he was stubborn, preferring to stand on his asserted position rather than argue its acceptability. He was vain and perhaps unduly appreciative of the physical advantages which his position provided him. I met Hartini in his presence. She was undoubtedly an outstandingly beautiful woman. He was evidently a willing victim of such beauty.

I had the benefit of our military assessments from which I concluded that neither the Indonesians nor the Dutch had the logistical capacity to support organised military operations in West New Guinea. Australia had no territorial claims in the region though its responsibility for the security of Papua New Guinea could possibly call for the exercise of military force. It was important that there should be no such conflict close to our shores; we would not welcome the creation of a running sore affecting our nearest neighbours. Overall it seemed to me that Australia had every reason to see the differences over West New Guinea peaceably settled. I saw no possibility of a peaceful settlement under which Indonesia abandoned its claim to the territory.

So I returned to Australia and reported to the Prime Minister. Later, at the General Assembly in New York, I met Dr Joseph Luns, the Netherlands Foreign Minister. I had quite a few discussions with him, not specifically about West New Guinea but generally about Dutch relations with Indonesia and Australia. He was very forthright about his government's unwillingness to yield to the threat of force and its intention to retain West New Guinea, but I nonetheless formed the impression that if pressed, the Dutch would negotiate on West New Guinea, making some reservation as to self-determination for the local people.

One other circumstance had a quite powerful influence on my thinking about West New Guinea, beginning while I was only Attorney-General. Pat Shaw, the Australian Ambassador in Indonesia, was a fervent advocate of closer relations between the two nations. He saw the logic of Indonesia's claim to West New

Guinea and persisted in trying to persuade the government to take a more favourable view of Indonesians and not encourage the Dutch to resist their claim. Each time Pat Shaw came to Australia he made it his business to call on me, although I was not the responsible minister.

Pat was an enthusiast and expressed himself quite strongly. I realised early that in dealing with departmental officers who are or have recently been in post abroad one should be cautious in considering their recommendations, particularly if they contain any emotional content. Quite rightly the officers become immersed in the local affairs of their post. They have a primary duty to report on them objectively, but there is a natural tendency to develop an understanding of, if not sympathy with, local sentiment in areas of international controversy.

I had found Tom Critchley very well informed on Indonesian local affairs and attitudes. He also thought that our relations with Indonesia should be softened. Perhaps I found Critchley more objective in his conclusions than Shaw; he seemed to have his feet very firmly on the ground, and I came to respect his assessment and was grateful for his help. The same came to be true of my relations with Pat Shaw. He was absolutely sincere, honest and, though enthusiastic, perfectly rational. In the end I was very much influenced by what he recommended. Apart from Pat Shaw's views, I also became aware that Jones, the American Ambassador in Jakarta, insisted on the need for his country to adopt a more friendly and supportive attitude towards Indonesia.

* * * * *

Through 1960 and 1961 I observed the attitudes of my colleagues in Cabinet, watching for any softening towards Indonesia and its leaders. I knew from the dispatches I read when acting Minister the sort of reports the External Affairs Department was receiving from Jakarta. Our traditional attachment to the Netherlands, and a distrust of Soekarno and Subandrio as having communist links, prevented Australians accepting Indonesia's claim that it merely wanted to round off its independence. Over this period I think I became more inclined to give credence to the Indonesians for having no territorial ambitions beyond West New Guinea. They already had a great deal of territory, thousands of islands of which only about 3000 were inhabited and even those, with the exception of Java, were very sparsely populated. So the acquisition of more territory could scarcely be regarded as a solution for population density in Java, even allowing for the fact that the Javanese were unwilling to live elsewhere, even in Sumatra. But of course national aspirations are not always logical. And the Indonesians were not then making any move to oust the Portuguese from Timor.

I also explored in my own mind what motives the Dutch could have for wanting to remain in West New Guinea. Once Indonesia had been given independence I could not see any economic reason for the Dutch wanting to maintain a colony there, dissociated from Indonesia and its resources. There was talk of granting self-determination, but I questioned Dutch sincerity in this: from the Dutch point of view an independent West New Guinea was likely to make financial demands on the former colonial power. But the possibility that they would grant self-determination did exist. I concluded that the Dutch attitude was based on little more than a sense of national pride in not wishing to give in to their former colonists, particularly under the threat of force.

I also realised that the Dutch were in no position to maintain their situation in West New Guinea indefinitely. They had been refused military overflight both by the American and Australian administrations. They could no longer rely on the United Kingdom for any logistic support.

Self-determination as a principle lingered very strongly with the Australian Government and particularly with part of the back bench; I heard continuing talk of freedom of choice for the people of West New Guinea. The idea of an independent West New Guinea beside an independent and antagonistic Indonesia on the one side, and on the other a Papua New Guinea which might soon hope to be independent, called for close thought. What would be the consequences for Australia of an independent West New Guinea? As far as I could see, such a state would not be economically viable, certainly not in the short term. And I doubted if the indigenous population had a national consensus which could lead to national unity and a stable administration.

To set up such a state in the face of Indonesian opposition might be a provocation to military action. It could endanger international stability in the area. From the Australian point of view, this would be most unwelcome; in a conflict between Indonesia and an independent West New Guinea, we might find ourselves involved even to the point of military intervention. Of course similar consequences could possibly arise out of an Indonesian province of West Irian in conflict with Papua New Guinea.

From the point of view of an Indonesian administration, the existence of an economically weak and perhaps politically unstable state to its north-east would at the least create tension and at worst armed conflict. I could not see Indonesians accepting such a creation without making an armed attempt to prevent or overturn it. Neither could I see any advantage in it for Australia. So from these various points of view, the idea of self-determination was neither practicable nor desirable.

So far as Papua New Guinea was concerned, any change in the status of West New Guinea was likely to create problems. And there were ethnic and tribal differences to be considered. So here again, it seemed there was no Australian national interest in supporting an independent West New Guinea. Though an Indonesian-controlled West New Guinea might pose like problems for us, on balance Indonesian control seemed the more likely to produce stability in the area, and in any case avoid armed conflict.

But in the climate of the times, Australia would be bound to favour the principle of self-determination and publicly to express support for it. So

Indonesia's claim must be approached with that principle as part of any resolution of the problem. My personal views, if publicly expressed, were bound to be dubbed appeasement, a politically powerful description at the time. Later, when I did express myself publicly, I was said to be merely an appeaser.

So far I had no ministerial responsibility in the matter, though I shared responsibility for the Cabinet's attitude and policy. Acceptance of the portfolio in 1961 altered all this. I had now to propose the policy for the future.

By January 1962 I felt I had a fair appreciation of the attitudes of some of the countries of Asia and South East Asia and had made a reasonable assessment of the West New Guinea problem from Australia's point of view. Menzies' longstanding attitudes towards change, towards developing countries in general and Asians in particular, added to our traditional associations with Europe, would make it difficult for him to change course. I did not think his years as Foreign Minister had markedly weakened these influences. But I had great respect for his capacity to accept rational argument.

When I took on the full responsibilities of External Affairs in 1961 I started with the advantage of Menzies' statement on the occasion of Dr Subandrio's visit. The government had publicly affirmed that Australia, though not a principal party to the dispute over West New Guinea, would accept any resolution of it which the principal parties reached by voluntary negotiations, not under the threat or use of force. This was a considerable step forward and an encouragement to the parties to negotiate their differences. It was certainly a base on which I could hope to build. So in deciding to attempt the modification of Australian policy towards the Indonesian claim and indeed towards Indonesia itself, I felt that in the long run I could induce Menzies' support. With it I thought I could carry the day. Some of the back bench were openly and implacably opposed but not, I thought, the majority.

As the time approached for making a Cabinet submission which I hoped would lay the ground for a radical change of policy, I had a number of discussions with Sir Arthur Tange and other External Affairs officers. The departmental submission to the Cabinet was to set out in full the course of the dispute and the government's attitudes and policies. When it had been developed to my satisfaction it was long and comprehensive. But I felt compelled to write a memorandum to supplement it, not because of any deficiency in what Tange and his officers had prepared but out of my own need to reshape policy and to express in my own words the attitude at which I had arrived, after much thought. I could not have expected the officers to put forward these views as the views of the department.

My personal memorandum was built upon five main points:

- the avoidance of armed conflict in the region;
- adherence to the principle of self-determination;

- the desirability of developing friendly and co-operative relations with Indonesia;
- the promotion of negotiation between the principal parties to reach a peaceful solution;
- withdrawal of support of Dutch administration and acceptance of Indonesian control of the territory, if that resulted from an agreement between the parties.

My memorandum, which I read to the Cabinet, has recently been released from the Archives. A facsimile copy is in Appendix III. It pointed out that the Government had for some time been following two opposed policies on West New Guinea. It had supported the maintenance of Dutch sovereignty and had collaborated with the Dutch in the administration of New Guinea, with the purpose of excluding Indonesia from any control of this territory. At the same time it had had a policy of advancing friendly relations with Indonesia. With the development of the Dutch-Indonesian dispute over West New Guinea the clash between these policies became apparent.

It discussed the reasons for giving priority to the first policy: the strategic value to Australia of a European occupation of West New Guinea; alarm that Indonesia might become dominated by Communists and attach itself to the Soviet Bloc; and insistence on the principle of self-determination of West New Guinea. I emphasised some of the disadvantages of continuing a Dutch administration: the revolutionary elements which had produced the independence of other parts of the former colony were likely to be a cause of instability in the region; support of the Dutch was unlikely to promote good relations with Indonesia; the Dutch presence was in any case likely to be temporary; an independent West New Guinea was unlikely to be economically and politically stable, and being incapable of defending itself would be a standing provocation to Indonesian military assault; the Indonesians had sought Soviet aid and might well receive it.

Our present policy must really be grounded on the view that there was no Indonesian national sentiment for the possession of West New Guinea but only a desire on the part of Soekarno as a distraction from the state of the Indonesian economy. But very many informed Indonesians felt that the possession of West New Guinea was necessary to complete their wresting of independence from the Dutch.

My substantial proposal was that we withdraw our support of the Dutch, accept a transfer by peaceful agreement of the territory to the Indonesians provided they accepted an obligation to afford self-determination to the indigenous people. I did not propose that we initiate discussions between the parties to this end but that we encourage a major power to do so with our support.

I read the memorandum to Cabinet on 12 January 1962. By then my colleagues had had time to read the departmental submission, so both documents were aired. John McEwen said that what I had read made the best sense he had so far heard on the matter. Other ministers expressed diverse views, some adhering to the existing policies, others inclined to make a departure and accept my proposal for solution.

If Indonesia's claim was but a precursor to an expansionist policy which would place Papua New Guinea at risk, there would be considerable force in the view that it would be better to "put the plug in" now rather than later. This aspect of the matter was put forward by some in the Liberal Party and had had its place in my own thinking.

Though my paper made an impact, Cabinet remained divided. The result was an adherence to existing positions while giving an added emphasis to maintaining Indonesian friendship as an article of Australia's long-term interest. The decision was as follows:

> The Cabinet considered the particular question posed by the Minister in his memorandum concerning action by Australia to influence the course of negotiations between Indonesia and the Netherlands, but concluded that initiative on the part of Australia was unnecessary and inappropriate. It decided that it would leave to the Prime Minister and the Minister for External Affairs, both being in possession of the mind of Cabinet, the matter of communicating Australia's views to other governments as necessary. Cabinet expressed the view that in whatever messages are sent to the British and American Governments, consideration should be given to including strong expressions bearing on the enduring importance to the western world of the principle of strength in the face of threats of aggression for territorial purposes and to the possible embarrassment to Australia of the continuance of threats of the use of force.

It is quite clear that Cabinet had decided to temporise rather than take any step towards changing direction. Because of the decision I could not propagate my suggested solution in stimulating the Americans to thinking along the same lines.

Up to then the Americans had not made any change in their approach to the West New Guinea dispute. While discouraging the use or threat of force, they were unwilling to place pressure on either party. Along with ourselves, they had supported the Netherlands Government in its failed attempt to place the dispute on the agenda of the United Nations. Their ambivalent attitude was in some part due to a desire to avoid cutting across Australia's position, which seemed to favour the Dutch.

As the Cabinet had left the further progress of the matter to Menzies and me, we discussed my proposal during the following days and weeks. I made some progress with him, for he appreciated the logic of my argument. Steadily he came to be at least less resistant to it, if not indeed to view it with sympathy.

* * * * *

After the decision had been taken, early in 1962, I told Menzies that I would like very much to have a press conference to persuade the press to publish factual material about the Indonesians, their way of life and their problems, to give Australians some awareness of their neighbours. The insularity of our community, "girt by sea", is very deep-seated. I realised that Australians had no idea whatever about Indonesia's situation or of its people's problems. Australians have not had to fight for their separation from the British Empire, so we have no experience of a revolutionary conflict.

While matters were still in limbo, I thought we would do well to act on the assumption that the Netherlands would ultimately agree to hand over West New Guinea, and so create a common land border with an Asian people. My idea was to lessen the impact of the change by stimulating the Australian population to think about their neighbours as people with human problems, problems of the kind to excite sympathy rather than animosity. The press, if it was so minded, could play a significant part in exciting that interest.

Menzies counselled against it. He said the press was unreliable and that I ought not to count on their honest co-operation. I replied that I was very anxious that the Australian public should not wake up one morning to find they had a land border with an Asian people about whom they knew nothing. He thought quietly about my suggestion. After a time he said, "Well, perhaps it's worth taking the risk but you'd better be extremely careful".

"I won't talk to the scrubbers", I said. "I'll get the head men of the press to meet me all together. I'll do what I can to avoid any damage."

"Very well", said Menzies, "but do be careful".

So I arranged with all the principal newspapers that they should have their top brass meet me in Melbourne on a given day. I would that day be on my way to Tasmania where there was a meeting of the Standing Committee of Attorneys-General. I met privately in my Melbourne office senior representatives of the *Sydney Morning Herald*, the *Sun*, the *Daily Telegraph*, the *Age* and the *Melbourne Herald*.

I told them I wanted to talk to them privately about Indonesia, completely off the record and not in any sense for publication. I was not there to solicit their support for any policy of mine or of the Government. I did not wish to alter or compromise their own attitudes on those policies. I was there in the interests of the Australian public generally. I said that they could read the signs as well as anyone and they must know that Australians might soon wake up to find themselves with a land border with the Indonesians. I said that as a community we were extremely ignorant of these people and inclined to be suspicious of all Asians and particularly our Indonesian neighbours; that by a concerted effort the press could increase the community's knowledge of people destined to be their neighbours.

Fort Street Boys High, Petersham, Sydney, 4R Class, Garfield Barwick third from right in front row

Garfield Barwick aged 24 just before admission to the Bar

Established at the Bar: Garfield Barwick at top end of King St, Sydney, in early 1940s

"Stepping out" – Day of Investiture, 1954 –
Sir Garfield and Lady Barwick

Garfield Barwick on ski slopes,
Snowy Mountains, New South Wales

Sir Garfield and Lady Barwick in their garden
with son Ross and daughter Diane

Left: Portrait of Sir Garfield by William Pidgeon done for the opening of Selborne and Wentworth Chambers and which now hangs in the Bar Common Room.

Menzies Ministry 1960-61 (clockwise from front): Hugh Roberton (Social Services); John Gorton (Navy); Allen Fairhall (Supply); Paul Hasluck (Territories); William Spooner (National Development); John McEwen (Trade); Robert Menzies (Prime Minister); Harold Holt (Treasurer); Athol Townley (Defence); Charles Adermann (Primary Industry); Harrie Wade (Air); Hubert Opperman (Shipping & Transport); John Cramer (Army); Garfield Barwick (Attorney-General); David Fairbairn (Air); Shane Paltridge (Civil Aviation); William McMahon (Labour & National Service); Denham Henty (Customs & Excise); Alexander Downer (Immigration); Reginald Swartz (Repatriation).

Sir Garfield, Minister for External Affairs, meets with President JF Kennedy at the White House, October 1963

Sir Garfield (far right) at reception at Elysée Palace with President de Gaulle, 1963

Sir Garfield and Prime Minister Robert Menzies at UN General Assembly, New York, 1960

Sir Garfield with Sir Harold Macmillan, British Prime Minister, in Australia

Sir Garfield with the King and Queen of Thailand, Bangkok, 1962

Sir Garfield on appointment as Chief Justice, 1964.

High Court of Australia, on the occasion of the swearing in of Sir Cyril Walsh as a Justice of the Court, October 1969. (from left to right) Owen J, Menzies J, McTiernan J, Barwick CJ, Kitto J, Windeyer J, Walsh J

The Queen with the Justices of the High Court, 1980 (from left to right) Wilson J, Murphy J, Gibbs J, The Queen, Barwick CJ, Stephen, J, Mason J, Aickin J

Above: The Queen, with Sir Garfield, planting a tree at the opening of the new High Court Building in Canberra, 1980

Right: The Queen and Sir Garfield at the opening of the new High Court building, 1980.

Right: Sir Garfield and Lady Barwick with granddaughter Amy on their 60th wedding anniversary

At the end of the conference they said they would consider whether they should do as I asked. No one scouted my proposal as impossible. I was pleased with the outcome, though I could not regard them as committed.

I went on to Tasmania. Perhaps I was unworldly in thinking that I might have succeeded, but I felt I had set in train something useful. But I was badly mistaken. When I woke next morning in Hobart the Melbourne *Herald* carried banner headlines: "Minister Announces Change of Policy", and there was a whole screed about a supposed statement of such a change. I was furious. I rang Williams at the *Herald* and I suppose from his point of view I abused him. From my point of view I berated him for a gross breach of faith. I made it clear that I strongly resented the paper's false statement. But I doubt if I did more than ease my own feelings. I later found out that the *Herald* had actually sent a cable to The Hague saying that its publication was based on an off-the-record conversation with the Minister. So Menzies' repeated warning was justified. He commiserated with me but offered no criticism.

The next time I was interviewed by a journalist there was a microphone on the table. The visitor called attention to it. I said, "That's something that will always stand between you and me. I will never have an interview but that I have my own record of it".

The experience indicated to me that the press have no real sense of responsibility for the welfare of the country. Their interest is in scoops, exclusive interviews, and tragedies or disasters in human events. And that, I may say, is a serious indictment. They have the capacity to exert considerable influence. But in general journalists do not convey information, particularly information objectively treated; they almost invariably offer comment, if in no other way than in the adjectival description of people and events.

In retrospect, I accept that I was naive to think my plan would work. But it is a sorry reflection that the press showed no willingness to educate the people, to help them to understand the problems which beset others.

* * * * *

The Indonesians had won control of the Archipelago by violence. I had reason to think that they believed that only by violent revolution had former colonies achieved their independence, and that consequently West New Guinea could only be obtained by force. This attitude was understandable but in my view wrong. Certainly we could expect a continuation of threats of violence and a willingness to exercise it as part of the Indonesian campaign to coerce the Dutch into handing over West New Guinea. It seemed that diplomatic action was necessary to persuade them to desist from threatened or actual attack and to negotiate a settlement. Diplomatic efforts by the Dutch to persuade the Americans to pressure Soekarno into abandoning violent action had not so far produced results.

The Americans had no part or influence in the formation of my proposal to Cabinet. My memorandum was written well before we had any knowledge of the change in American policy that now came.

Between the taking of the Cabinet decision and the announcement of the Bunker plan, I had to tread fairly warily with the members of my own party. There was within it a quite powerful group which was not only anti-Indonesian but had an aggressive stance towards them and was very much pro-Dutch. I had to try progressively to reduce resistance to the direction I wanted policy to go. I feel that even in the long run I did not satisfy all the members, some of whom regarded me as a weak-minded appeaser. Recognition of the existence and strength of this group I am sure made me appear at times almost ambivalent towards Indonesia.

In discussion with the Indonesians, of course, I discouraged the use or threat of force and at the same time encouraged peaceful negotiation. I could not put any pressure on the United States to follow the course proposed in my memorandum. But sometime in April, the Americans put forward the Bunker plan, which at least closely resembled my own proposal. The Americans now actively promoted the Bunker formula. The softening of the Australian attitude towards Indonesia and the progressive movement away from the Netherlands probably gained momentum from the American support for the plan. Once it was launched, Australia's willingness to go along with it contributed to the emergence of Indonesia's willingness to negotiate peacefully. Ultimately, and not without difficulty, an agreement was reached under which the control of West New Guinea passed to Jakarta, the Indonesians undertaking to give self-determination to the local people.

Now I had to turn to working out the details such as the identification of the border between East and West New Guinea — a difficult operation because of the mountainous terrain and the tortuous Fly River which forms part of the border — the treatment of the indigenous people and the development of neighbourly relations. In Indonesia there was still in fact a considerable struggle going on between the Communists and the government, with the government at times seeming to be in the weaker political position. After a dramatic struggle the anti-communist elements of the Indonesian hierarchy triumphed, but only by a narrow margin. Soekarno disappeared and was replaced by Soeharto, one of his generals. We now had to build our bridges with a new and largely unknown group in government.

* * * * *

Once the agreement between the Netherlands and Indonesia on handing over West New Guinea was finalised, the task of building good relations with Indonesia began. We had to ensure that the takeover would have no disadvantageous impact on Papua New Guinea, and the boundary between the two parts of New Guinea had to be marked. The terminal points of the boundary were already fixed, but much of it had still to be marked; it was difficult to ensure observance of the border because it might intersect tribal territory. But Foreign Minister Subandrio proved co-operative, agreeing that there should be no intrusion of the West New Guineans over the border.

Soon, however, we had to cope with the development of the federation of Malaysia. The plan was to incorporate Malaya, Singapore, Sabah, Sarawak, and in the original intention, Brunei. Early on the Government of Brunei expressed its unwillingness to join the federation and stood out as it is today, an independent state. This was a blow to the federation because Brunei was extremely rich in oil and timber.

I had always felt in conversation with the Tunku that he was aware of the difficulties of the proposed federation. He had had experience of trying to administer a state which contained diverse ethnic minorities and all the difficulties that entailed. He had been successful when the constitution of an independent Malaya had been formulated by the Commission over which Lord Reid presided and on which Sir William McKell served, that the predominance of Malays should be entrenched. Malaya had a large population of Indians and of Chinese. The neighbouring colony of Singapore was predominantly composed of Chinese. The Malays were not a vigorous people and were not given to business activity. Indeed I suppose it was their unwillingness to work for the rubber plantations and the mines which caused the influx of Indians and Chinese as labourers to service those industries.

I remember the Tunku saying to me that he understood Australia maintaining a European population: "Why should you have my insoluble problem? The problem of ethnic diversity is insoluble. I have Malays, Indians and Chinese and it is insoluble". So I always had a feeling that the Tunku was not all that keen on the proposal, which had emanated from the British Government, to enlarge Malaya into Malaysia. Federation would increase this ethnic diversity. In particular, I realised the Tunku was apprehensive about the inclusion of Singapore with Lee Kuan Yew as its Prime Minister.

Before Malaysia was launched I attended a conference in the Cameron Highlands. Lee was present and my quarters were set up with him rather than with the Tunku. I soon worked out the reason for this; the Tunku knew that I had some knowledge of the way finances were worked in a federation and he was attempting to get a larger contribution to federal funds from Singapore than Lee was then prepared to make. I think the Tunku thought that I might give Lee some advice which would rebound to the Tunku's benefit. In fact Lee did open with me the question of financial management of a federation. I had to tell him that I would not offer him any opinion on that point. Those relationships would have to be ironed out between himself and the Tunku. I did not want to appear to be a partisan in any way. I did remark, however, that in a federation you ought not to have any poor cousins. The participating members of the federation must, as far as possible, meet on an equal financial footing.

As a result of this conference the Tunku did manage to get an extra $5 million contributed to the federal funds by Lee. I heard subsequently that Lee had said that I was the cause of this result as I had been giving the Tunku some financial advice. But in fact I had not; I had kept myself very clear of the argument between the two.

In the long run I think the Tunku got some form of undertaking from Lee that he would not field candidates in Malaya when general elections for Malaysia were held. Later when Chinese candidates were nominated for elections in mainland Malaya, the Tunku decided to take steps to exclude Singapore from the federation, something which in the long run was not, I think, to the disadvantage of Singapore, particularly as it had the great advantage of having Lee as its Prime Minister. After Singapore's withdrawal, I think relations between the Tunku and Lee were fairly good.

Now the proposal for the Malaysian federation was in the hands of Duncan Sandys. Duncan was a dogged, persistent man. I remember him addressing Federal Cabinet at the time that Britain was proposing entry into the European Common Market. He tried to persuade Australia to agree with the British proposal. That of course, as far as Australia was concerned, was impossible. But Sandys kept battering away, working back and forth over the same ground. The Cabinet went on into the late evening, and at last Menzies suggested we adjourn as a respite from Sandys' advocacy. Menzies, like the rest of us, had had enough of him. I remember saying to Menzies during the adjournment, "I think you ought to tell Sandys, as Isaacs once did to counsel, that there is a point at which laudable persistence becomes sheer stupidity". Bob laughed and said, "I believe you would". I said, "I think I might". When we resumed Sandys went over it all again and all to no point. He was the same about Malaysia.

From the Indonesian point of view, the proposal for the federation wore the aspect of an attempt by the British Government to encircle Indonesia. Soekarno could not get it out of his head that the federation would be very much under the thumb of the British Government. The fact that the Tunku was an Anglophile and that the proposal evidently emanated from the British gave Soekarno some basis for this attitude. But it was not wholly true. There were advantages to the local population of federation and, as well as I know, no continuing benefits to the British Government beyond the immediate loss of responsibility for the federated territories.

From my point of view and left to myself, I doubt if I would have favoured the proposal. As I saw it, the attempt to administer Sabah and Sarawak from the mainland of Malaysia was fraught with difficulty. I remember saying to the Tunku that he would find the administration of these new territories very difficult. I asked him, "Where are you going to get the administrators able to manage the affairs of widely separated territories?". He said jokingly, "Oh, I'll borrow some from you", but I had quickly to disabuse him of any idea that Australia might assist in the administrative problems I could see emerging.

But Sandys persisted; he even set the date, 16 September 1963, for the declaration of a new federation, a day which could well be before the result of a United Nations investigation of the wishes of the people of Sabah and Sarawak was known.

The United Nations assessment of the views of the indigenous populations of Borneo on the question of their joining the federation had not been completed at the time Sandys set the date for the declaration. The Tunku was quite willing that a much later date be set. He had complete confidence that the United Nations' assessment would show that the indigenous people were favourable to the proposal. But Sandys persisted. In my view the speed with which Sandys furthered the scheme tended to furnish Soekarno with reasons for opposition.

As it turned out, the result of the United Nations' assessment became known on the morning of 14 September. It was favourable to the proposal. I received news of the result in the early morning of that day in Jakarta where I had called to confer with Soekarno on my way to Kuala Lumpur for the inauguration ceremonies. I had an interview with Soekarno at a time when I was sure he had not received the result of the assessment and I talked to him on the footing that he did not know of it. The interview with Soekarno, Subandrio being present, was a lengthy one. Soekarno was adamant that the proposal was only a British ploy which he would oppose. There would be a confrontation.

I put the Australian point of view, namely that Australia favoured the new federation and thought that it would be beneficial to the whole of the region including Indonesia. It represented a further reduction in colonialism and would be democratically based. I pressed him to give weight to Australian support for the federation, emphasising Australia's place in this region of the world.

In any discussion with him, Soekarno was prone to emphasise the numerical strength of the Indonesian people, 100 million or more, contrasting it, without statistical comparison, to the relative smallness of the Australian population. I contrasted the productive capacity of the Australian population, small as it was, with the productive capacity of the Indonesian population. I think I did this with some forcefulness. And towards the end Soekarno said to me, "So what?" I had to say that I thought the opinion of the Australian people mattered and should be put in the scales when Indonesia was making up its mind about Malaysia. The Australian people's favour of the proposal ought to weigh with him.

But I did not turn Soekarno's mind. For stubbornness there was little to choose between Soekarno and Duncan Sandys. Soekarno was unalterably committed to confronting Malaysia. It seems that he did not intend to do so by putting an army in the field. He was more inclined to weakening the Malaysian position by guerrilla tactics. He got together a number of dissident Malays, probably mostly Chinese Malays, whom he trained as guerrillas to be dropped into Malayan territory, there to act as a guerrilla force. In this he was fairly successful. I think in all he managed to have about 12,000 British troops bogged down in Borneo without committing any great number of Indonesian troops to the field. In my period as Minister, Cabinet had not agreed to any Australian combat troops being deployed in Borneo. We were prepared to offer the British or Malaysian forces some logistic support but no more. The proposal to form Malaysia was not an Australian initiative although we had gone along with it largely because of our British association, though our own long-term interests were to maintain the goodwill of the Indonesians. So my own policy was as far as possible to keep clear, if at all possible.

Soekarno and I did not part on this occasion in an unfriendly mood although I had been very firm in my talk with him. I made some impression on him because he told Hasluck at a later date that in this interview I had "scolded" him. I did not see it that way. But it seemed neither Soekarno nor Subandrio had taken my emphatic words amiss.

I went straight from Jakarta to Kuala Lumpur where the inauguration ceremony took place in a torrent of rain. The skies fairly opened up. The new federation was ushered in with suitable pomp and ceremony and with the support of Australia. Indeed, apart from the withdrawal of Singapore, the federation has survived and with the abandonment of the "confrontasi" has lived with Indonesia even if at times uneasily.

I really had not hoped to change Soekarno's mind but I still thought it very much worthwhile to press him and to try to make a dent in his resolution. As well as I recall, I did not try in this interview to dangle the effect of the ANZUS Treaty in front of him. I had a firm view that Borneo would properly be regarded as within the area of ANZUS; so that if Australian troops were attacked we could expect the Americans to respond in some way. Subsequently I had an interview with John Kennedy on this very point. But I acted in this interview with Soekarno on the footing that there could be no question of Indonesia attacking Australia.

From Australia's point of view, I saw no particular advantages in a larger Malaya, certainly not in the short term. But the government felt bound to support the scheme, seeing that the Tunku, though perhaps with reluctance, favoured it. If it worked there could be some advantages in the co-operation between Kuala Lumpur and Singapore.

16 Journey to South East Asia

Before my appointment as Minister for External Affairs in 1961, I had formed the view that Asia, and particularly South East Asia, would become increasingly important to us in forming both our domestic and international policies. This did not mean we should become Asians or to any extent cease to be Europeans with our own national institutions and behavioural standards, but it did mean that European solutions to our relationship with Asia would be inadequate and inappropriate. So far as British folk are European, I am a European. But while I would much prefer that my family and I should remain European, I have no antipathy to or sense of superiority over other peoples, in particular Asians. I am conscious of the difference between the European and the Asian, Melanesian or Polynesian, but none of those differences excites me to adverse reactions.

Beyond my visit to sound out Asian policy on West New Guinea, I had had little experience of the countries to our north. However, on my appointment as Minister, I thought that I should visit them. So over ten weeks in mid-1962 Norma and I visited Singapore, Saigon, Hong Kong, Taipeh, Seoul, Tokyo, Pnom Penh, Bangkok, Rangoon, Kuala Lumpur, and Jakarta, a vigorous and stimulating itinerary. It was more an exercise in mutual acquaintance than a diplomatic event. In any case I believe routine diplomacy should be left to diplomats.

The participation of the United States and Australia in the war between North and South Vietnam gave rise to much bitter controversy which exhibited considerable ignorance of the facts which led to that participation. At times there has been deliberate misrepresentation of them. The controversy has lasted long after the cessation of hostilities. A clear understanding of the causes of and the justification for the American and Australian intervention is rarely evident.

It is proper that at this point I record my own activity in connection with that conflict and indicate on which basis I think that participation was justified.

My first ministerial contact with affairs in Vietnam was in 1960. I was returning from London where as Attorney-General I had appeared for the Commonwealth in an appeal to the Judicial Committee of the Privy Council. In Singapore I met and discussed events in South East Asia with a high-ranking diplomat from the British Foreign Office. I received much information about activities in that area. Though I did not become Minister for External Affairs till 1961, I had also had the benefit of discussions about Vietnam with officers of the Department of External Affairs.

In what follows I set out my understanding of the situation in South East Asia at relevant times, that is, 1960-1964.

As a result of the earlier conflict between the French and the North Vietnamese, three sovereign states had been created in Laos, North Vietnam and South Vietnam, each with territorial boundaries internationally recognised.

In the second half of the 1950s and throughout the early days of the 1960s China, under Mao, had built a road in and through Ladakh to facilitate its movement towards Tibet, which later it subjugated. It also built a road across the northern border between itself and Laos and for some distance into Laotian territory.

By 1960 North Vietnam was building or had already completed a bridge over a river within Laotian territory and was constructing a road therefrom into that defile along the border between Laos and Vietnam which became known as the Ho Chi Minh Trail. This defile was so obscured by the canopy of the rainforest that activity taking place along it could not be observed even from the air. Norma and I flew over this area on our way to Da Nang, a town proximate to the border between South and North Vietnam. The North Vietnamese were already conducting a campaign of terror against the villagers of South Vietnam. The wide plain which stretches from the rainforested range of hills to the sea is wholly within the territory of South Vietnam. It consists of rich and deep alluvial soil through which the North Vietnamese constructed tunnels for considerable distances, even as far as two or three miles. Air vents were left in the tunnels so that Vietnamese raiders, being physically small, were able to move from the forest to the areas of the plain adjacent to the villages without being observed. They emerged from the tunnel, terrorised the villagers both physically and psychologically, took whatever they fancied, whether it be food or materials, and then quickly disappeared through the tunnel.

As a result of this and other forms of terrorism, the villagers were unwilling to co-operate with the South Vietnamese Government authorities in their endeavour to halt the threat of the North Vietnamese. Their activities represented aggression of a very formidable kind. It placed the South Vietnamese in an increasingly desperate position. If successful, the North Vietnamese were likely to overrun and spread communism through South Vietnam into Cambodia, with the possibility of threatening Thailand.

In the 1960s communist terrorists had caused the villagers in Malaya to live in a state of fear and apprehension. They were unprepared to co-operate with the government in its defence against the communists. There, terrorism and the threat of communism were brought to an end by two factors: one, a system of fortified villages introduced and supervised by an officer of the British Army named Thompson, and two, by the arrival of Sir Gerald Templar to take control of Malayan military operations. Incidentally, it happened that I travelled on the same plane as Sir Gerald. During flight I conversed with him about affairs in South East Asia.

Thompson's scheme in Malaya was to fortify a village, demonstrating to its occupants that the authorities would maintain the fortifications and protect them from the communists. Having cleansed and fortified one village, Thompson moved to an adjacent village, repeated the process and so on from one village to the next until he had a chain of fortified villages, the inhabitants of which had been persuaded to co-operate with the Malayan authorities.

Diem, the President of South Vietnam, a fervent anti-communist, no doubt with the encouragement of American diplomats engaged Thompson to repeat in South Vietnam his Malayan performance. Thompson commenced to do so. With Cabinet's approval Richard Casey, my predecessor in office, had assisted Diem by providing materials for this fortification of villages: barbed and fencing wire, steel fencing posts and some corrugated iron. After I became minister, I continued to provide Diem with materials for Thompson's scheme.

Also, Casey had established a dairy at Ben Cat some miles from Saigon under the control of an Australian. The dairy was to provide Saigon with fresh milk. I think as things turned out all the milk did not reach Saigon; sticky fingers of some Vietnamese public servants intercepted much of it. I visited the dairy in 1962 and found it in good shape.

Unfortunately Diem was not prepared to be as patient as Thompson and the Malayan authorities had been in developing a chain of fortified villages. Thompson was quite successful in fortifying villages in South Vietnam. But Diem directed the fortification of villages which were not contiguous and which did not form a fortified chain. The result was that the North Vietnamese terrorists were able to raid the isolated fortified villages, take away a great deal of the fortifying material and do violence to the villagers. In short Thompson's scheme, for this reason, broke down.

I have spoken of the Chinese thrusts towards Tibet and into Laos. The Russians for their part were supporting North Vietnam in its aggression of the South. They supplied armament and funds to enable that aggression to expand. The Russians' motivation was not merely to spread communism but also to gain access to a warm water port in the East — Vladivostok, its only port there, was closed in winter. In this they were successful; they gained access to Cam Ranh Bay, a harbour in North Vietnam open the year round.

The precise relationship between China and Russia was unknown to the West. Both had communist governments and in that sense shared the same objectives and methods of attaining them. But whether they were in a close-knit alliance or merely shared common beliefs and objectives was unclear.

Whilst the relationship between Russia and North Vietnam was quite apparent, that between China and North Vietnam was far from evident. Traditionally, because of ethnic differences, the North Vietnamese would be expected to dislike and distrust the Chinese. But whether the common adherence of both governments to communism with its ready recourse to aggressive action caused the North Vietnamese to be willing to accept Chinese support, if offered, was uncertain. Wisdom, however, would require the assumption that if appropriate circumstances arose, the Chinese might well come to the assistance of North Vietnam.

Today, the evil of communism and its destructive capacity have become evident. The downfall of the Russian economy and the disarray of its people are eloquent testimony. But in the 1950s and 1960s opinion in Australia as to the dangers of communism was sharply divided. From the point of view of the then Australian Government, and in my own opinion, Australia had a very vital interest to prevent the spread of communism throughout South East Asia, with which Australia must cultivate good relations and perhaps trading connections. Australia therefore had a very real interest in halting North Vietnamese aggression.

Indonesia had not fallen to communist subversion though the balance in that country might not be so firmly established that we should put out of mind the possibility of communism taking hold there. The consequences if the North Vietnamese were successful in their aggression against South Vietnam were, as I have mentioned, quite evident.

During Casey's time as Minister for External Affairs Australia had joined the South East Asian Treaty Organisation (SEATO). The mainspring of its formation was the need to impede and if possible prevent the spread of communism throughout South East Asia. After I became minister, I regularly attended its meetings at its headquarters in Bangkok.

Dean Rusk, Secretary of State of the United States, also attended these meetings. We became firm friends. We were both disappointed by the unwillingness of the British and French governments, also members of that organisation, to take any joint steps to prevent the spread of communism. But in considering the constitution of the organisation, it became apparent that the members of the organisation were not limited to joint action but could take individual action under its aegis and for its purposes. It was this view of the treaty which enabled the United States to intervene militarily on the side of South Vietnam in the war of aggression and terrorism carried on by the North Vietnamese.

In 1963 Dean Rusk came to Canberra for a meeting of the ANZUS council. I had many discussions with him during the meeting about the course of events in Vietnam. He remarked on the need to upgrade the American troops' performance in jungle warfare. At no stage did he suggest that there was any obligation on Australia by reason of ANZUS to join in those military operations.

Australia at this time maintained a jungle warfare training school in Queensland which had developed considerable experience in such training. Colonel Serong was in charge of this unit and was himself an outstanding jungle warfare expert.

Dean Rusk, in discussion with me, said that it would be a distinct advantage if Australia would lend America the services of Colonel Serong and a few of his trainers. Athol Townley, Minister for Defence, attended the conference with me and joined in these discussions.

Townley and I discussed the possible effects of agreeing to Dean Rusk's suggestion. Both of us realised that whilst it carried no present suggestion for combat troops, the fact that Colonel Serong's services had been made available could make refusal of a request for combat troops much more difficult. But Townley was prepared to make Serong and three or four trainers available and I, for my part, was satisfied that the request ought to be granted. We both felt that the Cabinet's authority to assist the Americans was ample to cover our agreement. So I promised Dean Rusk that Australia would make Colonel Serong and three or four trainers available. Townley and I met the press at the conclusion of the ANZUS meeting and informed them of our decision, emphasising its limited nature. We later reported to Cabinet and whilst I think some members of the Cabinet felt apprehensive of the possible consequences of making Serong's services available, there was no dissent. And there, for the remainder of my term of office, the matter remained. I think in subsequent negotiations with Townley the number of trainees was increased, but otherwise the position remained unchanged until the end of my term of office in April 1964.

I therefore did not have to decide whether or not Australian combat troops should be sent to Vietnam. But I considered what should be done if such a request were made. I felt that if practicable we should go along with the Americans. We shared their opposition to communism and we had a distinct Australian interest in preventing it taking hold throughout South East Asia. Also, we had an interest to withstand aggressive territorial expansion, the overrunning by force of one nation by another. We had entered two world wars to oppose aggression of that kind.

We had a limited number of regular troops, probably insufficient to enable us to reinforce an expeditionary force in Vietnam. If that were so, it would be necessary to call up servicemen and because of the limited numbers involved, do so by a ballot to select them. Such a ballot, with its appearance of discrimination, was likely to meet with opposition. When Mrs Jones' son was called up and Mrs Smith's was not, jealousy and a sense of unfair treatment was likely to be engendered. Coupled with a certain amount of anti-war and anti-American sentiment, a quite difficult situation might be experienced. But whilst conscious of this possibility I might well have thought its risks were outweighed by the need to support a valued ally, particularly as our interests coincided. Thus, as I had no need to decide, I left the matter.

Later Harold Holt went "all the way with LBJ".[1] The situation I had thought possible became actual and actively so. Both in America and in Australia these forces of jealousy and a sense of unfair treatment, coupled with anti-war and pro-communist sentiment, caused LBJ to withdraw from Vietnam at the very moment the war was being won. Of course, Australia had to withdraw with LBJ. What I feared might happen did happen. Communist North Vietnam overran Cambodia but it did not reach Thailand.

Latterly we have put troops into Cambodia in an endeavour to stabilise that nation. There seems to be little opposition to this course.

When seen in its proper perspective, history will justify Australia's support of America in resisting communist North Vietnam's aggression against South Vietnam.

One final thing about the Vietnamese war. It was not lost, as is so frequently said. I think it was in substance won, but the Americans, under pressure of the demonstrations, withdrew from the conflict before its result was clear. I also felt that the Americans had been half-hearted in their conduct of it. I realise the great difficulty there was in fighting the Vietnamese in the jungle. The pockets of North Vietnamese in South Vietnam left over from the earlier conflict added to those difficulties. But with all those disadvantages in mind, one feels that a more determined effort might well have brought the conflict to an earlier and more decisive end.

I have always had in mind the possibility of Chinese assistance to this aggression southward. Whether that materialised or not, there was every reason to have Vietnam, Cambodia and Thailand under a non-communist government. Thus it was in my opinion in Australia's interests both honourable and appropriate to participate in the Vietnamese war.

There is one incident during my term of office that I should mention. I became aware that the American military command was apprehensive that China might move in force to assist the North Vietnamese. I felt that if this occurred, the Americans might be tempted to use nuclear warheads to stem a Chinese advance. I was convinced that Australia should not be party to or concur in such a use of nuclear power. I felt so strongly about this that I took a journey to Honolulu to meet with Admiral Felt, in charge of American operations. I pressed him to agree that in no circumstances would nuclear warheads be used, but he was unwilling to give such an assurance. He did, however, say that there was no present intention to do so. With this I had to be content.

Perhaps I should digress to say that I had noticed that Menzies had no brotherly feeling towards coloured people, whether of Africa or in South East

Asia. Not that he was unkind or antipathetic to their concerns; it was rather that he was more affected by his difference from them than impelled by a sense of common humanity. I remember an occasion when he was off to a Commonwealth prime ministers' meeting and we were talking about some of the things up for discussion.

"Well", I said, "you'll meet Jomo", meaning Kenyatta, who had just succeeded in his bid for power.

"Oh, he's a murderer."

"You can't say that of him. You must remember that once the English cut off a sovereign's head. He's been through a somewhat similar struggle, though perhaps of a different dimension."

"He's much more viciously violent", said Menzies.

But I suggested that he meet him on a friendly basis. When Menzies came back from that meeting he told me he had met Jomo and found him a very interesting and intelligent character. This points up the fact that Menzies had lived a life segregated from the great populations of black and coloured people round the world. Indeed, in general, we all had been, mostly making contact through missionaries who brought home stories of their work among primitive people.

* * * * *

We next went to Tokyo for a weekend's respite. We stayed with Ambassador McIntyre in the splendid Embassy which the Australian Government has in Tokyo. On the weekend we went up to the mountains to Karuizawa where our government kept a cottage for the recreation of the Embassy staff. We went up by train through terraced paddy fields. The air at Karuizawa was very bracing, but unfortunately it rained most of the weekend though the Ambassador and I managed to do some walking, which was very pleasant after the time I had spent in Saigon.

My party arrived in Rangoon within a day or so of the flight of President U Nu and the assumption of office by Ne Win. His regime was to be in practice a military dictatorship. In a conversation I had with him, Ne Win presented himself as intent on ruling the country well, which seemed to include the implementation of a little booklet of which I was given a copy, entitled "The Burmese Way to Socialism". I must say this struck me as a somewhat childish exercise but evidently the Burmese were dead serious about it. They had of course already excluded the non-indigenous people, who had done much to open up Burma. They were not intending to take anything from the outside world in their socialist plan; they were turning in upon themselves.

Mr Homer was in post in Rangoon at the time and made arrangements for me to meet quite a number of Burmese officials. I was also able to see the diplomatic corps of the city and for a reason I will soon mention, was able to use the services of the British Ambassador.

The constitution of Burma provided that when there was no president in office a regency council must be assembled of which the Chief Justice of Burma formed an integral part. Of course it did not suit Ne Win and his associates to have such a council, so to prevent the possibility of it being assembled Ne Win incarcerated the Chief Justice. His name was U Myint Thein. I had met him at the United Nations in 1960 when he was the Burmese representative, and again after his appointment as Chief Justice in legal conferences. I remember inviting him as a guest to my house in Beecroft one evening when I had a sizeable party in progress. As I met him at the front door of the house, he could see into the drawing room and there he saw a Miss Smith, a bulky lady with whom he had worked at the United Nations.

He immediately said, "You must protect me from that woman. Just keep her away from me".

"I can't do anything of the kind. She is a guest here as you are".

"Well, I know what I'll do. I'll see her and suggest that she ask you why you don't have women on the High Court bench. She is a great feminist and she would do that if I put her up to it".

I asked him not to do so but he was a playful man and he said he most certainly would; and he did.

By and by Miss Smith bore down on me like a galleon in full sail. She immediately targeted me with "Why don't you have women on the High Court?". Well, I was not looking for an argument on this social occasion and I parried her by saying, "Well, we don't get very many women offering their services or available for appointment". This did not satisfy the lady, and she persisted. She kept on, no matter how I parried her assaults. Eventually I felt I should counter-attack. I said, "Well, if you must know, Miss Smith, the reason we don't have women on the High Court bench is because a woman can't bear to be wrong, certainly to acknowledge a mistake. She's got to be always right and you know, none of us ever are". She hotly disputed this and I eventually had to stop the conversation and look after my other guests. But throughout the whole of my sally with Miss Smith, U Myint Thein was enjoying himself, and visibly so; he thought it amusing to see me incommoded.

But we were very good friends and one of the first things I wanted to do in Rangoon was to see him. But Ne Win refused to allow me to see or even communicate with him. The British Ambassador did take a message from me which he said by one devious means or another he would get to Myint Thein.

Myint Thein's wife died at the time I was in Rangoon and Ne Win refused to allow Myint to attend her funeral, which I thought singularly harsh. The Burmese are often painted as a gentle people; well, I saw none of that in Ne Win.

Myint Thein was kept in close arrest for seven or eight years. During that time he managed to get some letters out to me and I managed to get some in to him. He remained always cheerful. He had a considerable knowledge of the Old Testament as well the New, and was also familiar with the many proverbs that the Burmese have. He published a translation of them along with some cross-references to the Book of Proverbs. He sent me the volume and I treasure it. He was a little older than I. Sadly, he died late in 1994.

I went to the Burma oil wells at Mandalay during this visit and spoke to the Burma Oil officials there. Norma and I went to the Great Temple (the Shwe Dagoon), which we both thought particularly filthy because the Burma chew betel nut and spit a reddish mess freely on the pavements. The marble floors of the temple showed much evidence of this habit, and since the Burmese insisted on bare feet in the temple our visit was somewhat agonising. But I must say the structure was magnificent in concept and execution.

Our visits injected an Australian presence into the area though it was not possible to establish any vital links because of the inward-looking nature of the Burmese mind at the time.

One of the fond recollections we have of Rangoon was an evening's entertainment of Burmese dancing. We particularly remember the dancing of the Shan tribes, which was free and unstylised and singularly happy. It contrasted greatly with the stylised dancing we had seen in Vietnam, Tokyo and Korea.

* * * * *

My encounter with Prince Sihanouk of Cambodia began with a rather awkward tussle over international boundaries in 1962. Cambodia and Thailand were in litigation before the International Court of Justice at The Hague. The question was the ownership of the Temple Prehar, which stood on or near a disputed part of the boundary between the two countries. The dispute was about on which side of the boundary the temple really stood. The boundary was in a precipitous area; the steep flight of stairs that had formerly led to it, up a near vertical face, had become unusable, so that Cambodians could no longer gain direct access to the temple but had to travel through Thai territory to reach it. Nonetheless possession of the temple had become a point of Cambodian national pride and honour. When the boundary had been delineated, its position was expressed both in words and in diagram. If one went by the words the temple was in Thailand, but if the diagram was taken as the authentic definition, the temple was in Cambodia.

The International Court is mostly composed of diplomat lawyers, those who have become prominent in international diplomacy, particularly in the United Nations. It is representative in that its members are elected by various regions of the world. Thus the judge so elected is regarded in some sense as representing the nations of the electoral region. This and the uncertainties and ambiguities of international law means that international politics can at times play a part in the court's decisions.

Prince Sihanouk, then Prime Minister of Cambodia, was intensely interested in this litigation. When I became Minister, the Cambodian Ambassador, Poc Tuan, was instructed to ask me to secure for Cambodia Sir Percy Spender's vote in the resolution of this dispute. Spender was at the time a member of the court; later he was to become its president. Poc Tuan explained to me that although Spender had not been elected by the region in which Australia is placed, he was an Australian and the Prince thought that I would have great influence with him. I had to explain that I had no such influence: Spender was an Australian but that was all there was to it. The Ambassador undertook to inform Sihanouk that I could and would do nothing. I might add that I think Poc Tuan understood the situation perfectly well, though he no doubt felt he was in no position to say so.

But my message quite evidently did not satisfy the Prince. A few months later the Ambassador called on me again and renewed his request. Again I had to assure Sihanouk that I had no influence and in any case would not have thought it proper that I should interfere. I am quite sure Sihanouk was displeased by my attitude and unconvinced by my reasons. But for the time being I heard no more. Naturally I had no communication with Spender. Before I left on my journey through South East Asia, Poc Tuan told me that he would be in Pnom Penh when I called there. He gave me some indication of local custom and ceremony.

Because our ambassador to Cambodia was on leave the chargé d'affaires at this time was the senior official at the Embassy. A number of functions had been organised for me. I was to meet Prince Sihanouk, Cambodian ministers and departmental officers. Naturally I was looking forward to this round of discussions.

When the Air France plane touched down at Pnom Penh and the doors of the cabin opened, the chargé immediately came aboard with the news that all my engagements with Sihanouk and his ministry had been cancelled. The reason he gave was that that morning a decision in the case of the Temple Prehar had been announced by the International Court. Cambodia had succeeded: a majority of the court had favoured following the diagrammatic description of the boundary rather than the written one. But the judge from the United Kingdom and Sir Percy Spender, relying on the written description, had dissented and had held that Thailand owned the temple. Sihanouk was very displeased, indeed offended by what he regarded as the unfriendly attitude of Australia. My earlier refusal to get Spender's vote for him obviously confirmed our supposed unfriendliness.

I was in an awkward situation. I was not due at my next port of call for several days, so had time to spend in Pnom Penh. I told the chargé that as soon as we had finished the formal welcome on the tarmac I wanted to call on Prince Sihanouk to discuss matters with him. The chargé left to make the necessary arrangement and we had the ceremonial reception, the guard of honour and the playing of the national anthems. I thought the Cambodian anthem musically attractive, so much so that when I was later able to ask him, the Prince responded and gave me a tape of it.

In the flurry caused by the chargé's message, a small valise Norma always kept by her, which held her jewellery, cosmetics and medication, was overlooked and left on the plane; it was not until we were settled at the end of the day in the residence provided for us that it was missed. By then the plane had taken off. Its next stop was Bangkok but because the two nations were not "playing speaks" we were not able either to communicate with the plane or with Bangkok. We had to improvise until the valise came back from Paris several days later. The British Embassy had arranged its return. Obviously it had been opened by customs but nothing was disturbed.

A call on Sihanouk was arranged by the chargé. He was and still is a very ebullient person, vivacious, demonstrative but always charming. He gave the impression of being, and I think he is, a very cultivated man. He was concerned to reduce the harm caused to the people by their social problems, due in some part to the lack of capital. This made him a very popular leader and gave him quite some strength in running Cambodia. On this occasion, however, when I called on him he was, to begin with, unfriendly and almost sullen. He forcefully declared what to him was Australia's obvious unfriendliness. I had to be most diplomatic in impressing upon him my inability to have done anything for him, and explaining our standards of judicial independence and propriety. I assured him that, on the other hand, I had done nothing against him or his country's interests. I congratulated him on his success in the case. I pointed out that Anglo-Saxon judges and lawyers often disagreed and were seldom unanimous, and that Spender's decision did not indicate hostility.

Well, over an hour or so I seemed to make progress with him and at last he was able to find a way to exculpate us both from the difficulty which Spender's dissent had seemed to create. He said that if I would publicly state that I had no objection to his neutralist attitude towards China he would restore all the arrangements, and things would go ahead as planned. I told him that so far from merely making such a public statement, I could tell him that in fact I did not quarrel with his attitude in relation to China; that I understood it and that if I were in his shoes, with the shadow of a very great power over me, I would also be inclined not to take sides in matters in which that power would be concerned. This seemed both to reassure and to please him.

One of the planned events was a visit to the Prince's mother who, I rather suspect, was a considerable power in the land. Norma and I went to see her in her home. Now the Cambodian requirement was that no one in the presence of Royalty should have his head at any time higher than that of the Royal personage; when Royalty was seated, servants and officials therefore moved on their knees. On this occasion the Prince's mother was seated, so we were faced with this rather alarming protocol. Fortunately we were excused, but we were expected to bow low several times on entering the room. We sat at the same level as she, but when leaving we had to walk backwards with our heads bowed, right from the point where she was sitting to the door, a considerable distance away.

At that point we were to bow low several times before departure. All this we did and, though with some difficulty, were none the worse for it.

We conversed with the Royal mother sentence by sentence through an interpreter. She was a very lively person, well versed in the politics of the day, and showed the vivacity so apparent in her son. I must say I enjoyed our conversation. We touched on many of the current events and to some extent on the possible future trend of affairs. The conflict between North and South Vietnam was well afoot and the anxieties which later became realities were evident in the minds of the Cambodians, who I gather had no great affinity with the Vietnamese. Communism and the intrusive Soviet Union were both to be distrusted and feared.

I found Sihanouk in high contrast to Diem. Sihanouk's was no cloistered existence. He was interested in administration and understood the importance of regular contact with his people and knew something of their personal problems. His PR, as we would say, was excellent.

In conversations both alone with Sihanouk and in those I had with his ministers I sensed the deep and enduring ethnic antipathies between the Cambodians and the Vietnamese on the one hand, and between themselves and the Thais on the other. These ethnic antagonisms might well prove ineradicable, as such differences tend to be. Sihanouk I felt was fearful of the Chinese and was anxious to maintain an accommodation with them. He seemed to feel that the Chinese felt that they could deal with him and that to an extent he was acceptable to them. He was alarmed at the possible movement of the North Vietnamese and expressed his concern quite clearly.

Pnom Penh was a pleasant city, neither large nor complex; bicycles were the main form of private transport, with pedicabs and small motor bikes for public transport. The people seemed happy and contented though, I thought, apprehensive. There seemed to be plenty of food — fruit and vegetables in fair supply, ducks, geese and chickens, and fish from the river and the great lake. I gathered that their chief desire was to be left alone. To those who were informed about international affairs, the Vietnamese threat seemed close at hand, while China, as a very great power, seemed to be feared if for no other reason than that its intentions appeared uncertain and possibly hostile. Its leaders had already shown expansionist tendencies. It had built a road through Ladakh and taken over Tibet.

I left Pnom Penh feeling that it was not in Australia's interests should Cambodian fears about Vietnam become a reality. The North should not be allowed to overrun the South and thus have a springboard from which to overrun Cambodia.

We were entertained by an evening of Cambodian classical dancing, which I enjoyed though I did not understand the symbolism of the gestures and movements. Then there was a great dinner in our honour at which I was to speak. The dinner was a wonderful affair. The table was laid out with delightful cut glass and silver, and we dined off gold plate; the food was fine French cooking, and French wines were abundant. Sihanouk was in a most expansive mood, voluble and cheerful. I spoke on Cambodia's neutrality towards China, with a young Australian diplomat, Ronald Walker, acting as interpreter. (He was the son of our Ambassador in Paris of the same name, and a boyhood friend of mine.) My speech was very well received by the audience but particularly by Sihanouk. I did say explicitly that I quite understood and did not disapprove of his neutral attitude towards China.

During the dancing Sihanouk asked me was I intending to view Angkor Wat. When I said it had not been planned because of time restrictions, he said it was quite possible for me to visit the temple and still maintain my programme. He would make his private plane available to us next morning.

So the next day we had a marvellous visit to Angkor Wat. We flew over the Mekong River and the Great Lake and landed close to Angkor Wat, having first had a good view of it from the air; from ground level, its size and architectural complexity were vastly impressive. We climbed up its great staircase and saw the views from its top terraces. Its staircases were designed so that the risers between steps progressively diminished so that as one tired, the effort to take successive steps became less. We particularly admired the long wall at ground level with its remarkable sculpture depicting historical events of very ancient times. Unfortunately, though we had a knowledgeable guide, we did not know enough Cambodian history really to appreciate the significance of its details. Before we left Pnom Penh I thanked the Prince for his great kindness in making this visit possible and congratulated him on the work done in exposing and repairing the temple.

17 I Leave Politics

By early 1963 I had been administering my double portfolio for two years. Although I had assistant ministers, I had had a very busy time. My physical ability to withstand the constant pressure was fully taxed. I had constantly to observe my diabetic reactions; the risk of hypoglycemia seemed likely to increase. I knew of the risk to my sight and to my lower limbs and feet which my condition could present and maintained a close check on likely points of breakdown. I particularly watched the condition of my eyes. So far my sight remained extremely good, but I felt, just the same, a continual anxiety. Perhaps needlessly, I still told no one about my diabetes, and as far as I knew no one in the law or in political life even suspected it. Such secrecy given my otherwise open nature gave me some concern.

But though I did not particularly enjoy parliamentary life, I did enjoy ministerial office and the work of the Cabinet. When I ceased to act as Minister, and Tange and Waller thanked me for attending to departmental affairs, I was surprised and pleased that they had found me "accessible". Towards the middle of 1963, however, I had had enough experience of the strains of office to realise that it was by no means certain that I could sustain high political office in the long term. I had no burning ambition for the prime ministership, which would have been a spur to accepting the risks of office, though I would have been more than pleased to have assumed it. Apart from my diabetes, my health was extremely good. Not unnaturally, I canvassed in my mind the possibilities of the future.

I was then sixty years of age. I saw no sign of impending resignation by Menzies. He was enjoying what for him must have been halcyon days. The 1961 experience had, I thought, shaken him. But I admired the way he had come back during 1962 and the first half of 1963. Any lack of confidence at election time had evaporated. Except in the case of restrictive trade practices, the government had carried out its policies in that time unhampered by its narrow majority. There was little reason for Menzies to contemplate leaving office. He seemed to be in good health, if somewhat overweight. With the assistance of a good Cabinet (he remarked to me that it was the best in his experience) he was coping with the strain of office quite comfortably. It would be late 1964 before an election was due.

I had an idea — though the subject had never been discussed between us, except for a chance remark in 1958 — that he would have liked me to succeed him, though he must have been conscious of my greater interest in the law than in party politics and my weaknesses as a politician. Yet he had not raised the matter with me. I had come into Parliament without prior party experience. I was a newcomer, an outsider, and had not tried to build a support base in the party. I had got along quite well with my party colleagues and had the best of relations with fellow ministers. But high office, if it is to be successfully carried, needs a solid basis of loyal support, available through thick and thin, never more necessary than when the inevitable mistake has been made. I had no reason to think I had or could have this.

Further, Harold Holt and I had become good friends. I liked and trusted him. I knew he had aspirations to be Menzies' successor and many in the party so regarded him. I would not have contested his leadership if Menzies were to resign: he had solid party support, and my own nature would have prevented me from being so political as to put aside friendship and personal loyalties. No doubt that was a fundamental weakness in political life, and there is no doubt that I had such a weakness. I felt Holt had earned the opportunity to succeed Menzies.

My private estimate of Harold Holt was that, while affable, easygoing and possessing great political experience, he would find the Prime Minister's office heavy going. He compared very unfavourably with Menzies, and I doubted his capacity for judgment and leadership. I noted the attitudes of William McMahon and John Gorton and I thought they would eventually white-ant him. But I also realised that McEwen's antipathy to McMahon and Gorton's political weakness through being a senator would assist Holt. Although I thought McEwen would accept Holt, I thought their relationship would in time prove difficult for Holt. McEwen was a strong character, quite capable of going his own way and of protecting the interests of the Country Party and himself as he saw them.

Menzies gave the appearance that the Prime Minister's job was not overly difficult. He had a certain serenity, seeming always to be in control of the situation. In his early days he had the reputation that had been ascribed to Sir Walter Raleigh that "he was prepared to lose a friend to coin a joke". But I saw none of this. He had matured, and while he could score off Opposition politicians like Eddie Ward, he was very much less inclined to score off a friend. He had the enormous advantage of being able to sleep through the night, no matter what anxieties the day or the morrow carried. Each morning he would appear with clear eyes and a clear skin, completely refreshed. I think this led Holt to assume that his own prime ministership would be just as easy. I thought at the time that, bearing in mind the disarray of the Labor Party and the presence of the DLP

(Democratic Labour Party), Holt, if he were to succeed Menzies in the near future, would survive two parliamentary terms. Calwell was being undermined by Gough Whitlam, who was unrestrainedly ambitious. Though Calwell was still surviving in 1963, I realised that Whitlam, now deputy leader, would ultimately displace him. I doubted whether Whitlam, whom I regarded as an amateur as far as government administration went and who was arrogant and dictatorial in manner, could hold the Labor Party together. He did not seem to me to be a Labor man of a kind traditional Labor would rally round. Strangely, that party has fallen for career men, particularly those with academic records, such as Evatt and Whitlam, who have led to its undoing. Thus I did not think that the Labor Party would be able to defeat Holt for at least two terms.

On this timetable, even if Menzies retired soon, I would be in my late sixties or early seventies before I would feel free to contest the leadership of the party. The longer Menzies stayed, the more my own age would increase and add to the disquiet of any medical condition.

Having thought a great deal about the matter, I decided that I should retire from politics in four or five years' time. I would then be in my mid-sixties and still able to build another career for myself, most likely (but not necessarily) in the law. I decided to speak to Menzies about the future. We had a conversation one evening in late June 1963 in his room in the House; except for special official occasions, I never visited him at the Lodge. Having for so long kept my diabetic condition to myself, I felt no need on this occasion to tell him of it and did not do so. In retrospect, I think I was wrong in this and in a real sense unfair to him.

In the course of the interview I told him that I had made up my mind to leave politics in 1967, some time after the next election; that I would then leave in time for another man to be in place before that election. I gave no reason for my decision beyond saying that it was the result of much thought. He expressed his surprise and great disappointment. I think he thought I was enjoying my work as a minister (as I was) though I am sure he was conscious of my shortcomings as a parliamentarian.

During the discussion I indicated my feelings about Harold Holt and said I would not contest his leadership. Menzies did not canvass that matter with me at all, merely accepting my attitude. Nothing was said of any possibility of his resignation but it was tacitly assumed that it was not too far off. The upshot of our meeting was that I would fight another election with him and resign at or just before the following election. In my mind this timetable would enable me to complete the principal activities on which I was then engaged, particularly the restrictive trade practices legislation which was then in abeyance because of our electoral position, and the consolidation of our relations with Indonesia. I expected some party dissension about such matters and believed the government would need more than a bare majority of one to carry them through.

I had not decided what I would do after leaving politics. Menzies asked me about this. I could not give him any indication. There was always the law in which I could rely on a comfortable living. There might even be a place for me in commerce. But all that was in the future, which I thought at the time would take care of itself.

About this time, Menzies asked me what I thought about an early election. I said I would have had one well before the budget, which in my view could not enhance our electoral chances. Though an astute politician, Menzies was not given to making electoral promises. There would be no pork-barrelling.

But it was then too late to call an election before the budget. I said that I thought that we should have an election as soon as possible after the effects of the budget had passed off. Menzies asked me how I would fare in Parramatta if the government decided to subsidise the private schools. I said I might well lose my seat as I thought the Parramatta electorate would show strong opposition to such a change. But, I said, why go so far? Everyone is crying out for more to be done for the education of science students. Why not provide all the schools, public and private, with science laboratories? It would be a more useful step and would not excite opposition. It might even provide a basis for subsequent subsidisation. He quickly said that this seemed like a good idea. Later on Cabinet decided upon it and ultimately Gorton, as Minister for Education, was given the task of implementing the scheme. But at the time of our first chat about an early election this initiative had not been taken.

Although we were carrying on quite as usual, the narrow majority did put a strain on the Ministry. In any case it placed the government at risk in the event of the death of a member and the loss of the subsequent by-election. Menzies asked me why I thought we should have an early election. I said that though we had done well with a majority of one, living with it was risky and should be ended as soon as possible. Times were good, bellies were full, and the electorate had no discernible complaint. The Opposition was still in disarray and the DLP remained supportive of the government.

He asked me how I would fare in my electorate if there were an early election. This enquiry was no doubt prompted by my narrow victory in the 1961 election. I said I felt quite safe. I thought the electorate was quite content with the government's performance and little inclined to transfer its support to Labor. As well, I had actively attended to the electorate.

A few days later, Menzies raised the matter again. He said he had checked with the pundits and had been told that in an early election I was fairly certain to lose my seat, that there had been extensive building activity in Parramatta which would contribute to my downfall. I asked him who the pundits were. He said Senator Spooner and William McMahon. I said I thought they were wrong. I repeated that I had looked after the electorate and, while it was true that there had been a good deal of home-building, it was not of government housing, as had earlier happened in the Dundas Valley, but of private and mostly very substantial houses.

For the moment the matter was left there, but a week or so later, Menzies told me that he had checked again with the pundits and again been told that I was likely to lose my seat. Again I disputed this and expressed my confidence that, unless the Government were swept from office in a landslide, I would retain Parramatta. I assured him that he could consider the question of an early election on the assumption that I would be returned.

There the matter rested until one evening in November when Menzies rang me in Washington, where I had been talking with President Kennedy. He asked me to return home as he had become a "November man". I quickly finished what I was doing in Washington and returned to Sydney. Apropos of my confidence of surviving in an election, I might record my last few words with President Kennedy.

At the conclusion of our formal discussion, which had been about Malaysia, Borneo and Vietnam, and after the usual taking of photographs in the Oval Office, the President led me out of the room to the side verandah. I had earlier told him that I was going home straight away to face a general election. He asked me what the issues would be in the election. I said that I thought that perhaps — unusually — foreign affairs and my own conduct of them would figure prominently. He quickly responded, "Then you will lose". I asked him why he thought that. He said, "They will say that you have tied yourself to American apron strings and that will work fatally against you". I said I did not agree. I didn't think Australians were as gullible and foolish as that. I thought Australians understood the need for loyalty to one's allies, that they valued the American alliance and realised that it was necessary to work with America, and that doing so did not compromise national independence. I said I thought we would win — and perhaps quite comfortably. He had listened to me intently and replied, "You seem confident of your re-election. I wish I were of mine". They were the last words which passed between us as we parted from each other, other than words of personal farewell.

I had only returned to Australia a few days when in the early morning of 23 November Keith Waller rang to tell me of the President's assassination. As I had seen him so recently it seemed like a personal loss and apart from a sense of insecurity which the news engendered, I felt deep regret. As a boy I had learned of the impacts of Lincoln and Garfield. I felt great sympathy for the American people that yet another and, at least in their eyes, a promising young president had been violently taken from them.

The shock was not only personal. While I was in no position to assess the President and his work, my recent conversations with him and the result they produced made me regard him as potentially a good friend of Australia. The full import of the ANZUS Treaty, the possibility that America might be drawn into armed conflict by Australian actions, had come as a shock to him. But he did not show any signs of wishing to retreat from these implications. Indeed, the inferential result of our recent discussions was that the treaty would operate in relation to possibly warlike events in Borneo. Thus, by the news I received that morning, I felt that Australia had lost a friend. But I had little time to philosophise. The election was upon us.

I took no chances. I organised an intensive coverage of the electorate. I equipped three station wagons with up-to-date cassette-playing gear with speakers capable of being heard from a distance of half a mile. I recorded a number of three-minute speeches on self-rewinding tapes. With my son's assistance, three positions in the electorate were fixed for each week night for each of the three wagons. Friendly members of the Bar and party supporters manned the wagons, each taking up the planned three separate locations successively each night, remaining at each one only long enough to play my speech and to give the voting prescription before moving on. Thus no inconvenience was caused in neighbourhoods which valued their privacy. Several days a week, at lunchtime, the station wagons were taken to the shopping centres. Nancy Bird, Nancy Wake and Marion Hearnshaw (wife of the State Member for Eastwood) each took a wagon and made addresses to the shoppers. Other three-minute speeches were played over the loudspeakers.

I held a number of public meetings where I ridiculed the unilateral declaration of a nuclear-free zone in our hemisphere then a plank of Opposition policy, pointing out its danger to the nation. As geography is not a common strength in Australians, I had a slide made which I projected at the meetings to alert the audience to the position of the equator — that invisible line which marks out our hemisphere from that of much of Asia. When I emphasised the realities of a nuclear-free zone in our hemisphere, while in the hemisphere to our north nations were free to deploy nuclear weapons, one could hear some part of the audience gasp, the proposition was so obviously dangerous. I did not think that my more politically experienced colleagues thought at the outset that the proposal of showing a map to electors was such a good idea. But before the campaign ended I had requests to borrow the slides and the projection gear.

It was a vigorous campaign. My result in Parramatta was the second best in the Commonwealth for the Liberal Party in point of majority, exceeded only by the result obtained by John Cramer in Bennelong.

The Government was returned with a substantial majority, a very big turnaround from the narrow margin of 1961. It was that small majority which had justified to the Governor-General Menzies' request for a dissolution before the expiry of the full term of the Parliament. But incidentally it created the situation that a half-Senate election had to be held separately from a general election, which was not a good thing. Slim might of course have refused Menzies' request for a dissolution. Generally speaking, parliaments should run their full term of three years, a period which in any case is short enough. A multiplicity of elections is a most destabilising phenomenon. Much has been said about too frequent elections in Australia, and there is much substance in these complaints. It is the firm exercise of the Governor-General's discretion to dissolve the House which should ensure that parliaments do run their full term.

With the Government's attainment of a good working majority in 1963, I looked forward to preparing a Restrictive Trade Practices Bill and assumed without question that I would remain Attorney-General to carry it through. But I was to be disappointed. I had to bow to Menzies' wish that I give up the portfolio of Attorney-General and continue in External Affairs.

At the time, I accepted as genuine Menzies' stated reason for moving me from Attorney-General; I did not then suspect that he had yielded to pressure from the business community to prevent me from carrying my proposal through. Later, I must confess, I began to doubt this. Yet I held to the belief that if he had been questioning what I was proposing, he would have done so frankly in our discussion. Not only were we both lawyers, but over time we had become good friends and he had no occasion to be deceitful in dealing with me. Throughout my whole time in the ministry he had supported me and he never interfered in any way with my conduct of either portfolio. I can understand that he might have found it politically necessary to differ from me in my perception of what was required to check unacceptable restrictive practices in business. Throughout I had realised the party's political difficulties in accepting restrictive practices legislation, if for no other reason than that the party depended to some extent on the electoral support of industry leaders and industrial funding. But quite apart from that, the philosophy of the party was against undue government intervention in community affairs.

So I was deeply disappointed and frustrated, but on the announcement of the new Menzies administration, with Snedden as Attorney-General (whom naturally I congratulated), I settled down to the work of the Department of External Affairs. Although I remained in Cabinet until the following April, I was not consulted by Snedden or his department about the provisions of the Trade Practices Bill being prepared. But of course the Department had all the records of the work done in devising my scheme. When it emerged the Bill quite obviously owed more to American precedents than to my scheme.

While I gathered that the senior officers of the Attorney-General's Department were very disappointed that I did not continue as Attorney-General, I quickly appreciated that the senior officers of the Department of External Affairs were more than pleased that I would be able to devote my whole time and effort to External Affairs.

*****

One of my last actions as Minister for External Affairs was appointing a new ambassador to the United States. Towards the end of 1963 Sir Howard Beale's term was running out. The post in Washington had come to be regarded as one to be filled by a parliamentarian or an ex-parliamentarian, preferably one with ministerial experience. There was an advantage in having an ambassador with such experience; there might be added rapport between himself and his government because of it.

After some weeks I came to the view that Shane Paltridge was the only member of the Ministry I could recommend. Shane had performed very well in his portfolios and was a very useful member of Cabinet. He seemed to me to have excellent judgment and a capacity for communicating with others. And he had a very good wife, Molly, who would have filled the role of ambassadress splendidly.

So I had a good chat with Shane and suggested that he accept the appointment. I disclosed to him that I had already decided I would not remain in politics and that he ought to know that in making up his mind whether he would accept a post abroad. I had already told Menzies this. Shane declined the offer because he wanted to stay in active political life in Australia.

Since there were no other suitable men in the Ministry I decided that it might be better to appoint a good departmental officer. Keith Waller was my choice. Then I asked the Prime Minister if I might see him about the appointment.

As I have mentioned, the Menzies Government was very much a ministerial government where the minister took initiatives and responsibility conforming to Cabinet policy but making his own decisions in implementing it. It was a form of government which I much favoured; perhaps you may think this is because I like getting my own way, and there is an element of truth in this. But in this case I would be departing from political convention. Menzies arranged to see me at Kirribilli House in Sydney.

Kirribilli House had been in somewhat derelict condition when the Menzies Government decided to restore and refurbish it. It turned out to be a very comfortable small house, very conveniently placed and generally of great use. Its availability had a very interesting side effect. Menzies was a Melburnian and like many Melburnians tended to regard Sydneysiders as being mostly sharp businessmen somewhat too eager to succeed and even more eager to do so quickly no matter what the opposition. In short, they were considered brash. But when he began to use Kirribilli House, Menzies' attitude towards Sydneysiders visibly changed. He got to know more Sydney business and professional people, and I encouraged him to become familiar with the members of the Sydney Bar. I think his stiff Melbourne attitude was much softened by the fact that he stayed from time to time at Kirribilli House and saw much more of Sydneysiders than he might otherwise.

When Dick Casey, another Melburnian, became Governor-General and began to use Admiralty House, he said to me one day, "Gar, you've never told me how beautiful Sydney is", and I remember replying, "Well, what good would that have been, Dick? You're a Melburnian, and to you the world ends at the top end of Collins Street".

My remark contained a grain or two of truth. When I appeared in the Melbourne Supreme Court or before the High Court in Melbourne I had always felt, particularly in the early days of practice, that I was viewed somewhat askance. I really was not one of "us". I think some of this standoffishness wore off in the course of time, largely I think through my friendship with Douglas Menzies, but I could not say that I ever felt I had "arrived" in Melbourne.

When I saw the Prime Minister about appointing a departmental officer as Ambassador to Washington if there was no one suitable in the Ministry, he did not readily agree. Ultimately he came to accept that it was better in the circumstances to appoint a good officer than an inadequate parliamentarian, but he quickly said, "But you won't appoint Tange". I said no, I was not thinking of Tange. I never discovered the reason for the antipathy Menzies had to Tange, but I knew it was deep-seated and persistent. I said I was contemplating Keith Waller, who had had a long experience of association with government and politicians. I remembered that he had once been secretary to Billy Hughes, which was a very good introduction I am sure to the uncertainties of political fortune.

He had also had a long experience in the department and as an international diplomat. He had a good presence and a wife used to diplomatic life. To my mind he had good judgment and communication skills and would be a very loyal ambassador; he would carry out the government's policy no matter what he might think about it, at the same time giving the government the best of his honest advice. Menzies did not have any objection to Waller. I was pleased with the discussion, though aware that I was stepping away from tradition and likely to experience repercussions from some members of the Ministry.

Two days later Menzies asked me had I spoken to Waller yet. I said I had not.

"For the moment don't go any further with the matter. Your colleagues are very dissatisfied that you're not going to appoint a minister."

"Well, of course I realise that my point of view won't be generally accepted and undoubtedly there'll be disappointment. But we've been through the list and I don't think there's any minister apart from Shane I'd feel confident to recommend."

"Would you offer it to Gorton?"

"I will if you ask me to do so, but he wouldn't take it."

"Why do you say that?"

"He's been my assistant minister in External Affairs and I've had an opportunity to observe him. He's rather headstrong, he likes going his own way, he doesn't readily accept discipline and he doesn't like being told what to do, particularly by me. If I were to offer him the post I'd have to tell him there'd be no freelancing. He wouldn't like that."

Menzies listened intently. He smiled and said, "Well, he won't take it, but for a different reason".

"What reason?"

"He wants to be Prime Minister."

I was surprised. "Sitting up in the Senate will give him no chance of building a base in the Reps."

"Never mind, that's what he wants to be and he's likely to want to pursue it."

"Since you've asked me, I will offer him the appointment but it will be coupled with the emphasis that he'll do as he's told."

Menzies nodded his assent and we parted, each of us I think a little bemused at the turn the conversation had taken.

A few days later, after a Liberal Party dinner in the old Canberra Hotel, I had a chance to speak to Gorton. We went for a walk along Constitution Avenue, across the bridge towards Civic and back again. I offered him the post, stipulating as I had told Menzies I would that there would be no freelancing. Gorton received all this without demur and in an almost offhand way said he would think about it. After a day or so Gorton told me he would not accept the offer. I told Menzies and he confirmed that I could now approach Waller.

As events turned out, I did not appoint Waller because I ceased to be a minister before the time to do so arrived. But I did offer him the post after discussion with Arthur Tange, and obtained his acceptance. It was left to my successor, Paul Hasluck, to make the recommendation of the appointment. It may be doubtful whether left to himself my successor would have nominated Keith Waller or for that matter any other officer. But Waller was appointed and he served very well indeed. It was quite a notable event that for the first time a good officer rather than a parliamentarian had been appointed to Washington.

* * * * *

In the New Year Arthur Tange discussed with me the possibility of a ministerial tour of European capitals. The aim would be to present Australia to Europe as a complex society of high cultural sensitivity and of wide and diverse artistic as well as commercial achievement, not merely an agricultural country producing wool and wheat. Arthur's initial approach to me was to establish whether I was willing to undertake such a strenuous journey. After discussion of the pros and cons, I expressed my willingness to do so.

For my part, I held and still hold the view that it is no part of the Foreign Minister's function to do the work of the diplomat. The minister is neither suitably trained nor possessed by nature of the necessary professional talents for this work. Also, if the minister in effect displaces the professional diplomat, the morale of the department may well be detrimentally affected. Of course, there are occasions when the participation of the minister in the country's representation to a particular country on some matter of unusual critical national importance is of advantage. But for the most part the minister, in my view, should be at home supervising the Department, contributing to the formation and direction of policy, weighing its political content and consequence. But as in 1962 in the case of Asia, I thought ministerial contact with Europe would be advantageous. Tange and I both thought that my wife should accompany me.

In early March, the Prime Minister called me in to tell me that Sir Owen Dixon had expressed his intention to retire as Chief Justice. This surprised me. I had appeared as counsel before Sir Owen over many years and had had many personal discussions with him. Although he never looked robust, I thought him physically tough and resilient. Yet I had noticed over the past six years that he was not quite as consistently alert as I had known him earlier, though I saw little evidence that the quality of his work had declined. Indeed, I had formed the opinion that he was likely to remain in office till disabling ill health compelled his retirement; I saw no signs of such a condition having arrived. It must be remembered that in his generation, members of the High Court Bench had served well into their eighties. I had seen no reason to think that Sir Owen would not do likewise. The introduction of a retiring age was to come much later. (I must say I could not approve of compulsory retirement, particularly as it set the retiring age as low as seventy. To do so is to deny the community the service of many well-furnished lawyers of long experience during which the capacity for wise judgment has been developed.)

So I was much disturbed by Menzies' news. My initial reaction was to tell him that Dixon's early retirement raised problems for the Government which would need time to resolve. An obvious replacement from the practising Bar was not available. I suggested that to make time for consultation, Menzies might suggest to Dixon that he take leave of absence, something which was due to him for he had served long and unstintingly. He could decide at the end of this period whether he still wished to retire; he might feel sufficiently recovered to want to continue. I reminded Menzies that Sir John Latham had taken this course before he retired in April 1952.

Menzies put my suggestion to Sir Owen but he insisted on retiring immediately. When the Prime Minister told me this, I said that I had already given some thought to finding a candidate whom I could recommend for appointment as Chief Justice. Of course, I was no longer Attorney-General but I expected that, because of my background and our personal relationship, I would be consulted. I said I was familiar with both the Sydney and the Melbourne Bars, and for that matter, members of the Queensland Bar and the practitioners in South and Western Australia. I did not see any member of those Bars who in my view could adequately fill the position. I said I was not in favour of promoting anyone from the existing Bench. I held the view that once a judicial officer was appointed he should have nothing to expect and that promotion within the same court ought to be avoided unless circumstances were unusual. In any case, I would not favour any one of the judges to fill the vacancy. I said that of the Melbourne Bar, Keith Aickin was an outstanding lawyer, the best among them. But I thought the office of Chief Justice needed a lawyer with general experience, including common-law experience and most importantly, administrative capacity and experience. I did not think Aickin, although having had wide commercial experience, filled that bill.

To my mind, the High Court badly needed an administrator. I said that really, only the two of us, Menzies and myself, might satisfy the requirements. Of the two of us, I thought he was indispensable to the government and I was not. I was content in my ministerial life though I had already indicated my intention not to remain in political life, an intention if anything confirmed by my loss of the Attorney-General portfolio. So, though I was not seeking the position of Chief Justice, I was prepared to go if the Cabinet felt that way. It was a matter for him and our colleagues. I was not pressing a request though I would both welcome the appointment and fulfil the office, if it was so decided. The matter was left there and I went on with my ministerial plans. I said nothing whatever of our conversation or my own position to anyone outside my family. I had no wish to raise expectations or to give cause for mischievous rumour.

I did ask the Prime Minister that in fixing the date for Sir Owen's retirement he remember my own commitments as I particularly wished to be present at the farewell ceremony. Among my engagements was an attendance in Manila at an ECAFE conference in April. To my dismay, however, Sir Owen insisted on retiring while I was at this conference, and I missed his farewell in Melbourne on 13 April 1964.

On my return from Manila on 20 April, the arrangements for the European journey had been finalised and cleared with the Prime Minister. I was to leave Sydney on Thursday, 23 April. This necessitated my leaving Canberra on the evening of Wednesday, 22 April. Between the date of my return from Manila and 22 April, Snedden, now Attorney-General, had spoken to me, asking me if I would accept appointment as Chief Justice, if it were offered to me. I said that I would. I had heard nothing from the Prime Minister about the replacement of Sir Owen but obviously some discussion must have been taking place between Menzies and Snedden. Holt had spoken to me and suggested to me that I take the appointment. He spoke in terms commending my suitability for the office and indicated his personal support. I think from our conversation that Holt genuinely thought that judicial life would be less strenuous for me. It will be remembered that he had been most considerate to me during the debate on the Crimes Bill. McMahon also spoke to me as we crossed the tarmac in Canberra airport one morning, saying I ought to accept the office. At some time on the Wednesday, Senator Spooner asked me what my own wishes were and I said that if offered it, I would accept and be pleased to fill the office.

That afternoon I made a speech in the House about the Foreign Affairs Committee of the House, which I was encouraging the Labor Opposition to join, something that it had so far refused to do, largely because of the requirement of confidentiality of sensitive material made available to the committee. Immediately afterwards I went to Menzies' office to say farewell before leaving for Europe. John Bunting told me the Prime Minister was occupied but likely at any moment to go into a meeting of a committee of Cabinet. I said I would wait and speak to him as he passed through the Cabinet anteroom. After a few moments Menzies bustled out of his office. I told him I had come to say farewell. He said he would have to get the Cabinet together to consider the position of Chief Justice. I said I would be away only three weeks and he should consider leaving that matter till my return. He said he did not like that idea and would get Cabinet together. That of course was a matter for him: I was off to Sydney and then to Europe. I said goodbye and went straight to the airport. There I met Arthur Tange who was to accompany me to Sydney. During the flight, for the first time I alerted Tange to the possibilities. He was very disturbed by my news. He said that he had enjoyed working with me and that he looked forward to a continuance of our association. I reciprocated these sentiments and said I would be loathe to leave the department. But, I said, ministers are easy to replace, chief justices difficult to find.

When the plane landed on that part of Mascot Airport set aside for non-commercial flights, there was a message asking me to ring a number in Canberra. Snedden answered the phone and informed me that Cabinet had accepted his nomination of me to be Chief Justice and had made the appointment. I received this information with very mixed feelings. The news was hardly a shock, but this was an unsatisfactory situation brought about by the unnecessary haste with which the appointment had been made and which in any case had resulted from Menzies not having dealt with the matter earlier. There would have been no problem whatsoever in allowing the office to be vacant for three weeks or more, even though such a course left room for undesirable press speculation.

For me personally there was disappointment that I was denied an opportunity to represent Australia to European capitals as more than a producer of agricultural products, something which I thought was very necessary. As well, I would have little or no opportunity to speak to my officers in both the departments I had headed. As it turned out I had no opportunity to farewell my parliamentary colleagues and to thank them for their friendship and support. But, believing that the High Court needed an administrative head as well as a widely-experienced lawyer, and realising that my successor in the ministerial office could pick up where I left off, the departmental officers, as is usual, providing the necessary continuity, I felt no real regret in accepting the new office. But undoubtedly there was no feeling of elation: the disarray of the department resulting from the suddenness of the change loomed large in my feelings.

I immediately told Tange what I had heard from Snedden. We walked out on the tarmac discussing the situation. He again expressed his considerable disappointment that I was leaving the Ministry, but he had urgent work to do. The immediate problem was the itinerary which had been arranged with our embassies and the governments of a number of European countries. Tange had straight away to organise messages to those countries cancelling a multitude of engagements. I was indeed sorry for him.

For a time, after I had made a personal phone call, we strolled about the tarmac together. The more we examined the new situation, the more the Cabinet decision seemed unnecessarily to have complicated life for Tange and the Department and indeed for me. Altogether, I think it was an unpleasant moment, a sudden change with new restraints on what I could be able to do and say, for I took the view that once appointed, I should stand aloof from my former associates.

Norma, who was to accompany me on the journey, had packed her bags against our departure on the following morning. I rang her from the air facilities terminal to tell her what had happened. I think she was put out by the drastic change in our plans, though I think that in her heart she was glad that I was returning to the law and leaving behind the strains of political life. She was then, and she still is, most solicitous for my health, knowing what my diabetic condition entails. Also, she has always felt more comfortable with lawyers than she did with politicians, though she made many friends among them.

So Arthur Tange and I parted at the airport, he to return to Canberra to rearrange the European appointments and to undertake the task of supporting a new Minister, I to my home on the Pittwater to ready myself for another change in the direction of my life.

* * * * *

My appointment was announced by the Prime Minister when the House met on Thursday morning, 23 April 1964. This must have come as a great surprise to all the members who had not been in on the decision to appoint me. I do not know — and indeed have never enquired — who attended the Cabinet or what passed between them. All that I know is that Snedden proposed me as the sole nominee. Nor, except for my conversations with Menzies, have I heard any explanation for the haste with which the decision was taken. That is not to say that I have not felt curious about the matter. I took the view, however, that once appointed to judicial office I should immediately and entirely sever my relationship with government and the party except in so far as matters concerning the administration of the court might require my dealing with government.

The press, ever prone to find fault with Menzies, said that I had been "kicked upstairs" by Menzies because he regarded me as a competitor for his office. That was nonsense of the first order. Nobody in his right mind would for one moment have thought that I represented any threat to Menzies' position as Prime Minister. But the idea nonetheless received an airing.

Menzies, I knew, would feel badly about such a press suggestion. To have appointed me merely as a political manoeuvre he would have regarded not only as shoddy but as a failure to perform his duty to maintain the standing and integrity of the judiciary. I am sure he prided himself on his own high sense of duty, and his adherence to the rule of law and integrity in its administration. The choice of those who would be responsible for such administration was integral to the maintenance of that integrity. I felt sure he was extremely sorry to lose my services to the government and would have been glad of a solution which did not involve my leaving the Ministry.

Because I sensed the extent of Menzies' hurt, I seriously considered making a public disavowal to put the record straight. But I decided against it. For one thing, in my view, the press assertion should not be dignified by any statement of mine: but more importantly, once appointed, I felt I should not indulge in any public self-justification, or in any defence of the government.

I think that there were those, including Dame Pattie, who were disappointed that I had not made the statement. It may be that I disappointed the Prime Minister as well as his Lady. But even on reflection now, I feel that I took the right course. I did resolve, however, that at my swearing-in speech I should make it clear that I had come to the office by my own choice.

A new door had opened and through it I must go. My days in parliamentary and ministerial life were at an end. The years 1958 to 1964 had been full of intense interest and I think of a good deal of accomplishment. It had been different from any experience I had formerly had. Though I did not show it, and was not unduly disturbed by it, I entertained a sense of inadequacy. I was at times called upon to do something for which I was not trained but which challenged my own drive and capacity to succeed. Although my legal training and experience fitted me quite well for the performance of the Attorney's task, in External Affairs I had had no preparation beyond a distant and I hope intelligent interest. Nevertheless I had enjoyed all of it and deeply regretted leaving it.

The control of each of the two departments with their many well-trained officers had quickly to be learned and performed with generous perspicacity. With them I had formed friendships and always felt respect for them and their instructing support. I would resent the application to them of the ugly description of bureaucrats. In my experience of and with them, so far from deserving such an epithet, they deserve praise; and I am pleased to give it.

I think I was better prepared to assume my new office when I did than I would have been had I accepted a seat on the Bench in 1958. But, of course, the estimate of my performance in it and my ministerial performance must be left to time and another generation.

I had now to arrange for my resignation from the House and for my swearing in on the following Monday morning. On Friday, 24 April, I went to Canberra and handed to the Speaker my written resignation as Member for Parramatta. I saw a few members to say farewell but there were very few around, as Parliament was not sitting that day. Also I did not have an opportunity to speak to the Prime Minister because of his engagements. I left the House, without any send-off by my colleagues, and much as I had entered it — as an outsider, or at any rate, so I felt myself. Although I had established firm relationships and many friends in the Government parties, my own judgment was that I never really became a fellow politician. Perhaps this derived as much as anything from my own failure to cultivate support for myself. Perhaps it was due in no small part to that self-sufficiency engendered by having had to make my own way through life.

The reaction of the members of the Opposition to the announcement of my appointment interested me. They quite understandably were affected by the almost unceremonious and hasty way in which the appointment was made. Although doubtless a poor politician, I had successfully promoted a great deal of legislation and been engaged with some matters in the international affairs of the country. So to have unceremoniously disappeared from the Parliament and the Ministry must have seemed, to say the least, unusual. Arthur Calwell was generous in his comment so far as it concerned me. He rightly thought that my parliamentary experience would enhance my ability to perform the duties of my new office. None questioned my own qualification for the office or attributed improper motives or conduct to me, but Calwell and others took the occasion to assault Menzies.

Menzies responded to Calwell's criticisms. On the timing of my appointment, he said that it would have been wrong for me to have made my proposed international journey as the Chief Justice elect. There had been press speculation before I had been nominated for the office.

On Monday, 27 April, at a sitting of the High Court, very well attended by the Bar and by solicitors and members of the public, I presented to the Senior Justice, Sir Edward McTiernan, who had been acting Chief Justice pending an appointment, the Letters Patent appointing me. He received them and administered the oaths of allegiance and of office. Then followed the speeches of the Attorneys-General of the Commonwealth and of New South Wales and representatives from the Bar and the solicitors.

To these generous welcoming speeches I replied, I am afraid, at some length. I concluded my remarks by saying: "I can only hope that at the end of my time with all my work, good and bad, in retrospect, it will be possible to say with kindness and yet with truth that my decision to come to this great office was among the better decisions I shall have made." And next day I began presiding over the court's daily activities.

After my appointment, I regularly visited Sir Owen and Lady Dixon when I was in Melbourne until her death; and thereafter, I called on Sir Owen quite regularly. On those visits we had many friendly conversations and I received from him much useful advice.

As well as calling on Sir Owen Dixon when in Melbourne I regularly called on Menzies, Sir Robert as he now was, after his retirement. I saw him when he was in the Mercy Hospital where he was being treated for a cardiac condition. I recall that on one such occasion he commended "our health insurance policy", the benefits of which he was then experiencing. There was an understandable degree of pride in the tone of his remarks. On later occasions when I saw him at his house in Haverbrack Avenue, it was clear from our conversations that he was still keenly interested in public affairs and followed the fortunes of the Liberal Party closely. One thing struck me from time to time: his reference to my office as Chief Justice. It was clear to me that he regarded highly the office and the honour of being appointed to fill it. There was never any questioning of the appropriateness of my appointment nor any tinge of jealousy in his references. But the manner of his remarks about the office recalled to my mind his statement to me in 1958 that he would like to have been Chief Justice of Victoria.

The position of Chief Justice, I venture to think, would have been for him a welcome office. I wondered whether if he had had the choice between being Prime Minister or Chief Justice he might have chosen the latter. It was not impossible. He was an able lawyer, well imbued with the fundamentals of the law, devoted to the rule of law and the separation of powers, matters he fully understood to be basic to the maintenance of individual freedom. I always felt he was at home in the company of lawyers and it seemed at times that he felt political life less worthy and less satisfactory than the pursuit of the law.

I called on Sir Robert early in the Melbourne sittings of the High Court in October 1975. He was far from well, confined to a wheelchair and irked by the restraints imposed by his physical condition. We had a fairly wide-ranging conversation but I got the impression that he was seriously ill. So at the end of the sittings, as I was leaving to return to Sydney, I decided to call on him again. This time I saw him in his office in Collins House. Just after we began to converse, his secretary brought him a message from Malcolm Fraser. The message was simply that "we are acting". I had been following the newspaper accounts of events in the Parliament and consequently understood the purport of the message. It also alerted me, by inference, to the fact that there had already been some earlier communication between Fraser and Menzies.

The arrival of the message very obviously disturbed Sir Robert. He was somewhat angered by it. He said to me, quite testily, "The young fools are too impatient. If they give this fellow (meaning Gough Whitlam) enough rope he will hang himself".

He then turned to me and said, "Gar, what would you do?".

"Assuming a proper occasion", I said, "I would not be troubled by a refusal of Supply by the Senate. After all, it is the Parliament's traditional and ultimate means of control of the Executive. Whether or not there is an occasion to do so now, I cannot really say. I do not know enough of the facts. But I do not think Fraser realises how bad things are with the country. If they are to be put right, Fraser if in government must do some very unpopular things. So what would trouble me would be the certainty that in three years the government would be most unpopular. On political grounds, I would not refuse Supply unless I felt very certain of such a large majority from the electorate in the ensuing election that, at the end of three years, the government could stand the loss of a substantial number of seats and still survive. If it did, things would be easier three years later. I cannot see such an electoral result at the present time".

He smiled at me and said, "That would be asking too much".

"Yes it would. But that is what I think."

After some pleasantries, I left to catch my plane. In all, the interview was brief and in a sense casual, yet to my mind memorable.

Part IV

Chief Justice

18 Justice in the High Court

When I joined the High Court in 1964, I became one of a group of men who had known each other over long periods. With the exceptions of Mr Justice McTiernan and Mr Justice Owen, all the members of the court at some time had been my junior and, of course, at times my opponent. We had been friends at the Bar. I had appeared before Mr Justice Owen quite often when he was a judge of the Supreme Court and in the Petrov Commission when he was its chairman. Certainly when I joined the High Court I made no attempt to give these men leadership in the decision of cases, though I did make many administrative changes to speed up the work of the court. Later as younger men replaced those with whom I first came to sit, the disparity between our ages and to some extent our professional experience would have made it very ill-fitting indeed that I should attempt to influence their views otherwise than by the circulation of my own reasons for judgment.

During my practising days I had formed firm views of the function of the judiciary, having experienced its work at various levels. On assuming office I intended to confine myself to the administration of the law as it exists. I had no intention of attempting to make law in the sense of performing a legislative act to change it. I did not intend to engage in any form of social engineering. While quite prepared to correct a precedent which I thought to have been erroneous when made, I did not intend to alter one when I thought it to have been correctly decided in order to bring it up to date. To do so, in my philosophy, would be a legislative act solely in the province of the appropriate legislature. Consequently, few if any of my judgments attracted the attention of the imaginative journalists.

The most important function of the Chief Justice during a hearing, and the one I sought to perform, is to identify and bring to the fore the problems the case presents, to establish the issues of fact and law which arise for solution, and to put aside peripheral and irrelevant considerations. My colleagues of course were quite at liberty to think and say that I had not found the relevant issues or that I had not correctly formulated them or that counsel were unduly confined in their argument. But generally speaking that rarely happened. My colleagues seemed content with what I had done.

Some barristers disliked this form of judicial intervention. They preferred a Bench which sat quiet, allowing them an uninterrupted opportunity to address it, however far from the point they strayed or however repetitive they became. That, I am afraid, I did not always tolerate. I was ever conscious of the passage of public time, of which the court never had a surplus. I had had the experience of conducting cases before an interrogative court, exchanging points of view with its members. To no small extent my success as an advocate had been due to an ability to find the critical issue and by concentrating on it, persuade my hearers to acceptance of my submissions. In the course of doing so, an ability to receive and respond to judicial interventions was no disadvantage.

Another feature, perhaps not a function of the Chief Justice's office but undoubtedly a characteristic of my own tenure, was that I regarded court time as working time, during which I had not merely to listen but to evaluate and think about the propositions put forward on each side and in appropriate moments to indicate my own reactions to them. An advocate of quality will welcome the opportunity of eliciting from the Bench its reactions to his or her propositions and the opportunity to deal with those reactions. After all, the courtroom is a place for a friendly exchange between counsel and Bench, none the less friendly because views may be forcefully expressed. A court which treats court time as wasted time (as I have known some judges to do) constitutes a risk to the due administration of the law. On the contrary, in my view the court hearing is a time not merely to identify the issues arising but to work towards a resolution of them.

Those who regard the time in court as wasted rely on reading the transcript later on. This seems to me to forfeit the great advantage of an oral discussion in which an evaluation of submissions tends to clarify an understanding of the issues. Such judges would have to rely on written submissions to present counsel's argument. To my mind, written submissions cannot take the place of oral discussion, useful as they may prove as summaries of or supplements to oral discussion.

In more recent times, when a hearing involves the presentation of many documents, there is likely to be a greater tendency to the presentation of written arguments. While I understand the difficulties in presenting complex commercial issues, I retain the view that the description of such detail that allows of an oral presentation of argument is worth the effort of performing it. Thinking back over my years in office, I am unrepentant about my endeavours to keep argument to the relevant and to avoid the waste of public time. This was, to my mind, a vital function of the presiding judge.

To keep the High Court's work up to date, a system was developed by me under which the likely length of the hearing of each appeal was assessed as the appeal books were brought to my notice. The court had seven judges upon my assumption of office. In general the hearing of an appeal needed five judges and in some instances only three, or four in the case of an appeal from the decision of a judge of the court. But in constitutional cases all the available judges sat. I resolved early in my term of office that I would preside in all cases unless there was some compelling reason for my absence.

During the period up to 1973, the court not only heard appeals but tried cases at first instance. Most of these were presented as appeals from the assessment of the Commissioner of Taxation or from a decision of the Taxation Board of Review, but they were in part trials upon oral evidence. They were heard by a single judge, sitting in the No 2 Court contemporaneously with a full court hearing appeals in No 1. This list of single judges had to be taken into account in making up the lists for hearing. The name of the judge proposed for the hearing of these cases appeared in the weekly proposal.

The purpose of this listing procedure was to avoid waste of the court's time and to avoid bringing counsel to the courthouse to wait unnecessarily for their cases to be heard. Also, judges, on being left free to do so, had the time to complete reserved judgments. Each Thursday a proposal for the ensuing week was circulated, listing the cases and the judge or judges by whom each would be heard. My colleagues understood that the proposal was tentative and would yield to their individual convenience or preference.

This arrangement worked excellently. Judges knew in advance for what cases they should prepare themselves. Those not listed to sit could devote themselves to reserved judgments. The scheme became so accepted that if the proposal was not circulated by the Thursday, my associate would receive an enquiry for the list from the associates of the other judges. The effect was to reduce the backlog of cases so that in quite a short while after my appointment the lists came up to date and remained so. I think that the Bar appreciated not having to attend the court fruitlessly because too many cases had been listed in a day.

*****

During my term of office, some of my colleagues suggested that I approach the government to arrange for all rights of appeal to the High Court to be removed so that the only appeals to be heard would be those which the court itself chose to hear. I considered the proposal but declined to act upon it.

At the time I joined the High Court, there was a considerable range of matters in which citizens had the right to appeal to the court. Included in those matters were objections to taxation assessments of income tax. Although these taxation matters came to the court in the form of appeals, they mostly involved an original hearing, the taking of evidence and the determination of liability under a complex and cumbersome statutory code. From a judge's decision there was a right of appeal to the full bench, a right not infrequently exercised both by the taxpayer and by the Crown. One result of this process was that a final decision on the meaning and operation of the Income Tax Assessment Act could be fairly quickly obtained. Being a decision of the High Court, it was definitive and binding throughout Australia.

There were also applications and contests under the Patents Copyright and Trade Mark Acts and occasionally suits for damages for negligence on the part of federal officers or statutory bodies, and very occasionally, compensation claims between citizens. In all these there were rights of appeal.

Soon after my appointment, I began to take my share of this trial work. Sir Owen Dixon, on an occasion when I had called to see him, said that he had noticed that I was sitting at first instance. He strongly advised me not to continue to do so. He said he had not sat at first instance after his appointment as Chief Justice and he gave me his reasons for this. I accepted them and took his advice. Accordingly, I ceased to sit at first instance, but did once sit as a court of disputed returns. This attempt on my part to reduce the burden on the other members of the court came to an end.

However, later I decided to approach the government asking that the Parliament relieve the court of some of this work. In consequence, the original jurisdiction in taxation and industrial property was removed from the court and vested in the State Supreme Courts. But the right of appeal to the High Court from the Supreme Court's decision remained. This change effected a considerable reduction in the load of litigation falling on the court. For the Parliament to remove all rights of appeal, however, would, I thought, transform the existing supplementary power to give special leave to appeal into something quite different, namely an uncontrolled discretion to entertain or to refuse to entertain any appeal.

It also seemed to me quite unlikely that in the exercise of such a discretion reasons for its exercise would regularly be given. Thus it was unlikely that there would develop any consistent body of precedent which might on the one hand provide some control of the exercise of this discretion and on the other provide some predictability for the citizen and the legal profession. To my mind, to have removed all rights of appeal would have created an absolute and uncontrolled discretion, something I consider would be anathema in a society built on the rule of law, which ever involves and should produce predictability.

*****

The layman often places an unwarranted emphasis on the position of the Chief Justice of the High Court. It seems sometimes to be thought that he should lead his colleagues so as to obtain as much unanimity (and presumably in the sense of his own opinion) as possible. But in my view, this is not the function of the Chief Justice. He ought to administer the court, manage its business, control its staff and arrange its lists, taking into account in all these matters the opinions and wishes of his colleagues, whom he should consult as necessary. For the rest he is only one among equals.

Judges worked independently on their judgments. The High Court never had, and did not develop, a practice of formal consultation among all members of the Bench before reasons were prepared, though discussion did take place between individual judges. As far as I was aware, however, there was no lobbying by one judge of others: the individual's judgment was respected and was very much his own. Not only was there no formal discussion before the hearing but also the court did not formally decide as a body on the result. That only emerged when the individual reasons for judgment were circulated, sometimes not till the last of such reasons came to hand.

The advantage to the public and the practising profession of a unanimous decision of the High Court may seem obvious. It certainly contributes to the certainty of the law and perhaps to the simplicity of its expression. But it can have disadvantages. Unanimous expression of a decision may involve compromise in language and even in substance, which could mean that the community may not receive the benefit of the full effort of all the judges on the case. It is easier simply to agree with a reasoned view presented for consideration than it would be to work out and write one's own opinion; and considerations may emerge from one's own work which may not have been apparent from reading another's opinion. It is therefore possible that apparent unanimity may result from a too ready concurrence in a solution presented.

In Britain some law lords, given to expressing individual opinions when delivering judgment in the House of Lords, have been disinclined to sit on a board of the Privy Council because of its need to express its advice with a single expression of reasons. When later I sat as one of the members of the Privy Council, I took steps to persuade the Lord Chancellor to vary the 600-year rule which precluded the public expression of dissent by a member of the Council. Lord Gardiner yielded to my suggestion and varied the rules so that a member of the Council could publicly dissent from its decision, both in point of expression and in point of substance.

On the other hand, the disadvantage of diverse expressions of opinions supporting the same result is that it often leads to uncertainty and confusion, particularly if the individual opinions are expressed discursively and at great length. But I am inclined to think that nonetheless the expression of individual opinion is in most cases preferable as long as it is brief and clear, without *obiter dicta*.

Holding these views, I never at any time lobbied any fellow judge to seek his concurrence in any view of mine. I think it would be a very bad thing for the public if any Chief Justice, or for that matter any judge, did that. There is of course plenty of room for consultation between judges, leading as it does at times to joint judgments. For me, the acceptable way of influencing my colleagues' views was to circulate to them my reasons for judgment as soon as I had completed them, just as they may influence my views by circulating theirs.

In any case there was little time or opportunity for the frequent meetings and discussions that would have been necessary to produce a unanimous decision. The habit of individual expression was also so well ingrained among those with whom I came to sit that I thought a radical change in this respect would be disruptive and doubtful of success.

But with the arrival of new members of the court I did try to make some changes. My first suggestion was that instead of each judge reciting the facts of the case in his reasons for judgment, one judge at the conclusion of the hearing should be asked to prepare and circulate a draft of the facts, from which any judge could request a variation. There was little room for differences on the facts and ample opportunity for agreement in an accurate narration; any particular emphasis desired by a judge could be made in his own reasons. The exercise of setting out the facts of a case often leads to a clarification of the issues. I felt that perusal and, if need be, correction of such a draft statement of the facts could perform much the same function. When agreed, this statement of the facts could be made part of the law report and no recital of the facts need form part of the individual reasons for judgment. This proposal, however, proved unacceptable.

Later, and in relation to a particular case, I suggested holding a conference at or soon after the conclusion of a hearing so that the fundamental issues could be determined and perhaps the general inclination of the individual minds exposed. This found no favour either.

One other attempt at a means of moving towards common ground is worth mentioning. It was the practice for judges not to circulate anything until they had a complete and final statement of their reasons for judgment. It was unusual for all judges who had heard a case, or even a majority of them, to circulate reasons in that case at or about the same time. There was often a substantial interval between the circulation of the first set of reasons and the last, or even the next to be circulated. The gap between the appearance of reasons may tend to lessen the impact which the later reasons have. I had the idea that if judges could be persuaded to circulate a tentative draft set of reasons while their minds had not finally resolved the problem in hand, these tentative drafts might be circulated earlier than final reasons and thus reduce the effect of the gap. But my suggestion was not adopted. Indeed, some judges told me they could not do as I suggested: that they did not really feel able to produce even tentative reasons and preferred to hold any circulation of reasons till they had reached a final conclusion. I respected my colleagues' view and accepted that my proposal was impracticable.

A member of the High Court is, for Australian purposes, a judge of ultimate authority. It is his view which if accepted or concurred in by a majority of his colleagues becomes part of a definitive statement of the law. Reasons he must give for his view and they should convince by their logic. Of course all the relevant books must be read and reread as part of the judicial process. The unwritten law is to be found in the decisions of earlier courts which form precedents which the courts must respect and from which they should not depart unless convinced that such a precedent is erroneously decided. But to bolster the judge's conclusions formed after this process has been followed by citation of the views of others, however eminent and authoritative, may reduce the authority of the judge and present him as no more than a research student recording by citation his researched material. Of course, a mere *ipse dixit* would not be acceptable. The supporting reasoning must be convincing and if citation is necessary to complete the logical process, then of course it must be made. But otherwise it can become an exercise in essay-writing rather than the statement of reason for an authoritative judgment. I did try to follow this belief in writing my own judgments.

I have little doubt that discursive reasons for judgment contribute little to the law's certainty and much to its confusion, particularly if opinions are expressed as *obiter dicta*, views expressed which are unnecessary to the resolution of the dispute before the court. After all, the primary and fundamental function of the court is to resolve that dispute; it is the issues which their controversy raises which must be resolved. That dispute ought not be made an occasion for the expression of views on matters not essentially relevant to that resolution. The precedent resulting from the court's decision is the conclusion of law on the particular facts of the case. The application of established principle to a new and perhaps uncontemplated situation of fact is of course part of the regular activity of a court. In doing so it may be said that the court decides what the law ought to be. But this is not to change the law: it is but to apply it, albeit in a novel situation. But to overturn accepted precedent, and do so on the basis of the personal philosophy of a judge, is to my mind a legislative act not authorised by the grant of judicial power. Of course — and the two situations must be distinguished from each other — if the court is convinced that an earlier statement of principle or an earlier application of some accepted principle was erroneous when made, the court can rectify the error and replace it by a statement of principle or conclusion which in its view was correct at the time of the earlier pronouncement. This both in theory and in practice does involve a change in the precedent, which later forms part of the law. This correction of error does not involve a change in principle: it affirms what the principle was at the earlier time but misapplied. I am aware that this view of mine is not universally accepted by today's judiciary. But I fear that judges who feel themselves free generally to change the law are not limited to the restraints I have mentioned and will ultimately bring the judiciary into controversy and weaken the respect on which its authority really depends.

* * * * *

Much is said of the independence of the judiciary but not always with complete understanding of what the description involves. In the unitary systems of parliamentary government, the basic separation of powers rests not on statutory prescriptions but on constitutional principle derived over time from the inherited traditions and experience of the English people.

But in a federal system regulated by a written constitution, this doctrine may have a statutory basis. However secured, the maintenance in fundamental respects of a separation of legislative, executive and judicial powers is essential to the maintenance of individual freedom and the protection of the citizen, in person and property, from any risk of tyranny in government. A wise community should ever be alert to the possibility of its institutions being weakened by the encroachment by one of the separated powers upon or over another of them. This is particularly so in the case of the judicial power, which should be kept strictly independent of the executive power and not exercise any legislative power, except such as is strictly incidental to the exercise of judicial power. The important thing is that liberty is not necessarily secured by verbal formulae, as in a Bill of Rights, however precise in their expression. Rather, it is an independent judiciary, by developing and applying the principles of the common law with its emphasis on the essential importance of the individual and the citizen's duty to his neighbours, its insistence on the observance of natural justice where the citizen is likely to be affected in person or property and the use of habeas corpus in relation to physical restraint, and requiring the executive and legislative arms under their allotted limits, which will ensure that tyranny does not gain sway.

The Australian Constitution is based on a separation of powers. All legislative power is vested in the Parliament consisting of the Crown and two chambers, each independent of the other and each equally possessing legislative power, with, in the case of the Senate, a limitation on initiation and amendment of money Bills.

The executive power is exclusively vested in the Governor-General acting upon the advice of ministers who are members of and responsible to the Parliament for the advice they give. This is not the place to discuss the dangers which may ensue from the dominance of the Parliament by the executive government. The party system, in so far as it involves loss of personal independence of action on the part of the party-sponsored members of Parliament, may lead to a serious inroad by the Executive into the independence of the Parliament itself and calls for serious consideration.

But whatever interaction of the legislative and executive power may be tolerated, the independence of the judiciary as the sole repository of judicial power cannot be allowed to be compromised.

I should say two things about this independence. First, the judiciary must be independent both of the Parliament and of the Executive in the exercise of its judicial power. But while this independence of decision and application of the law must not be compromised, it must be remembered that the High Court, for which constitutional provision was made, owes its structure to the Parliament as well as its recurrent funding. That it should account to the Parliament for its expenditure of those funds does not, in my view, in the least impinge on its judicial independence. Ideally the High Court should present its own budget, compiled by itself with the aid of its officers, to the Parliament and, as in the United States, if need be a judge attend before the appropriate committee to justify it. Here in Australia, the court's budget is presented through the Attorney-General who, in doing so, represents the executive government. Just as the court should itself put forward its requirement of funds, so it should directly account to the Parliament or to its chosen parliamentary committee for the expenditure of those funds: in doing so, the attendance and the answering of relevant enquiries by a judge would not, in my view, represent any intrusion into the independence of the judicial power.

Any request by the Parliament for an account of the High Court's judicial work would, in my opinion, be a totally different matter. Such a request ought to be resisted as a real intrusion into the independence of the judicial power.

The Constitution provides for the removal of a judge at the request of the Parliament for proved misbehaviour or incompetence. This is conformable to the tradition of judicial independence. The Crown on the advice of a ministry responsible to the Parliament appoints the judge. It does not impinge upon the independence of the judiciary for the Parliament, satisfied of misbehaviour or incompetence, to request the judge's removal by the Crown. But the Parliament may not delegate to any person or body the judgment that misbehaviour or incompetence has occurred or is present. It may delegate its ability to ascertain the facts, for example to a parliamentary committee or commission to do so. But it may not authorise such a body to determine whether or not misbehaviour has occurred or incompetence has supervened. To commit to any person or body the ability to decide on the quality of a judge's conduct or on judicial competence would, in my view, be a clear invasion of the independence of the judiciary.

It might also properly be said that whereas the legislature in a statute may indicate the sense in which it has used words, either generally or particularly, in its statutes, it may not in any sense instruct the court on the manner in which it may exercise its judicial power in construing the words of an enactment. To do so would, in my view, be to intrude into and usurp judicial power. The formation of rules of construction and the interpretation of statutes and regulations is exclusively a judicial function.

The court decided in the *Boilermakers* case[1] that, as the enforcement of an award was essentially judicial, involving as it did the decision of matters of fact between contesting parties and also at times the construction of the award itself, the penalty provisions of the then Arbitration Act were void. Thus while the Arbitration Commission could make awards it could not enforce them by penalties for their breach. As a result, a separate tribunal, a court to exercise judicial power, was legislatively created to enforce the awards. Its main if not its sole substantial function was to impose penalties on those who were in breach of the awards of the Arbitration Commission. Generally speaking, these two functions, the making and the enforcement of awards by penalties, are better performed by the one body, which, having made the award, has a close understanding of the substance of the matter. Also, its authority to amend the award might resolve a disputation which has led to its breach. But the spectacle of a tribunal bereft of real knowledge of the nuances of the making of the award, with no power to vary its terms and simply engaged in imposing penalties, ultimately brought industrial revolt and the loss of the power of enforcement of awards by the imposition of penalties.

So, as matters stand, the legislative grant of any judicial function, even as a necessary incident of the execution of some validly granted power, must necessarily be constitutionally invalid. Just as a rule-making power and the ability to enforce a judicial resolution of a case can be validly given to a court, though such powers are in a real sense executive powers, so it may well be thought that the powers to enforce an award of arbitral authority was an incident, if not indeed a necessary incident of the executive power to make the award.

In each instance the essentially incidental nature of enforcement may justify its vesting in the executive, as it is by the judicial.

* * * * *

After its new premises were built in Canberra, I worked to secure the independence of the High Court. First of all, it seemed to me that there should be a statute giving the court control of its own affairs, including the care of the new building and its grounds. Before this the Attorney-General sought funds for the running of the court as part of the budget of his Department. He decided what funds were necessary with, in my experience, only limited consultation with the members of the court. No doubt specific requests by the court were considered. But such requests were few. Further, the funds obtained through the budget were wholly administered by the Attorney-General's Department.

The time had arrived, I thought, for the court to take over the control of the whole of its function including budgeting for and expenditure of the necessary funds. At first my proposal for the promotion of a statute met opposition. Some appeared to prefer that the administration of the court remained under the control of the Attorney-General. Among other anxieties, the possibility of the court's staff being affected by industrial disputes was of particular concern. The employment of a clerk of the court in addition to a registrar, who would employ the staff, though under the court's direction, disposed of the worst of these anxieties; the clerk would be the respondent in any arbitration proceedings that might arise. Agreement was reached for the promotion of a Bill for a statute, which provided for a clerk.

In setting up the Federal Court, the relevant statute gave the administration of this court to the Chief Judge. With this I agreed. I had in fact administered the High Court from the time of my appointment in 1964. I expected that the Bill for the statute would expressly give me responsibility for administering its non-judicial affairs. While the Bill was under consideration, some of the judges told me that while they had no quarrel with my administration, they were not prepared to give the Chief Justice the authority to administer the court, as this power would apply to my successor, of whose identity, naturally, they were unaware and whose choice in any case they could not necessarily affect. It was not till shortly before I retired that any question of a successor arose, and then it was because of my failing sight. So my colleagues' intervention meant that during the remainder of my occupancy of the office my ability to administer the court would lapse.

I had no desire to create a division in the court by insisting on my point of view. Unlike my colleagues, except Mr Justice Murphy, I had had experience of administration as a minister of the Crown. My colleagues were proposing that the court should be administered by the judges operating as a committee of the whole, an idea which I thought both undesirable and impractical. In the end, the Bill did not include a provision for the Chief Justice to administer the court. In the committee of the whole, he was to be merely one, with no special significance beyond its chairmanship.

I tried to eliminate any function of the Attorney-General from the proposed Bill for the High Court. As I have said, I thought it no impairment of judicial independence for the court to be accountable to Parliament for the expenditure of funds. But this must be clearly distinguished from any Executive or parliamentary interference, or for that matter oversight in any form, of the court's judicial work.

But I was unsuccessful. I hope that another generation will see the importance of the complete independence of the court and seek direct access by the court to Parliament, not merely in budgetary matters but in the proposal of legislative measures to remedy defects in the administration of the court and of defects in the substantive law itself as they are perceived by the court in the course of its judicial work.

*****

My work as a judge is to be found in the volumes of the *Commonwealth Law Reports* which record all the reported decisions of the court. There is no public report of the many other decisions not accounted as reportable. But there are few of them of such public interest as to be worth mention here.

Some of the judgments, particularly those touching on the Constitution, did provide additions to constitutional history. For example, the judgments adopting Isaacs' view of the commerce power of the Commonwealth (*Huddart Parker Ltd v Commonwealth*[2]) greatly increased the scope of Commonwealth power. In particular, it ensured the validity of many statutory provisions relating to restrictive trade practices. No doubt there are others of a like nature. But in these pages I have not attempted to highlight any of them.

However, criticism from some quarters of my decisions in taxation cases warrants a brief reference to them. They are fairly numerous and relate to many aspects of the assessment of taxation. As I remark elsewhere, the Commonwealth statute of 1936 which resulted from Mr Justice Ferguson's efforts and those of David Roper (later Chief Judge in Equity), his assistant secretary, was generally understood and gave no undue difficulty in its administration. It has, however, suffered frequent amendment, so that now it is a patchwork which often lacks consistency. Into the detail of my decisions on this hotchpotch of legislation I will not go, but I will indicate the principle upon which I acted, a principle denied by some politicians but one which is fundamental to the operation of income tax law and has had the endorsement of earlier courts.

The liability to pay income tax is wholly derived from the law imposing and providing for the assessment of that tax. The obligation to pay it is a legal one. Some politicians try to treat it as a moral obligation. But it is not. The citizen is bound to pay no more tax than the statute requires him to pay according to the relevant state of his affairs.

Consistently with this view, it has long been a principle of the law of income taxation that the citizen may so arrange his affairs as to render him less liable to pay tax than would be the case if his affairs were cast in some different form. In the language of the layman, the citizen is entitled to minimise his liability to pay tax. This is sometimes expressed as a right to avoid tax, an expression which is in contradiction to the evasion of tax, a failure to pay tax which is properly due.

On this principle, I regularly acted. Provided the citizen's transactions were not shams, pretences, the form of his transactions and their legal consequences would affect his liability to tax, even though that form might be unusual and adopted for the express purpose of limiting the liability to pay tax.

I do not countenance fraudulent dealings, or give effect to sham transactions or the destruction of records. But clearly I did not accept the view that there was a moral duty to pay tax. Further, I held the view that it is for the Parliament in passing laws imposing taxation to make its meaning as unambiguously clear and certain as the use of language will permit. In the event of ambiguity in such legislation, the citizen, not the executive government, should have the benefit of that construction of the language of the statute which is most favourable to his or her interest.

* * * * *

I wish to say something about the selection and appointment of judges, particularly the judges of the High Court. The Crown, in legal theory being the fount of justice, traditionally has had the exclusive power of selection and appointment of the judiciary. That in present-day terms means that politicians who for the time being form the executive government alone select and appoint the judges.

I have long thought this procedure inappropriate in our society. Left to politicians, the appointments are not always made exclusively upon the professional standing, character and competence of the appointee. At times, political party affiliation, or at least an expected affinity in judgment to the philosophies of the party, form some of the criteria for choice. Sometimes party-political considerations are the dominant reason for it, even to the point of choosing the appointee merely to resolve a possible threat to the leadership.

I have advocated for some time that the exclusive power of the Executive to choose and appoint the judiciary should be transferred to a standing commission, presided over by the appropriate Chief Justice and consisting of senior representatives of the Bar and of the solicitors, representatives of academic lawyers and of an appropriate section of the general public.

The process of appointment should begin with the Attorney-General proposing the names of suggested appointees. If the commission should be unwilling to appoint any of these, it would request a further nomination. None of this process should take place in public and none of it should be publicly reported other than the final result. That is to say, the initiative should remain with the Executive, but the commission should have the final say.

Under such a process the Crown, in making the choice of nominee, would be most likely to confine itself to the professional eminence, competence, integrity and capacity for judgment of its nominees. Politicians who respect the judicial function and realise its significance for the community and for the freedom of the individual accept the need for its competence, integrity and independence and ought to be prepared to implement such a regime.

I think there is one further change which ought to be made in the appointment of the judiciary. Judges are now lured from the Bench by the prospect of earning much more as arbitrators, conciliators or consultants. Having qualified for the judicial pension but not having reached the age of compulsory retirement, they leave the Bench and become more gainfully employed in some such capacity. As younger men are appointed to the Bench this attraction will deprive the Bench of many experienced judges, and professional men in active practice are seriously disadvantaged. The disparity between the salary offered to an interested appointee and what a suitably qualified lawyer might make in practice has in recent times been so great that many suitable practising men cannot afford to accept judicial office.

My suggestion is that the commencing judicial salary be at a level commensurate with the earning capacity of those who could qualify for appointment. That salary, indexed for inflation, should be paid for life. A retiring age would be provided but the full salary would remain payable for life provided the judge had served his full term, with appropriate provision for retirement caused by ill health or like considerations. But in any case the retired judge should not be able to be gainfully employed under private circumstances. The community, through its parsimony, deprives itself of the benefit of the services of many competent lawyers and in the case of early retiring judges, of what may be their most productive years as competent judges.

* * * * *

I must now digress to provide an introduction to what I wish to say about the appointment in 1975 of Lionel Murphy as a Justice of the High Court of Australia.

When, in anticipation of his retirement from the House of Representatives in 1980, Clyde Cameron made his final speech to the House, he included some very kind and generous remarks about me, both as a parliamentarian and as a politician. When I read these unexpected references I wrote to Clyde and thanked him for his generosity. He responded by telephoning me and saying that I was a puzzle to him, that he thought me the most Tory man he had ever met and yet I had introduced a liberal form of divorce and was prepared to advocate legislation to restrain restrictive trade practices.

He asked me would I be prepared to sit down with him and with a microphone between us converse about our respective points of view and our experiences in public life. The tapes and any transcription of them would be placed in the Commonwealth Archives in Canberra with an embargo on their public disclosure without our consent before the year 2006. I was prepared to do so because I had a high opinion of Clyde and felt I could rely on his probity.

Accordingly we met in my house at Careel Bay whenever Clyde was in Sydney. These frank and friendly interviews began in February 1981 and continued deep into 1982. They covered a wide variety of topics and filled a great number of tapes; transcriptions fill five stout volumes. Both the tapes and these volumes have been lodged with the Commonwealth Archives under the embargo just described.

Until now we have not agreed to any disclosure of this material. However, in discussing with him the appointment of Lionel Murphy, Clyde Cameron informed me that he would consent to my making public what he had told me about the appointment in the course of these interviews. From this material and from what Clyde has told me it would seem that the appointment of Lionel Murphy took place in the manner and circumstances which I now relate and which I believe to be true in every particular. I am disclosing this material primarily because it seems to me that this appointment does illustrate the need to make the changes I have suggested to the authority of the Executive to appoint the judiciary, something at present in its exclusive and uncontrolled discretion.

In February 1975 the Labor Party was holding a conference at Terrigal on the central coast of New South Wales. As you would expect the Cabinet ministers, of whom Clyde Cameron was one, were present. On Sunday, 9 February, a Cabinet meeting was called. All Cabinet members other than the Prime Minister, Jim Cairns (then Treasurer of the Commonwealth) and Lionel Murphy assembled ready for the meeting to open, but they were kept waiting quite some time for the Prime Minister to arrive.

Apparently during that time a meeting had taken place between Whitlam, Cairns and Murphy in which Murphy was offered the appointment to the vacancy in the High Court. As a term of his acceptance of it, Lionel Murphy insisted that Prime Minister Whitlam give him a firm assurance that should the position of Chief Justice fall vacant, he, Lionel Murphy, would be appointed. Whitlam gave a firm assurance and Murphy thereupon agreed to accept appointment to the High Court. Jim Cairns has assured Clyde Cameron that this took place. It seems from what Whitlam later told his colleagues that Lionel Murphy also thereupon resigned from the Senate.

It appears from this narrative that the appointment of Lionel Murphy to the High Court was cut and dried before Cabinet was consulted. The price for Murphy's acceptance had been paid, the firm assurance given, and he had already resigned from the Senate. Cabinet had little option but to endorse the Prime Minister's decision.

I had seen Mr Whitlam in Canberra after I had returned from The Hague where I had been sitting on the International Court of Justice. I discussed with him several members of the Bar as possible appointees to the vacancy caused by the sudden death of Sir Douglas Menzies. Lionel Murphy's name was not mentioned.

The motivation for this appointment seems predominantly, if not exclusively, party political, in which the personal interests of Prime Minister Whitlam had a significant part. The removal of the possibility of a challenge to his leadership would quite likely have been an attractive consideration for him; his readiness to assure Lionel Murphy of the chief justiceship may be thought to indicate an anxiety to have Murphy out of the way. But of course, on the material we have, no firm conclusion can be drawn.

On the evening of 10 February my wife and I were staying the night with Sir John Cameron, then Chancellor of the University of Tasmania, in his home at Ross in Tasmania. I was on my way to Hobart for a sitting of the High Court. During the evening Whitlam telephoned me. He said, and I recall his precise words, "Murphy has agreed to accept the appointment".

"But he is neither competent nor suitable for the position", I said.

"But he managed to have the Family Law Act passed", replied Whitlam. And with that somewhat irrelevant remark I closed the conversation. I confess I was considerably upset by the news.

So much of the information of the subsequent activities of Mr Justice Murphy which is available to the public (part of that information has been locked away from public view by the Hawke Government) supports what I said about Murphy's suitability for the office. But from whatever angle the appointment is viewed, it does I think lend weight to the need to change the process by which the judiciary is chosen.

From this narrative it is also clear that the alteration in the party political balance of the Senate which proved so disastrous for the Whitlam Ministry had its origin in the creation of the two vacancies in the Senate. As everyone knows, the Queensland Government filled the vacancy, caused by Senator Gair's appointment as Ambassador, by appointing a Labor Party man who did not support the Whitlam Ministry, and the New South Wales Government appointed a Liberal Party man to the vacancy caused by Murphy's appointment to the High Court. Both these appointments by the respective governments were lawful and authorised by s 15 of the Constitution. Evidently the legal position on the State's rights to fill the casual vacancies had not been understood.

Although not a necessary part of the narrative of these events, I think it is appropriate that I say something further about the so-called convention of filling casual vacancies in the Senate. Until 1975 and certainly in recent times the political parties had in fact filled such a vacancy by appointing a person of the same political persuasion as the deceased or retired senator. No doubt parliamentarians may claim that this habit had developed into a parliamentary convention, but I take leave to doubt that. But in any case if there were such a convention among politicians it could not override or qualify the written terms of s 15, which I quote below; nor would it have any sanction to ensure its observance. Consequently there could have been no doubt as the Constitution stood in 1975 that each State was at liberty to choose and approve whom it would as its representative in the Senate. Thus although there had been political manoeuvring, by both political parties, about the creation and the filling of the two casual vacancies, what the States did in 1975 was perfectly lawful, and the resulting composition of the Senate perfectly valid.

After 1975, because of bipartisan agreement amongst politicians, an amendment to the Constitution was made by referendum to require a State to appoint to a casual vacancy a person of the same political persuasion as the former incumbent. Strangely enough it appears that Labor politicians thought this amendment would mean that the State must appoint the party's nominee, but that clearly was not so. Under the amendment the State could still choose the appointee provided that that person was of the same political persuasion as the previous incumbent.

Section 15 of the Constitution is as follows:

> If the place of a senator becomes vacant before the expiration of his term of service, the Houses of Parliament of the State for which he was chosen shall, sitting and voting together, choose a person to hold the place until the expiration

> of the term, or until the election of a successor as hereinafter provided, whichever first happens. But if the Houses of Parliament of the State are not in session at the time when the vacancy is notified, the Governor of the State, with the advice of the Executive Council thereof, may appoint a person to hold the place until the expiration of fourteen days after the beginning of the next session of the Parliament of the State, or until the election of a successor, whichever first happens.
>
> At the next general election of members of the House of Representatives, or at the next election of senators for the State, whichever first happens, a successor shall, if the term has not then expired, be chosen to hold the place from the date of his election until the expiration of the term.
>
> The name of the senator so chosen or appointed shall be certified by the Governor of the State to the Governor-General.

This amendment of the Constitution turned the senator into a representative of a political party and not merely one of the State which elected or appointed him. This was a considerable inroad into the theory of the federation, and from that point of view it ought not to have been made. It further entrenched the party system and increased its dominant position in the Parliament. No doubt the party system has helped to maintain stability in government, but in my view it is time to consider ways by which that dominance can be reduced and greater freedom gained for the parliamentarian, whether as a senator or a member of the House of Representatives.

*****

One of the very pleasant and informative experiences I had in my extra-judicial life was to witness the development of the interior of the Sydney Opera House after Utzon resigned.

In the 1960s I had formed a close friendship with the architect David Littlemore. Later I was to persuade him to join the council of Macquarie University when I was its chancellor. The council greatly profited by his advice as the building of the university proceeded. David was one of the triumvirate appointed to complete the Opera House and I think had the task of supervising construction. He suggested that I might care to visit the site from time to time when he could explain to me what was going on. This I did at three-monthly intervals during construction.

When I first visited it, the ceilings had not been placed in the shells and the glass walls facing the water had not been installed. So I was able to see the internal structure of the shells and appreciate the rugged appearance of strength as well as the vastness of the space they enclosed. Later I was able to observe the tremendous amount of wiring, piping and ducting, which is now hidden from view. Behind those ceilings David explained to me the situation the building was in when Utzon departed. There were many unsolved problems: there were not enough working drawings; there was a lack of the trained staff that the project needed in great numbers. David explained to me the significant work Arup &

Partners had done on the engineering side, and the excellent construction work Hornibrook had done in placing the shells in position. My regular visits gave me a very good idea of the complexity of the project and the difficulties the trio had overcome.

On one of my visits I met Ted Farmer, the government architect, and from David I received an account of the quality of Farmer's contribution to the solving of many of the problems. Later I was delighted that he was appointed as one of the group to select the design of the High Court building; in this venture we profited greatly from his knowledge and judgment.

I thoroughly enjoyed these visits to the Opera House under construction, and particularly David's explanations of what was going on. When I sat beside Dame Pattie Menzies on the day the Queen opened it, I had a good understanding of the great merit, not merely of the conception but of the construction of this remarkable building.

*****

I have generally had a healthy life, after an indifferent start. But I have suffered two major disabilities, one over which I had hardly any control, the other to which my conduct contributed.

I inherited a tendency to diabetes: members of my father's family were diabetics, a fact I only learned in later life. I have already referred to its diagnosis while I was in London. I also inherited a fair and sun-sensitive skin. But I did little to protect it. I surfed, played on the beach, fished both on the beach and in inland rivers, went horse-riding in the Alps, golfed (often hatless) and became a yachtsman. As I passed middle age I had increasingly to have skin cancers removed, at times by surgery or by radiation (cobalt), but mostly by being burnt off.

I was early aware of the risks to my sight which my diabetic condition would pose. Consequently, once diagnosed diabetic, I had my eyes examined regularly. On such a visit to an ophthalmic specialist in 1978 I was told that serious changes were occurring in my retina and that I should immediately consult a practitioner familiar with the use of the laser beam. Although I had not observed any change in my sight, I heeded this warning and consulted Dr Frank Taylor.

It seems that in a diabetic, new blood vessels sometimes form in the retina. They are by their nature unstable and likely to break down. When they do, blood fills the eyes and this prevents sight. By the time I reached Dr Taylor this had already advanced in my right eye, whose sight had now become seriously affected. But though I now had sight in only one eye, I was not conscious of it and had no difficulty in seeing people or things or in reading. But the following year I became very conscious of diminishing sight and had received a gloomy prognosis.

Two new blood vessels had appeared in the retina of my left eye close to the macula. Skilful use of the laser over the next two years dried up these vessels, and later inspections have shown that they remain so. Use of the laser, however, necessarily extensive in my case, caused damage to my central sight. The ophthalmologists, I understand, experience this phenomenon from time to time but have no certain explanation for it. Until then I had not experienced any serious loss of sight in that eye, but since the conclusion of the laser treatment I see nothing in focus, unless it is within a foot or so of me. For the most part the scenes before me are shadowy and indistinct.

Because of the developments of 1980 I took some part of the leave due to me. I went to London and sat on the Judicial Committee of the Privy Council before returning to work on the High Court.

Shortly after my return to duty I decided I must retire. I clearly remember Sir John Harvey's poignant remark on his retirement. He had lost the sight of one eye because, I understand, of his philanthropic activities during World War I. He served long years thereafter but ultimately lost the sight of his other eye. In responding to the praise offered by the profession on his retirement, he said, "Justice may be blind, but justices may not".

Up till this point I had not disclosed to my colleagues this anticipated loss of sight. I had been able successfully to carry through the opening of the High Court building in Canberra. I had had to condition myself to being unable to remain long enough in office to establish the use of the Canberra building as the sole centre of operations of the court (as I would have wished). With the opening of the building behind me, I began to prepare for retirement. I retired from office in 1981, disclosing both my diabetic condition and the prospect of diminishing sight.

There is no need to emphasise the frustration which this loss of sight can cause. But I have now learned to live with it and do not allow it to overwhelm me. I still read, though slowly, and write, though I am afraid badly. With glasses I can see my own handwriting but can only read print with the aid of a magnifying Telesensory machine called the "Voyager".

Since retirement I have maintained my active presidency of the Royal New South Wales Institute for Deaf and Blind Children and my chairmanship of the Purves Foundation. Latterly I have also spent time in putting this book together, at times by dictation but most by writing its text by hand, increasingly in less legible script.

19 The Building on the Lakeside

In a splendid ceremony, in the presence of judges from Federal and State courts, and indeed judges from many parts of the Commonwealth, the High Court was opened by the Queen on 26 May 1980. It was for me the culmination of years of thought and planning in my capacity as Chief Justice.

During my practising days, the High Court sat in Sydney and Melbourne several times a year and in each of the other State capitals once a year. The Commonwealth did not own any of the courtrooms in which the court sat. In Sydney and in Melbourne there were premises identified with the court, but in the other capitals it sat in courtrooms in the Supreme Court building of that State. These varied in their adequacy. None provided an ideal environment for the work of the Australian final court of appeal.

The High Court's use of these premises in the State capitals involved some disruption of the work of the State Supreme Court and the displacement of some of its judges from their chambers. The court's sitting in these capitals rarely extended beyond six sitting days. If it were necessary to reserve judgment in a case heard in these States it was unlikely that there would be opportunity for the court to work on those cases. Further, there would be insufficient time before the next scheduled sitting to complete the investigation of the case. Consequently, work on the reserved cases would be most likely postponed for at least part of the next sitting. This could scarcely be deemed an efficient method of arriving at an early solution of the case.

In Sydney a building adjacent to the Criminal Court at Darlinghurst, that court itself a relic of the days of early settlement, was known as the High Court. This building had been built by the New South Wales Government during the chief justiceship of Sir Adrian Knox (1919-30) and the Commonwealth was a periodic tenant of it. In 1964, when I became Chief Justice, the Commonwealth was, or shortly thereafter became, a weekly tenant.

The Melbourne courthouse in which the court sat was by comparison a much grander edifice. It had been built for the High Court by the Victorian Government, immediately to the rear of the State Supreme Court building which faces William Street. It contained three courtrooms and chambers for seven judges. Though not of the same size, the courtrooms were all adequate for the performance of the court's function. Court premises owned by the Commonwealth in Canberra and Darwin were devoted to the use of the Supreme Courts of each Territory.

During my early days of appearing in the High Court, the cases each day were not necessarily heard in the same order, as the printed list gave no indication of the time each was likely to take. In Sydney, as Darlinghurst was some distance from Phillip Street where barristers' chambers were then mostly located, the uncertainty as to when counsel would be required to conduct an appeal or application was quite common: a highly inconvenient situation. Few counsel could devote themselves to work only in the High Court during its sittings, most accepting briefs in the State courts during that time. It was quite difficult to accommodate cases so as to avoid clashes with work of the Supreme Court.

In Melbourne, the distance from chambers to the High Court was much less, but even there counsel were expected to remain in court to await the time when their case was called for hearing. On one notable occasion, Hayden Starke was briefed to appear as counsel in the second case for the day. He attended the opening of the court and after receiving an estimate of the time that case would take, he returned to chambers to pursue his work. Unfortunately the case first listed ended sooner than expected. Starke's case was called but Starke was not present. A message ultimately brought him into court. The presiding Chief Justice, Sir Samuel Griffiths, somewhat tersely told him he was late. Starke was of a strongly independent turn of mind and quite fearless. His response was as immediate as the Chief Justice's rebuke.

"I beg Your Honour's pardon, I was not late, I was here at the time at which the court sat and for which the case was listed."

Sir Samuel retorted, "But it's counsel's duty to wait".

"I'll remind Your Honour", said Starke, "that Your Honour is paid for waiting, counsel is not".

And with that Sir Samuel had to be content, for Hayden Starke was no mean adversary. My own experience of trying to manage appearances in both the High Court and the Supreme Court was also difficult.

Since the men on the High Court were longstanding friends of mine I felt that I would have their goodwill in effecting some changes in courtroom arrangements and the listing procedure. With their concurrence I engaged an ABC technician to design a sound system for the Sydney and Melbourne courtrooms. In Sydney the recording machines were removed from the courtroom and two land lines established between the courtroom and the transcribing centre in the city. A small room was built on the outside of the courtroom, on the eastern side, by removing a high window which was replaced with a sheet of one-way glass. An operator in this room during a court sitting would be able to see what was happening in the court but himself remain unseen. He would also be able to hear what was said in the courtroom by the judges as well as by the advocates. He could interpolate on one of the land lines his own identification of the person speaking, including the spoken interventions of the judges. Thereafter, the transcripts correctly attributed to the appropriate judge any remarks which had been made during argument. He also controlled the level of sound in the courtroom. He could adjust it on a signal from the presiding judge, who was constantly in his view. About forty small speakers were placed around the courtroom so that the proceedings could readily be heard by all those in the room. Small speakers were also placed on or beneath the bench at each judge's place. This idea I developed from a visit I had once paid to the House of Commons. Inserted in the upper portion of the back of each chair in the public gallery was a small loudspeaker. If it became difficult to hear what a member was saying, the reception could be improved by simply leaning the head back a little, thus bringing the small speaker closer to the ear.

I also rearranged the lectern at the centre of The Bar table. The lectern could be raised or lowered hydraulically to suit the height of the advocate addressing the court. It carried a microphone connected to the land lines and to the speakers in the courtroom. A clock was placed on the lectern to remind the advocate of the passage of time — something not always prominent in his consciousness. There was never a time limit placed on counsel as is the case in the United States Supreme Court. There the passage of time is brought to the advocate's attention by the sudden appearance of a light, by which time he must resume his seat. There being no set time limits in the High Court, the often necessary but ever unpopular task of keeping counsel within bounds fell to the presiding judge. The system I inaugurated proved satisfactory and was I think welcomed by the Bar.

These Sydney arrangements were substantially duplicated in the Melbourne courtroom with the exception that no adjustable lectern was installed but a portable lectern was placed on the Bar table.

When Attorney-General, I had tried to find temporary accommodation for the High Court in federally-owned premises. I knew that Sir Owen Dixon was emphatically opposed to the court regularly sitting in Canberra. There was some notion that in Canberra the judges would be at risk of being subject to political influence, a view I did not and do not share. But I realised that Sir Owen had great influence with Prime Minister Menzies, who had been one of his pupils and admired him very much. So while Sir Owen remained Chief Justice there was no point in proposing the erection in Canberra of a courthouse for the High Court.

During my time in that office, a courthouse was built in Canberra for the use of the Australian Capital Territory Supreme Court, and I had some part in its construction. It is a pleasant building clad with Wombeyan marble and having an enclosed garden in its foyer. With the design of the Supreme Court building in

Darwin I had only one contact. Sculptured figures were proposed for the principal outside wall of the courthouse. As presented to me, an upright figure was handing something to another figure in a begging attitude. I thought this a bad representation of the relationship of the citizen to the provision of justice. At my suggestion the attitude of the sculpture was changed to that which now appears on that wall of the courthouse.

For Sydney I considered at one stage using the old Union Club premises in Bligh Street as a temporary courthouse, but the building was demolished too quickly and the land turned into a car park for my thoughts to materialise. When the New South Wales Police Headquarters were to be removed from the building at the corner of Phillip and Hunter Streets, I tried to arrange for the Commonwealth to acquire the building for the High Court. I had plans prepared by the Department of the Interior for the reconstruction of the building, but this possibility fell through and the Goodsell Building was erected on the site.

In Melbourne the use of the old Mint Building in William Street was considered but not decided on. Land was acquired in Adelaide for High Court premises but the proposal was rejected, though the land was retained for federal use.

*****

I had early entertained the idea of a High Court building in the national capital and of abandoning the court's peripatetic visitation of the States in rotation. The High Court, to my mind, is the most important institution in the Australian federation. It has the function of interpreting and applying the Constitution. It stands between the Parliament and the Executive on the one hand and the citizens on the other to see that both remain within the bounds of their constitutional authority. It thus has the responsibility of maintaining the rule of law. Its complete independence of both those institutions is vital in the maintenance of individual freedom. It is, as Alfred Deakin said, the keystone of the federal arch. So it is right that it should have its place in the national capital, particularly now that Canberra has developed so significantly. The physical arch should be as prestigious and permanent as any structure housing the other elements of the federation. In addition, the High Court is a court of appeal for all classes of litigation in the Federal and State courts. It was destined to become in due course the final court of appeal from the State courts, as well as from judicial tribunals created by the Commonwealth. This appellate function provides a means of securing uniformity of the common law in Australia and also uniformity of construction and application of a great deal of the statutory law of the Commonwealth and the States so often cast in a common mould.

There are two ways in which the High Court differs radically from the United States Supreme Court. The latter could not, as a general rule, hear and decide appeals from the state court in respect of state as well as federal law.

Thus uniformity of law is more readily attainable in Australia than it is or can be in the United States.

The other radical difference is that, at least up to the present, there is no constitutionally entrenched Bill of Rights. The American Bill of Rights is to be found in the amendments to the Constitution. It is expressed in the form of slogans, incapable in themselves of application as is a statute of the Congress or the Parliament. Inevitably, the conversion of the slogans into decisions in concrete circumstances involved to no small degree political and even ideological concepts. It will result in political decisions which the Congress cannot override or amend.

To my mind, courts are ill-equipped to make such decisions, which are in their nature legislative and lead to public comment and denial, which can seriously jeopardise the authority of the court and its acceptance of its decisions. The slogans of one generation are not necessarily those of the next. I feel that no generation is warranted in entrenching its own slogans so as thereby to bind succeeding generations. Far better to leave such fundamental matters to be dealt with by each generation through the democratic processes.

I had another reason for wanting to house the High Court in the national capital. Legally-trained men are among the more useful members of a parliament, particularly in the parliament of a federation. In a State parliament, particularly in the days when it sat after court hours, a practising man could enter the House while relatively young and at the same time sufficiently maintain his practice and thus an income on which a family could be supported. This situation was at least partly satisfied in the federal area while the Commonwealth Parliament sat in Melbourne.

But when that Parliament moved to Canberra, the position of the young practising lawyer changed dramatically. He could not successfully practise and attend the House at the same time. Percy Spender, when elected to the House of Representatives as an independent, tried to do it but it proved too difficult. I practised with him and knew the problems which the isolation of Canberra created.

Thus, when thinking about the siting of the High Court building, I had the notion that a building in Canberra might in time enable some young barristers, anxious to serve in the House, to do so while maintaining a busy practice in Canberra and its environs. There would be available not only the High Court, but the Australian Capital Territory Supreme Court and the New South Wales Supreme Court on circuit in Goulburn and Yass and the various district courts.

As matters have developed, however, these ideas wear the appearance of a pipe dream. But I retain the hope that at some time in the future the work of the national Parliament will be enriched by the presence of actively practising men of legal distinction.

But there were more practical matters to be attended to. If the High Court were to be sited in Canberra, a library had to be built for the judges. There would also need to be a library for advocates working far from their own State libraries. I knew that it was unlikely that I would be able to persuade the Treasury to fund the second of these. Yet if a courthouse did emerge in Canberra, it would be essential to provide a well-stocked library for the Bar. There were the rudiments of a library in the books possessed by the court in Sydney and in Melbourne. As the court worked extensively both in Sydney and in Melbourne, there was justification for duplicating those libraries. This I did over a period of years within the restraints of an annual budget compiled by the Attorney-General's Department. The excellent libraries both for the court and counsel now in Canberra thus emerged. Early on in my chief justiceship, I obtained authority to purchase the books each High Court judge held in his chambers. From then on, all these books belonged to the court itself. They helped to form the nucleus of future libraries along with those the court already possessed.

* * * * *

In Prime Minister Holt's time, I succeeded in obtaining a decision for putting up a building for the High Court in the Parliamentary Triangle in Canberra. That decision would not have been likely in Menzies' time. Although he had been responsible for the growth of Canberra when in 1950 he began to move federal departments from Melbourne to Canberra, and though he closely watched the development of the city — and I think obtained satisfaction from it — it always retained for him an ersatz quality. Apart from the risk of political influence which in Sir Owen's view might follow the court's presence in Canberra, the judges would be removed from what, in his view, was valuable contact with the judiciary and citizenry of the States. Though I fully understood these views I did not and do not share them.

The original Burley Griffin plan for Canberra sited the permanent Parliament House on Camp Hill which lay immediately behind the present Parliament House. It provided 20-odd acres for a High Court building at the southern end of the lake frontage (Griffin's plan provided for the creation of the lake) bordering the bridge which now crosses the lake on the way to Russell and the airport. Griffin, an American, like his fellow citizens placed great store on the United States Supreme Court, of which the High Court was to be a counterpart.

The Menzies Government had enlisted the assistance of the distinguished architect Sir William Holford when considering the siting of the permanent Parliament House. After considering the physical situation, Holford asked Menzies whether the existing House would be demolished if a new House were erected on Camp Hill. Menzies said certainly not. His carefulness with government funds and his sense of tradition would have made him want to retain the existing building. Holford said that a building placed behind the existing structure would look in perspective like "a pimple on a pumpkin". The appearance of the temporary House would so dominate the perspective. No consideration was given to siting the House on the top of Capital Hill. This would have been influenced by the inadequacy of the available area.

Sir William Holford pointed out that a parliament should be on ground level and not on an elevated site. This, I think, followed from the thought that a parliament represents the daily life of a people and not some exalted view of its own importance: a place for dusty feet rather than for display, certainly not for magnificence. So with Holford's support, a lakeside site for the new House was decided on.

The new courthouse would not require all of the 20 acres of the site, even if a substantial area of garden was made around it. While we were deciding what to do with this remaining land, there was the tragic event of Prime Minister Holt's death, and John Gorton came into office. The Menzies Government's decision was overturned and the decision on the location of the new House passed to the Parliament. Perhaps that was unfortunate. I suppose there is much to be said for the Parliament deciding where it will sit. But the risk of building a palace rather than a meeting place became greater. The result is there for all to see. A decision by the ministry which had to foot the bill might have involved less risk.

The site of the court building had to be renegotiated. After some time, it was agreed that it be eastwards of a line drawn directly from the southern extremity of the existing Parliament House and the southern limit of the War Memorial enclosure.

From this point on, negotiations had to be conducted with the National Capital Development Commission ("NCDC"), then chaired by Sir John Overall. Sir John was sympathetic to my aims for the courthouse and I found no difficulty in negotiating with him and his staff.

The Commission in the beginning wanted to build a judicial complex to house not only the High Court but also the Australian Capital Territory Supreme Court, and to provide chambers and hearing rooms for the Industrial Arbitration Commission. No doubt the availability of sufficient land to carry such an extended building gave rise to this idea. But it was strongly opposed. I felt that the unique position of the High Court in the nation's affairs required that it have a building to itself, that the building have some monumental qualities and that it should stand alone free of any contiguous buildings. In the end the NCDC accepted my point of view; the suggestion of a judicial complex did not surface again.

It was agreed that the National Gallery would be a compatible neighbour of the courthouse but it was stipulated that the courthouse should stand alone, an island by itself, and that the gallery building should be distinctly lower than the court building. Sight lines were drawn, discussed and accepted; these ensured that from all points of view the court would be seen as quite separate from any adjacent building. None was intended on the north, the National Library being the nearest structure on that side. The unique quality of the High Court and its independence as a constitutional institution was thus physically prominent.

Twelve months followed during which I met frequently with Sir John Overall and staff members of the NCDC and Mr David Jackson, an architect practising in Melbourne, who joined all the conferences and whose contribution to the success of the building was considerable. The purpose of these conferences was to enable me to indicate in detail the functions the courthouse must be designed to perform. Ultimately a substantial booklet was produced by the NCDC detailing in schematic and diagrammatic form the essential functional features of the building and the expected movement of people within and through it: judges, counsel, jurors, suitors, members of High Court staff and members of the public generally, for whose presence and activity the building must also provide. The terms of a design competition were drawn up by the NCDC. David Marr in *Barwick* says that it is evident that I drew their terms because he can recognise my bad prose in their expression. Unfortunately for Mr Marr's intuitive certainty, I had absolutely nothing to do with the expression of those terms. I did have to do with their substance. These terms formed part of the design specification.

The competition for the design was inevitably lengthy. In the first stage of the judging, the designs of 158 competitors were housed in the partly completed Defence Department building in Campbell. The judges were Sir John Overall, New South Wales Government Architect EH Farmer, Professor PH Karmel of the Australian National University, David Jackson, and myself.

I well remember that when I arrived to begin the inspection of the entries, I was presented, as was each of the other judges, with a wheelchair in which to sit while studying the drawings. Still being young enough to be vainly proud of my physical stamina, I promptly rejected the offer and set about my task on foot. But it was not long before my vanity was punctured and I sought the solace of a wheelchair; in the end I was most grateful for the thoughtfulness of those who had provided it. It took two full days to complete our inspection.

Of the five finalists, all of whom were given time to amend their original drawings, we unanimously chose Mr Christopher Kringas, a member of the firm of Edwards, Madigan, Torzillo & Briggs. His design fulfilled all the functional requirements of the building and solved all the problems. Kringas worked with the view that the building should indicate externally what its interior provided; the bulk of the three courtrooms on the eastern side were represented by noticeable projections. The design also had a monumental quality. But it did not seek or profess any classical parentage; it bore the marks of utility and it typified essentially Australian features of vast space and light. Unfortunately Kringas did not survive to see the completion of his creation.

The building was to be of ferroconcrete. The prospect therefore of similarity to much commercial construction was a source of anxiety. But the firm decided upon a "bush-hammered" surface on the main parts of the building, which might in time acquire a pleasing patina. During construction a great deal of experimentation took place, testing the result of more or less depth and severity of bush hammering of the "off form" surfaces in order to get the best finish.

The same firm of architects won the competition for the National Gallery, and the same builders secured the contracts for the construction of each building, though the management of each project was quite separate. Because the High Court building required excavation below the water table of the lake, with consequent costly drainage and waterproofing, the construction of the Gallery above ground advanced quicker than the courthouse.

A decision (to which I was not a party or, indeed, of which I was not aware till later) was taken early to use the same aggregate in the ferroconcrete construction of each of the buildings. Indeed, a mixing plant to service both buildings had been built and quantities of material had been assembled before I became aware of this decision. While I understood the economy of the decision, it did not quite fit what I had hoped to achieve for the High Court. I had earlier obtained a decision of the NCDC that the external appearance of the building should be white. The Commission, in settling the constituents of the aggregate, decided to use off-white cement and to use blue metal as one of the main components of the aggregate, which would result in a bluish or grey surface, particularly when wet. An attempt to get white cement and white granite in the aggregate for the High Court (whatever was done for the Gallery) was turned down by the architects. I had hoped that a white external appearance would make the High Court building a more outstanding structure, particularly in the strong light of Canberra. One has only to observe the way the painted whiteness of the old Parliament House enhances its prominence to realise what might have been achieved.

The architects estimated that these changes would add about $700,000 to the cost of the building (when finished it cost around $50 million). This I was disinclined to accept, and pressed my point strongly. Failing to obtain the concurrence of the NCDC, I carried the matter to the Prime Minister.

My meeting with Mr Whitlam in this connection occurred in October 1975. While expressing his sympathy with my point of view, he said that the additional cost was more than the Government could bear and he refused to intervene. This was a time at which, for one cause or another, the financial fortunes of the Government were not rosy. So, although he had generally been quite co-operative over the construction of the building, on this occasion he refused to support me. So the same aggregate was used for both buildings, neither of which is truly white.

There was no difficulty in getting adequate funds for the interior finishes. Generally the press ignored the building operation and did not engage in its usual ploy of playing up the cost involved. There was one occasion, however, when the press highlighted the cost of the building, publishing fairly accurate figures of the then cost of construction. I suspect that their knowledge of the figures was the result of leakage from the construction staff on the Gallery.

At this time I had become anxious about the rate of progress. It appeared that management was short of cranes. I had seen quite a number of cranes on the Gallery site, some of which to my unpractised eye seemed to be less than fully employed. As the one company was building both buildings, I suggested to the manager of the High Court project that the builder divert some of the cranes from the Gallery to the courthouse. This was done. In consequence, work on the Gallery was said to be retarded, to the displeasure of the management of the Gallery building and doubtless of the Gallery authorities. It was not long after this incident that the press began quoting figures of the cost of the High Court. Actually, particularly in retrospect, the cost of the courthouse was modest. It would compare very favourably with the contemporary cost of any building approximating its national significance.

No account of the construction and furnishing of the High Court building would be complete without mention of the devoted and efficient service of Mr Neil Sainsbury, Administrative Officer of the Attorney-General's department during the whole period of the construction. Unfortunately he died suddenly a few weeks before the opening ceremony was held. He well deserved to be there. He participated, always constructively, in the work of the NCDC, prompting the adoption of many of the features of which I have spoken. Throughout he was loyal, reliable and whole-hearted in considering what was best to be done.

* * * * *

The design provided for three courtrooms: a ceremonial or main courtroom to be used when the presence of the whole court was required; a working courtroom with a bench which could comfortably accommodate five judges; and a small courtroom with a jury room attached in which a hearing by a single judge or a trial with a jury could take place.

The sound system was a matter of some concern. It was important that the judges as well as counsel should be heard in all parts of each of the courtrooms. Also, all that was said must be accurately recorded. It was not possible to use small speakers around each room as had been done in the buildings in Sydney and Melbourne. After discussion with sound engineers the consultative group decided to flood the courtrooms with sound emanating from speakers above and below the bench. Speakers were sited behind the panelling and behind the face of the bench, each set of speakers designed and sited to flood a different area of the courtroom, so that together they would make what was said by either Bench or Bar audible throughout the room.

The display of armorial bearings on the court building gave rise to much discussion. I sensed some reluctance in at least one member of the group to support the display of the bearings of the United Kingdom. The not unfamiliar assertion that their use involved a "cringe" to British tradition was perhaps in mind if unspoken. But the court derived its existence from an Act of Parliament at Westminster. Accordingly the British Arms should be displayed. The Arms of the Commonwealth should also be displayed, as the court's particular jurisdiction depends upon Commonwealth legislation.

On the parapet of the temporary Parliament House both British and Australian Arms were displayed, as is proper: the Parliament also derives authority from Westminster. After discussions, the Arms of the United Kingdom were to be displayed on the front of the courthouse which faces the lake. The Commonwealth Arms were to be displayed on the face of the building fronting the Administration building, the Robert Garran Building.

The walls on both these faces are of glass panels with vertical metallic mullions. No way could be found to incorporate the United Kingdom Arms in the glass wall on the lake side. The existence and spacing of the vertical mullions created a difficulty which was resolved by placing the Arms on a separate sheet of glass which could be affixed behind the vertical mullions. As the wall on this front is much smaller than the wall on the other side of the building, the area of the British Arms, being proportionate to the size of the wall, is smaller than the Commonwealth Arms. But its position is permanent. There was no idea, in placing them on a separate sheet of glass, of facilitating their removal or of treating the display of the British Arms as temporary.

A different and difficult problem arose with regard to the Commonwealth Arms. In heraldic terms the blazon or device on the shield constitutes the Arms. The animals, such as the kangaroo and emu on the Commonwealth Arms, are only supporters, notionally holding up the shield. Usually, as in this case, the animals face each other; further, being supporters, they should, and usually do, touch the shield. However, because of the position of the mullions on the western wall, the heads of the supporting animals, if they faced each other, would be cut by the vertical mullions. But enquiry elicited the fact that it was heraldically acceptable to turn the heads of the animals so that they looked forward. By designing them this way, the heads of the kangaroo and emu would fit within the lines of the mullions, but the animals could then not touch the shield, itself sitting between the mullions. So the Commonwealth Arms have the slight heraldic irregularity that the supporters do not actually touch the shield.

A quite different problem arose in connection with the display of Arms in the main courtroom. There was little difficulty with Nos 2 and 3 Courtrooms. In No 2 the back wall was adequate to bear the Commonwealth Arms carved in timber. They were carved out of Australian Cedar by two Dutch carvers who had become Australian citizens. Those in No 3 were fabricated out of copper rods.

But in No 1 Court there were problems of scale because of the size and particularly the height of this room. Early on I had received a suggestion that the Arms be fabricated in a woollen tapestry. I was referred to a tapestry in a courtroom at Parramatta, which I inspected. But I thought that the loosely woven tapestry would sag and distort the figures, so I decided against a tapestry.

However, Lady Aickin, wife of my colleague Sir Keith Aickin, was interested in the work of the Victorian Tapestry School. She suggested a visit to the school, where I saw some splendid examples of tightly woven tapestries, in particular one depicting ceremonial Arms of a local government authority. I took a suggestion to the committee and it was decided that the Arms be depicted in such a tightly woven tapestry for display in No 1 courtroom. Accordingly an artist was engaged to design the tapestry. In the design he provided the animals were, to my eye, inadequate. I suggested some amendments to the design. The artist put me in my place, saying that it was *his* design and he refused the suggestions. The committee rejected the design.

Meantime, an officer of the NCDC, having made some heraldic examination, informed me that if the blazon were displayed in a rectangular form, as distinct from a shield, there would be no need for supporters and that a rectangular tapestry displaying the blazon would be heraldically correct. This view having been verified, the Victorian Tapestry School was commissioned to weave such a tapestry and did so, with both expedition and great skill. The result was most satisfying and now hangs in No 1 Courtroom and is, I gather, much admired.

The interior of the building was finished in Australian timbers. Australian tulip oak, which has warmth and character, was chosen for the panelling of the two main courtrooms. Panelling was essential for several reasons, including the need for dignity and the need to cover the air-conditioning ducts and the sound-reinforcing apparatus. The result of the tulip oak panelling has been very satisfactory indeed. Western Australian jarrah was chosen for the surface of the benches and the tables for counsel in these two courtrooms. For the third courtroom Tasmanian myrtle was chosen. I already knew this handsome timber from the high table of the Bar Common Room in Sydney.

The only imported material was the Italian stone on the floor of the main hall and on the front of the bench in No 1 and No 2 Courtrooms. When used on the face of the bench, the stone is polished, but is left with a matt finish when used on the floor. I think this was a fortunate choice. Its supply was commissioned before any embargo was placed by the government on the use of imported materials.

A separate advisory group had the task of selecting artefacts for the decoration of the building. Individual tastes were not allowed to dominate any decision; in general, the advice of the group was accepted. I think that on the whole the decoration of the building has been found acceptable.

During the period of construction, the Memorials Committee of the Parliament approached me with the suggestion that my portrait, as Chief Justice, should be painted. The committee suggested Brian Dunlop as the artist. I accepted the nomination and sat or rather stood for him. I refused to wear a wig as I had done when I sat for William Pidgeon, who painted the portrait which hangs in the Bar Common Room in Sydney. But I agreed to wear my robes, to stand in my room in the Darlinghurst Courthouse and to have my full-bottomed ceremonial wig beside me. Mr Dunlop's portrait now hangs in No 3 Court. Some of my friends think that it makes me appear somewhat severe and even sullen, not suggesting such good humour as they think I exhibit. But I think the representation quite just, as it had to portray me in serious mood.

There were already available in the court's possession portraits of previous Chief Justices: Griffith, Gavan Duffy and Dixon, but none of Knox or Isaacs. The portrait of Sir Samuel Griffith which the court had was felt not to be as good as one in the Queensland Supreme Court that shows Sir Samuel in red robes as Chief Justice of Queensland. I did try to persuade the Queensland Chief Justice to allow the portrait to be moved to Canberra. Understandably he did not agree, but he did arrange for a copy of the portrait to be made and donated to the court. The Jewish society in Melbourne owned a portrait of Sir Isaac Isaacs which I was able to obtain for the High Court in exchange for a good copy.

I had asked the Memorials Committee to have the portraits of all the sitting judges painted before the courthouse was completed and that this course be followed for the future. This the committee refused, on the ground that, whereas as Chief Justice I ranked in the Commonwealth order of precedence before any of the ministers of the Crown other than the Prime Minister, the judges ranked below the ministers. If the judges were to be portrayed in oils, the ministers could rightly claim to have their portraits painted at government expense. That prospect was really daunting. So I had to be content with photographs. I resolved to collect photographs of all the judges of the High Court since its inception. They now appear on a section of the side wall of the main hall.

Another step which it was decided to take to memorialise the members of the court was the incision of their names and years of office in the wall by the staircase on the southern side of the building.

A fortuitous circumstance made the court temporary custodian of a significant painting. Tom Roberts painted the scene in the Exhibition Building, Melbourne, when George V, then Duke of York, proclaimed the inauguration of the Commonwealth of Australia. It is a remarkable painting with a great number of figures, all of whom I am told were recognisable by those who knew the individuals. I understand that painting the large canvas took a good deal of time and is itself a rare performance. In the course of the years the painting was relegated to the basement of the temporary Parliament House where it began to deteriorate.

About the time the High Court building was under consideration, the Memorials Committee had undertaken the restoration of the painting. In due course it was repaired and mounted on a firm substance. As mounted it measures 11 x 22 feet. When the court building was well advanced the Memorials Committee asked me if the court would be prepared to house the painting until a new Parliament House was ready for it. I was fascinated with the painting — I had earlier examined it in the basement of Parliament House. I took it on myself to say that the court would find a place for it. But the Memorials Committee said

I would need to have the consent of the Speaker of the House. I approached Mr Speaker, then Sir Billy Snedden. He bridled at the suggestion and said that the painting must stay in the House of Parliament. I conceded that that was its rightful place, but I ventured to ask him through which door of the Parliament building the painting would be taken. When I reminded him of its size — the painting now being rigid — he realised the difficulty and finally, though I think reluctantly, agreed. In fact part of the glass wall of the main hall of the court had to be removed to bring the painting in.

During the morning of the day the Queen opened the courthouse, she made an inspection of the entire building. I remember that she paused for a considerable time looking at this painting. The Duke of York was her grandfather, so that apart from its historical significance and its intrinsic quality, the painting had a sentimental interest for her. The Parliament has now reclaimed the canvas. Its removal has left a void which it will be hard to fill.

There was a competition for a work of art to be placed on the walls of the main hall. I participated in the final decision. I had no real difficulty with the choice of the winning design. I did ask its maker whether inclusion of the Eureka flag in the work was really necessary. But it was said — and I think rightly — that the event is part of our history and warranted a place in this representative sculpture. I accepted this point of view and, after all, the work was his conception, a matter into which I really had no right to intrude.

I decided that the judges' chambers should be ranged round the library provided for them. As with Wentworth Chambers in Sydney, I did not think that a large room was necessary for working on a case, so these rooms were not designed on any grand scale. Each comprised a sizeable working room with adequate bookshelves, with an associate's room, a secretary's room and an area for the tipstaff and his accoutrements. Each judicial suite has its own bathing and toilet facilities; each had access to an open verandah and each opened into the area of the judicial library.

I had to provide for the possibility of there being nine judges, though in the foreseeable future there would only be seven. I would hope that governments would realise that the greater the number of judges on the court, the slower and more discursive would be its work. Also, the nation is too small in population and too recent in history to generate more than a very few judges of the requisite knowledge, wide experience and judicial temperament appropriate for a court whose decisions are of such constitutional and general importance. I would also hope that no countenance will be given to the idea that the judges of the court should be representative of some sections of the national community. The court should never be regarded as in any sense a representative body. Its authority must be found in the quality of its members as independent minds, well qualified in constitutional and general law, and of such integrity that decisions are objectively made free of all forms of bias. But whatever my personal views, I could not attempt to foreclose the appointment of more than seven judges. Two additional spaces were therefore arranged to provide additional suites. These are mainly used for court activities.

One of the characteristics of the High Court Bench is the strong individualism of its members. A mechanism for consultation and for the search for common views has not so far existed. By placing the judicial suites around the library, and by placing chairs and tables in the library, I thought to furnish some stimulus to informal consultation between judges. Space adjacent to the Chief Justice's chambers was also provided for meetings of the judges. In this room was placed a circular table, whose design, much as King Arthur's Round Table was said to have done, allowed of no dominant presence. The table is a superb piece of craftsmanship.

* * * * *

I believe that the dignity and solemnity of ceremonial occasions is aided by a strict observance of traditional form and dress. Perhaps this particularly applies to the judiciary and its participation in such occasions. While the importance of traditional acts and dress is easily lost — or not understood in Australia — I feel their continuance is worthwhile. The people who in general have great respect for the judiciary carry the image of a judge bewigged in red robes. This perception is a continuing one and its existence needs to be remembered. Some part of the community respect and acceptance of judicial authority derives, I think, from that image.

The High Court is established by statute. Having no such traditional robes as have the Supreme Courts of the States, which have inherited the robes of the court of King's Bench, the High Court judges have used the working robes of a King's or Queen's counsel with a sergeant's wig as distinct from the common wig worn by counsel in court. On ceremonial occasions they have used the Windsor dress of a Queen's counsel at court: buckled shoes and stockings with knee breeches, a dress coat, full-bottomed wig, silk gown and a tricorn hat carried but not worn. Some of the judges were irked by the knee breeches and buckled shoes. So at their request I enquired and found that it would be in order for them to wear the trousers of a sack suit and ordinary shoes under their robes; this all members of the court began to do.

Early in my tenure of office, I arranged with the officers of Parliament for the court to attend, robed, at the opening of Parliament and at the swearing in of a Governor-General. In any case, the Chief Justice had long acted as the deputy of the Governor-General to perform the first part of the parliamentary opening ceremony.

But earlier the other judges had not attended any part of the morning's ceremony in the Senate Chamber. No change was made in this, but it was arranged that they should all attend in the afternoon when the Governor-General would be present. The President of the Senate, at my request, provided accommodation on the Senate side of Parliament House in which all the members of the court could don their ceremonial dress. In the case of the swearing in of a Governor-General in the Senate Chamber, there were no parliamentary officers at the Senate table. It was arranged that on such an occasion the judges should sit at the table, ceremonially robed, during the swearing-in ceremony.

Matters of dress in themselves may be thought peripheral to the substantive work of the High Court. But the distinctive appearance of the judge in any tribunal is, in my view, of considerable importance. While some may think it less so in a court of final resort — and point to the fact that the members of the Privy Council, being a committee, sit in mufti — I feel sure that the dress of members of the High Court has its place in marking the distinctiveness of their place in our constitutional system. The readiness of the public and particularly the litigant to accept the authority and decision of the judge and to respect his office derives, I feel sure, in some part from his distinctive dress.

Those who have experienced the simplicity and dignity of a sitting of the Privy Council may be tempted to think that that experience could be extrapolated to courts in Australia, and particularly to the High Court. For my part, I do not think it could.

20 Danger Zones

Both as Attorney-General and as Chief Justice I have had to deal with international issues which have aroused vehement debate in the community: the use of Australian territory for United States communications facilities and French testing of nuclear devices in the Pacific.

In 1963 Cabinet decided that it would allow the United States Government to install a communications station at North West Cape. The main purpose of the station was to enable messages to be transmitted to submerged submarines, particularly those in the Indian Ocean. But it was to be capable of much wider uses in communication, both transmitting and receiving. Menzies asked me would I head a committee to draft the agreement between the two nations. I said I would prefer not to have a committee but to do it myself with the aid of an officer. He agreed to this and I chose Keith Brennan of the Department of External Affairs to assist me.

The American Ambassador at the time was William Battle, a lawyer from Virginia. The United States Government sent out two other lawyers to assist him in the negotiations with me. One of these was Mr, now Professor, Alfred P Rubin from the United States Defense Department, and the other was from the State Department, both of them young men highly qualified as lawyers and keen negotiators.

The Americans had made agreements with a number of nations for the placement of facilities and in some cases weaponry in their territories; the United Kingdom figured prominently among these. The United States Government had been very successful in obtaining from these nations various concessions which they now sought from me. However, I was disinclined to go along with the sort of arrangement to which the other nations had agreed. We had a long negotiation while I maintained my point of view; in the end an agreement was reached with which I was satisfied. I also settled the terms of a letter of understanding by way of interpretation of the agreement to which we had come. It was clear that the Australian Government did not wish to seek access to American communications which concerned the affairs of the United States. The Cabinet accepted what I had agreed including the letter of understanding, and the agreement was duly signed between the two nations.

Dean Rusk, the American Secretary of State, sent me a cable at the end of the negotiations. It said, "Congratulations. You have negotiated the coat tails off us". And, indeed, I thought that from Australia's point of view the negotiations had been very successful. It was, of course, an agreement being made between unequal partners, unequal in resources and in responsibilities, so its negotiation was likely to throw up differences difficult to iron out.

When Whitlam was Prime Minister he several times chided me for having been a party to the agreement on North West Cape, and particularly for agreeing to the letter of understanding. The Labor Party wanted greater access by Australia to the communications system than we had sought at the time the agreement was made. It virtually wanted access to all the American correspondence through the communications base. The Americans subsequently made some adjustments with a view to allowing some Australian access to the messages passing through the North West Cape facility.

I think Labor politicians have great difficulty in trusting one another, an attitude deriving from the constant factionalism within their ranks. Equally, I think a Labor government does not make a good partner in international affairs. It lacks trust in its partners and unduly seeks means of monitoring its partners' activities. Of course, a nation must base its external policies on self-interest and self-protection, but solid international arrangements depend on trust between partners and are weakened by endemic suspicion.

Latterly the leader of the Labor Party has been very vocal about the possibility that without Australia's knowledge a pre-emptive strike by a nuclear power could be ordered by means of messages sent through North West Cape. But it is naive to think that, if an occasion arises for the United States to order a pre-emptive strike, this country will not itself also be involved in the circumstances which lead up to and warrant such a strike. Nor do I think the United States would wish to make such a strike without consulting its allies, of whom we must be accounted one, if we were likely to be affected. But this is not to deny that some unexpected occasions may arise to warrant unilateral action without consultation. But that possibility, I think, must be accepted.

*****

Early in 1973 the French Government announced its intention of exploding a nuclear device in the air over Mururoa Island in the Pacific. Although hundreds of miles to the east of Australia the Whitlam Government was advised that there was a real risk, having regard to the wind movements around the globe, and particularly of a westward flow over the South Pacific, of some fallout from this explosion being carried over the Australian continent.

The government decided on a challenge to the French in the International Court of Justice. After the legal process had been started Whitlam asked if I would accept nomination as judge ad hoc to the International Court for the hearing of the case. Under the rules of that court if a party to a litigation before it did not have a national among the permanent judges of the court it was entitled to nominate a judge ad hoc, not necessarily one of its own nationals. I accepted nomination at the urging of my colleagues.

The New Zealand Government was to join with Australia in this litigation, New Zealand being also at risk. There was some negotiation with the New Zealanders, who wanted to appoint Professor Baxter. In the end I was told that I was acceptable to both Governments. I then had to be accepted by the court. However, the matter was urgent because there was interim relief being sought.

In the short while I had between being approached by Mr Whitlam and leaving Australia I brushed up my international law and the procedure of the International Court, so that by the time I reached The Hague I was *au fait* with the court's practice and knew the relevant international law tolerably well.

When I arrived at the court I went to see the President, Mr Lachs, of Polish origin. He had recently been elected President of the court. There had been quite a bitter struggle and the French national, Manuel Gros, had been narrowly defeated. I sensed some animosity between the two men. I was vastly amused that when Lachs smoked a cigar during a conference, as he regularly did, Gros would pull out the wick of a bottle of Airwick on the table in front of him.

Gros had been longest on the court and sat on the President's right. I think the next senior judge was Bengzon from the Philippines. He had held office in the Supreme Court of the Philippines before joining the International Court. The other judges presiding included a judge named Ruda who derived from Argentina, a judge from Senegal who spoke no English — all the others did, although Gros insisted that everything be translated into French, though he was a most fluent speaker of English — there was Morozov, a Russian, who was dour but with whom I came to be on good terms; there was Waldock, the most recently elected, an English Professor of Law, a very pleasant companion indeed; there was an Indian named Singh; and de Arechaga from Uruguay. Also sitting were Petren, Onyeama, Dillard and Ignacio-Pinto. De Arechaga was, in my opinion, the best equipped both intellectually and professionally.

We sat in a shallow rectangular room in the Peace Palace with stained-glass windows forming a spectacular backdrop to the Bench. The rule of the court was that the advocate appearing should be dressed as would be required by the highest court of his own country.

The Commonwealth's team of counsel consisted of Lionel Murphy, Attorney-General, Robert Ellicott QC, Solicitor-General, and Mr Pat Brazil, a barrister of the Attorney-General's Department. Lionel Murphy appeared without a wig; the rest of the team were bewigged. When the court rose on the first day, Lachs sent for me. He asked how would counsel dress before the High Court of Australia. I said counsel would appear in wig and gown, otherwise he would not be heard. "Well", he said, "What's the Attorney-General trying to do, insult us?" I said I did not know what he was trying to do but I had no part in his dressing. Later I taxed Murphy with appearing without a wig before the International Court. He asserted that he had obtained Lachs's agreement that he might do so. Plainly there was duplicity on somebody's part. I doubt if the President was guilty of it.

The Australian case really rested in trespass. The effluvia from the atomic explosion which, according to the material produced, were more probably than not likely to move across Australia were physical particles which would invade and cause harm and possibly damage. The Australian argument did not put this point of view in the forefront. Murphy's argument took some ground which was I think unsustainable, emotional and ideological rather than legal. After such questioning as took place and the judicial consultations, a vote was taken in which a majority of judges favoured granting Australia interim relief. The majority was evidenced on a motion to appoint a judge to write the court's reasons. The result could not be announced until the formal judgment had been drawn up and published.

I was due to sit in London in the Privy Council a day or so after the decision was taken in the International Court. I left The Hague immediately and flew to London. I returned some time later to The Hague for the purpose of the approval and publication of the court's judgment.

Meantime Prime Minister Whitlam had attended a Bar function in Sydney where he had declared that Australia had won the application in the International Court. He had nominated almost accurately the majority by which he said it had won. He well knew of course that the judgment had not been published. A moment's consideration would have indicated the peril in which he placed me in making such a premature and unwarranted public statement.

I arrived back in The Hague to meet a very unpleasant situation. Naturally, eyes were turned on me, particularly by Gros. One can understand that I was likely to be suspect. I suppose in his heart to this day Gros believes I disclosed to Whitlam the result of our unpublished determination. I think I fully convinced at least the greater majority of the judges that I had not made any disclosure. When the President asked me what would happen if a like disclosure were made of an unpublished decision of the High Court, I made it plain that if the Prime Minister had done to that court what he had done to this he would be severely dealt with, probably for contempt, notwithstanding the high office he held.

I must say the incident left a bad taste in my mouth. I was the victim of a piece of egotistical exhibitionism of a very poor kind. I straight away expressed my indignation to Whitlam and said that the least he could do was to apologise forthwith to the President of the court, which I understand he did.

The case came on again in 1974 and I spent three months hearing the argument, conferring and ultimately writing a judgment. After we had retired to consider what we had heard and were in the course of preparing judgments, the President assembled the court claiming, with the support of other judges, that the case had become "moot". It seems that there had been a press statement that the French President d'Estaing had said in a press conference, in the course of rebuffing a journalist's suggestion, that of course there will be no more aerial atomic testing, or words which carried the same import.

Onyeama, Dillard, de Arechaga, de Castro, Waldock and myself wrote dissenting reasons for judgment. Perhaps I was the most vociferous in condemning as unjudicial what was being done, acting on a press report without giving the plaintiff parties an opportunity to be heard on the proper course to be taken. I have no doubt many of the nations were pleased to see the result because there were many instances in Europe of fumes and gases passing out of the territory of their origin to adjoining territory.

I enjoyed my stay in The Hague. It is a very pleasant place in summer, close to many interesting places. I was able to visit the Rijks Museum and the adjacent Van Gogh Gallery which has some very fine canvasses and drawings. I was able to see much of Amsterdam, Rotterdam and the Dutch coast; Brussels and parts of Germany beyond the bridge of Aachen, the "Bridge Too Far". There was a very pleasant gallery in the woods in Otterloo where Norma and I saw a number of Van Gogh canvasses, the whole glass-sided gallery being in a delightful setting.

When I first went to The Hague I stayed in a hotel which was visited constantly by "tourists". Later the Australian Embassy placed me in a private hotel in the woods at Wasenar. It was a late eighteenth-century castle fitted out as a residence for executives of international companies when moving through Europe. It was a lovely old building set in a very good garden. I became its longest resident, as the business executives stayed only brief periods. On my leaving I was presented by its staff with the book *A Bridge Too Far*, the management knowing of my interest in the area.

During the winter months there was always a nice fire by which to sit at evening. While I was there alone, I noticed an elderly couple coming to sit by the fire one evening. They had with them a French poodle which sat beside them. They spoke together in Dutch. On a later evening the lady spoke to the dog in English. I said quietly, "I see he understands English". She promptly said "And so do I". We fell into conversation and became quite friendly. After a couple of evenings, the gentleman asked me did I know a person in Australia by the name of Nygh, which he spelt for me. At that time I was Chancellor of Macquarie University; a little time before this I had joined in the council decision to appoint Peter Nygh as Professor of Law at Macquarie. I was able to tell the gentleman that I did, and of his appointment. "Well", he said, "he must be the son of my former business partner". Strange how small the world is and how some small circumstance can produce a quite remarkable result.

I found the period spent as judge ad hoc quite stimulating. I met quite a number of interesting people and I had some respite from the volume of work which I would have normally had to handle in Australia. I was disappointed that the case fizzled out in the way it did. It was the result of international politics, something I fear is always likely to bedevil the work of the International Court.

One day while I was in a conference of the International Court I was called out to take a telephone call from Sydney. Lionel Murphy informed me that Douglas Menzies had died suddenly at a function of the New South Wales Bar that evening. I was most upset. But matters were at such a stage that I could not come away to attend his funeral service in Melbourne, but Norma did and gave me an account of it. Both of us were terribly saddened by this event. Douglas and I had practised with each other and against each other in Australia and in London for years. Our wives were very friendly with each other and with each of us respectively. Helen, Douglas' wife, who was a very fine character and able to manage Doug's exuberance very well, had died earlier after a very long illness. He had missed her very much indeed and while at one time I think he had contemplated remarrying, he had decided against it and remained a widower for the rest of his days.

21 A Balanced View of Conservation

In 1965 the World Wildlife Fund was seeking some financial support from Australia. I was then in touch with a group of scientists in Canberra who were interested in the conservation of land, forests, plants and animals. My friends were aware of my experience with the Kosciusko State Park and of my abiding interest in land and forest conservation. They suggested that it was not wise to send money out of Australia to be spent on wildlife projects in various parts of the world when perhaps the money could be spent on some work in Australia. Not that we were against the work of the World Wildlife Fund, but that the funds available for conservation in Australia were naturally very limited, much more so than they are now.

My friends proposed the formation of a foundation to be known as the Australian Conservation Foundation. Its charter was to promote the education of the Australian public in the need to attend to soil degradation and erosion, and the protection of the natural forests and of native plants and animals, particularly any that were endangered by human activities, past or present. The emphasis was to be on education and the provision of accurate information. It was not designed as a protest body or a political lobby group, nor did it seek to enter into any large campaigns for funds or to acquire a large membership.

The group included informed conservationists such as RG Downes, CW Bonython, AD Butcher, MF Day, HG Frith and HNB Wettenhall. Among their number was Francis Ratcliffe, an Englishman who had come to this country for scientific investigation when he was a young man and had stayed here to become the chief of a department in the CSIRO. He had been responsible for the successful use of myxomatosis in the control of the rabbit plague. He was a fine scientist and a person of good quality, added to which he had a very good pen and could express scientific facts in a fashion which could be understood by the ordinary reader. He had written a splendid and most readable book entitled *Flying Fox and Drifting Sand.*[1]

I was asked to become president. I gave the matter a good deal of thought because I was in office as Chief Justice and, of course, not only had fairly heavy demands upon my time but I had to be careful not to become involved in political matters. On the other hand, I had a very firm view that the judicial office did not preclude me from taking part in the activities of citizens other than party-political activities. I realised that in a sense conservation, in so far as it was implemented by government action, would possibly have some political content, but I thought that its educational emphasis secured it from any suggestion of party politics.

My interest in land and forest had been excited by my work for the Kosciusko State Park and my association with my fellow trustees, who were all both conservationists and professionally knowledgeable on various aspects of conservation. I had by then had twenty years' experience of the conservation of the alpine region. I not only had developed a keen interest in conservation but felt that I had something to contribute to the spread of knowledge about it. I decided to accept the invitation and thus became the first and an active president of the Australian Conservation Foundation.

The foundation began to prepare a series of booklets on aspects of conservation. These were, in my opinion, first-class publications, attractive and readable, each written by an expert and presenting a balanced view of the particular need to conserve or protect. Each pamphlet had the consideration of all the members of the group before publication. They provided excellent educational material, even suitable for use in schools. They were freely distributed and progressively covered quite a number of topics. Meetings were also held and addressed from time to time in order to stimulate community awareness. I took part in them when I found the time, making addresses appropriate to the occasion.

Members of the foundation laboured mightily over what should be done about the kangaroo, particularly the red kangaroo. The red kangaroo favoured the short grass of a grazing pasture, something it could not readily find in the wild and in any case not in anything like the volume which our improved grazing lands presented. By the extension and improvement of their grazing properties, the graziers had increased the food supply of the kangaroo and therefore had added to its rate of reproduction, with the result that herds had increased exponentially. Strangely, it seemed that in good seasons, kangaroos and sheep and cattle might graze in the same area without the one denying the other the benefit of the pasture. But in leaner times, the kangaroo seriously depleted the pasture available to the sheep and cattle.

There was plenty of sentimental talk among the public and in the press about the dangers to which the kangaroos were exposed, but little attention had been paid to the damage they did. The grey kangaroo, which mainly inhabited the forest lands, was not in as much danger as the red; it was not so accessible to the hunter and therefore not so vulnerable. The red kangaroo, however, came out on to the plains in great numbers and was hunted by day and night with spotlights from moving vehicles with a great deal of success.

Our discussion of the question over a considerable time led us to think that the proper solution was to use the kangaroo, particularly the red kangaroo, as a resource and devise a system of controlled culling. The meat and the pelt of the animal both had commercial value. I remember the mental turmoil through which our members, particularly Francis Ratcliffe, went in reaching this conclusion, but in the end we reached it unanimously. I think our stance angered the demonstrating sort of conservationist who wanted absolute protection of the kangaroo.

In practice, the professional shooters delivered their carcasses to mobile freezing facilities. The operators of these facilities disposed commercially of the meat and hides. The hides made excellent leather and the meat good pet food. Indeed, some regard it as suitable for human consumption. We thought a system of regulating the culling through controls at the freezers could be developed but did not ourselves formally devise one.

Later on the New South Wales Government devised quite a good scheme of control. It licensed professional shooters and gave each a number of metal discs identified with the shooter which could be attached to the carcass. The freezer operators could not have in their possession any carcass of a kangaroo which did not bear one of these discs. While this quite effectively controlled the professional shooter, who being a marksmen killed outright with one shot, it did not solve the problem of the weekend or freelance shooter who had no pecuniary interest in the carcass and who left it where the animal fell. Only an alert public conscience would keep this within bounds.

Overall, I think the philosophy the foundation adopted has been justified, though I do not think there is community unanimity for the use of the kangaroo as a resource under proper control. I doubt if there can be a watertight scheme which eliminates completely the effects of fraudulent or reckless shooting. The recent disclosure of the substitution of kangaroo meat in the beef export trade indicates the difficulty which attends systems of control when common honesty is not observed.

The foundation joined in the opposition to the destruction of Lake Pedder by the Hydro-Electric Commission of Tasmania. As president, I wrote to the Tasmanian Premier, urging him to abandon the proposal. But the opposition was unsuccessful. The original Lake Pedder and its unique beach disappeared, and a new and larger lake was developed. While I still doubt if the destruction of the original was fully justified, what has developed is in itself a beautiful lake.

On this occasion I had some qualms about writing to the Premier. But after consideration I felt that in emphasising to him the conservation aspects of the matter I was not entering into any political controversy.

Later the question arose of tipping spoil into an area of the Shoalhaven River. I thought objection to this was justified on the grounds of preserving the Shoalhaven Valley. On behalf of the foundation I joined in public expression of that view. Tom Lewis, then Premier of New South Wales and a good friend of mine, publicly suggested that in joining the protest I had overstepped the line and had entered the political arena which, as Chief Justice, I ought not to have done. I did not think then, and do not think today that I had breached any rule against judicial participation in political affairs, however widely the rule might be expressed. But the margins of propriety in such matters are ill-defined. Individual members of the Privy Council who are law lords do speak in the House of Lords on public questions from time to time, though usually on topics of concern to the administration of the law. But that is an unusual situation derived from the passage of historical time. As members of the House of Lords they are free to express themselves on the merits or demerits of proposals before the House. In any case I think English society has a maturity we have not yet attained and thus a greater tolerance of judicial extramural activity. Although I felt I was not transgressing I thought more closely about the whole matter of my participation in conservation affairs.

There was about the same time a serious development in the affairs of the foundation. Since we were not a pressure group, as time went on we found we were not satisfying the conservation activists. At the outset we did not seek to build up a membership; it was intended to keep the foundation as a group of educators who would give their services voluntarily. There was enough money to cover the cost of printing and distributing our booklets, but no administrative structure was built. After some time it had been decided to encourage public membership for a small fee, at the one time consolidating the foundation's base and increasing its funds. In fact our membership grew rapidly.

A number of activists joined the foundation and apparently decided to take it over. They managed to stack an annual general meeting, which became noisy and difficult to control. I remember telling the leader of the activist members that if the foundation was taken along the political path he was intending to follow he would probably destroy its credibility, not only with the general public but with many of its members. I reminded the meeting that part of the foundation's success was the respect which the community evidently had for its balanced views and the known expertise of its principal speakers and writers. The conservation cause was one of rational education, not of political activism. But after what occurred at this meeting, I realised that I must remove myself from the foundation's affairs, otherwise I risked being drawn into political controversy.

I discussed retiring as president with my colleagues. Among our number was Mike Parker, who had been private secretary to the Duke of Edinburgh. Since coming to Australia he had maintained contact with the Duke, who was president of the World Wildlife Fund and very interested in conservation. Mike was anxious to induce the Duke's interest in the Australian foundation and kept him abreast of its activities. Now he canvassed with the Duke the possibility of his becoming president. In due course he brought me the news that if asked, the Duke would do so. So when the Duke visited Australia next, I went to see him at Government House in Canberra and made the proposal to him. The reaction was somewhat amusing. He said, "Me? They'd only call me an absentee pom". I said, "They probably would, but you could live with that. I think you would do the movement a great deal of good by identifying yourself with it". He took time to consider and later sent me a message that he would be prepared if asked by the foundation to become its president. So I resigned, sorry to part from the frequent association with the men with whom I had been dealing, but glad that any risks there may have been to the independence of my office had been removed.

Australians as a group are to a degree immature. A besetting sin is jealousy, the coveting of what the other fellow has and the desire that none should have what all cannot have. Next to jealousy is an inborn cynicism, fostered to some extent by journalists and those politicians who are more interested in party-political division than they are in national unity. I knew that the Duke would have to face a good deal of the combined effect of all these immaturities. I had hoped that with his presidency the activists who seemed bent on turning the foundation into a political weapon would pause. But I am afraid this did not happen, and eventually Prince Phillip felt he could no longer remain president.

Meantime, the Victorians had broken away and formed their own group and in New South Wales the Wildlife Foundation when set up did not associate itself with the Conservation Foundation. All this has been a matter of regret, for I had had high hopes of the foundation as a prime source of educational material objectively presented in the cause of national conservation. I had hoped that it could continue to do so without becoming identified with or supportive of any political party, but I fear that that has in substance happened. I think in its original efforts the foundation did do much to alert the Australian public to the need for care for the environment including wildlife in all its many manifestations.

There has been a noticeable change of public attitude in these matters over the past fifteen to twenty years and in that change I think the foundation certainly had its part. But the protests of extremists have given encouragement to anti-conservation sentiment. Whereas I had hoped for quiet, rational and balanced views which would seek accommodations between the need to conserve and the need to use, we have seen absolutes asserted by extremists and an opposition group gathering strength. The possibility of objective public discussion has not been realised. Commercial men, I am sure, would be ready to seek accommodations such as the use of the kangaroo as a resource, but I suspect many find difficulty in pursuing such a course. It is along that line, I think, that solid progress can be made: not by activism but by the exercise of calm reasoning and dispassionate judgment. Such progress will not be made by banner-carrying, shouting and the asserting of absolute and unqualified generalities. A man does not forfeit any principle who seeks an accommodation between two justifiable claims. He can of course refuse to compromise with a completely unjustifiable claim, but an accommodation with a justifiable claim is a different matter.

Now, I might add, politicians have taken up the cause of the environment as a means to the attainment of political power. A greenie group of activists holding the balance of political power will lead inevitably, I think, to instability in government and the abandonment of those very principles whose observance would lead to a national accommodation between the need to use and the need to conserve.

22 The Order of Australia

In 1962, when I was both Attorney-General and Minister for External Affairs, I had a conversation with Prime Minister Menzies about the possibility of inaugurating an Australian Order to replace some of the traditional orders and to provide a way of recognising merit in Australian citizens. Menzies and I often met at the beginning of the day in the lower part of the House. Menzies would enter the basement by a door that was closer to the Lodge than the front of the House. Its use would avoid the gathering of inquisitive journalists on the steps of the House, if the old House were still in use. (There are no like steps to the ministerial entrance to the new House, but there is now a car entrance which places the ministers out of reach.) Having passed through the basement, the Prime Minister would go upstairs to his office on the next floor. I had an office at that time on the same floor with a door leading on to the front terrace and another door which led into the passage which ran from Kings Hall to the end of the building where the Prime Minister had his rooms, and where the Cabinet rooms were located. I do not remember now just how on these occasions I came to get into the basement, but I think it was through a door off the area in front of the House.

On this morning, in a general conversation, I said that while he was such a favourite at the Palace, as indeed he was, it would be a good thing if he inaugurated an Australian Order of Chivalry to replace the traditional orders, particularly the Order of the British Empire, which I considered outmoded. The existence of such an Australian Order would enable Australians who did not care to accept honours in a traditional British Order to accept awards, including a knighthood, in an Australian Order. He said he thought it a good idea.

"You know", I said, "when you come to think of it, an Order of the Wattle or of the Waratah would be no sillier than the Order of the Thistle". Later Menzies was granted a knighthood in the Order of the Thistle. Had there been talk of it at the time, of course, I would probably not have said this. Menzies thought my suggestion a good one. But unfortunately he was not really an executive man. He forgot about it, no doubt because of more pressing things. I did not follow it up with any persistence, since I was busy as well.

When Whitlam came to power in 1972, he, following Labor's traditional aversion to knighthood, chose to inaugurate the Order of Australia, partly I am sure because of a degree of Anglophobia, partly also because of a desire to stimulate Australian nationalism and partly out of a general desire to be an innovator. He copied the Canadian scheme. But the Canadians had not had the problem of the acceptance or refusal of traditional British honours — since 1935 non-military honours had not been accepted in Canada. The Order of Canada was started in 1967 with, as it were, a clean slate and with no similar institution with which it would compete. The Canadian Order had no place for knighthood because the Canadians shared an American view that knighthood involves an undue distinction between individuals. At the time I thought, and still think, that this copying of Canada was unfortunate. The mere title of the Australian Order was unimaginative. There were possibly other models. But Mr Whitlam was in a hurry.

Having set up the machinery for the Order of Australia, probably with little consultation outside those immediately round him, Whitlam rang me to inform me that he proposed the inauguration of the order and to ask me if I would chair its Council, which would have the independent function of making the awards. I asked him if I might first see the order's charter, and studied it carefully. At once I realised that the specifications for the grant of the various levels of award were fairly demanding and that nominations were to come, not from government, but from citizens on their own initiative. I noticed the priority over equivalent awards in the traditional orders which awards in the new order would have, but this did not particularly trouble me. But I did foresee difficulty in finding many citizens whose activities could measure up to the specifications. The charter, however, was already settled and my misgivings would be unlikely to lead to any change.

I gave the matter some thought and decided that, as the order as I saw it would be apolitical, its Council quite independent of government, it would be a good thing if I were to chair it. I realised that there would be a degree of public opposition to the order, which would not be seen for what it was, a Royal order and one of national significance. That it emanated from a Labor administration might well cause opposition. I thought, however, that being Chief Justice my involvement as chairman might help the order's acceptability and that in its early steps I might be able to contribute to the respectability of the Council's work. So I agreed to chair the Council.

Not only was there no provision for a knighthood in the charter, but I understand that originally it was intended that the highest award should have seniority over all awards in the traditional orders, including that of the Knight

Grand Cross; the Companion in the Order of Australia, its then highest rank, was to have precedence over a Knight Grand Cross of any traditional order. Sir John Kerr later told me that he was instrumental in persuading Mr Whitlam that the only degrees in the traditional orders which had precedence over a Companion were the Knights Grand Cross of traditional orders. But when later Mr Fraser arranged for a knighthood to be introduced into the Order of Australia, that knighthood ranked before all awards in the traditional orders, including that of the Knight Grand Cross.

The basic idea of the order was a good one, namely, that it was exclusively for Australian citizens to nominate fellow Australians for recognition. The nomination is based upon individual initiative in which government has no part. An independent Council and not the government decides who is to be honoured. I particularly approved of these features since I was of the opinion that politicians already had undue opportunities for patronage. Government, however, was solely responsible for nominating citizens of other countries as honorary members. Early in my chairmanship I tried to have all honorary nominations processed through the Council, but failed. I understand that similar endeavours by my successors have also failed. These awards are still made on the sole authority of government without consultation with or notification to the Council.

The Council included a minister of a Commonwealth Department and the Secretary of the Premier's Department in each State; other members were the chairman of the Joint Chiefs of Staff, or his representative, and two or three prominent members of the general public. This composition of the Council subsequently had its effect on maintaining the policy of excluding government influence in the nomination of citizens. No doubt some of these government representatives from State departments had had considerable experience in the selection of citizens for honours and the Council profited greatly by their expertise. But they could also be vehicles by which government wishes could be furthered. I think a council composed of a decisive majority of citizens drawn from all the States would have been better, the Governor-General's Honours Secretariat providing the necessary advice and expertise. But doubtless the involvement of the States themselves in the work of the Council was justifiable and, indeed, in our federation, probably necessary. But the effect of the presence of these State officers required an independent stance on their part.

While awards in the Order of Australia and the awards in the traditional orders on the Queen's Birthday are published on the same day, announcement of the New Year awards is made later in the Australian order than in the traditional orders. It seems to me that the gap of three weeks or so between the publication of the honours might well have been removed by the adoption of New Year's Day (being the date of the proclamation of the Commonwealth in 1901), as the appropriate day for the publication of the both sets of awards. There is in any case much to be said for the view that New Year's Day is much more related to Australia as a nation than 26 January, a day which has little real symbolism for

South and Western Australia, being merely the beginning of European settlement in the Colony of New South Wales. It is not too late to make 1 January Australia Day. The inauguration of the Commonwealth ought to be regarded as the birth of the nation even if the change has to be postponed till the year 2001.

Since the specification of the various levels of awards in the order was early found to be pitched rather high, it was sometimes difficult conscientiously to recommend some of the nominees for particular awards, or indeed on occasions for any award at all. Accordingly the Council suggested the creation of the Medal and proposed to the Fraser Government that it be introduced into the order. This amendment has enabled recognition to be given to those who have done meritorious service but who could not properly satisfy the prescription of one of the higher ranks of the Order of Australia. It is in itself a substantial recognition of merit.

A question that arose early was that of a nomination of a judge still in office to be recognised for services done both in his judicial office and also in other areas of public service. In my view, a serving judge should not have any recognition by the award of an honour in this or any other order for any such service. I felt then, and still feel, that once appointed, a judge should have nothing to hope for as well as nothing to fear. He ought not to be placed in a position where it could be said that he could be tempted to curry favour with government or with anybody in authority. I do favour the participation of the judiciary in voluntary community service, but do not think of this, or exceptional performance of judicial duty, as reason for reward. At first the Council acted upon this view. Later, with a change of personnel on the Council, my view was regarded as too strict and was no longer followed.

My opinion was not and still is not shared by the States. Judges have been knighted after some years in office, their judicial seniority being observed when such awards have been made. The AK which I enjoy was awarded after I had retired from office and had ceased to be chairman of the Council.

As for the High Court of Australia, before the time of which I now speak, the practice of non-Labor governments had been to knight a judge of the High Court after a lapse of a number of years in office, and to nominate him for knighthood in the Order of St Michael and St George, that is to say that he should be made a KCMG. In deciding to nominate a judge for such preferment, his seniority on the Bench was observed.

When it came to Mr Justice Edward McTiernan's turn to be knighted, High Court judges who had been knighted KCMG had already retired. Thus, of the sitting members, only the Chief Justice, Sir Owen Dixon, was a knight, a KCMG. So there was room for change. Menzies was then Prime Minister. A knighthood in the Order of the British Empire was offered to McTiernan and accepted. He became Sir Edward McTiernan, KBE.

Some years later, in 1953-54, when it became Mr Justice Dudley Williams's turn to be knighted, he being next in seniority, Menzies proposed a knighthood in the Order of the British Empire. Williams at first demurred. At this time I had recently been president of the Law Council of Australia. Menzies came to see me in Sydney. He told me of the difficulty he was having over this proposal. I said that governments had brought this problem on themselves by, as it were, promoting a judge after his appointment. I stressed the view I have already expressed. I accepted that with Sir Edward a KBE, the government could not now do otherwise than offer other judges junior to Sir Edward a like award. There was no room for making any distinction here between one judge and another. I suggested that what he should now do, and what governments in the past should have done, was to propose a knighthood for each judge of the High Court on his appointment. Thereafter he could have nothing whatever to expect. I pointed out the possible implications of a judge wanting to be knighted and that while I thought it highly unlikely (yet something upon which the press was capable of seizing) there was a theoretical risk. The mere possibility of it was undesirable. I said that if a regime of knighting each member of the High Court as he was appointed were instituted, any difficulty in the case of Mr Justice Williams would be solved.

Menzies was satisfied. Williams accepted the KBE and subsequently all members of the High Court have been knighted in the Order of the British Empire on appointment until the appointment of Mr Justice Murphy.

When I was appointed Chief Justice, I was already a Knight Bachelor. So on my appointment I made no reference to the Prime Minister of the possibility of a knighthood. But after I had been in office a few weeks, I received a communication from Government House in Canberra that the Queen was prepared to make me a Knight Commander in the Order of St Michael and St George. The Governor-General's secretary, Murray Tyrrell, rang me and said that he would like me to accept this offer. I said that I was not prepared to, that the office of Chief Justice should carry the highest rank, a Grand Cross. There was an awkward moment while readjustments were made, but then I was offered nomination as a Knight Grand Cross (GCMG), which I accepted. Following this precedent, my successor was made a Knight Grand Cross in the order of St Michael and St George on or shortly after his appointment as Chief Justice.

It is to my mind of considerable importance that the high distinction of the office of Chief Justice of Australia be maintained. It is in itself a unique office and its place in the constitutional and judicial life of the nation is pre-eminent. If its occupant is to be honoured by knighthood, the honour should be of the highest order. I also think that it was proper that the judges should all be knighted on appointment. Their office warrants this distinction but, the Queen having requested the discontinuance of the practice of recommending British honours, a knighthood in the traditional order could no longer be possible.

* * * * *

Over time, perhaps partly because of the insufficiency of nominations made directly by the public, the secretaries of the Premier's Departments who were members of the Council began to forward nominations submitted by other citizens, nominations which on occasions I suspected had been inspired by their ministers or their own departments. I thought this an unfortunate development that would open the door to political patronage.

As Labor administrations do not favour awards in the traditional orders, and while more traditionally minded people may continue to look with disfavour on awards in the Order of Australia, there could arise a distinct imbalance in the awards in that order, particularly if political patronage of any kind were allowed. There could be a distinct risk that party-political divisions in the community might be repeated in the awards in the order. Such a divisive effect might even result in worthwhile citizens being overlooked altogether.

My perception of the possibility of the order becoming divisive grew during my period as chairman. I resolved to do something about it personally. I saw Prime Minister Fraser and suggested that it would be as well if the Commonwealth Government terminated resort to all traditional orders, but if not, at least to the Order of the British Empire, which had overtones of the past. The ideal thing would be the abandonment of all the traditional orders and the universal use of the Order of Australia. But if only the Order of the British Empire were abandoned, the government would still be able to recommend the creation of knights bachelor, awards in the Orders of St Michael and St George and of the Bath. I thought that if the Prime Minister accepted my advice those who may have preferred an award in the traditional orders might come to accept an award in the Order of Australia. In that way the possibility of the order working divisively in the nation would be substantially reduced.

Mr Fraser took heed of what I said and appointed Sir John Bunting to report on my suggestion and to advise him. Sir John's report did not favour the adoption of any part of my suggestion. Fraser said he intended to accept its recommendation. Though I had not discussed my proposals with any of the members of the Council, nor informed them of my meetings with Fraser, I asked him if the report was to be made available to the members of the Council. He said it would not but that he would give me a copy which I could treat confidentially. I told him that I would not accept the report on that basis. I was chairman of the Council and, although I had not consulted the Council members about making my suggestion to him, unless all the members of the Council were able to see the terms of the report, I did not wish to do so. Accordingly I have never read the report, nor have I discussed the matter at any time with Sir John Bunting, although I have seen him on quite a number of occasions as we remain quite close friends.

I very much regret that Sir John reported in that fashion, because I think it would have been a good thing to have reduced the possibility of a divisive quality in the operation of the order, and as well it would have reduced the area for government patronage and increased the authority of the Council. However, it was left for the Queen to request in February 1990 that all Australian Governments, Commonwealth and State, should no longer make recommendations to her for the grant of British honours to Australian citizens.

One other development which related to this question ought here to be mentioned, namely, that Malcolm Fraser while Prime Minister, had the terms of the order altered to include the rank of knight. I had no part in prompting or making this change. As far as I am aware none of the members of the Council took any initiative on this. Indeed at the time I had my doubts about the inclusion of a knighthood. But I thought that there was some possibility that the notion of chivalry (the sense of obligation, of duty, of compassion and of excellence in endeavour) might accompany the inclusion of a knighthood in the charter of the order.

After some thought, I came to the conclusion that, on balance, the addition would do no harm, particularly while resort to the traditional orders with their rank of knight was maintained. But I realised that the egalitarians and others in the community might be offended. Indeed the attraction of the order for many was that it had no provision for knighthood. In the event, the inclusion of a knighthood as a rank in the order led to some of those who had already received an award in the order returning their insignia in protest. Oddly enough, the differentiation of Companion, Officer and Member seemed quite acceptable to such people, though in the logic of the egalitarian there should have been no rank within the order at all. I sense that the current use of the given or Christian name in citizens addressing one another, and in being spoken of publicly, is probably an unconscious disdain of the rank involved in the address of "Mr". If it is, it at least shows some logical consistency. For my part, if we are born equal, we certainly do not perform equally: we do not die equal. Unless there is to be absolutely no recognition of unequal service to one's fellows, the inequality of merit may justify the inequality of rank. The important thing is not the existence of rank, but insistence that it be only for commensurate merit in community service and no more. Nor should the stimulus to effort, which the existence of rank may well afford, be overlooked.

I might add that when the award of knighthood became available to the Council, there was a unanimous view that RG Menzies, then retired from office, should be offered the first knighthood to be awarded. But members of the Council were apprehensive that he might reject the offer, favouring, as he well might, traditional institutions. So as its chairman I was given the task of interviewing him to foreshadow the offer before it was formally made.

I saw him in his house in Melbourne. I broached the question of the knighthood as diplomatically as I could. He was less than enthusiastic. But, perhaps because of our personal association, I was able to speak directly to him, saying among other things that he was a great Australian and had been pre-eminent in the service of his country. None could have a greater claim to the offer of knighthood in the order. Although he had otherwise been honoured, this was an Australian honour proffered by Australians — I knew he always craved the approval of his fellow Australians. I also said that the order needed such support as he could give if it were to become universally accepted in Australia. His acceptance of a knighthood would mark his approval. Ultimately he accepted, and the Queen invested him on her visit to Australia in 1976.

The Hawke Government removed the rank of knight from the order. This situation may change again. In referring to the Royal request of February 1990, the former Leader of the Opposition, Dr Hewson, gave some indication that he might restore it.

It is now probable that the aversion which some have had to the order may decrease. With the disappearance of traditional British honours any divisive competitiveness between the orders has disappeared. But a total absence of political patronage must be ensured and high standards in the selection of nominees for awards maintained.

An Order of Australia Association has been formed and it has had significant success. I think its appearance on the scene has been very beneficial and that it may be an added element in the development of a true patriotic sentiment. I use the word "patriotic" in clear contrast to "nationalist", which has a different significance. I feel we have as yet much nationalism, sometimes almost to the level of jingoism, but I suspect we have not as much patriotism.

23 The Rule of Law and the Constitution

The Australian colonies upon their settlement inherited the rule of law as developed by the English people over a considerable period of time. I set out here my understanding of that rule and my view of its operation.

The rule of law involves and carries with it the separation of powers, legislative, executive and judicial, each respectively reposing in a separate authority: the Parliament, the executive government and the judiciary.

The law binds everybody: the Crown, the Parliament, the executive government and its public servants of every description, all persons exercising authority, the judiciary and all citizens. Every act and dealing taking place between citizens, between governments, and between governments and citizens must be according to and justified by law. Every exercise of authority, no matter by whom, must accord with the law. No individual, group or body may exercise with respect to any citizen in any capacity or circumstances or with respect to any relationship between them an absolute and uncontrolled discretion. To do so would be tyrannical: tyranny in any form or to any degree is inconsistent with the rule of law.

The Parliament, which is representative of and responsible to the people, is bound by the law as it exists. But Parliament has the exclusive power and authority to change it, other than the Constitution. In doing so the Parliament ought not to create in any individual, group or body an absolute and uncontrolled discretion. Every parliamentary grant of authority of any kind should stipulate the purpose for which, the manner in which and the extent to which such authority can be exercised. The rule of law requires this.

In the Australian Parliament the Senate's power of disallowance of regulations made under parliamentary authority is most useful in avoiding misuse of such delegated legislative authority. But it is no substitute for the Parliament's regular refusal to give absolute and uncontrolled discretion to any individual, group or body.

It is by the rule of law and its observance that the freedom of the citizen is secured. I should emphasise that it is freedom, not licence to unrestrainedly act according to personal will, that is secured. Personal freedom does not mean that any citizen can do as he or she pleases. By description a citizen is a member of a community, whether large or small. The citizen owes his or her significance as a person to the fact that he or she is a member of a community. Robinson Crusoe on his lonely island, even with his companion Friday, not being a member of a community, had no real significance. Each member of the community owes duties of a definable nature to all fellow citizens. Because of such mutual duties between citizens, freedom in a community involves restraint and forbearance on the part of each citizen. At the lowest, the citizen must not act so as to diminish or weaken the freedom of other citizens. Every other member of that community is entitled to the same freedom, and each citizen owes a duty to respect the other's freedom.

The illustration of the use of the public highway epitomises this restraint and forbearance. That the rules of the road must be observed does not reduce the road user's freedom to use it. By observing them the freedom of other citizens is secured. Licence to go as you please must result in chaos and diminish the freedom of all. So it is throughout our life's activities.

All are equal under the law. No distinction of class, race or religion is made in its observance and administration.

That some citizens may lack the financial resources to exert and enjoy the rights which the law accords them does not deny that they are equal before the law. The law can take no account of such financial inequality. It may be different when a judicial discretion is being exercised. It is a function of government to endeavour to reduce the disadvantage which lack of resources may involve in this connection.

The law is to be found in the totality of the Federal Constitution and those of the States as affected by it, the statutory provisions enacted by a parliament or under its authority and the common law which, though unwritten, is considered as objectively existing. When not expressed in binding precedents, the common law is discoverable by the judiciary. The common law originated in the customs and attitudes of the community, identified and formulated from time to time as the courts decided according to disputes brought before them. This development case by case provides the many recorded precedents which bind the judiciary. When a precedent is found to have been incorrectly made the error may be corrected. But otherwise the precedent may not be disregarded whether or not the court may entertain a view that the law should be otherwise. If in a case before it there is no precedent, or combination of precedents by the application of which the dispute before the court can be resolved, the court must nonetheless decide the case according to law. In doing so the court may create a new precedent. But it will not do so according to personal philosophy or inclination. The court will decide according to the principles of the law and any necessary development of them by logical reasoning from them. To do otherwise would reduce that certainty and predictability which is a feature of the rule of law. It will also introduce an element of tyranny.

It is often said that by this process of decision in such a case the court determines what the law should be: and so in a sense it does. But it does not make the law, in the sense of reshaping it. But a clear distinction must be made between the logical process of applying the law, which as I have said is considered as objectively existing, and an attempt to resolve the dispute according to personal philosophy or inclination.

In any event, what might be acceptable in a developing community and before the parliamentary process has become highly developed is unlikely to be accepted by a community accustomed to a parliamentary democracy and insistent on the Parliament's representative and accountable quality.

This power to decide disputes brought before it is exclusive to the judiciary. Because of this exclusive authority vested in it, it is of the utmost importance that the judiciary confine itself to the administration of the law and eschew all tendencies to reform it or to indulge in social engineering. To do either is to legislate and invade the Parliament's exclusive area of authority.

If the judiciary does not so confine itself and attempts to change the existing law — to make law according to its own ideas — it enters the area of authority exclusively vested in the Parliament which, as I have pointed out, is representative of and accountable to the community and controlled by it. The judiciary, on the contrary, is neither elected nor representative. Indeed, it should not in any respect be representative. Its members should be chosen on merit, knowledge of the law and capacity for objective, dispassionate and logical judgment. It has the function of administering the law, and in my view has no other function. The community cannot be expected to accept the idiosyncratic changes in the law made by unelected and unaccountable judges.

If the judiciary does not so confine itself to the administration of the law it must, probably in a short time, lose that respect of the community on which its authority so largely depends. It is therefore of paramount importance that it strictly confines itself to the administration of the law. To subject the citizen to the arbitrary discretion of an unelected judiciary is as dangerous to the maintenance of individual freedom as would submission to the arbitrary discretion of a dictator. In either case, the outcome is tyrannical.

If by some chance the judiciary were accorded the function of reforming the law, shaping it according to the personal philosophies and inclinations of its members, the community would require more frequent unanimity and unambiguous clarity in their judgments than is now the case. Yet even if these requirements were attained, predictability and consistency of the law would suffer grievously.

If the law is contained in written material, the language in which it is expressed must be construed. Construction of this material and its application forms part of the exclusive function of the judiciary.

For this purpose, rules or canons of construction have been gradually developed over time. Their existence and use tends to give certainty and predictability to the law. The medium by which sighted and hearing people communicate with each other is spoken or written language, composed of words related to each other. This in particular circumstances may be supplemented by drawings or pictures of one kind or another. Words of which language is composed have definable meaning derived from common usage and the context in which they are used. Thus language is the exclusive means by which the authors of written material communicate their intention in creating it.

The creator of a written instrument however may specify the sense in which its language is used. The Parliament in general indicates the sense in which it uses words by an Acts Interpretation Act, but it may also do so by some particular provision. In either case, the specified sense must be respected. But Parliament may not otherwise direct the judiciary as to the construction of the statutory language.

Legislatures in statutes, and the executive in regulations, at times fail to convey by the language they choose the message they had intended. The language now does not mean what the legislature intended.

The language employed can only be assigned a meaning which the words used are capable of carrying, even in any special context or circumstance of their use. The creator of the language must be taken to intend that meaning. In other words, it is only the expressed intention which can be operative. The unexpressed intention can have no effect, nor can the judiciary give it any other meaning; to do otherwise would be to legislate, a function deemed to the executive. It must always be remembered that statutes and regulations bind the citizenry, who must act upon the meaning which the language itself conveys both in personal conduct and in proprietary dealings. In construing statutory language therefore it must be borne in mind that to attribute a meaning to the language which the citizen could not have taken from it would be a denial of that certainty and predictability of the law which, even if sometimes difficult of attainment, the rule of law requires.

*****

Before I became Attorney-General a joint parliamentary committee had published a report on the Commonwealth Constitution making recommendations for its change. Some of these may have stemmed from a desire for uniformity of law throughout Australia, others were spurred by nationalist sentiment, and others appear to be based simply on a desire for more power in the Commonwealth. I studied this report for some time but in the end made up my mind that I should not take any steps to implement any of its recommendations.

I had had some experience of the operation of the Constitution and thought it worked very well. Being federal, it naturally posed some difficulties both of construction and of application. It did not give much legislative power exclusively to the Commonwealth: in fact only those matters which fall within s 52. All other powers are held concurrently with the States — that is to say, both Commonwealth and State may legislate on all or any of those subject-matters. But paramountcy is given to Commonwealth legislation. To the extent of any inconsistency between Commonwealth and State statutes, the Commonwealth statute prevails. This is something to be borne in mind in considering any addition of subject-matter to s 51.

It is evident that any proposed constitutional change is unlikely to succeed unless there is a complete consensus between the political parties on both the principle and the detail of the proposed change. Such a consensus is in general highly unlikely. Although not a reason for my decision not to implement the report, I could not see any prospect of such a consensus with respect to the alterations recommended. In any case, I thought that it would be better if those defects in the Constitution which could be remedied by parliamentary action were left to be so dealt with on some suitable — though I must confess, unexpected — occasion.

To my mind there were two principal defects in the Constitution. First, our forefathers did not provide a long-term formula for sharing as between the Commonwealth and the States the major part of the national revenues. These revenues, as of 1900, took the form of customs and excise, topics handed over to the Commonwealth exclusively. The short-term solution provided by s 87 covered only the first ten years and thereafter left the matter to be dealt with by the Commonwealth Parliament alone. The disadvantage of s 87 to the States was for a time partly ameliorated by the development of State income tax. But the enactment by the Commonwealth in wartime of the uniform taxation legislation and its survival of a challenge to its validity in postwar days exacerbated the situation. The greater part of the national revenue now came under the exclusive control of the Commonwealth.

The other defect left by our forefathers was the open-ended nature of s 96 — the power in the Commonwealth to make financial grants to the States on terms fixed by the Commonwealth. It has been this open-endedness both in the power not being limited to making grants to those States less naturally endowed, those who became known as the claimant States, and more significantly in the generality of the terms which might be imposed by the Commonwealth on the grant. This power given by s 96 has enabled the Commonwealth (beginning with the Federal Road Act) to devise the system of tied grants by means of which legislative power has in substance been exercised by the Commonwealth over subject-matters not granted to it by s 51. This has resulted in Commonwealth departments of education, housing, etc, duplicating to a substantial degree those of the States.

Both these defects, given the necessary party-political goodwill or government resolve, can be removed without constitutional change. For the rest, except for the removal of harmless vestigial provisions, I found no need to promote constitutional reform. In particular I saw no need, certainly no pressing need, to increase Commonwealth legislative power. Subsequent gatherings of politicians, academics and lawyers have failed to produce any proposals likely to attract such a political consensus and popular support as constitutional amendment usually requires.

Granted adherence to federation and parliamentary democracy the Constitution works well. So far from being outdated, it is on that footing as modern and up to date as could be wished. Its federal structure appears to suit this country, with its States with diverse natural resources and historical development. It is worth remembering that the people of the States are the people of the Commonwealth which as a legal entity has no citizens other than those of the federal territories.

The Constitution embodies the basic principles of the Westminster system of government, a system of parliamentary democracy under a constitutional monarchy. It is the result of a long historical process by which the parliament changed an absolute monarch into a constitutional monarch who, though still having a formal place in the system of Government has, as I think, no power to act except on ministerial advice. Consequently when transcribed into the Australian Constitution in Australia the monarch remains a formal but powerless part of the parliament.

To understand this unique form of government, which has provided such stable government, a knowledge of the history of the English people is at least advantageous. The Commonwealth Parliament as the Parliament of a federation of States is essentially bicameral. Unlike the situation in Great Britain where the members of the House of Commons are elected whilst the members of the House of Lords are not, each chamber of the Australian Parliament is elected by the same people — the House of Representatives on the basis of constituencies which reflect local concerns; the Senate by all the residents of the State voting as one constituency. Though the franchise for each chamber is identical, the method of vote-counting differs as between them.

The Queen of Australia is a constitutional monarch, without personal power of any kind, bound in every case to act only on the advice of the Prime Minister of Australia who expresses the views of the ministry he leads. Without political association such a monarchy is symbolic of national unity.

Every legislative power given by the Constitution to the Commonwealth Parliament is conditioned on the terms of ss 51 and 52, "Subject to this

Constitution". That at least means that there is no legislative power to destroy the federation or weaken any of its essential features.

The Constitution resulted exclusively from the initiative of the people of the Australian colonies. With the exception of some parts of s 74 relating to appeals to the Judicial Committee of the Privy Council, the Constitution was wholly devised by the people who sanctioned it by popular referenda.

Although devised as the constitution of a colony within the British Empire, the Constitution was expressed in a manner which would make it appropriate for the emergence of an independent Australia, an event which in 1900 could not have been considered remote. The Constitution gave the monarch only the power to appoint and by inference to dismiss the Governor-General, to give him instructions, and to disallow Commonwealth legislation within two years of its enactment.

Power to summons, prorogue and dissolve the House of Representatives was given not to the monarch but to the Governor-General personally. Section 58 also gives to the Governor-General personally the power in stated circumstances to dissolve both chambers of the Parliament simultaneously. He appoints the ministry to hold office not for a fixed term but during his pleasure, which means so long as the ministry retains the confidence of the Parliament. Thus these important discretionary powers are not derived by the Governor-General from his vice-regal position but directly from the Constitution itself. The exercise of these powers is not dependent upon or controlled by ministerial advice, unlike the ordinary acts of government which are to be effected by the Governor-General in Council, whose actions depend upon and are controlled by ministerial advice.

Independence came to Australia, as I think, by the time of the making of the Balfour Declaration but at latest upon its adoption by the Commonwealth Parliament during the administration of the Chifley government (1945-1949). At the time of independence, whenever it came, a severance of the Australian territory from the imperial realm occurred so that then on the one hand the monarchy of Great Britain, whose authority is limited to the realm of Great Britain, lost all authority over and in respect of the territory of Australia, and on the other hand there developed a constitutional monarchy of Australia, separate and distinct from that of the United Kingdom. But the law of the United Kingdom, already binding in Australia, remained in force. The "Queen" in s 1 of the Constitution became the Queen of Australia.

By that independence as Queen of Australia, a constitutional monarch became bound to exercise all powers given the Queen by the Constitution only on the advice of the Australian Ministry expressed by its Prime Minister. Thus the Queen became bound to appoint as Governor-General the person nominated to her by the Australian Prime Minister. Any instruction given to the Governor-General must be decided by the Australian Ministry. Although occasion for its exercise is unlikely to arise, the power of disallowance is only exercisable on that advice.

So the Constitution as drawn was apt for the attainment of Australian independence, and its provisions operate appropriately for the conduct of an independent Australia's affairs.

Of course, if Australians came to form a congressional system of government or abandoned federation for a unitary form for all Australia — both perhaps unlikely events — the Constitution would need to be replaced by a totally different document.

Granted, however, that it is accepted that a federation of the Australian States with a parliamentary democracy under a constitutional monarchy is the best arrangement for Australia, the Constitution is quite suitable and practical for present day Australia.

An uninstructed community may well have difficulty in understanding that the Queen is at the same time the constitutional monarch in the government of a number of independent states, each having its own international identity unaffected in any respect by the fact that the Queen is the constitutional monarch of the other independent and separately identified nations. But as a matter of substance and not merely of titular form, she is at the same time Queen of Canada, of New Zealand and of Australia. Neither Canada nor New Zealand has any impact upon Australia's government. The same is true of Great Britain. Her occupancy of the British throne does not affect in any respect the government or affairs of international identity of Australia.

In Empire days, it used to be said that the Crown was "one and indivisible". So it was. But as former colonies became independent nations, the Crown did split, not physically, but emblematically into a number of separate and distinct crowns.

The difficulty of an uninstructed community recognising the reality of these separate and independent constitutional monarchies must be realised and countered by education of the community. Meantime, those who oppose the constitutional monarchy of Australia profit by the confusion which that difficulty of perception causes.

24 1975

Sir John Kerr died on Sunday, 18 March 1991. There was a church service in St James' Church in Sydney early on the morning of 24 March, attended only, I understand, by his family. He was buried in the Northern District's Cemetery at Ryde on that Monday afternoon, again in the presence only of his family.

The insistence by his family on this degree of privacy was prompted no doubt by the understandable apprehension that any public ceremony would be marred by the noisy protests of those who still maintained the "rage" that had been counselled by the Prime Minister whose commission Sir John had been in duty bound to withdraw. It is a sad commentary on our humanity that one of our great sons should go to his rest without affording those of his fellows — and probably a majority of the community — an opportunity to express by their presence their appreciation of his many public services and of the quality of his character; some of them doubtless anxious also — and there were many — to show their warm affection.

But smallness of mind, ignorance and bitter political partisanship are unfortunately rife. Too few have the virtue of magnanimity, and fewer that of tolerance. Even fewer understand the events of 1975 and the constitutional importance of Sir John's performance of a duty rendered necessary not by anything he had done, but solely by the dishonourable, unparliamentary conduct of the Whitlam Ministry.

I paid a tribute to Sir John Kerr in an interview I gave to Paul Murphy of the ABC's *PM* programme on Tuesday, 26 March 1991.[1] I made two conditions on which I would give an interview: first, that the tape would not be edited before being broadcast; second, that a duplicate would be lodged in the National Archives in Canberra. I remember saying to Paul Murphy, who accepted both conditions, that I had little chance of convincing journalists of the error of their attitude towards Sir John and the events of 1975, but that the historians would take a different view. Of necessity my remarks were brief and largely responsive to the insinuating questions of the interviewer. They did not fully reflect the respect and affection I had for Sir John, whom I had known in professional and personal life for half a century.

Sir John, who had been an outstanding student both at Fort Street High and in university, maintained throughout his life wide intellectual interests covering government, the Constitution, politics and international affairs. He was ever thoughtful and imaginative in his thinking. He had an abiding interest in the intellectual development of young people, was kind and considerate to others, perhaps slightly withdrawn in manner and at times uncertain of the conclusions he drew for himself. He was a good companion and a loyal friend. He was a very good and much-loved family man. John Kerr and I had practised as barristers, though in general in different departments of the law, and had been active in the corporate affairs and activities of the Bar. We had become personal friends.

In 1983, eight years after the events of 1975, because of what I considered to be continuing misunderstanding of the import of those events, I wrote an account and legal explanation of them, *Sir John Did His Duty*.[2] Because of its structure and because it was written for the constitutionally uninformed, the text is considerably repetitive. The repetition aimed to ensure that the fundamentals of our parliamentary democracy and the relation to it of Sir John's action would be understood.

The booklet contains one erroneous observation. On p 55 I wrote that "until 1975 no Prime Minister in any Westminster System, including the United Kingdom, had ever failed to resign or advise a dissolution if unable to secure supply". But there were exceptions which I had overlooked, namely instances in the colony of Victoria in what might be called its frontier days. With those exceptions, my statement was accurate.

Thus in Australia the Parliament is summoned, adjourned and dissolved by the Governor-General, though in general on the advice of the Prime Minister of the day. There must be a Royal Assent to make the parliamentary provisions into law and legally all acts of government are done by the Governor-General in council. But in all these matters the Governor-General acts and can only act on the advice of a member of the government who, being a member of Parliament, is responsible to it for the advice given and the action taken on it. So although politically powerless, the Governor-General is an integral part of the Westminster system of government.

Government under this form of constitutional monarchy is truly democratic. The members of Parliament are elected by universal suffrage. Thus every citizen has a say as to who shall form the Parliament.

Then the Parliament controls the finances of the country. All the revenues received are paid into a consolidated fund which cannot be drawn upon without parliamentary authority. To implement this, each year Parliament approves a budget submitted by the ministry which specifies what receipts there will be, both by way of taxes and charges and by way of borrowings. The budget sets out in detail the manner in which those receipts will be expended.

If Parliament will not approve the annual budget, the ministry must resign or ask for the House of Representatives to be dissolved so that there will be a general election at which the electorate can decide the future course of government. The resignation of the ministry once Parliament rejects its budget is to avoid the embarrassment to the Crown in having to dismiss the ministry, something which must happen if the ministry does not resign or advise a dissolution of the House of Representatives.

It must be remembered that under our parliamentary democracy the electorate chooses the Parliament. The ministry to form the executive government is not elected as such. As I have said, it is appointed by the Governor-General not for a fixed term but to hold office during the Governor-General's pleasure. That does not mean during his personal pleasure: it means for so long as a ministry retains the confidence of the Parliament. Parliamentary democracy involves the control of the executive government by the Parliament throughout the whole life of the Parliament. The Governor-General's power to choose and to dismiss the ministry is to be exercised according to the parliamentary wishes. If the Parliament indicates that it will not support the ministry, the ministry must go to the people for their endorsement either voluntarily or involuntarily by dismissal. In other words, the Governor-General's function in this connection is to see that the parliamentary wishes are carried out and he acts as the link in the chain which will give the electorate the opportunity to express itself. Thus when Parliament will not support the ministry it is not the Governor-General who, though bound to dismiss the ministry, decides the future government. It is the people who do so, returning if they wish the former ministry, or if unwilling to do so, electing a differently composed House which will support a different ministry.

It is undoubtedly a time-honoured and honourable parliamentary convention that a ministry unable to obtain supply from the Parliament, or which suffers a vote of no confidence, immediately takes steps to face the electorate so as to give the people the opportunity to decide whether or not they wish to retain the government in office: those steps call for resignation or advice that the Parliament be dissolved. In either case a general election follows. The purpose of this longstanding parliamentary convention is to avoid the inevitable embarrassment to the Crown or, in Australia's case, to the Governor-General, in having to dismiss the ministry. So the event proved in 1975. Sir John, in carrying out his duty, was embarrassed: it was the ministry which caused the embarrassment. The press exacerbated and prolonged that embarrassment. Academic lawyers who intervened to support the ministry increased the embarrassment and displayed their own ignorance of our parliamentary democracy.

Our parliamentary democracy requires the Governor-General to have advisers who take responsibility to Parliament for the acts of the executive government, that is, for the advice they give and for the action taken upon it.

The ministers of state are not elected as such. The expression "the elected government" is a misnomer and quite inaccurate: the ministry is appointed by the Governor-General, though as members of Parliament they were elected. The Governor-General has a duty to appoint his advisers. For the performance of this duty he needs no advice. In fact he is required to make his appointment at a time when there may be no ministry in office. He normally does so immediately after the results of a general election are known. In practice a general election produces a majority of members of a political party and the Governor-General has no difficulty in selecting their leader for appointment as Prime Minister; thereafter he takes the Prime Minister's advice as to the identity of the other members of the ministry.

But there may be circumstances, as in what is called a "hung" parliament, in which the Governor-General has to make a judgment of his own as to whom he will appoint. In technical terms, his action in appointing and also in dismissing a ministry is not justiciable. It is an exercise of the personal discretion given him by the Constitution. This does not mean that the exercise of this discretion is uncontrolled. The control of the Governor-General's action in choosing or in dismissing a ministry is not through the courts but through the Parliament. In every case the Governor-General's choice of a ministry, if it is to be effective, must have the approval of the Parliament. That approval is normally given by passage of the budget presented to the Parliament by the ministry. Its disapproval of the Governor-General's choice is by the refusal to pass the budget and thus provide funds to enable the ministry to carry on, or by passing a resolution of no confidence.

During the life of a Parliament the ministry must continue to have the confidence of the Parliament. The lack of that confidence is expressed by a resolution of no confidence by the House of Representatives, or by the failure to pass a legislative proposal vital to the execution of a major policy of the ministry or, of course, by the failure to carry the budget which must be presented annually throughout the life of the Parliament.

A longstanding parliamentary convention, of which I have spoken, calls for a ministry which has lost the confidence of the Parliament by any of these events to resign forthwith or to advise the Governor-General to dissolve the House of Representatives. It is worth repeating that the purpose of the resignation or the dissolution is to pass to the electorate the decision as to whether or not the ministry is to remain in office or, if it has already resigned, is to be returned to office.

Differences between the ministry and the Parliament resulting in a lack of confidence cannot be resolved by the Governor-General nor by the courts. They can only be resolved by the people expressing themselves through a general election. It follows that this process of resignation or advice of a dissolution, or failing resignation or that advice, the dismissal of the ministry, is at the very heart of our parliamentary democracy; it constitutes an essential step in the operation of that democracy. This process ensures that the ministry has the Parliament's approval and is thus the means of securing the electorate's control of the executive government through its parliamentary representatives.

The Parliament has the exclusive control of all government funds. All moneys received by the executive government, whether revenues or moneys borrowed, must be paid into one consolidated fund. No money can be withdrawn from that fund except with the Parliament's approval expressed through a legislative act.

It is by this control that the Parliament can express its approval or its disapproval of the ministry. This is also an essential feature of our parliamentary democracy. It follows that the Governor-General cannot allow a ministry to continue in office which cannot obtain supply from the Parliament or has otherwise lost the confidence of the Parliament. He cannot retain such a ministry as his advisers. He forms part of the executive government, the ministry forming the other part. He presides over the Executive Council, which in law is the executive government. All initiatives of the ministry must become acts of the Executive Council if they are to have legal effect. The Governor-General could scarce preside over a meeting of its members of whom the Parliament does not approve. It would be an intolerable threat to our democratically secured liberties if a Governor-General could allow such a ministry to remain in office. For a Governor-General to retain in office a ministry of whom the Parliament has disapproved would represent a defiance by him of the Parliament's expressed wish. To do so would transgress a fundamental tenet of our parliamentary democracy.

If, when supply is not forthcoming, the Governor-General could find in the Parliament a group which could unconditionally provide supply, he could appoint their leader to head a ministry. But if there is no such group in the Parliament (as there was not in 1975) he must dissolve the House of Representatives and thus allow the electorate to decide which party should provide the ministry. Pending an election he can appoint a caretaker ministry.

Another small matter I have observed on rereading the booklet is that at p 121 I spoke of the Prime Minister's course requiring "the exercise of Vice Regal power". But none of the powers of the Governor-General given to him by the Constitution, including the power to dismiss a ministry and choose another, is vice-regal in the sense of having been derived from the monarch or exercisable in her place. The description I used was intended to acknowledge that the Governor-General is the monarch's representative in Australia. But the powers exercisable by him are his personal powers expressly given him by the Constitution.

Before the events of October and November 1975, the ministry had been trying to improve its political position by removing from the ranks of its supporters in Parliament those who were dissident or posed a threat to its leadership. Appointments were made to the diplomatic service and the High Court. These appointments created casual vacancies in the Senate, vacancies which could be filled by the parliaments of the States pursuant to s 15 of the Constitution as it then stood.

One consequence of Australia's federation is that a Senate forms part of the Parliament and is given equal legislative power to that given to the House of Representatives — with one exception which I will mention later. Each State necessarily has equal representation in the Senate, each senator representing the State for which he or she is elected. Therefore the State through its Parliament or its executive chooses the person to represent it when filling any casual vacancy. Until 1975 it had been customary in filling such vacancies for persons of the same political party as the retired or deceased senator to be chosen as the replacement. This, a concession to the dominance of the party system, and however convenient for politicians, has been claimed by some to have attained the status of a parliamentary convention. But, by whatever description it is known, this practice did not and could not override the constitutional power of the State to choose a person to represent it rather than choose one to represent a political party.

Since 1975 there has been a constitutional amendment carried with bipartisan support (*Constitution Amendment Senate Casual Vacancies Act* 1977) which requires a casual vacancy in the Senate to be filled by a member of the same political party as the retired or deceased senator. This, a significant departure from the principle of the federalism, tended to convert the senator into a representative of a political party rather than the representative of a State. It also gave undue significance to the party system and the distortion of our parliamentary system which it has effected. But the amendment did not go so far as to require the appointment of the nominee of a political party; the choice of the person to fill the vacancy still remained with the State provided that person was a member of the same political party as the retired or deceased senator.

In 1975 two States filled the casual vacancies caused by these political manoeuvres with persons who would not necessarily support the ministry. Because of these appointments, and the death of another senator, the control of the Senate passed out of the hands of the ministry. What had been done in filling the casual vacancies was lawful; so was the resultant composition of the Senate. Its actions, to which I will refer, were lawful, quite constitutionally unaffected in that respect by the antecedent political manoeuvring of both parties which had affected its composition. Too often commentators and parliamentarians have been unable to separate the political manoeuvring, about which there may be different views, from the constitutional situation which resulted, about which there can, in my opinion, be no doubt.

I now record what ensued.

The House of Representatives, having passed Appropriation Bills to support the ministry's budget, presented them to the Senate, for its concurrence, on 14 October. This was an essential step towards obtaining supply.

I must emphasise here that each of the two chambers of the Parliament — the House of Representatives and the Senate — has the same legislative power as the other, with one exception: the Senate may not initiate or amend a money Bill. Only an act of the Parliament can warrant the withdrawal of money from the consolidated fund. Only a Bill in which the Senate as well as the House of Representatives has concurred can be presented to the Governor-General for the Royal Assent. There can be no act of Parliament without the concurrence of the Senate.

I now recite what precisely happened to the Appropriation Bills. The Senate resolved to defer consideration of each Appropriation Bill in terms of a resolution as follows:

> That these bills be not further proceeded with until the Government agrees to submit itself to the judgment of the people, the Senate being of the opinion that the Prime Minister and his Government no longer have the trust and confidence of the Australian people because of:
>
> (a) the continuing incompetence, evasion, deceit and duplicity of the Prime Minister and his Ministers as exemplified in the overseas loan scandal which was an attempt by the Government to subvert the Constitution, to by-pass Parliament and to evade its responsibilities to the States and the Loan Council;
>
> (b) the Prime Minister's failure to maintain proper control over the activities of his Ministers and Government to the detriment of the Australian nation and people; and
>
> (c) the continuing mismanagement of the Australian economy by the Prime Minister and this Government with policies which have caused a lack of confidence in this nation's potential and created inflation and unemployment not experienced for 40 years.
>
> 2. That the foregoing Resolution be communicated to the House of Representatives by Message.

This was clearly a course constitutionally open to the Senate. Its lawfulness, as I have indicated, was quite unaffected by the political manoeuvring which had affected the political balance of the Senate. This resolution clearly amounted to a failure to pass the Appropriation Bills within the meaning of s 57 of the Constitution. It made it clear that the Senate would not approve the continuance in office of the ministry. It would only provide funds to enable a general election to be held.

On 22 October and on 5 November Appropriation Bills were again presented to the Senate by the House. Resolutions in the same terms as I have set out here were carried on each occasion.

By taking this course rather than rejecting the Bills outright, the Senate both kept the Appropriation Bills alive and ensured its own control of them. It was, however, a course the Senate could lawfully take.

It could properly be said, therefore, that as from 14 October the ministry had been unable to obtain supply; it had lost the confidence of the Parliament though it still had the confidence of the House of Representatives. It then came under a parliamentary obligation to resign or advise a dissolution. From that date it had no legitimate claim to govern.

Whether or not it was proper or appropriate, in a political sense, for the Senate to have used its legislative power in this way cannot affect the validity of the action it took. One of the causes of popular misunderstanding of the events of 1975 has been the failure to distinguish between the Senate's legal powers to do what it did and the political advisability or propriety of its doing so. Surely no one of any standing as a constitutional lawyer today can doubt the necessity for the concurrence of the Senate in the passage of Appropriation Bills. Not only was the Senate not bound to concur in them but it had constitutional power to take the course it did. Its failure to pass the Bills was an exercise of its legislative power.

In the debates which took place at the time it was claimed by some that the Senate was obliged to pass the Appropriation Bills, principally for the claimed lack of constitutional power to do otherwise, but in any case because a parliamentary convention was claimed to exist. I doubt if today there exists any informed support for that view. But it is worth recalling that when in opposition in 1970 both Mr Whitlam and the then shadow Attorney-General, Senator Murphy, had publicly affirmed the Senate's ability to refuse to join in an Appropriation Bill. Further, both expressed an intention to cause the Senate at that time to exercise this power and thus bring about a general election.

Our Constitution is an amalgam of the Westminster system as it was in 1900 and part of the federal system of the United States. Some of the misunderstanding in 1975 came from a failure to appreciate the effect the federal elements of the Constitution have upon the Westminster elements. The claim for dominance of the House of Representatives over the Senate may well have come from this failure. The dominance of the House of Commons in the Westminster system and its claim to be the popular house, whereas the House of Lords composed at that time of hereditary peers, was not elected or representative, really has no counterpart in Australia, where the Senate is also an elected representative body. It is designed, as I have said, to protect the interests of the States and their people, individually and collectively. It is not merely a house of review.

Perhaps we have not yet worked out the full effect of this basic federal element upon the concepts of the Westminster elements. Failure to realise that the Senate is a representative body produced surprise that the Senate could bring down what was said to be "an elected government". This description was in any case a misnomer, as I have indicated. The ministry is appointed with no fixed term, but only during the Governor-General's pleasure. This means only for so long as it has the approval of the Parliament, that is, of both House and Senate and not merely the House alone.

In the booklet *Sir John Did His Duty* I set out fully my own part in the events of 1975. Here I will summarise my part before the events of 11 November.

During the time I was Chief Justice, I kept myself very much aloof from government and from party politics. I did call on the Prime Minister when I wanted something done by the government for the Court or for its members.

During 1975 I had no communication about political matters at any time with any members of the government or opposition parties, Senators or members, or any other person outside my immediate family and close friends. The same is true of the period of the confrontation between the Prime Minister and the Leader of the Opposition and of that between the Senate and the House of Representatives.

Since 1974 I have been Chairman of the New South Wales and Australian Capital Territory Group of Members of the Order of St Michael and St George. This Group meets annually for dinner on a Saturday evening in September close to the Feast of St Michael.

On the night of 20 September 1975, the Group held its annual dinner at which I presided as Chairman. On my right was the Governor-General. On my left was Sir Roden Cutler then Governor of New South Wales. During a lull in conversation during the latter part of the dinner, the Governor-General attracted my attention and said that he was very worried about what was going on at Canberra. He felt that neither of the protagonists was disposed to give way and that if each maintained his stand serious difficulties were likely to arise. He asked me did I see any way in which the High Court could be called upon to resolve the situation should it develop. The Governor-General did not formulate the situation he had in mind but I took it to be an impasse between the two chambers over supply. This I could see was made likely by the attitude of the protagonists reflected in the relationship of the two chambers of the Parliament. At that date the Senate had not actually received the Appropriation Bills but the Leader of the Opposition had indicated the Opposition's attitude towards the grant of supply.

I was disinclined to answer or discuss the Governor-General's question, particularly in any constitutional discussion. So I was quite unwilling to be drawn. But I said that the matter appeared to be for the Parliament itself and not for the Court to resolve. I added that, in the long run, the matter might land on his, the Governor-General's table. I was then thinking of the possibilities of s 57. What I had in mind was whether or not the Governor-General could dissolve both chambers of the Parliament without being advised to do so by the ministry, a point about which there was no precedent and one of some difficulty.

The Governor-General then asked me if I would be prepared to advise him as to his own position if need arose. This raised a matter to which I had had no need to give any specific attention. I was content to temporise. I said that that would depend upon what I was asked and the circumstances in which I was asked. There the matter rested and nothing more was said that evening. I am bound on reflection to say that I had left the door open for the Governor-General to approach me.

I should say that I was not surprised that the Governor-General should contemplate seeking my advice. Governors-General seemed to have had the idea that they could seek personal advice from the Chief Justice, and at times from other justices, in matters in which the courts cannot be concerned. It is worth mentioning here that Richard Casey when Governor-General sought my advice on whether after Mr Holt's disappearance he should immediately appoint an acting Prime Minister or wait for fresher news about Mr Holt. He further asked whether he should appoint Mr McEwen, or wait until the Liberal Party elected a leader. I expressed the view that an acting Prime Minister should be immediately appointed and that John McEwen should be appointed on terms that he resign when the Liberal Party had elected a leader. Later Mr Hasluck, when he was Governor-General, asked me to read an article he proposed publishing about his office and advise him if it was correct.

Between the evening of the dinner and the evening of Sunday 9 November I did not have any conversation or any communication, direct or indirect, with the Governor-General. Nor did I have any communication with anybody else about the parliamentary or the political situation. In particular, I was not approached by anybody about these matters or about any possible action by the Governor-General. I should add, to avoid any misunderstanding, that I had no conversation or communication of any kind with Mr RJ Ellicott QC at any time during 1975.

During the latter part of this time I considered the constitutional possibilities which might arise from a failure to obtain supply. These included the obligation of the ministry and the duty of the Governor-General.

Between 20 September and 9 November I also thought about the propriety of a Chief Justice giving advice to the Governor-General. I realised that I had not rebuffed the Governor-General's approach by what I had said on 20 September. I considered this matter on principle though there were precedents.

On principle, it seemed to me that if the matter on which advice was sought was not a justiciable matter, the advice given would in reality not be advice given in a judicial capacity. It would rank no higher than personal advice though undoubtedly, because of the office of Chief Justice, it might appear to carry more weight and even to be the likelier to be correct.

The giving of advice on a non-justiciable question or matter seemed to me then and now quite clear on principle. To give such advice to the representative of the Crown at his request did not seem to me to compromise the independence of the Chief Justice, including his independence of the executive, or that of the judiciary. Nor did it involve any admixture of constitutional power. I considered also whether it would be proper to give advice on a justiciable matter and decided that it would not.

On Monday 10 November between 9 and 10 am, at his request, I called on the Governor-General at Admiralty House, Sydney (actually on my way to the court in Darlinghurst). He had decided to terminate the ministry's commission and to appoint a caretaker Prime Minister who could obtain supply and would advise a double dissolution. He asked me if what he proposed to do was within his constitutional power with the then prevailing circumstances.

I responded to a request by the Governor-General for an answer to a question he asked. It was a legal question — not a political question — and its answer did not involve the expression of any political opinion, though of course Sir John's action in withdrawing the ministry's commission was likely to have, and did in fact have, political consequences.

Having heard his question and having decided to give the Governor-General an answer to his question, I knew of instances in which a Chief Justice and other judges of the High Court had given legal advice personally to a Governor-General. I knew also that the Chief Justice of the High Court had on an occasion given such advice to a State governor. Other instances of which I was then unaware have been disclosed by Don Markwell.[3]

I was satisfied that what I was asked did not involve a justiciable question; no court would interfere with the exercise of the Governor-General's discretion to choose or dismiss a ministry. In the case of his choice, the Parliament alone can approve or disapprove it. In the case of a dismissal it is the electorate which will decide whether or not the dismissed ministry will or will not be returned to office. What the Governor-General proposed to do was to dismiss a ministry of which the Parliament, that is to say the whole Parliament, did not approve. That was not a matter in which any court could interfere.

I put my answer to the question in writing, in a letter to the Governor-General as follows:

> Dear Sir John,
>
> In response to Your Excellency's invitation I attended this day at Admiralty House. In our conversations I indicated that I considered myself, as Chief Justice of Australia, free, on Your Excellency's request, to offer you legal advice as to your Excellency's constitutional rights and duties in relation to an existing situation which, of its nature, was unlikely to come before the Court. We both clearly understood that I was not in any way concerned with matters of a purely political kind, or with any political consequences of the advice I might give.
>
> In response to Your Excellency's request for my legal advice as to whether a course on which you had determined was consistent with your constitutional authority and duty, I respectfully offer the following.
>
> The Constitution of Australia is a federal constitution which embodies the principle of Ministerial responsibility. The Parliament consists of two houses, the House of Representatives and the Senate, each popularly elected, and each with

> the same legislative power, with the one exception that the Senate may not originate nor amend a money Bill.
>
> Two relevant constitutional consequences flow from this structure of the Parliament. First, the Senate has constitutional power to refuse to pass a money Bill; it has power to refuse supply to the Government of the day. Secondly, a Prime Minister who cannot ensure supply to the Crown, including funds for carrying on the ordinary services of Government, must either advise a general election (of a kind which the constitutional situation may then allow) or resign. If, being unable to secure supply, he refuses to take either course, Your Excellency has constitutional authority to withdraw his Commission as Prime Minister.
>
> There is no analogy in respect of a Prime Minister's duty between the situation of the Parliament under the federal Constitution of Australia and the relationship between the House of Commons, a popularly elected body, and the House of Lords, a non-elected body, in the unitary form of Government functioning in the United Kingdom. Under that system, a Government having the confidence of the House of Commons can secure supply, despite a recalcitrant House of Lords. But it is otherwise under our federal Constitution. A Government having the confidence of the House of Representatives but not that of the Senate, both elected Houses, cannot secure supply to the Crown.
>
> But, there is an analogy between the situation of a Prime Minister who has lost the confidence of the House of Commons and a Prime Minister who does not have the confidence of the Parliament, ie., of the House of Representatives and of the Senate. The duty and responsibility of the Prime Minister to the Crown in each case is the same: if unable to secure supply to the Crown, to resign or to advise an election.
>
> In the event that, conformably to this advice, the Prime Minister ceases to retain his Commission, Your Excellency's constitutional authority and duty would be to invite the Leader of the Opposition, if he can undertake to secure supply, to form a caretaker government (ie., one which makes no appointments or initiates any policies) pending a general election, whether of the House of Representatives, or of both Houses of the Parliament, as that Government may advise.
>
> Accordingly, my opinion is that, if Your Excellency is satisfied in the current situation that the present Government is unable to secure supply, the course upon which Your Excellency has determined is consistent with your constitutional authority and duty.

I have already indicated the democratic nature of government in this country. It is safeguarded first by Parliament being elected by the people; second, by the ministry being composed only of members of Parliament having the approval of Parliament; third, the Parliament's absolute control of all moneys received by the Government. Plainly, an attempt to govern without supply provided by the Parliament would be both essentially undemocratic and subversive of our parliamentary system. It represented an attempt to govern without parliamentary approval and indeed in defiance of its disapproval.

It is true that in 1975 the ministry was supported by a majority of members of the House of Representatives. But that Chamber is only part of the Parliament.

It has been said that the Whitlam Ministry was "toughing it out". This was in order to put pressure on the senators that at least a significant number of them would defect from their party allegiance and vote to grant supply.

But is that sort of conduct acceptable? Is it acceptable in a parliamentary democracy where the members are expected to do their parliamentary duties honourably and free of coercion of any kind? Brinkmanship of this kind might be accepted in the factional infighting in a political or industrial group, but to my mind not in an assembly of honourable representatives of the people.

With Mr Whitlam's approval, Sir John saw Mr Fraser to satisfy himself of the unlikelihood of a senator or senators succumbing to this pressure. After that interview Sir John was satisfied that the thrice-repeated refusal to provide supply was unlikely to be reversed. After the event, one senator is claimed to have said that eventually he would have defected, abandoned his colleagues and voted for the granting of supply. The credibility of such a person, if there really was one, must at best be suspect.

One aspect of "toughing it out" is worth mentioning. At best, following this tactic was a gamble. If it did not come off, a chaotic situation of the most dangerous proportions would follow. There would be no funds to carry on government, not even to pay for an election. By 11 November the private banks had indicated their unwillingness to fund the government. Both leaders knew that because of logistic constraints 13 December was the last day of the year on which a general election could be held as a month must elapse between the calling of an election and the election itself. Failing an election that day, there could be no election till the New Year, perhaps not till February at the earliest.

I think it is important that I point out the enormity of the Whitlam Ministry's proposal to continue to govern without supply but with the aid of funds provided by the banks, including the private banks, funds over the provision of which Parliament could have no direct control. The consequence of not resolving the matter on 11 November would have been that the Whitlam Ministry would remain in office without parliamentary approval and without funds. Public servants would be unpaid, creditors unpaid, social services unpaid. One could properly call it a catastrophe of gigantic proportions.

Yet it was with this possibility that the Whitlam Ministry was prepared to gamble, refusing to face the people, refusing to fulfil its democratic and honourable obligation to resign.

I might mention here that one still hears the scurrilous and childish suggestion of a conspiracy to which Malcolm Fraser, Robert Ellicott, Sir John Kerr and I, or some pair of us, were parties. There is no substance whatever in this. For the record, I have referred to what I wrote in *Sir John Did His Duty* stating what contacts I had with the other suggested conspirators. With Mr Fraser I had none.

As matters stood in the second half of 1975, there was ample ground for a double dissolution as the Senate had already rejected twenty-one earlier Bills presented and re-presented by the government and in most instances the necessary interval of time had elapsed.

Section 57 of the Constitution provides a means of overcoming a deadlock between the two chambers of Parliament with respect to particular proposed laws. It provides that if the Senate rejects or fails to pass a proposed law which has been passed by the House, or amends it in a way to which the House will not agree, and if after an interval of three months the House again passes the proposed law with or without any such Senate amendment and the Senate rejects or fails to pass it, the Governor-General may dissolve the Senate and the House simultaneously.

As a general rule the initiative to set in train such a dissolution is taken by the ministry. Also as a general rule, although the power of dissolution is not given to the Governor-General in council but to the Governor-General in person, the Governor-General awaits advice from the ministry before considering the exercise of his discretion. Whether the Governor-General could act without advice has not been decided.

It has been suggested that instead of dismissing the ministry, resort should have been had in 1975 to s 57. But it will be apparent that s 57 provides no real solution to a deadlock over the grant of supply. The urgency to provide funds to carry on government may (and in 1975 did) make a waiting time of more than three months in order to satisfy the terms of the section quite inappropriate. If parliamentary practices and usages are followed, this will itself bring about a general election though not necessarily a double dissolution.

The ministry should follow the same course if the House by resolution expresses its lack of confidence in the government or rejects a government measure in circumstances in which that rejection amounts to a vote of no confidence. Such a resolution or rejection is in reality an anticipatory statement that supply would not be granted. It would not matter that existing supply had not then run out. It would be intolerable that after such a resolution or rejection the ministry should continue in office until supply ran out.

To a community, a great part of which is ill-informed about our federal form of parliamentary government, the 1975 dismissal was dramatic, the more so as the ministry had a majority in the House. Journalists who live on drama and tragedy had something to their taste; and they made the most of it. So instead of providing information which might assist the public to understand the true situation in which the Governor-General had been placed, the media inflamed the situation, treating the Governor-General and not the ministry as the cause of the crisis. This worked to the great disadvantage of the community.

It is said Sir John acted too soon: he ought to have waited till temporary supply ran out or at any rate until some illegality was committed by the ministry. It is also said that he should have informed the Prime Minister of what he was contemplating — he ought to have "warned" him. This last criticism is based on Bagehot's expression of the courses open to the Crown when ministerial advice is received, advice that must be accepted and acted upon. Included in Bagehot's options is the ability to "warn" the ministry. First of all this is a power or ability, not an obligation. Then the power is to warn the ministry in relation to the proffered advice, for example warning of the likely public disquiet about acting upon that advice. But Bagehot's expression had no relevance whatever to the situation in 1975. He was not referring to the performance of a discretionary act in respect of which no advice was necessary or given. For the Governor-General to have "warned" the Prime Minister that he might exercise his power of dismissal would not only not fall within Bagehot's concept but would clearly have worn the aspect of a threat. This is something which certainly should not be done by the Governor-General.

Further, in the particular circumstances obtaining in 1975 the Prime Minister had a full appreciation of what courses the Governor-General could take. He himself alluded to the power of dismissal — as he says, in jest — in front of the Prime Minister of Malaysia, saying that it might come down to "who got to the palace first". But jesting or not, the Prime Minister's remark contained an ill-disguised threat to cause the dismissal of the Governor-General if he contemplated the dismissal of the ministry. At the very least, the remark shows that the Prime Minister was aware of the possible action of the Governor-General. From Sir John's account of his interview with the Prime Minister on 11 November and notwithstanding Mr Whitlam's denial, there would seem to be at least a high probability that Mr Whitlam had it in mind to advise the dismissal of the Governor-General if it were thought that he was about to dismiss the ministry.

The remark, jocular though it may have been, nonetheless emphasised to the Governor-General that he was at risk of dismissal, something of which I suppose he was already acutely aware. I would expect that he understood the embarrassment to the Queen which could be caused by the receipt of prime ministerial advice to dismiss him. If the Queen accepted the advice, as she must, and acted immediately upon it, a substantial section of the Australian public might be critical of her having done so, expecting her perhaps at least to have temporised. On the other hand, if she took time to consider her position, a different but again substantial part of that community might suggest partisanship on her part. I think it may be accepted that Sir John had come to the conclusion that he should not give the Prime Minister the opportunity to embarrass the Queen. It is I think, in all the circumstances, quite understandable that he did not take the Prime Minister into his confidence.

On 11 November the Prime Minister intended to advise the Governor-General to call an election for a "half Senate". Some have said that the tendering of this advice would have satisfied the need to consult the electorate and even justify the ministry's refusal to resign. But obviously the holding of a half-Senate election could not overcome the deadlock between the two chambers; only a general election would resolve it.

Sir John Kerr is journalistically described as the "man who divided the nation", so that some "healing" process was called for. Did Sir John Kerr's action divide the nation? I doubt very much that the nation was divided by the ending of the parliamentary stalemate. The incident probably intensified the existing party-political division largely built on dichotomy of rich and poor.

It may be that the public did not then realise the gravity of the situation created by the ministry's refusal to face the electorate or the important and beneficial function of the Governor-General in giving the electorate its opportunity to express its choice between the warring political parties. I am sure it did not recognise the strength of our Constitution in that it provided a mechanism to "cut the knot" tied by the politicians and avoid the violence which a continuing stalemate could possibly cause as it would in other systems of government where no such resolving mechanism exists. But the electoral results of 1975 and 1977 do not look like a nation divided as the journalists have suggested. The Whitlam ministry was roundly defeated on both occasions. I think there has been much nonsensical talk about the so-called healing process.

There is currently talk of a departure from the monarchy into a republic. But it is worth remembering that in a republic, particularly if parliamentary democracy were maintained, there would need to be the same authority to resolve a 1975 situation as is now placed in hands of the Governor-General.

Then there is the claim that Sir John should have waited till temporary supply had run out, or more nearly run out than was the case on 11 November. I have already indicated the disaster which would have befallen if the Senate, notwithstanding the pressure put upon it, had maintained its attitude to the grant of supply and that supply had run out without the deadlock having been resolved. But in any case, the fact that temporary supply had not been exhausted may be quite irrelevant. Suppose that at the time a resolution of no confidence had been passed by the House there remained sufficient supply to see out the rest of the year. The passage of the resolution required nonetheless immediate resignation or advice of a dissolution. In default of that action, the Governor-General's duty would be to dismiss the ministry. The existence of unexpended supply would afford no reason not to do so. Equally, it seems to me that the continuance of temporary supply, if indeed it does continue, does not afford an excuse for not resigning or for the withholding of dismissal in default of the ministry's doing so.

It might be as well to consider the effect of the refusal of or failure to grant supply upon the grant of temporary supply. The purpose of the grant of temporary supply is to allow government to be carried on while the budget and the estimates are examined. No doubt if the House refused to accept the budget the inevitable consequence would be that the ministry would have to resign, advise dissolution or be dismissed. The authority to continue to use temporary supply would lapse.

Though temporary supply is usually given until a specified date to allow these budgetary processes, it must be taken as granted on the unexpressed condition that the budget is carried, that is, the Appropriation Bills are carried by the Parliament. There is at least much to be said for the view that upon the rejection of the budget, on the refusal to pass Appropriation Bills, the temporary supply lapses unconditionally. So it is far from clear that after the resolutions of the Senate in October and November temporary supply remained available.

Another approach to the question may be to regard the refusal of unconditional supply as terminating the ministry's claim to remain in government. It would seem clear that once Parliament will not provide supply, the legitimacy of the ministry disappears.

I would make two observations upon Sir John's handling of the situation. First, there has been some suggestion that he should have sought to arbitrate between the warring politicians. I feel that an attempt to arbitrate would not only be unwise but might endanger the office itself. I think Sir John, who was by nature a kindly man, would have liked to see the opponents compromise their positions. To some extent he held his hand to give them an opportunity to do so. But I do not think any arbitration between them should have been attempted.

My other observation is that it may be that Sir John delayed too long in taking action. I incline to the view that he ought to have acted, at the latest, by 25 October. I think this because by the delay after that date, the Prime Minister had a party-political advantage enabling him to indulge in brinkmanship to coerce some, no doubt the weaker, of the senators to break ranks. In fact the Prime Minister did have the advantage of Sir John's delay until 11 November.

I think Sir John had a better appreciation of the place which the office of Governor-General has in our system of government than some who have occupied the office both before and since. He rightly did not regard it as having a mere ceremonial function and its occupant as a cipher. He realised, I think, that the office created by the Constitution provided a means of ending a parliamentary deadlock for the resolution of which s 57 was quite inadequate when parliamentary conventions were ignored. 1975 demonstrated the validity of that view. There was a deadlock which, because of the Whitlam Ministry's failure to follow that time-honoured and honourable parliamentary course, was incapable of parliamentary solution. It was the existence of the Governor-General's office with its powers and duties which ended the deadlock in a democratic way, that is, by a general election.

Those who say that by exercising the powers of the office he damaged it fail to perceive that Sir John had demonstrated the place and strength of the office in the operation of a parliamentary democracy. Due performance of parliamentary obligation will render resort to the Governor-General's powers unnecessary. But when the conventions of the Parliament are ignored as they were in 1975, parliamentary democracy requires a mechanism to return the effective decision to the electorate. The office of Governor-General and the willingness of its occupant to exercise its authority and perform its duty provide that mechanism.

It was indeed for Sir John a tragedy that because of the defaults of others he was compelled to take a quite proper but highly unusual step in which the press could have assisted an ill-equipped community to understand the position as I have outlined it. But it did not. It helped to create the tragedy which remained with Sir John till his death, but which he bore with dignity and forbearance.

*****

Since completing the text of this chapter there has been a telecast of an interview which I gave to the Australian Broadcasting Corporation. In that interview in response to a question by the interviewer, I disclosed that I had spoken to Sir Anthony Mason on 10 November 1975. Having done so, I now record what actually happened in that connection.

My letter to Sir John Kerr was delivered during the afternoon on 10 November by my driver, Bert Reid. At that time I was still presiding in the court. After I had returned to chambers when the court rose, I received a telephone call from Sir John Kerr. He acknowledged receipt of my letter and he then said that he was curious to know what the former Solicitors-General would have thought of the matter. He said he knew what one of them, Robert Ellicott, thought because he had publicly stated his views. But he would like to know what the other retired Solicitor-General, Sir Anthony Mason, thought. He asked me would I mind asking him. I said I did not mind doing that and after I had concluded the conversation I went downstairs to Sir Anthony's chambers. Sir Anthony had been sitting with me during the afternoon though he was then unaware of what had passed between Sir John and myself earlier that day. I told him what had occurred and I told him the substance of my letter. I told him that Sir John had asked me to ask him his view and I was now doing so. He said he quite agreed with the view I had expressed and I may say he did so without any reluctance. I returned to my chambers and phoned Sir John and informed him of what had passed between Sir Anthony and myself.

It is worth observing that by this time Sir John had both decided himself on the course of action he was to take and had received my letter. I doubt if Sir Anthony's opinion had any effect whatever upon Sir John's decision to take the course on which he had already decided and indeed as I have pointed out, to one he was in duty bound to take.

Epilogue

I have been favoured with a long life, most of it in good health but latterly experiencing some of the ailments of age. But I continue to enjoy Norma's companionship. Life has provided me with a variety of experience: the practice of the law, politics and government, and the judicial bench. Each in turn has given me pleasure and satisfaction, and opportunities for public service.

In this book of recollections there are parts of my story that have had to be left out. I would like to have told of the expansion of services to deaf and blind children during my term in office in the Royal New South Wales Institute for Deaf and Blind Children. But the limitations of space have not allowed this.

I began my practice in the law like the judge in *Trial by Jury* — "an impecunious party". Like many others I had no patron or mentor to open any door or smooth any pathway. Apart from my two bursaries to high school and university, I have never received any unearned payment from government, or from any other source. Of necessity I have had to be self-reliant. This in turn has led me to accept responsibility and to be decisive in judgment and action. Throughout my days I have been able to maintain my personal independence. The motto of Fort Street High School is "Each man the maker of his own fortune". I have fulfilled its prescription, aided only by beneficent incidents and accidents of circumstance.

When in 1953 I became a knight bachelor and received from the College of Arms armorial bearings I took as my motto "Work with courage to achieve". That expressed my philosophy and the course of my life. I think that in the end I did achieve much both for my family and for the community at large.

My parents' families derived from England — my father's from Lincolnshire, my mother's from Devon and Cornwall — so it may be said that I am an Anglo-Saxon by derivation, though Australian by birth and sentiment. The Anglo-Saxon population which came to this country whether voluntarily or under restraint brought with them a great heritage of parliamentary democracy, separation of powers, the rule of law, a rare capacity to govern themselves with stability, a desire for and love of personal freedom, tolerance of the beliefs and attitudes of others, a desire for justice and fair dealing whether by government or between fellow citizens. Perhaps above all, they brought us the English language, now of universal currency, and the language of commerce, both in Asia and in Europe.

I have witnessed in latter days with regret a considerable dilution of this Anglo-Celtic stock and wonder if the elements of this heritage will be understood and respected by those of our citizens who have recently arrived from elsewhere. I fear that those who have adopted the fashion of multiculturalism fail to realise the depths and intractability of the mutual disapproval of some ethnic groups, an antipathy which may prove ineradicable and is often attended by violence. At the lowest, the cause of national unity is not aided by this ethnic diversity.

As well, Marxian philosophy has weakened if not in some areas fully destroyed that mutual trust and confidence of one citizen of and in another without which civilised life is scarce possible. In any case national unity is made less likely.

I have also witnessed in more recent times the weakening of the moral fibre of our people by the welfare state with its creation of such a large proportion of the population dependent upon and, it seems to me, often content with, the handouts from government, handouts which are provided by their fellow citizens who work to produce wealth but lose much of the benefit of their endeavours in high taxation and government charges of one sort or another. None of this encourages personal initiative and endeavour.

I hope this pessimism is misplaced. We are a young and vigorous people. Our forefathers learned to master a most difficult climate and terrain. We have developed great natural resources and discovered and mined much mineral wealth. But the shelter of a tariff wall has failed to produce a great manufacturing base capable of competing with the world in exportable goods (indeed it has tended to destroy it). It may be that we will turn back to hard work and restraint of short-term individual gain in pursuit of long-term national advantage and by unremitting effort and national unity learn to process our raw materials into manufactured exportable form and ultimately find our proper place as a leading nation in the Asia-Pacific region of so much promise.

Appendix I
Curriculum Vitae

Born 22 June 1903

1906-08	St John's Parish School, Darlinghurst
1908-13	Bourke Street State Primary School
1914-15	Cleveland Street High School
1916-19	Fort Street High School
1919-21	Sydney University
1922	Received Arts degree
1925	Received Law degree
1927	Admitted to NSW Bar
1929	Married Norma Mountier Symons
	Elected Member of Barrister's Admissions Board
1942	Appointed King's Counsel
1943	Elected to office in NSW Bar Association
	Chairman, Wentworth Chambers Ltd
1944-64	Founding and active Trustee of Kosciusko State Park
1950-58	Director, Royal Prince Alfred Hospital, Camperdown
1952	Chairman, Law Council of Australia
1953	Created Knight Bachelor
1958	Entered House of Representatives as Member for Federal Division of Parramatta
1958-63	Attorney-General of the Commonwealth
1958-76	Director, Royal NSW Institute for Deaf and Blind Children

1961-64	Minister for External Affairs
1964	Appointed Chief Justice of Australia
1967-78	First Chancellor of Macquarie University
1972-83	President, Australian Institute of International Affairs
1973-74	Served as Judge ad hoc of International Court of Justice, The Hague
1976-present	President, Royal NSW Institute for Deaf and Blind Children
1981	Retired as Chief Justice

Appendix II Interview with Sir Garfield

The following is a transcript of Paul Murphy's interview with Sir Garfield Barwick, ABC Radio *PM*, 28 March 1991:

Paul Murphy	This is PM, I'm Paul Murphy, and this evening an exclusive interview. A state memorial service for the late Sir John Kerr will be held in Sydney next week. Sir John died in Sydney last Sunday and was buried yesterday. Last night PM approached a distinguished Australian who knew Sir John well, for an appreciation of his friend and he asked for a day to think about it. Today, Sir Garfield Barwick agreed to talk about a former Governor-General who ignited the most explosive constitutional crisis in Australian history — the dismissal of an elected Prime Minister of Australia, Gough Whitlam, a decision which Sir John consulted Sir Garfield about before November 11, 1975. Fairly or unfairly it's this titanic struggle between a prime minister and the representative of the Crown for which Sir John Kerr will be principally remembered. This afternoon I talked to Sir Garfield Barwick in his Sydney chambers.
Murphy	Sir Garfield, thanks very much indeed for speaking to PM. You knew Sir John Kerr very well. What sort of man was he?
Barwick	I knew him very well. He used to bring briefs to me when he was an articled clerk and I was a barrister building a practice. So I've known him a long time. He was a very intellectually gifted man. He was a very thoughtful man. He had very wide-ranging intellectual interests. They included of course the law, politics and international affairs. And in these areas he not merely read, he thought. And he was very thoughtful and constructive in some of his ideas.
Murphy	In fact you shared the same school. You both went to Fort Street, which was the real proving ground of brilliant minds who didn't have the benefit of wealthy parents.

Barwick That's true enough. As a matter of fact we had the benefit of not having them. And the difference is so very awful in favour of the chap who hasn't, and I have never been the least bit jealous of the fellow that had, because I know how much working for myself and relying on myself has meant in my lifetime.

Murphy Which is why Clyde Cameron found you such an interesting fellow parliamentarian perhaps.

Barwick Oh yes, well he thinks of me as the most Tory man he ever met who had strange radical ideas. That's how I think I struck Clyde Cameron.

Murphy And some people think of Sir John as Tory although of course he was a member of the ALP and I think you could have fairly described him as a person who was leftish of centre for most of his career.

Barwick Yes, I think John thought life through for himself and like a lot of young men there is an attraction in ideological concepts, but slowly as life goes on you realise their impracticality and you realise the consequence of them and I think he followed that sort of path and towards mid- or late mid-life he began to be not Tory — I don't think he was ever Tory in my sense of the word — but he was no longer radical in thought. He was more practical in thought.

Murphy And yet some critics say that he was attracted to power and that perhaps that a rightward progression is the way to get closer to that.

Barwick No, I would acquit him of that. I don't think that's right. I think he had an interest in affairs and he liked to be close to them. But I don't think he himself really yearned for power or the exercise of it. I don't think that.

Murphy When he was offered the chance to go to Yarralumla apparently he really thought deeply about it and he was reluctant to begin with because after all he was Chief Justice of New South Wales, but then he took it. Do you think that might have been, in hindsight, a mistake, that he should have stayed with the law on the bench?

Barwick Well, that's a matter of personality. He came to tell me that he had been offered. I was then Chief Justice and I remember saying to him wild horses couldn't take me out of that office. But he felt that he wanted to do it. I do remember saying to him that if you do do it, I want to tell you there is no pension to the office. You see we have been used to expatriate Governors-General who had money and could look after themselves and to switch over to Australian Governors-General was not accompanied by a pension. So I said to him, "If you're going to take this office you'd better get a pension". And I said, "You've got a fellow dealing with it who's not much good at looking after money, so you get a pension". And he did.

Murphy Right, so he asked Gough Whitlam for that, and got it?

Barwick Of course.

Murphy From a man who wasn't too good looking after money?

Barwick That's right, particularly other people's money.

Murphy And so Sir John was a confidante of yours or I mean you were his mentor for quite some time?

Barwick Oh, I think I had been his senior in practice and I had developed a certain amount of old man qualities, I suppose, and that brought him to me. I think no other relationship because I never advised him in any other aspects of life and I didn't advise him on this. He merely out of courtesy told me what he was likely to do.

Murphy And so you said well, if you want it go for it, but get a pension.

Barwick That's right. It was his business. I wouldn't tell him to go for it. I'd say it's his decision, not mine.

Murphy And then of course only a year after taking that job in Yarralumla he found himself in the middle of the most enormous constitutional convulsion that this country's ever seen?

Barwick Yes, well what happened — and it's just as well to put this rather straight — what happened was that there was a struggle between two political parties quite bitterly conducted, both of them manoeuvring politically — both of them, not only one — and they reached a stalemate. The Parliament was stalled. Now our Constitution is a singularly good one. In other countries when two political parties get into that sort of stalemate there is fighting, there is violence, but there is none under our Constitution because the Governor-General can act as an arbiter, in this sense, that he can cut the knot and send the question to the electorate to be solved, let them choose between the two warring parties.

Murphy You're the most eminent jurist of your generation, possibly ever in this country, and yet what you're saying is that Sir John was right to sack an elected government and install a caretaker prime minister?

Barwick You want to be careful when you use the word elected government. The ministry is not elected. The parliamentarians are elected and the government is appointed. Of course it has to be appointed out of the Parliament, one House or the other, and that's because of our sense of ministerial responsibility. We must have those who advise the Governor-General in the Parliament and responsible to the Parliament. And so the government is appointed, it is not elected, it is appointed.

Murphy But he did sack an elected government, a group of ministers with a Prime Minister at its head, and you're saying that that was a courageous act.

Barwick I'm saying it was a correct act and indeed it was courageous for any man. You see there's a longstanding, time-honoured and honourable way in which a ministry acts when it cannot get from the Parliament the money to carry on government. Now it's time-honoured and it's honourable and it is a process of course which facilitates an election so that the people can resolve the dispute that exists between the parties and choose one of them and so resolve the dispute. And that's what happened, and that's all that happened in '75.

Murphy And he suffered for it. But Sir Garfield . . .

Barwick Yes, I want to say he suffered for it, and that what I call the time-honoured and honourable course has been adopted over long years in order to avoid the person in the position of the Governor-General — whether it be the Crown or the Governor-General — save them the embarrassment of having to sack the ministry. And what happened in 1975 was that because the ministry refused to follow this honourable course they caused embarrassment to the Governor-General, because he had to dismiss them.

Murphy So they embarrassed Sir John Kerr and he had no choice but to do what he did, that's what you're saying?

Barwick That's right.

Murphy Let me put to you another point of view, that that government had another two years to run, that Mr Whitlam had offered a half Senate election. That was going back to the people. Why shouldn't that government have served its full term?

Barwick Because it wasn't going back to the people in that sense. The issue between the parties was not in connection with the Senate — it was that the Parliament would not give the government the money to carry on business. So you couldn't have carried on — there would have been chaos — unless something had been done smartly.

Murphy Yes, well, obviously Malcolm Fraser and his allies in the Senate weren't going to give, were they?

Barwick No they were not and of course you will remember historically that the Governor-General asked Whitlam might he see Fraser and Whitlam agreed that he might see Fraser in order to satisfy himself that the Liberals wouldn't give, and he did that before he acted. He satisfied himself that the Liberals, the people in the Senate, were firm.

Murphy Sir Garfield, there was enormous pressure on Sir John Kerr as he came to that decision. He sought your advice didn't he?

Barwick Well he did, because he was a very conscientious man. He, like all of us who are lawyers, have got to feel satisfied about doing things and we do like to have our view confirmed. There's no question about that. And all he asked me was a legal question, as to whether what he was proposing and he had made up his mind to do was lawful. And it was not only lawful but it was constitutionally valid, and I told him. I may say there's really, today, nobody who would say it was wrong.

Murphy Well, there are some people who would say it was wrong but . . .

Barwick By nobody I mean nobody who really knows, who is really skilled and knowledgeable.

Murphy In the law.

Barwick Yes, that's right because it's a legal question.

Murphy It's also a political question.

Barwick It wasn't a political question.

Murphy To sack an elected government is not a political question?

Barwick No, it was a legal question not political at all. That's where I think your trade seems to mix it up. It wasn't political, it was legal and just let me add this. You know we live under the rule of law. That means that acts have got to be lawful. They've not got to be political, they've got to be lawful. And that's why every law that you make is formally endorsed by the Governor-General in council, it's lawful.

Murphy So Sir John came to see you, his mentor in the law, you of course a distinguished minister in the Menzies government. He came with a blueprint; he said he'd already made up his mind but what did you think.

Barwick No he didn't ask me what I thought. He simply asked me the one question — was the course he proposed which was to dismiss the ministry, to appoint a caretaker government and ensure a double dissolution so that there should be an election, whether that was constitutionally valid, and that's all I told him.

Murphy Sir Garfield, over the weekend of course, Sir John Kerr died and a lot of people have said that towards the end of his career and life he was a tragic figure, an exile who came back here and even then lived in obscurity. Is that too harsh a judgment? Do you think his final years were happy?

Barwick Depends who the judgment is on. There is a degree of truth in it because the press and the media generally have created and kept creating that tragedy. They at no time have turned the searchlight on to the real cause of the difficulty. It was the refusal to resign and to take the honourable course, the time-honoured course of facing the people.

Murphy Inevitably that happened, though, didn't it?

Barwick Only because Sir John intervened and did his duty.

Murphy	A great Australian?
Barwick	Yes, a great Australian.
Murphy	The former Chief Justice of the High Court, Sir Garfield Barwick.

Appendix III
Extracts from Garfield Barwick's Personal Memorandum on West New Guinea

From annexure 3 to the Cabinet submission it is clear that Australia has been pursuing two policy targets concurrently:

> *Firstly*, to ensure that the Dutch remain in West New Guinea and in their administration pursue policies in relation to the native population compatible with those being pursued by Australia in East New Guinea;
>
> *Secondly*, to secure the friendship of the Indonesian people.

If I may say so, it seems to me that the targets were in truth from the beginning antithetical. The antinomy has progressively increased in emphasis and the targets are now fast moving to the point where they are mutually exclusive, if indeed that time has not already passed.

* * * *

The point has now arrived, it seems to me, when the Dutch inevitably must go. Even granted their willingness to resist militarily an organised Indonesian assault on West New Guinea, a willingness I take leave to doubt notwithstanding a Dutch affirmative assertion, they could not hope to succeed in more than the short run, even if the Soviet afforded no more than the aid already given, but certainly not if the Soviet provided additional aid. I think the Soviet would find means of ensuring that the Indonesians did not fail in the long run and perhaps succeed in doing so without directly involving itself in a belligerency which could be sheeted home to it. As matters presently stand, the Dutch would be unsupported.

Not having received commitments for military assistance from the United States or the United Kingdom the Dutch recently undertook an initiative in the United Nations, an exercise which we did not counsel, and indeed sought to dissuade, but which we assisted vigorously once taken. The attempt was to internationalise the administration of New Guinea on the basis of self-determination for the indigenous inhabitants and Indonesia's exclusion from the administration. Further reference to this exercise is made in annexure 2 to the Cabinet Submission. Largely, I think, out of respect for our views, the United States gave the Dutch a substantial degree of support in the United Nations. But the exercise nonetheless failed even after modification of the Dutch proposals to make room for Indonesia's access to the indigenous inhabitants, and after its conversion by the French African group into an endeavour to obtain no more than United Nations commendation of negotiation between the parties "without prejudice to respect for the will and self-determination of the peoples".

Though, as appears from annexure 4 there may be some small hope of a better result following on Indonesia's aggressive threats of unilateral action, the Dutch cannot really hope for such an overwhelming United Nations view as would support it as the continuing authority administering the Territory in the face of Indonesia's dissent.

Thus, neither upon the basis of force nor on the basis of the support of international opinion can the Dutch hope to remain in possession of the Territory. There is no chance whatever, in my opinion, of an agreement with the Indonesians which will permit the Dutch to remain. The choice either now or in the near future is whether the Dutch go before or after a military attack or go in pursuance of a negotiated agreement.

The information available to me up to this time suggests that Indonesia is not in any present position to launch an organised attack upon West New Guinea and that indeed Soekarno has no present intention of so doing immediately. My information suggests that the dramatics in which he is presently indulging are part of a considered campaign to terrorise the United States into exerting greater pressure on the Dutch and also to ensure that the Dutch do at least adhere to, if not improve, their offer of negotiation without pre-conditions. But Soekarno is not incapable of taking a gambler's risk and launching an attack which he could not hope would succeed but which he could hope would bring forward United Nations activity initiated perhaps by a power friendly to him and resulting in a cease-fire before the Dutch had opportunity to do him much damage, followed by a negotiation which brought him the sovereignty of the Territory on better terms than the Dutch are presently willing to offer. It must be remembered that such a course, not merely accords with what one knows of his personality but would also give him the satisfaction of completing his revolution and having himself by an exercise of force, if only for a brief moment, brought about the result.

But even if no hostilities began for some months my information suggests that at least by the end of the year Indonesia will have the capacity to mount a very substantial attempt on New Guinea, an attempt which the Dutch unaided would not in the long run defeat. Again Soekarno might well contemplate, and with good reason, that he would not need to do more than begin such an attempt before United Nations intervention of the kind and with the results to which I have already made reference.

I ought here to interpolate that there is a distinct possibility that an outbreak of hostilities between the Indonesians and the Dutch may flare up into global proportions with the use of nuclear weapons. Indeed, some quite informed opinion would say that the risk of these results is greater here than in Berlin. No doubt this possibility has been in the minds of the Americans and the British in deciding not to commit themselves, and it is also no doubt present in the minds of the Soviet who at this very time may well be persuading Soekarno against his military enterprise. But, in any case, the possibility lends great point, I think, to what I later say as to the paramount necessity to prevent the outbreak of any hostilities whatever between the two parties to this dispute.

The course of these events, it seems to me, has made the pursuit of the first target now quite impossible, and it does present Cabinet with the need to re-appraise our policy and to broadly delineate the steps we ought not to take.

I would like at this point to say something of what I conceive to be Australia's real interest in this area of international affairs, both in the long term and in the short term. First, as to the long term.

I am quite sure myself that Australia's interest lies above all with a friendly and cooperative, and, if at all possible, a non-Communist, Indonesia; the friendship to be real and mutual as well as the cooperation.

The Chinese nation is, it seems to me, on the verge of a great expansive period of its history, an expansion which will increase its tempo as the industrialisation of the country increases. It is likely to move south by land, rather than by sea. In that event particularly, but in any event, the friendship of the occupants of the Indonesian Archipelago, particularly if they remain anti-Chinese and anti-Communist, will be of cardinal importance to Australia even if a Greater Malaysia eventuates and the countries of former Indo-China do not pass into the Communist orbit completely.

In speaking of developing that friendship which ought not to be casual, but deep, one must be conscious of the present tendency of the world to divide along lines of colour, the Soviet at the moment exploiting the emotional reactions of newly emerging coloured peoples for its own purposes and successfully creating an impatience with colonialism which often overbears reason and judgment. Support for continued Dutch administration of the coloured people of West New Guinea is regarded, in my view, by Asia as an assertion of white superiority and coloured inferiority. Asia, to my mind, does not regard self-determination of the Papuan natives of West New Guinea as a practical matter of the moment. I think it regards insistence on the application of the principle of self-determination to them as no more than subterfuge or gimmick, thus confirming its view that the issue really is one of racial superiority of the white man and of a claim to the right for that reason to continue a colonial domination. That it is Dutch Colonial domination which is involved makes the point, to my mind, much more significant. Further, if we are to maintain our immigration policy, as I am convinced we must, and secure its acceptance by Asia, and Indonesia in particular, we must be able to demonstrate that we feel no racial superiority, have no colour sense and are able to treat Asians as equals.

The desire to keep Indonesia non-Communist must, in my opinion, be an integral part of that policy. Although not thoroughly convinced that the acquisition of sovereignty of West New Guinea by Indonesia will by itself reduce by as much as has been suggested in some quarters, the risk of Communism in Indonesia, I do think that the removal of the West New Guinea issue, an issue played up by the Communists posing as great nationalists might well reduce their appeal in the Indonesian community and might well increase the scope of responsible non-Communist leaders for greater influence politically and also in improving the economy, thus removing a constant encouragement of Communist success. But, the continuance of the provocation which either Dutch administration or an independent state of West New Guinea would constitute, would in my mind, significantly contribute to communist influence.

In addition to these considerations, weighty in themselves, increasing friendship with Indonesia and greater scope for our effective co-operation and influence with its Government and people would assist to reduce the risk of Communist domination in Indonesia.

Of course nothing we do nor anything which I propose in this memorandum can guarantee Indonesian friendship or the defeat of Communism in Indonesia, but it seems to me that to continue to support the Dutch, and to fail to move towards the Indonesian position, is to do great and perhaps irreparable harm to our chances of such a friendship with the Indonesians as will make them reliable allies and possibly a greater bulwark against the southward march of Communism than a Papuan State of New Guinea created and existing without Indonesian goodwill could ever prove.

Thus, in my submission, the development of friendship with Indonesia is the paramount policy to be pursued as a long-term and, for that matter, as an immediate, objective. I would think this was so, even if there is substance in the prognosis that the rift between Moscow and Peking, which I think is deep and real, and probably now irremediable leads the Soviet, in the foreseeable future, to a realisation that the tremendous population and population potential of China constitutes such a threat to the Soviet bloc itself that it ought to seek to join the "White West".

Then as to the short term policy which of course is bent to achieving the long term objective. In my submission the short term policy must be to avoid at all costs the out-break of a shooting war to our north, a war in which white is opposed to coloured. I feel that the effect of such an event will be great and lasting detriment to Australia, even if its extension into global proportions does not eventuate and even if it is of but short duration because of UN political intervention.

* * * *

We have already publicly announced our willingness to respect an agreement giving Indonesia sovereignty if the agreement is peacefully obtained and if it contains provision for respect for the principle of self-determination. I think this is the direct implication of the Casey-Subandrio communiqué and of the Prime Minister's subsequent statement in the House. My recent statements were based upon the assumption that we had already gone so far. If I may put to one side for the moment the difficult question of domestic politics, I think we should consider whether or not we should take an initiative now before there is any outbreak of actual hostilities however limited in extent and before there is any United Nations activity. The purpose of the initiative would be to ensure agreement between the parties for the transfer of sovereignty with some provision for respect for the principle of self-determination and to improve our position with the Indonesians so as to minimise the accusation which no doubt will be made hereafter that we came to their side only after actual hostilities and when we had no other real alternative. It is already late enough in the day in this respect.

The United Kingdom has conveyed to us a suggestion which involves a transfer of sovereignty to Indonesia with an obligation with respect to self-determination. The United Kingdom suggestion is as follows:

The Dutch would agree to recognise Indonesian sovereignty over West New Guinea. The administration would be conducted by an authority set up by the United Nations on the lines of the Dutch proposal to the United Nations. The Dutch or the Indonesians or both could be associated in some way with such an administration but they could not exercise administrative authority. At the end of a period of tutelage, when the United Nations so determine, the administration would be handed over. Before this was done the Papuans would have the right to decide by popular referendum whether they wished to secede from Indonesia and the future political status of the country would be decided by this act.

I do not find its expression happy, particularly in the use of the words "to secede" but it does seem to me that it could be varied somewhat as follows and that as varied it would not significantly depart from what I think the United Kingdom has in mind.

Indonesian sovereignty to be recognised. The territory to be administered for a period by some form of international authority (not necessarily exclusive of some Indonesian association therewith) followed, either immediately or after a period of Indonesian administration, by an opportunity for the Papuans to choose between continued association with Indonesia, independence, or some other status.

My submission is that rather than allow the matter to drift we should promote this proposal or some acceptable variant of it. The choice in the manner of promotion would be between asking the United Kingdom to propound it to the Dutch and obtain their concurrence to its being propounded to the Indonesians, or to ask the Americans to do so, or to do so ourselves. I am inclined to think that however much we might like to take this initiative ourselves we have gone too far internationally in stating the significance of West New Guinea to us to be able, with any show of respectable consistency, to attempt ourselves to carry the proposition of the Dutch. My inclination is to think that we should first consult with the Americans and ask them whether such a proposal by them to the Dutch would be consistent with the activity which has been promoted by America in New York and that, if it is not inconsistent, that we should press the Americans or the United Kingdom to put the proposal to the Dutch and to press it upon them. If Dutch concurrence were obtained, the proposal should be put to the Indonesians by the Americans or the UK and we should so far openly associate ourselves with it as to commend to the Indonesians its acceptance, indicating to them that the conditions of the proposal satisfied our views with respect to the indigenous inhabitants.

Notes

Chapter 2

1 *Dennis Hotels v State of Victoria* (1960) 104 CLR 529.
2 *Whitehouse v State of Queensland* (1960) 104 CLR 609.
3 *Australian National Airways Pty Ltd v Commonwealth (No 2)* (1946) 71 CLR 115.
4 *Nelungaloo v Commonwealth (No 2)* (1947) 81 CLR 144.
5 *Commonwealth v Bank of New South Wales* (1949) 79 CLR 497.
6 *Bullen and Leake*, the bible on common-law pleading.

Chapter 4

1 Section 92 of the Constitution provides that "On the imposition of uniform duties of customs, trade, commerce and intercourse among the States, whether by means of internal carriage or ocean navigation, shall be absolutely free . . ."
2 *Gratwick v Johnson* (1945) 70 CLR 1.
3 Under s 51(xiii) of the Constitution the Commonwealth Parliament has power to enact laws with respect to "Banking other than State banking; also State banking extending beyond the limits of the State concerned ..."
4 (1947) 74 CLR 31.
5 *Bank of New South Wales v Commonwealth* (1948) 76 CLR 1 (High Court), affirmed (1949) 79 CLR 497 (Privy Council).

Chapter 5

1 *Gratwick v Johnson* (1945) 70 CLR 1.
2 *ANA Pty Ltd v Commonwealth* (1945) 71 CLR 29.
3 *Nelungaloo v Commonwealth (No 2)* (1947) 81 CLR 144
4 *James v Commonwealth* (1928) 41 CLR 442.
5 *Milk Board of New South Wales v Metropolitan Cream Pty Limited* (1939) 62 CLR 116.
6 (1932) 47 CLR 386.
7 *Hughes & Vale Pty Ltd v New South Wales (No 1)* (1954) 93 CLR 1 (Privy Council).
8 *Dennis Hotels v State of Victoria* (1960) 104 CLR 529.

Chapter 7

1 *Gratwick v Johnson* (1945) 70 CLR 1.

Chapter 8

1 I had no proprietary interest in Mundroola.

Chapter 9

1 *Bank of New South Wales v Commonwealth* (1948) 76 CLR 1 (High Court), affirmed (1949) 79 CLR 497 (Privy Council).
2 *Australian Communist Party v Commonwealth* (1951) 83 CLR 1.

Chapter 10

1 Constitution, s 51(xxii).

Chapter 11

1 Dash, Schwartz and Knowlton, *The Eavesdroppers*, Rutgers University Press, New Brunswick, 1959.

Chapter 15

1 *Dennis Hotels v State of Victoria* (1960) 104 CLR 621 (Privy Council).

Chapter 16

1 "LBJ": Lyndon Baines Johnson, the President of the United States 1963-1968.

Chapter 18

1 *R v Kirby; Ex parte Boilermakers Society of Australia* (1956) 94 CLR 254 (High Court), on appeal (1957) 95 CLR 529 (Privy Council).
2 *Huddart Parker Ltd v Commonwealth* (1931) 44 CLR 492

Chapter 21

1 F Ratcliffe, *Flying Fox and Drifting Sand*, Sirius Books, Angus & Robertson, Sydney.

Chapter 24

1 See Appendix II.
2 Serendip Publications, 11-22 Frederick Street, Hornsby, NSW 2077.
3 *Quadrant*, June and July 1985.

Index

As far as possible Garfield Barwick's life is set out in segmented chronological sequence; his family relationships are expressed in parenthesis; he is referred to as GB.
Illustrations are not indexed.

Index